1|25|16
$27.95
AS-14

2|16

LET THE
People Rule

LET THE

People Rule

THEODORE ROOSEVELT AND
THE BIRTH OF THE
PRESIDENTIAL PRIMARY

Geoffrey Cowan

W. W. NORTON & COMPANY
Independent Publishers Since 1923
New York | London

For information about permission to reproduce selections from this book,
write to Permissions, W. W. Norton & Company, Inc.,
500 Fifth Avenue, New York, NY 10110

For information about special discounts for bulk purchases, please contact W. W.
Norton Special Sales at specialsales@wwnorton.com or 800-233-4830

Manufacturing by R.R. Donnelley North Harrisonburg
Book design by Chris Welch
Production manager: Louise Mattarelliano

Library of Congress Cataloging-in-Publication Data

ISBN 978-0-393-24984-2

W. W. Norton & Company, Inc.
500 Fifth Avenue, New York, N.Y. 10110
www.wwnorton.com

W. W. Norton & Company Ltd.
Castle House, 75/76 Wells Street, London W1T 3QT

1 2 3 4 5 6 7 8 9 0

To Aileen, Gabe, and Mandy

AND

To those who tried to expand the franchise in 1912—
and those who are trying today

CONTENTS

LET THE
People Rule

PROLOGUE

When the Republican Party's national convention opened in Chicago on June 18, 1912, the eyes of the world were riveted on the looming battle between two presidents seeking the same nomination—Theodore Roosevelt, who had held the office from 1901–1909, and his hand-picked successor, William Howard Taft. They had been the closest of friends who had become the bitterest of enemies, intimate political allies who had come to represent two different visions for America. Privileged graduates of Harvard and Yale respectively, they had split the nation's electorate. Taft had more delegates in his corner, but there were so many credentials challenges that the public believed that the outcome was in doubt. If Roosevelt could win a few of those challenges, he would be the Republican Party nominee.

For the first time in American history, many of the delegates had been selected by voters in presidential primaries, where voters could express a preference for a specific candidate. Thirteen states allowed such voting, including several where primaries had been created during the past few months as the result of legislation promoted by Roosevelt's operatives and supporters. His moral claim to the Republican Party nomination rested largely on the fact that he had won nine of those primary contests and that in those thirteen states he had won two-thirds of the delegates and more than half of the popular vote.

In his most important speeches, starting with a stem-winder delivered on March 20 in New York City's Carnegie Hall, TR insisted that "the right of the people to rule" is "the great fundamental issue now before the Republican party and before our people." He shortened his demand into one pithy phrase: "Let the People Rule." That refrain became the theme of his campaign. Less than five months later, TR amended his views, arguing that only some people should rule. But when the 1912 Republican Convention opened, Roosevelt was the champion of popular democracy.

Taft controlled most of the delegates who had been named in the traditional way, by the party's machinery, selected by men (and in that era the Republican Party's leaders were all men) derided by reformers as corrupt party bosses, federal officeholders, and political cronies. It would take 540 delegates to win the Republican Party nomination. According to most observers, Taft had at least 566. TR could claim about 466. Thirty-six delegates were pledged to Senator Robert La Follette, who had become Roosevelt's bitter rival.

To win, TR would need to pick up about 70 delegates. If 27 were to change hands, Taft would lose his majority and the momentum might shift. Knowing that they could not count on converting La Follette's supporters, however, Roosevelt's managers waged fights in the Republican National Committee, the Credentials Committee and finally on the floor of the convention, claiming that at least 72 of Taft's delegates had been won by fraud or theft. But since Taft controlled the party's apparatus, including the Credentials Committee, political insiders knew that that effort was almost certainly doomed.

TR's managers had one other strategy. Using a range of tactics, some less savory than others, they tried to convince the black delegates from the South, selected in old-style, Taft-controlled party conventions run primarily by a few officeholders and special interests, to switch sides. "The hopes of the Roosevelt managers for controlling the convention," the *New York Times* reported, "rest today more strongly than anything else on their hopes of winning over enough of the Taft negro delegates from the South to make up the deficit that still separates them from a majority." When most of those men stayed with Taft, Roosevelt's quest for the Republican nomination effectively ended.

Claiming that Taft had committed political larceny, Roosevelt and his supporters walked out of the convention and started their own party—formally called the Progressive Party but, based on TR's quip that he felt as strong as a Bull Moose, more popularly known as the Bull Moose Party. In the election that fall, Roosevelt did far better than Taft, but by splitting the Republican Party vote, the rivalry between the two former friends allowed the Democrat, Woodrow Wilson, to emerge as the winner.

When I started research on this book, my inquiry was animated by an interest in the origins of the presidential primary. In 1968 both Eugene McCarthy and Robert Kennedy challenged Lyndon Johnson in a series of primaries and caucuses, taking on a sitting president much as TR had done in 1912. Like TR, they won almost every primary. On March 31, 1968, LBJ withdrew from the race, ultimately giving his support to Hubert Humphrey, his vice president. Throughout that spring, McCarthy and Kennedy captured the public imagination. Yet because of the power of incumbency, Humphrey, who had not won a single primary, seemed certain to capture the nomination, particularly after Robert Kennedy was assassinated on June 6, 1968.

In order to prevent that from ever happening again, I helped to create a commission that led the 1968 Democratic Convention to change the party's delegate selection rules for the future. My role in that effort led famed journalist Howard K. Smith to air a commentary four years later on ABC's nightly television newscast. Sitting in a control room high above the cavernous convention center in Miami Beach on the opening night of the 1972 Democratic Convention, Smith, in a bit of inflated rhetoric, said that "Over the hall tonight you'll see hanging huge pictures of the men who made the Democratic Party what it is. But one is oddly missing. That of young Geoffrey Cowan, the man who did more to change Democratic Conventions than anyone since Andrew Jackson first started them."

My inspiration in 1968 was TR and the role that he had played in opening up the political process some fifty-six years earlier. Though we could not predict it at the time, political scientists now see the reforms of 1968, along with those of 1912, as pivotal moments in the development of the presidential nominating process. They often divide the history of presidential nominations into four periods: (1) nomination by members of Congress meeting by party faction, sometimes derisively called "King Caucus" (1792–1828); (2) the Pure Convention System (1832–1908); (3) the Mixed System created by the rise of the primaries (1912–1968); and (4) the Dominant Primary System (1972 to the present).

In writing this book, I hoped to gain a better understanding of the ideas and forces that led Roosevelt to champion the creation of the presidential primary; of the impact that the primaries had on the political process in that first year; and of the ways in which the lessons from 1912 still resonate with us today.

Since successful politicians so often wait for fresh ideas to mature before embracing them, I should not have been surprised or disappointed to learn that Roosevelt was a late and somewhat reluctant convert to popular democracy and the importance of presidential primaries. The first political leaders to champion the cause were a small group of men that included Senator Robert La Follette of Wisconsin, Governor Hiram Johnson of California and especially Senator Jonathan Bourne of Oregon. TR did not join that group—indeed he generally resisted their efforts until it suited his political needs. To be fair, something similar could also be said of men like La Follette, Johnson, and Bourne; they, too, tended to have self-interested motives and were animated, at least in part, by the ways in which procedural changes could advance their personal ambitions or their particular political agenda. As some activists in the 1960s used to say, "Revolutionaries are just another special interest group." Moreover, the meaning of democracy is flexible enough to accommodate a wide range of laws and policies. Seasoned professionals know that procedural nuances can be and often are shaped in ways that favor a particular insurgent or incumbent.

The week after the Republican Party nominated Taft in Chicago in 1912, the Democratic Party held a convention in Baltimore to select its nominee. The two political parties followed different sets of rules. The Republican Party awarded the nomination to the first candidate to win a majority of delegate votes on any ballot. The Democratic Party did not declare a winner until a candidate had the support of two-thirds of the delegates. If the Democratic Party had adhered to the Republican Party's rules in 1912, the Democratic nominee would have been Champ Clark of Missouri, the Speaker of the House of Representatives, who went over that threshold on the tenth ballot. But since 1832, the Democratic Party's rules had required a nominee to earn the support of two-thirds of the delegates. As a result, the convention nominated Woodrow Wilson on the forty-sixth ballot.

As a political scientist and reformer, Wilson actually opposed the two-thirds rule, which he considered undemocratic. But that rule put him in power. Unlike TR, who won most of the Republican primaries, Wilson won only five of the twelve Democratic primaries. Ironically, many historians have concluded that if the Democrats had nominated Champ Clark, who was allied with the established interest groups and party bosses, instead of Wilson, who was a political reformer, TR and his Bull Moose Party might have won the election in 1912.

BY THE TIME I finished my research on TR and the role of presidential primaries in the 1912 campaign, I was equally interested in what happened when he created his own party. The man who had championed "the right of the people to rule" somehow decided to exclude blacks from the delegations of the states of the Deep South. As a young civil rights worker, I helped to organize the Mississippi Freedom Democratic Party (MFDP) in 1964. Because most blacks were not allowed to participate in the delegate selection process in the state, the MFDP conducted its own caucuses and brought a slate of challenge delegates to the Democratic National Convention in Atlantic City that year. Though they were not seated, their cause captured the nation's attention, epitomized by the powerful testimony of Fannie Lou Hamer, a former sharecropper from Ruleville, Mississippi.

No book has ever explored Roosevelt's decision to exclude the black delegates from the Deep South, but as Sidney M. Milkis pointed out in *Theodore Roosevelt, the Progressive Party and the Transformation of American Democracy,* "there are striking parallels between the delegate selection battles of 1912 and those over the challenge of the Mississippi Freedom Party at the 1964 Democratic Convention." I wanted to try to understand how TR could reconcile his professed belief in the right of the people to rule with his decision to exclude blacks from Mississippi and other states of the Deep South from his party. Was it purely a cynical tactical decision? After all, there were almost no black voters in the South and he needed to win white votes to win any electoral votes in the region. Or did he have other more noble motives; could his actions, for example, be compared to those of Lyndon Johnson, who did everything in his power to ensure the seating of the all-white delegation from Mississippi in 1964, but then used the power of his office to press for the Voting Rights Act of 1965?

Like everyone who worked in the civil rights movement, I was inspired by Fannie Lou Hamer, by farmers, ministers, small business leaders, teachers, sharecroppers, and field hands who risked their jobs and even lives to try to vote in 1964. Those people, including those I had known in Batesville, Mississippi, were in my mind as I started to conduct research about the men TR had excluded. In explaining the campaign's decision, TR's twenty-four-year-old son Ted, who later became a civil rights champion, said that the delegates "represent the very worst type of citizen of the south," called them "absolutely venal in every way," and claimed that "the majority have no intelligence at all." Those shameful comments undoubtedly echoed the deep racial prejudices of some of TR's advisors, but they proved to be particularly inaccurate once I learned more about the people he had so derisively dismissed. In fact, the delegation was filled with successful lawyers, poets, surgeons, and business leaders. Many were polymaths with multiple degrees and occupations. They were men of uncommon eloquence, learning, and grit. Most of them moved north during the following decade as part of the Great Migration.

Trying to discover more information about those men—hoping to find a suitcase filled with old letters that would shed light on their lives and perspectives—I began to learn about and even meet their heirs. Their offspring include the first black federal judge in the history of the continental United States; the author of a number of popular books, screenplays and songs, including "The Banana Boat Song," also known as "Day-O," which was made famous by Harry Belafonte; and a slew of successful lawyers, academics, artists, and business leaders.

Yet those impressive black Mississippians were the citizens that TR kept out of the political party that he had created based on the premise and the promise that the people have a right to rule.

The man who embraced democracy as his core campaign theme and had done so much to open up the political system, had been a skeptic if not an opponent of presidential primaries and suffrage for women only weeks before he embraced them; and he had pleaded for the support of southern blacks in the Republican Party only weeks before he excluded them from his own new party. During the campaign, he used a range of tactics that were less than fully honorable. Looking at the way he conducted his campaign led me to wonder what, if anything, TR would not have done—and what any serious candidate today would not do—in order to be elected President.

Though his decision to exclude southern blacks is hard to forgive, his inconsistencies about the meaning and requirements of various aspects of democracy offer a way of understanding some of our own attitudes. Almost everyone in public life has good reason to conflate means and ends and, in some instances, to write rules that favor their cause or to try to use existing rules to game the system. Ground rules for the use of political caucuses rather than open primaries; for the right of non–party members to vote in a party's primary; for the acceptable start and end date of primaries and for their approved order; for the legitimacy or illegitimacy of winner-take-all primaries; of the power of party leaders to name "superdelegates" who do not have to face the electorate; for the number of delegates to be given to each state at the national convention; for the requirements to win an election or face a runoff; for initiatives, referenda, and recalls; for the creation of third or fourth parties; for some form of voter identification; for the participation of felons; for participation in public debates; for the role of reporters and news organizations; for political contributions to campaigns or independent committees; and for the shape of electoral districts—all these have changed throughout American history and have varied from state to state and from party to party.

The rules that control political participation in each party's presidential selection process change from year to year and from convention to convention, and the laws used to achieve democracy vary from state to state and from nation to nation. Americans are committed to democracy as a core value. But, like TR, we often define democracy in ways that suit our own desired outcomes.

Chapter One

On Saturday, February 24, 1912, Theodore Roosevelt literally jumped off the train at Boston's Back Bay Station, greeted by a "wildly enthusiastic crowd," feeling the kind of youthful energy that had become a distant memory. Since 1910, when he returned from a year-long game hunting safari in Africa that began as soon as he left the White House, he had been feeling, looking, and sounding fatigued. Though only fifty-three, he told friends that "I am really an old man." He complained of rheumatism and even doubted that he could ever take long walks again. But he loved the smell of battle, and he was putting on his armor for one last great fight. He was about to challenge William Howard Taft, the incumbent President, his handpicked successor, the man he once said has "the most loveable personality I have ever come in contact with," to a political duel.

More than 1,000 admirers shouted "Teddy, Teddy," as the train pulled into the lower level of the station. "Here he is," someone yelled, catching sight of him in his dark suit and black fedora. The crowd burst into cheers again and at least 50 men tried to grab his hand as the former President and his party moved along the platform. The crush of humanity was frightening—and exhilarating.

"Make way, men," he yelled, bearing his famous teeth and taking the lead in a human wedge. He was heavier and a bit flabbier than in his days as a boxer at Harvard in the 1870s, but he used his still-powerful arms and shoulders to press through the mass of humanity, aided by a porter pushing a cart with the group's luggage and by a few other strong men, including his twenty-four-year-old son Ted and his son-in-law, Congressman Nicholas Longworth of Cincinnati.

As they squeezed their way up the stairway, people kept pressing in and yelling out questions, shouting at him, trying to grab his hands, thrusting envelopes in his direction.

"Don't talk to me now," he pleaded, "I must get out of this human box."

Roosevelt finally pushed his way out of the stairwell and onto the open sidewalk. He was greeted by another huge crowd and a gaggle of reporters from around the world. They were there to find out if he was definitely running for President.

"By George," he told the pressmen, "that was hard work." He was panting, perspiring, and happy.

As he moved toward a waiting limousine, he refused to answer their questions. Was he planning to run for President, to challenge President Taft for the Republican Party nomination? "Boys," he said, "you're a bully good lot and I like you every one." He had not lost his ability to charm the press corps. But as he climbed into the car he told them that they would have to read the statement that he would issue from his headquarters in New York City the next day.

Two men in the crowd had the last word.

"Where's your hat?" one asked.

"It's in the ring," someone else shouted, echoing TR's instantly famous statement in Cleveland a few days earlier that his hat was in the ring, a bon mot quickly interpreted as meaning that he had decided to run.

As TR drove away, followed by a dozen taxicabs filled with reporters and cameramen, he conspicuously removed his black fedora and waved it at his supporters.

He was back in the game.

———

PEOPLE WONDERED AT the time why he had left the game—and why he had returned. He had never really wanted to leave office. When he stepped down as President of the United States on March 4, 1909, Theodore Roosevelt was deeply ambivalent about his decision. He had been President for more than seven and a half years, using his power and podium, and seizing the public's imagination in ways that were unprecedented. The public loved his background as a western cowboy who had brought thieves to justice; as a crime-busting New York City police commissioner who had cracked crime by roaming the streets; as a naturalist who collected, studied, and discovered countless new forms of life and contributed to New York's Museum of Natural History; as a reform-minded political leader who had fought against corruption as a member of the nation's Civil Service Commission; as the author of important books of history, biography, and naturalism; as a military strategist and hero who had championed a large fleet as assistant secretary of the navy and later led a troop of his own "Rough Riders" in the Spanish-American War; and as a remarkably successful New York State governor who became the nation's Vice President under William McKinley and ascended to the presidency when McKinley was assassinated on September 6, 1901.

Even before he became President, the public knew about all of this—and about the hijinks of his youthful and athletic family—through Roosevelt's own popular writing and through the adoring accounts of his life that regularly appeared in the press. And then as President, he had inspired millions by championing conservation of the nation's majestic natural resources, by using new antitrust laws to bust monopolies, and by building the Panama Canal. By 1908, the country was flooded by "Teddy bears," named for the President himself.

He could easily have been reelected in 1908, but TR had tied his own hands on the night of his election in 1904. "Under no circumstances," he told reporters as a crowd gathered for a celebration party at the White House, "will I be a candidate for or accept another nomination."

In one sense, he was following what he called "the wise custom which limits the President to two terms," a tradition established by George Washington. Though he had only been elected once, by the end of his second term TR would have been in office for almost two full terms. But he was still very young. At fifty, he would become the youngest former President in the nation's history. He loved the opportunities and trappings of the office, the chance to have what he called the "bully pulpit"; and there was so much left to do. Still, as the election of 1908 approached, he felt obliged to keep to his word.

Roosevelt's popularity was so great that he was able to name his own successor. After considering a few alternatives—including his first choice, Secretary of State Elihu Root*—TR asked his Secretary of War, William Howard Taft, to take on the task. They were close friends, had a similar sense of humor, and seemed to share a common political philosophy.

"When the two were in the White House together their laughs, Roosevelt's high pitched, Taft's rumbling, would reverberate through the corridors." As TR's wife Edith recalled, "it's always that way when they're together."

"He is going to be greatly beloved as President," TR told his military aide, Archie Butt. "I almost envy a man having a personality like Taft's. People are always prepossessed by it." With his handlebar mustache, warm laugh, and huge physique—he often weighed over 300 pounds—Taft cut a warm and surprisingly graceful figure. "One loves him at first sight."

"No one could accuse me of having a charming personality," Roosevelt added jokingly.

---

* Roosevelt told H. H. Kohlsaat that "Root would make the best President, but Taft the best candidate." Kohlsaat, "From McKinley to Harding," p. 161. On July 30, 1907, he wrote William Allen White that "Root would be a better President than Taft or me or anyone else I know. I could not express too highly my feeling for him. But at present it does not seem to me that there would be much chance of nominating or electing him." TR Letters, Volume V, p. 735.

Though it did not seem particularly important at the time, Roosevelt's and Taft's temperaments could not have been more different. Where Roosevelt was a politician, activist, and warrior, Taft was an executive, mediator, and judge. Taft had been a talented and loyal lieutenant, serving brilliantly as governor of the Philippines before joining TR's cabinet as Secretary of War. But he was ambivalent about Roosevelt's offer. He had never run for a major elective office. His background was as a lawyer and judge, and he had served with distinction on the U.S. Court of Appeals for the 6th Circuit. His real dream was to become a member or, better yet, Chief Justice of the U.S. Supreme Court.

Nevertheless, Roosevelt was convinced that Taft would be a wonderful successor. He felt that the skills of a great judge and a great political leader could be harmonized. As early as September 1901, when TR was still Vice President and Taft the governor of the Philippines, Roosevelt had publicly described Taft as the only man that he knew with "the qualities that would make a first class Chief Justice of the United States" and also "make a first class President of the United States."

Their experiences working, laughing, and talking together over the next seven years only magnified Roosevelt's admiration for Taft. "Always excepting Washington and Lincoln," he told one friend, "I believe that Taft as president will rank with any other man who has been in the White House."

Out of weakness, or ambition—or perhaps simply out of a desire to please others—Taft acceded to Roosevelt's wish and to the ambitions of his outspoken and somewhat adventurous wife, Nellie, who wanted the presidency for him—and the opportunities afforded a brilliant First Lady for herself and her causes.

HAVING ANOINTED TAFT as his successor, TR's next challenge was to make sure that he was nominated by the Republican Party and elected by the public—no easy task for a man who had never held elective office. Roosevelt proceeded to tutor Taft on the skills needed by a politician. Show them your radiant personality, Roosevelt coached. "Let the audience see you smile, always, because I feel that your nature shines out so transparently when you do smile—you big, generous, high-minded fellow," he wrote to his friend.

But he also urged Taft to "Hit them hard, old man! . . . [L]et them realize the truth, which is that for all your gentleness and kindliness and generous good nature, there never existed a man who was a better fighter when the need arose."

He advised Taft to stay in hotels, giving "everybody a fair shot at you," rather than in private homes. He warned him not to be photographed playing golf. He did not want Taft to look too elite, too far removed from the lives of the people he hoped to lead. "It's true that I myself play tennis," he told journalist Mark Sullivan, his chosen messenger. "But you never saw a photograph of me playing tennis. I'm careful about that. Photographs on horseback, yes; tennis, no. And golf is fatal."

He even tutored Taft on how to speak and what to discuss. In her memoir, Alice Roosevelt Longworth claims that her father, "who had thrown himself wholeheartedly into the business of nominating him," told Taft what subjects to discuss and how to present them.

With the benefit of TR's endorsement, tutelage, and use of the levers of political power, Taft was nominated and then elected by a margin of 1.2 million votes.

TO GIVE HIS SUCCESSOR some space, and to remove himself from the inevitable feelings of remorse and regret, Roosevelt did what he always did in such moments: he went on an adventure. In 1884, when his wife and mother died on the same day, TR had left New York for the Badlands of North Dakota. This time, with backing from the industrialist-philanthropist Andrew Carnegie and from *Scribner's Magazine*, which planned to publish accounts of his exploits, he left America immediately after Taft's inauguration for a safari to parts of Africa that were still uncharted.

Almost as soon as he left American soil, friends started to send Roosevelt letters suggesting that he might find it necessary to run again in

1912. Perhaps his best correspondent was Henry Cabot Lodge, the senator from Massachusetts and fellow historian, who was one of TR's most reliable sources of information and advice. Twelve years TR's senior, with a patrician manner, thick Edwardian mustache and goatee, and elegant dress, Lodge was an unlikely but nevertheless intimate friend.

On December 27, 1909, in a long, detailed, confidential message, Lodge brilliantly laid out the problems with Taft's nine months in office and predicted that if the Republicans lost the midterm elections in 1910 (as later happened) the pressure for TR "to enter the field and take the nomination away from him" (which "you would not want") will become so strong that "neither you nor anyone in your place can control" it. The party's leaders "will insist on having you both because they want you anyway and because they want to win."

That refrain stayed with TR for the next two years. At least on some level, he believed that Lodge was right: there was a good chance that the party's leaders would "insist" that he run. Having no inkling that presidential primaries might change the dynamics of the selection process, both Lodge and Roosevelt assumed that if they were dissatisfied with Taft, the party's leaders would have the power to hand him the nomination.

With that background, Lodge pleaded with TR to "say nothing about your own political intentions . . . until you get home and we can talk it over."

Four days later, Gifford Pinchot sent Roosevelt an even more insistent missive. A tall, lean, and athletic graduate of Yale, with a dark, drooping mustache, Pinchot, the chief of the U.S. Forest Service, was popularly known as the nation's forester. With the unyielding conviction of a true believer, Pinchot could be a zealot for causes he held dear. With more than a touch of irony, one acquaintance called him a "descendant of old New York merchant families, whose dominant inner passion was to flee from the ease that inherited wealth invited him to." In order to harden his flesh "he slept on the floor with a wooden pillow and each morning for his bath had his valet throw buckets of icy water over his sinewy body."

Pinchot had been TR's partner in championing the cause of conservation throughout Roosevelt's years in office. They had been on outdoor adventures, enjoyed wrestling and boxing, and spent hours on the White House floor going over maps, finding areas to turn into national parks. He was a charter member of TR's famed (but seldom photographed) "tennis cabinet." Roosevelt assumed that Pinchot would be able to champion conservation causes under his successor.

Soon after assuming office, however, in one of his most notorious and controversial acts, Taft backed his new Secretary of the Interior, Richard Ballinger, in a series of decisions that seemed to backtrack on TR's cherished conservation plans. When Pinchot led a public campaign against Ballinger, Taft felt compelled to fire him for insubordination.

"The tendency of the administration thus far, taken as a whole," Pinchot told his friend and former boss, "has been directly away from the Roosevelt policies." While he was a good man, Taft had allowed himself to become aligned with the more conservative forces in Congress, those who refused to accept change, men widely derided as "stand-patters." Pinchot's letter set forth a sixteen-point indictment, listing failure after failure of the new administration, some personal, some substantive. "I have known, admired, and respected Mr. Taft since my boyhood and have wanted to give him every benefit of the doubt," Pinchot wrote. But he held out little hope. The problem was Taft's temperament. He has shown "a most surprising weakness and indecision, and . . . [a] desire to act as a judge, dealing with issues only when they are brought to him, and not as what the President really is, the advocate and active guardian of the general welfare."

"We have fallen back down the hill you led us up."

The letters from Lodge and Pinchot reached Roosevelt two months later, as he emerged from the African jungle and arrived at Gondokoro, a trading station on the east bank of the Nile in what is now South Sudan. By that time, a special runner from a press agency had reached TR at his safari's encampment on Lake Albert Nyanza with the news that Taft had fired Pinchot. Making it clear that he did not intend to criticize Taft, Roosevelt arranged for Pinchot to meet him in Italy in mid-April, at the start of a two-month trip on the continent where TR met world leaders and old friends, gave lectures, and represented President Taft as the official American representative at the funeral of England's King Edward VII.

By the time TR returned to a hero's welcome in New York on June 18, 1910, a "Back from Elba" movement had captured the country's attention. Though it was, in part, a tongue-in-cheek concept, a play on the experience of Napoleon a hundred years earlier, it was also very serious. So serious that Roosevelt, who did not want to be blamed for Taft's faults, or drafted (or, at least, drafted yet) as his replacement, wished he could just stay in Europe. In letter after letter, he told friends that "it is a very unpleasant situation." As he told Lodge: "Ugh! I do dread getting back to America and having to plunge into the cauldron of politics."

For the next year, Roosevelt continued to be plagued by political nightmares. As historian H. W. Brands shrewdly observed, his mood reflected an uncharacteristic uncertainty about the right course of action. There was no clear role for a relatively young ex-president. He had reached the peaks and there was no new hill to climb. Thanks to the Former Presidents Act adopted in 1958, presidents after leaving office are now entitled to a pension, staff, office expenses, medical care, and Secret Service protection. But none of those assets were available to TR. Although his family had once been deemed wealthy, Roosevelt needed to earn an income.

Lyman Abbott, the editor of *The Outlook* magazine offered what seemed an ideal solution. With roots in the social gospel movement, *The Outlook* (originally named *The Christian Union*) had been edited by famed abolitionist Henry Ward Beecher. Abbott succeeded Beecher as the pastor of Plymouth Church and as editor of *The Outlook*. On November 4, 1908, while Roosevelt was still in the White House, Abbott announced that TR would join the magazine as a "Special Contributing Editor" immediately after the inauguration. *The Outlook* provided him with a healthy salary, a good office, a group of bright colleagues, a ready outlet for his ideas, and occasional support when he traveled around the country. TR told his son that the magazine paid him $12,000 a year (the equivalent of more than $300,000 a century later) "which is very important to me to have as long as the family are being brought up." He intended to work there until 1918, when he would be sixty years old.

Roosevelt constantly wrote to friends about his physical limitations, complained about his critics in the party and the press, and said that he wanted to be out of public life. Yet his role at *The Outlook* and as a senior statesman was not fully satisfying. Somehow he could never stay out of, or above, the fray. Though some thought it undignified for a former president, when friends asked him to serve as temporary chair of the 1910 New York State Republican Convention, in order to combat the forces of reaction, he jumped into a bitter and mean-spirited intraparty dispute. When supporters in the West asked him to come out their way on a speaking tour, he let *The Outlook* charter a special train for a three-week trip. On one level, for all of their substantive and personal differences, he did not want to interfere with his old friend who was now in the White House; on another he could not resist the lure of public life, public pronouncements, and public acclaim.

During a 5,500-mile, sixteen-state tour in the late summer of 1910, he spoke to huge, sometimes frenzied, crowds, espousing ideas that he labeled "The New Nationalism." In comments that many observers considered tantamount to a manifesto for a new campaign, he called for workman's compensation laws, job training, a progressive income tax, a graduated and effective inheritance tax, workplace protections for women and children, a commission to set tariff policies that would remove the decisions from the inevitably corrupt political process, and closer government control of business as an effective alternative to anti-trust laws. In late 1910, *The Outlook* published his speeches from that tour in a book called *The New Nationalism*.

Roosevelt's rhetoric became particularly inflamed on August 31 when he dedicated a park in Osawatomie, Kansas, named in memory of John Brown, the abolitionist who became a martyr to the antislavery cause when he was hanged for treason in 1859 after he and his men killed five supporters of slavery in Pottawatomie, Kansas, and later seized the U.S. arsenal at Harpers Ferry, Virginia. Standing on a kitchen table, Roosevelt spoke for ninety minutes to a crowd of more than 30,000 people as sandwiches and drinks were sold in a gathering that resembled a county fair more than a political rally. The throng cheered as TR warned that Americans faced a new war "between the men who possess more than they have earned and the men who have earned more than they possess." Many reporters were convinced that he planned to challenge Taft. This region "takes it for granted that Theodore Roosevelt will be the next Republican candidate for President," a *New York World* correspondent wired from Cheyenne, Wyoming. But while there were those who hoped that he might be amenable to some form of draft, TR had no intention of running.

Much of the powerful rhetoric on that trip was written by Gifford Pinchot, who was traveling on the train with him. Roosevelt's original draft of the Osawatomie speech consisted of what Pinchot's brother, Amos, called "seven thousand words of safe platitudes." Gifford Pinchot wrote a muscular alternative draft, but Roosevelt continued to vacillate. Having been out of the country for a year, he had not been forced to choose sides between his friends and sympathizers in the establishment and the insurgent camps. In Amos Pinchot's words, TR was "still fluctuating between a very radical and a very conservative state of mind."

Wanting to be sure that he was aligned with the insurgents, the Pinchot brothers lobbied him mercilessly. "I made it my business to haunt the *Outlook* offices," Amos said, "to try to persuade the Colonel to adopt [Gifford's draft] as rewritten." Finally, Roosevelt used the Pinchot version, delivering what many deemed the most radical speech of his life. His words thrilled audiences in the West and leaders of what TR deemed the "ultra-insurgent" faction. But they stunned and disturbed a great many of his other friends. "Its delivery proved the signal for his reactionary friends to close in on him with more determination than ever" Amos recalled. He said that TR quickly "maneuvered a retreat from Osawatomie."

"I have never had a more unpleasant summer," TR wrote Elihu Root after his "New Nationalism" tour. He told Root that he did not like Taft's policies but that he was at least equally offended by "the wild irresponsible folly of the ultra-insurgents."

Taft was a disappointment, but TR had supported mediocre candidates before. He wrote a series of letters to his son Ted, who had moved to San Francisco after graduating from Harvard. The letters offered an ongoing tutorial about his philosophy and his concept of political leadership.

Taft is "a flubdub with a streak of the second rate and the common in him," TR told Ted. "He has not the slightest idea of what is necessary if this country is to make social and industrial progress."

Nevertheless, he expected to support his former protégé. "During my thirty years in politics, for nine-tenths of the time I have been accustomed to make the best I could of the second rate," he said. "I think Taft a better president than McKinley or Harrison."

THE DRUMBEAT PERSISTED, but Roosevelt continued to resist until late 1911. Why did he finally relent? Over the years, Roosevelt and his followers would offer countless explanations for his return to active duty. As he told his friend Charles G. Washburn, "Any change of decision like that or any reaching of a decision comes as a result of a cumulative process—whether it is a determination to run for President or to adopt the Declaration of Independence."

Part of the cumulative process was certainly based on mounting differences in policy, ideology, and style. While they agreed on many issues, there were areas of bitter disagreement, including Taft's support of an arbitration treaty to resolve international disputes, his reliance on antitrust laws rather than regulation to control business excesses, and his failure to use the executive authority of the President aggressively on behalf of conservation. TR also started to attack certain policies that he had originally endorsed, such as Taft's efforts to establish a reciprocity agreement for trade with Canada. One hundred years later, however, those issues—unlike a split over a war or over slavery—do not seem sufficiently dramatic to explain the decision to challenge Taft.

Roosevelt also told friends he had been offended by what seemed Taft's personal slights to TR's former cabinet members, his family, and to the former president himself, notably a letter giving his brother Charley more credit for his victory than TR. Taft had certainly given shoddy treatment to his former colleagues, particularly those who had been led to believe they would remain in the cabinet and were then summarily replaced. In 1916, TR said that Taft's decision to abandon the Country Life Commission that he had created to make rural life more attractive in the modern world had been "the last straw." Moreover, he was deeply affected by Taft's decision to dismiss Gifford Pinchot, the crusading forester who had been Roosevelt's great ally.

There were those who marked the filing of the Justice Department's brief in an antitrust case against U.S. Steel in late October 1911 as the decisive moment in their relationship since Taft's lawyers included a section suggesting that TR had been naïve in not allowing the case to be filed while he was in office. The government's brief implied that he had been duped by Wall Street financiers. While it was not the single cause of his decision to run, the document was needlessly embarrassing. Equally important, the case provided TR with a powerful argument that he could use when recruiting important financial and political figures, and with a reason to ask policy-makers and the public to rethink the proper uses of antitrust laws and to reimagine the best ways to control large corporations.

None of those issues fully explains Roosevelt's decision to run. It seems far more likely that he had been hoping to avoid a direct conflict with Taft and to run in 1916. But then on January 21, 1911, men he considered to be the more extreme insurgent forces in the party met at the home of Senator Robert M. "Fighting Bob" La Follette to create an organization they called the National Progressive Republican

League, which adopted a political agenda and then led an effort to create presidential primaries in as many states as possible. Though many members of the group were his friends, TR refused to join. Since TR insisted on remaining on the sidelines, in June 1911, Senator La Follette entered the race for President himself with the enthusiastic support of men, including some longtime TR friends like Pinchot, that TR considered "wild-eyed ultra-radicals." La Follette was a true crusader from the Middle West, and he and his National Progressive Republican League were defining the reformers' agenda.

With his French name, radical reputation, and strident tone, La Follette was anathema in some parts of the country. "What the people of the Middle West do not understand," *Collier's* editor Mark Sullivan observed later that year, "is that La Follette has never made the faintest impression, practically, East of Ohio." But by late October, thanks to the advent of presidential primaries, La Follette was looking like a serious candidate. Even if he couldn't get the party's nomination, he was capturing the imagination and endorsements of men who would otherwise have been in Roosevelt's camp.

La Follette later concluded that TR was influenced by jealousy, by competitive juices, and by the fear that even if La Follette were to lose in 1912 he would be the reformers' first choice to run for the party's nomination in 1916. TR had a more public-spirited way of seeing the same facts: he was even more troubled by La Follette's temperament and views than by Taft's policies, weakness, and corporate and political associates.

In a confidential letter to a college friend, TR said that he decided to run largely because "the professed reformers were coming more and more under the lead of La Follette and in all the United States there does not exist a worse type of public man." He called La Follette the "most dangerous" man in public life. TR's views on "Fighting Bob" reflected the consensus of leaders in the East. Trying to understand their differences, one scholar concluded that Roosevelt believed that La Follette-like progressives were too radical because they had too much faith in direct democracy and too great a sense of moral outrage toward corporate capitalism. By late fall, TR was becoming convinced (or had begun to convince himself) that only he could represent and save the party's responsible reformist center. If he wanted to be a factor in the 1912 election, he could not remain on the sidelines.

Once he began to think seriously about running, the scent of battle made the fight irresistible. Less than a year earlier, TR had tried to recapture the thrill of youth, his days as a Rough Rider, by asking President Taft, in the event of war with Mexico, to allow him to "raise a division of cavalry, such as the regiment that I commanded in Cuba." But there was no war with Mexico, and Taft was not so foolhardy as to give TR a hunting license to create one. A presidential campaign, though, and one with fresh recruits: now that was a fight worth making, a fight to restore the spirits.

Some people can enjoy life after power and the limelight, but Roosevelt needed action and conflict as other men need oxygen. His friend Henry Adams insisted that "his restless and combative energy was more than abnormal . . . he was pure act . . . he lived naturally in restless agitation." During the past year, he had been miserable. He was living on the north shore of Long Island, near Oyster Bay, in the twenty-two-room home that he called Sagamore Hill, and spending part of the week in New York City at his office at *The Outlook*. Arguing that there was only one president at a time, Roosevelt preferred to be called "Colonel," the title that he had earned in the Spanish-American War.

After a visit to Roosevelt in Oyster Bay, one friend "found the Colonel in a most depressed state of mind; all his old buoyancy was gone, and he really seemed to be a changed man." Roosevelt's mood was captured in a series of remarkable letters written by Archie Butt, the White House military attaché who was like a son to both TR and Taft.

Edith Roosevelt was unhappy, too, apparently because of her husband's depression. But she prayed that he would not enter into a political campaign as the way to better health. "If she could have her wish," Archie Butt reported, "it would be never to hear of politics again."

President Taft, who still loved his old friend and mentor, knew that only a good fight could revive him. "It depresses me very deeply, more deeply than anyone can know, to think of him sitting there at Oyster Bay alone and feeling himself deserted," he told Archie. "It is a dreary spot in winter. . . . To feel everything slipping away from him, all the popularity, the power which he loved, and above all the ability to do what he thought was of real benefit to the country, to feel it all going and then to be alone!"

With Roosevelt's character, there was really only one remedy. "If he could only fight!" Taft said. "That is what he delights in and what is denied to him now."

"All great souls have their hours of darkness, and the Colonel is having his now," Archie told his sister-in-law. "But it is heart-breaking."

Senator Elihu Root, whom Roosevelt admired as much as any man in public life, had a firm grasp on his friend's emotions. He told Roosevelt that his character would make it impossible for him to remain on the sidelines as a willing but reluctant candidate. You won't be able to refrain from battle, Root said, "because of your temperament; because of the urgent need of your nature for prompt decision and action which must make an attitude like this for you a condition of unstable equilibrium against which your whole nature will frequently cry out and urge you to end it."

"No thirsty sinner ever took a pledge which was harder for him to keep than it will be for you to maintain this position."

FOUR DAYS BEFORE he arrived in Boston, Roosevelt had made a speech in Columbus, Ohio, that energized his supporters but, fatefully, made it impossible for many of his friends to join his campaign. He had been invited there to address the state's Constitutional Convention, a fit setting for a thoughtful reexamination of the principles of government. Predictably, the Columbus speech generated headlines everywhere; it was widely reprinted and distributed with the title "A Charter of Democracy."

"We Progressives believe that the people have the right, the power, and the duty to protect themselves and their own welfare; that human rights are supreme over all other rights; that wealth should be the servant, not the master, of the people," he told the crowd in what amounted to a platform for his presidential campaign, and a call to arms for progressives. "We believe that unless representative government does absolutely represent the people it is not representative government at all."

Much of Roosevelt's speech that day was conventional progressive dogma, but he added one important new idea—a proposal that inspired progressives and stunned many of his friends. He had been infuriated by a series of state court decisions that had invalidated important pieces of social legislation that he had advocated in New York. In response, Roosevelt said that the people should have the right to overturn such decisions by popular vote.

He lavished particular scorn on a decision a few months earlier in which the top court in New York overturned the state's workmen's compensation act. "In their decision the judges admitted the wrong and the suffering caused by the practices against which the law was aimed," he said. "They admitted that other civilized nations had abolished these wrongs and practices. But they took the ground that the Constitution of the United States, instead of being an instrument to secure justice, had been ingeniously devised absolutely to prevent justice. . . . No anarchist or orator, raving against the Constitution, ever framed an indictment of it so severe as these worthy and well-meaning judges must be held to have framed if their reasoning be accepted as true."

"I wish I could make you visualize to yourselves what these decisions against which I so vehemently protest really represent of suffering and injustice.

"I wish I had the power to bring before you the men maimed or dead, the women and children left to struggle against bitter poverty because the bread-winner has gone.

"In such a case the fault is not with the Constitution; the fault is in the judges' construction of the Constitution; and what is required is power for the people to reverse this false and wrong construction."

Many people believed that the speech was designed to appeal to reformers in the West, particularly California's new crusading governor, Hiram Johnson, whose state had recently given the people the ability to vote to remove judges from office if they did not like decisions that they had rendered. Since many of the California reformers considered La Follette much more reliable than Roosevelt, it was important for him to find a way to win their hearts.

The speech also addressed the concerns of the "wild-eyed ultra-radicals" such as Amos Pinchot who were torn between La Follette and TR. Though he was almost a decade younger than his more famous brother, Gifford, and had never attained important office, the thirty-nine-year-old Amos was a powerful force in the progressive movement. Like Gifford, he had been a member of Skull and Bones, the elite secret society at Yale, and thanks to wealth and position inherited from his parents, he belonged to the right clubs and could afford to provide financial support to candidates and causes that he deemed important. With deep-set blue eyes and a strong chin, he could be at least as intense as his brother, and even less practical.

Unimpressed with earlier drafts, Amos warned the Colonel that he needed to show that he had spine. "I differ with you, Colonel, radically as to the need of your showing just how progressive you are," he said. "No man has a right to be in public life without taking the people absolutely into his confidence. The Progressives who have doubted your progressiveness are not few. But their doubts are not as to your progressive spirit or your desire to help the Progressive cause, but to the methods by which you may see fit to carry on your fight for the people."

With its powerful statement about the courts, the speech stirred the hearts of progressives who had doubted Roosevelt's resolve. One California congressman who had been a bitter private critic, now said that "Roosevelt's Columbus speech is sufficiently clear and definite to satisfy any of us." A reporter from Detroit called it "the greatest speech

I have ever had the profit of reading. If the legislature will now kindly pass the presidential primary act for Michigan, we will send to Chicago a delegation that will be an inspiring example."

But within hours the Columbus speech produced a firestorm of criticism, much of it from Roosevelt's friends and former cabinet members. Many of them were lawyers steeped in legal training and thinking and perhaps influenced by their association with corporate clients. They believed deeply in the sanctity of the courts to protect the rights and processes guaranteed by the Constitution. To them, it seemed that Roosevelt had capitulated to the views of those who believed absolutely in the wisdom of the "majority" and of their power to overrule the courts, even if the majority wanted a law that would violate the Constitution; even if the law would crush the rights of the minority as protected in the Bill of Rights and in the constitutional amendments that followed the Civil War; even where the majority's wishes would undermine any and all right to private property.

Longtime friends such as Elihu Root and Henry Stimson, his Long Island neighbor who had just run with TR's backing for governor of New York in 1910, could not support him after that speech. At least one of TR's top campaign aides later argued that that speech alone, by pushing men like Root into Taft's camp, was "responsible for the determination of the Republican National Committee that Colonel Roosevelt should not be the nominee of the Chicago Convention."

The speech even compromised his relations with Senator Henry Cabot Lodge, who had been urging TR to run for more than two years. Before Columbus, newspapers reported that his campaign in Massachusetts would be headed by Lodge, along with Lodge's son-in-law, Congressman Augustus Gardner.

But Roosevelt's speech had made that impossible.

Shortly after dinner on the night of Roosevelt's formal announcement, Lodge and Gardner called on Alice Roosevelt Longworth at her home to tell her that as much as they loved her father, they could not support his campaign. They disagreed too deeply with his position on the recall of judicial opinions.

"I never thought that any situation could arise which would have made me so miserably unhappy as I have been during the last week," Lodge told Roosevelt in a handwritten note. "I had not realized that our differences were so wide."

With regret, he told a friend that "Roosevelt's Columbus speech has turned Taft from a man into a principle."

Scores of Roosevelt's oldest friends and advisors defected, saying that they could not support him after his speech in Ohio. After that, as Alice said, "He had few advisors with whom he could really consult."

Alice, who had never wanted her father to run, "missed the old friends." But her father had new friends and a great battle to wage.

AS TR HAPPILY greeted the crowd in Boston, Edith Roosevelt was at the Port of New York, boarding the United Fruit liner *Turrialba*, headed for Colón, the sea port on the Isthmus of Panama, and a monthlong visit to South America. The press said that she was leaving for her health, to recover from an almost fatal horseback riding accident the previous fall. But she actually had other reasons for leaving. She had a feeling of foreboding. She hated the thought of another campaign, particularly one that was so certain to become unbearably bitter, inviting new attacks by the heavily partisan press, taking Theodore off on exhausting campaign trips, and pitting her husband against a man he had once loved. She knew that those pressing him to run had their own interests in mind, not his, and she resented what her biographer called "the Republican intriguers thronging around Sagamore," their home on Long Island.

"Politics are hateful," she had told her son Kermit two weeks earlier. "There is no possible result which could give me aught but deep regret."

As she boarded the ship with Ethel, her twenty-one-year-old daughter, a reporter called out a question.

"What are your plans for the trip?" he asked.

"You know I never, never talk," Edith said.

Keeping pace with her as she walked to her stateroom, the reporter tried again. "Is the Colonel to join you on the isthmus?"

"You had better ask him. I never, never, never talk," she said, trying to back away. "Never."

Ethel was a bit more forthcoming. When several large hatboxes arrived in the room, the reporter asked Ethel: "Is any one of those hats to go into the ring?"

"Father's hat is not among them," Ethel said tartly. "I guess he has that one with him."

Edith despised this new foray into public life. "I was forced to be away," she wrote a family friend. "In all my life I was never so unhappy."

ROOSEVELT'S OFFICIAL ANNOUNCEMENT came in the form of a letter issued by his office at *The Outlook* at 6 p.m. on Sunday, February 25. While Sunday was usually reserved for observation of the Sabbath, TR's team knew that the story was certain to dominate the next morning's headlines. He attended church in the morning, had lunch with friends, and then went to the home of his host for the night, Judge Robert Grant, a novelist and fellow member of the Harvard Board of Overseers.

As soon as the story hit the wires, Roosevelt, dressed in evening clothes, stepped out of Grant's house. "Beaming" and "unusually happy," he was greeted by dozens of reporters.

Everyone in the press noted his newly buoyant mood. He was "bubbling over with enthusiasm," the *New York World* observed, "as smiling and happy as a man who deliberately takes a plunge into an icy pool and comes up all panting and glowing for a rub-off."

Reporters fired dozens of political questions at him as soon as he appeared.

"It has been a very quiet day," Roosevelt laughed. "I have not seen one human being who is interested in politics." The reporters knew that he was playing with them.

And what about tonight?

"I'm having a quiet literary evening," he chuckled. "I plan to spend the evening discussing Dickens, Thackeray, and Scott with a certain Harvard professor with whose views I don't entirely agree."

It was the kind of banter that he loved—and that led most working reporters to love him—combining philosophy, literature, and the cat-and-mouse game of politics.

ROOSEVELT HAD DICTATED the names on the sparkling guest list for Robert Grant's small dinner party that evening. The group included William Allen White, a progressive writer and editor from Emporia, Kansas, who was a charter member of La Follette's Progressive Republican League and Arthur Hill, a prominent young Boston attorney.

For more than three hours, as waiters brought out wine and a splendid repast, Roosevelt held forth in a fascinating monologue punctuated by a series of questions. Lacing his conversation with stories about the kings that he had met during his year abroad and with a discussion of great literature, he spent most of the dinner discussing what Grant called "the burning question."

Arthur Hill, who had hoped that Taft would name him to the federal bench, was so enthralled that he was prepared to give up his personal ambitions. "The effect of the Colonel's personality on those he meets is really extraordinary," Hill told his mother. "Even the women waiting on the table were carried away." One said that she "wanted to just stand with my mouth open and listen to him talking." A woman who was sewing upstairs begged for the privilege of waiting on the table just for a few minutes, saying "All we Germans love Mr. Roosevelt, because he is not afraid of anything."

"It's good-bye to my chances for a federal judgeship," Hill concluded. "But hang it all, I would rather have two or three lunches with Teddy than any office you could mention."

But when it came to the "burning question," Judge Grant and his guests expressed deep reservations about Roosevelt's planned campaign. Roosevelt joyfully parried each critique.

"Will any of the party leaders be with you?" Grant asked.

"No," Roosevelt said, "None of them. Not even Lodge, I think. I don't see how he can. My support will come from the people, officered by a few young lieutenants." Men like Arthur Hill.

Much of the evening was devoted to TR's view of the courts. One guest objected that the proposal to recall judicial decisions would "destroy representative government and substitute the whims of the populace at the moment."

Nonsense, Roosevelt responded. We don't have representative government as it is. "I can name forty-six Senators who secured their seats and hold them by the favor of a Wall Street magnate," he said. "Do you call that popular government?"

To the group's amazement, he could not explain how his proposed recall of judicial decisions would work in practice. Much as he was enthralled by his personality, Arthur Hill, Roosevelt's prospective young lieutenant, was stunned by the new candidate's intellectual incoherence. Roosevelt didn't seem to understand the differences between state and federal law, nor could he describe how his proposal would relate to the responsibility of courts to protect property rights or the rights of political minorities.*

Judge Grant called TR's proposal "an 'indigestible mole'—an ethical social idea not yet properly worked out."

"I wouldn't have believed that a man could have been President of

---

* "He is entirely incoherent in his thought and that is one reason why he is such an excellent representative of American feeling," Hill told his mother before the dinner in one of a series of insightful and self-deprecating letters. "We ought to be led by an enthusiast and a man of vigor, and Roosevelt is all of that. But as for his thought, I do not think it is worth thinking about except as far as it reveals his personality. The best he does is to read good books and imperfectly understand their contents." Hill to Caroline Inches Hill, February 25, 1912, ADH.

the United States and know so little law," Hill wrote to his mother after the dinner.

Judge Grant described the remarkable evening in a detailed letter a month later. TR "realized that the probabilities were all against his nomination; that a President in office has all the machinery on his side; but . . ." And there was a but.

"But," Grant wrote, Roosevelt believed that "if he could reach the popular vote through direct primaries, he could hope to win."

Chapter Two

When he announced his candidacy, Roosevelt's campaign and campaign strategy were based on the importance of popular democracy, with particular emphasis on presidential primaries. But until a month earlier, when he concluded they had the potential to revolutionize the political process and offered the best and perhaps only way to wrest the nomination from a sitting president, he and his supporters had been privately and publicly skeptical about the virtues of such primaries.

As a student of history and politics, Roosevelt knew how candidates had been chosen in the past. For the first several elections after the adoption of the Constitution, presidential nominees were selected by members of Congress sitting as party caucuses—a group widely derided as "King Caucus" because it gave so much power to a small group of elected officials. Some critics also claimed that the system violated the separation of powers principle by giving the legislature so much power over the choice of the executive. Moreover, it was inherently undemocratic since those states and congressional districts that lacked congressional representation in the party's caucus were denied any voice in the selection of the party's nominee.

Starting in 1832, in an innovation often credited to, and in any case certainly popularized by, Andrew Jackson, the major political parties started to pick their nominees at national conventions for which each state was allowed to determine its own method of selecting delegates. In some states, delegates were chosen by the party's representatives in the state legislature; in others, by the state party leadership; in still others, by local caucuses and state conventions open to all members of the party. As a practical matter, all of these systems had a key characteristic in common: they could be controlled by a small group of political insiders.

Through patronage and the other powers of the office, a sitting president and his allies typically controlled his party's political machinery in almost every state. Having spent most of his life in politics, Roosevelt knew that it would be virtually impossible to take the nomination away from an elected president who wanted to be renominated. In the life of the Republic, it had never happened. But without any support from Roosevelt, a revolution was going on, largely below the radar.

At the end of the nineteenth century and in the first decade of the twentieth, a few states began to experiment with new means of popular government by creating primaries that allowed voters to participate directly in the selection of candidates for local and state office. Those reforms were part of the larger set of issues that constituted the progressive agenda, many of which were designed to use the power of government to reduce the power of the large corporations that had burst onto the scene after the Civil War as part of the Industrial Revolution.

Large railroads had become indispensable means of transportation for farmers, manufacturers, and local merchants; if unchecked by government regulations, they had the ability to—and often did—set rates for goods and services that could destroy or at least impoverish enterprises and communities everywhere. They and other new industries such as oil, coal, steel, and farm machinery were spending lavish amounts of money to select and control government representatives at the local, state, and national level. The new superrich owners and managers became known derisively as "Robber Barons." Some reformers wanted laws that would protect workers and children from horrendous working conditions; others wanted to protect consumers from unsafe and unhealthy products; still others, such as farmers and small business owners who did not want to pay what they deemed exorbitant prices to buy raw material or to ship their products, called for laws that would protect their own interests.

The villainy of the powerful companies was described in new national magazines and in novels such as Frank Norris's *Octopus*, published in 1901, which portrayed an evil railroad in conflict with ranchers in California, and Upton Sinclair's *The Jungle*, published in 1906, which showed the grinding poverty and unsanitary conditions in the meatpacking industry. The reformers had some successes, including the creation of the Interstate Commerce Commission in 1887, the adoption of federal antitrust laws in 1890, and a series of reforms under Theodore Roosevelt that included passage of the Pure Food and Drug Act in 1906. But large corporate interests often controlled the legislatures and courts. As a counterweight, progressive reformers wanted to put more power into the hands of citizens, giving them the ability to enact laws directly through a process that they labeled the "initiative and referendum"; to recall elected officials and judges; and to allow the public rather than state legislatures to elect the members of the United States Senate. Efforts to allow the public to play a direct role in the selection of presidential nominees became an important part of that movement.

In 1905, under the leadership of Governor Robert M. La Follette, Wisconsin adopted a law calling for the direct election of delegates to national conventions. He had a deeply personal reason for wanting the reform. In May of 1904, La Follette's progressive faction of the Republican Party had organized a convention at the University of Wisconsin's red brick gymnasium to nominate candidates for state office and to select delegates to the national Republican Convention to be held in Chicago the next month. He had been told that the conservative faction of the state party would try to steal the convention by rushing into the auditorium past the ticket-takers and seating scores of men with fake credentials and badges, so La Follette arranged for the installation of a barbed wire fence leading to the entrance of the gym so that people could only approach the building single file along a passageway lined by what some called "menacing guards" and others called college athletes. Those with what La Follette called "counterfeit credentials" were excluded. The men in the gym then nominated La Follette as the party's nominee for governor, his group of progressive reformers for other state offices, and his slate of delegates to the national convention.

Denouncing what they labeled La Follette's strong-arm tactics, the conservatives, known as the Stalwarts, held their own convention the next day at the Madison Opera House, where they selected former congressman Samuel Cook as the Republican nominee for governor, a group of Stalwart candidates for state office, and a competing slate of delegates to the national convention.

The Wisconsin Supreme Court ruled that La Follette and the other men nominated for state office at the red brick gym were the legal candidates of the party. As a result, La Follette and his group of reformers ran for state office and were reelected as Republicans. But even though the delegates had been selected at the same convention as the state officeholders, it was up to the national Republican Party, not the courts, to decide which slate of delegates should be seated at the convention. A month later, at the Republican National Convention in Chicago, the Credentials Committee voted unanimously to seat the Stalwarts who had been selected at the Madison Opera House rather than La Follette's delegates.

One of the delegates denied a seat in Chicago was Robert M. La Follette. He was later told that Credentials Committee members had been warned that "under no circumstances should this Wisconsin movement be allowed to spread; that La Follette was a dangerous man." The Republican National Convention that year was controlled by Theodore Roosevelt, who was about to be named the party's nominee for President; but TR refused to intervene on behalf of La Follette and his delegates. That experience led La Follette to support the direct election of delegates to future conventions. It also helped poison his relationship with TR.

Pennsylvania adopted a somewhat similar law the next year. However, while the new primaries in Wisconsin and Pennsylvania permitted voters to select delegates, neither of these laws allowed voters to express a preference for the presidential candidate those delegates would support. Those and one or two similar delegate selection laws were not a factor in the 1908 conventions.

IN OCTOBER 1910, thanks to a crusade led and funded by Senator Jonathan Bourne, a man largely forgotten by history, Oregon adopted the nation's first law allowing voters to cast a preference vote for the candidate that they would like to see nominated for President and to select the delegates to the national convention. Bourne's somewhat zealous enthusiasm sparked what became a national movement that transformed American elections, creating primaries of the kind that now dominate the nation's political life.

The scion of one of the wealthiest families in Massachusetts, Bourne had a reputation as an adventurous bon vivant who had dropped out of Harvard, been sent to sea by his father, been shipwrecked in a typhoon in the China Sea, and landed in Oregon on his way back home. He was also known as a fun-loving daredevil prepared to defy authority and convention. According to legend, he once made a series of $500 bets with some Harvard classmates. First he bet that he could eat a dozen raw eggs. They took the bet and he ate the eggs. Then he bet that he could drink a fifth of champagne without removing the bottle from his lips. He won that bet, too. Then he bet them that he could eat the window curtain in their dorm room. There were no takers. Years later, one of his friends said that she was sure that he would have eaten the curtain, too, "because that's the type of man he is."

With a flair for business, his varied career included successful stints as a cotton goods manufacturer, real estate speculator, plantation owner, and mining promoter. Close observers commented that his "political interests tended to coincide with his mining interests." In 1903, while President Roosevelt was desperately trying to prevent the private exploitation of federal forests, Bourne was lobbying friends in Congress to amend the federal mining law to permit operators to cut timber from government land.

One student of his career argued that Bourne became a progressive because he realized that "the political potential of the initiative and referendum amendment might be useful to his own interest in being elected to the United States Senate." In that era before the Seventeenth Amendment, the Constitution gave state legislatures the power to select U.S. senators. Bourne supported an unusual Oregon "Direct Primary" law that allowed voters to express their preferences and that effectively required the legislature to follow the public's wishes. Once the law was adopted, he became a candidate himself, pouring substantial amounts of his own money into his winning campaign, sending personal letters to every voter in the state and paying for advertisements and editorials wherever he could place them.

Shortly after arriving in Washington in early 1907, the cadaverously thin new senator became known for his hospitality, charm, large and varied cigar collection, and for hosting what soon became known as a "millionaire dinner." Bourne did his best to befriend the President, convincing TR to take him along on his strenuous walks through Rock Creek Park. He claimed that he saw the President "almost daily." Bourne genuinely admired and perhaps even adored Roosevelt. One reporter described him as a "fanatic" on the subject.

But his affection became too intense, too extreme. Before long he became an unwelcome pest, especially when he launched a crusade to have Roosevelt renominated in 1908. Roosevelt had made it clear that he did not want to be renominated or reelected; that having served for almost two full terms, since McKinley's assassination in September 1901, he was following the two-term tradition that had been begun by George Washington; and that Taft was his heir apparent. Nevertheless, Bourne kept pressing TR to seek what he called a "second elected term," a phrase that, thanks to Bourne's campaign, became a recurring refrain in the media. He even offered a cash prize for the best essay on why Roosevelt should run again.

At first TR dismissed him as "a sincere fanatic." But Bourne wouldn't give up. When Roosevelt continued to resist, Bourne issued a statement that attacked him for his tactics and coined a new and far more incendiary phrase. By attempting to anoint his own successor, Bourne said, Roosevelt was creating a "residuary legateeship" that was even worse than "dynastic succession under a monarchy." For progressives concerned with popular democracy, those words carried a powerful sting.

Roosevelt was finally fed up. Bourne "has ceased to amuse me," he told his attorney general.

APPARENTLY NOT A man of great emotional intelligence, Bourne didn't understand that he had lost Roosevelt's affections. When he first started to launch his idea for presidential primaries in which voters could express their candidate preferences, he hoped that Roosevelt would champion a national movement. In May 1910, on the eve of Roosevelt's return to America from his hunting trip in Africa and triumphant tour of Europe, Bourne sent TR a letter asking him to lead the movement for direct presidential primaries.

"I wish you would become the world's champion for popular government," Bourne wrote. By doing so, Roosevelt could "offset the evil" of the precedent he had established four years earlier by the "dictation of residuary legateeship."

TR didn't respond. He may have been otherwise occupied by the last month of his travels, disturbed by the tone of the letter, or offended by the continuing accusation that he had created a near-monarchy by supporting Taft. In any case, he didn't much like his pursuer. He considered Bourne "below average" as a senator and typical of the worst insurgents—"good for nothing except to insurge."

During the months that followed, Bourne sent a torrent of increasingly nasty and sarcastic letters. Once again, he was the unwanted suitor. Many letters enclosed speeches and articles touting the importance of presidential primaries, including a ninety-minute speech that he had delivered to the Senate. His remarks on the Oregon experiment would only take an hour to read, he told TR in mid-June, a week after Roosevelt's return to the United States. "Without being egotistical, I believe it would be an hour well spent."

Roosevelt brushed him off. "As soon as I get any time I shall look into it," he wrote in a terse reply, "but I simply have not one moment to myself right now."

Bourne did not like being dismissed so quickly. Even while traveling, TR famously consumed several books a week, works of fiction, history, ornithology. He had time for things that interested him. "I know you are a very busy man," Bourne persisted, but "I assume you welcome other people's viewpoints." This time he enclosed an article from *Collier's* magazine.

The following day, Bourne fired off yet another offensive letter; this one enclosed the draft of an article. He asked TR, in his capacity as an editor of *The Outlook*, to show it to the real power at the magazine, Editor-in-Chief Lyman Abbott. "If the *Outlook* does not care for the article," Bourne said, "I assume other magazines will."

"Kindly have your secretary acknowledge receipt," Bourne said tartly, "and notify me immediately of Mr. Abbott's decision." Bourne enclosed a 10-cent stamp.

His tone was challenging, partly because he felt betrayed by a man he had once admired, and partly because he was on a crusade. Whatever his original reasons for joining the cause of popular government, Bourne had become its chief spokesman. He had drafted Oregon's presidential primary bill and personally funded the winning campaign for its adoption. Now he hoped to take the movement national.

But TR wasn't buying it. He was skeptical about both the messenger and the message. While he claimed to be generally supportive of the package of political reforms being pressed by the progressives, he considered it "nonsense to make the Initiative and Referendum an article of National faith."

True social reforms, issues such as workers' compensation, were what really mattered, he finally told Bourne in early 1911, not the machinery by which they were adopted. The direct primary—along with other direct democracy measures such as the initiative and referendum—were not important in and of themselves. They were useful "merely as means to ends."

TR did speak out for a direct primary in New York State in 1910, a bit reluctantly, when called to do so by Governor Charles Evans Hughes, who represented the party's reform wing now fighting the conservatives. The two men sat next to each other at the Harvard Commencement ceremony on June 29, 1910, less than two weeks after TR's return to the country. Hughes asked for his support on the direct primary fight.

"I don't wish to say anything about this matter," Roosevelt replied. He had intended to keep out of any political battles for at least a few months.

"Colonel," Hughes persisted, "silence means opposition." He pointed out that some New York papers had been reporting that TR opposed the primaries.

"Opposition!" Roosevelt said. "If silence means opposition, I'll speak."

Even though he supported the direct primary in New York State, Roosevelt questioned its universal applicability. In a series of letters to progressives who were much more committed to the cause of popular democracy, Roosevelt stressed that the direct primary was far from an unqualified success in states where it had been adopted. He pointed to the results in New Jersey, in Cincinnati (where boss rule remained), in New Hampshire (which had just elected two conservative congressmen), and in California (where it had recently produced three reactionary judges.) In one of his more revealing moments, he told Robert La Follette, who had championed popular government for more than a decade, that it was "half amusing and half pathetic to see so many good people convinced that the world can be reformed without difficulty merely by reforming the machinery of government."

THROUGHOUT 1911, TR continued to try to find a middle course. Part reformer, part pragmatist, he hoped Taft could succeed but sympathized with many of the points made by critics. Roosevelt sent countless notes to friends distancing himself from the most extreme elements of the insurgent movement and the men who had managed to take hold of the label "progressive," calling them "fanatics" and "ultra-radicals." "I get almost as disgusted with the progressives as with the standpat crowd," he told Oscar King (O. K.) Davis, a *New York Times* reporter who later served as his press secretary.

He refused to embrace popular democracy as the cornerstone of the progressive agenda. He described his concerns in a revealing exchange of letters with Charles Dwight Willard, a leading Los Angeles progressive. Willard confessed that he and others in the movement believed in popular democracy as a religion, an end in itself. He called it "Godlike as a maker of men."

"The one thing in the whole scheme of human affairs that we can believe in without limitation and without reservation," Willard wrote, "[is] that the people should rule."

Roosevelt couldn't agree. In his view, the progressives were neither realistic nor pragmatic. He ticked off a series of places where the people were not educated well enough to vote, such as Haiti; places where reactionary forces had used the initiative process to thwart reforms, such as Switzerland; and places where the public had voted for corrupt politicians rather than for reformers, including his own state of New York.

The Colonel's letters reflected the class- and race-based views of some of his establishment contemporaries. "If you literally applied this without qualification and reservation in California," he told Willard, "it would of course mean that the Chinese and Japanese should come in in unlimited quantities, and should rule you." Then, in a comment that presaged the discriminatory policies that he would later adopt for his own party, he added: "Now you don't mean this, any more than the Texan and Mississippian who use the same phraseology mean that the negroes in the black belt should rule."

Every real proponent of democracy, Roosevelt said, "acts and always must act on the perfectly sound (although unacknowledged, and often hotly contested) belief that only certain people are fit for democracy."

To illustrate his point, to underline his belief that *only certain people are fit for democracy,*" Roosevelt pointed to what he deemed the short-comings of popular government in the South during the years after the Civil War. His views on that subject would, in time, become an impor-tant issue in the campaign and, in the opinion of many of his contem-poraries, a serious stain on his record. "No one now seriously contends that during reconstruction days the negro majority in Mississippi and South Carolina acted wisely, or that it was possible to continue the gov-ernment in the hands of that majority," he said.

Roosevelt had been President of the United States during the years when hundreds of thousands of blacks were removed from the voting rolls in the South. TR had found ways to extend the reach and power of government in other important areas, yet he did nothing to preserve popular suffrage in the region. His friend Henry Cabot Lodge had once suggested a way for the federal government to preserve the rights of black voters in the South. In 1890, Lodge authored a bill to provide fed-eral supervision for elections in the South in order to protect the rights of black (and overwhelmingly Republican) voters in federal elections. The legislation passed in the House but was defeated in the Senate by a filibuster. Roosevelt backed the Lodge bill in 1890 but later expressed opposition to such efforts. In any case, the Lodge bill illustrated one way in which the federal government could have intervened. Whether he could have slowed it down or not, the disenfranchisement process that continued to take place during his years in office had the practical result of assuring that government in those states did not continue "in the hands of that majority."

Willard and other progressives started to dismiss Roosevelt, concluding that he was simply unsympathetic to the progressives' core beliefs and, perhaps due to his year abroad, out of touch.

You are not yet "the great moral leader of the people," Willard told TR. You will join us later, but you are "not quite here yet."

Others were less charitable. "Roosevelt needs time to think and to grow," a new and very outspoken California congressman explained in September 1911. "He is definitely not inherently a believer in democracy."

FINALLY BOURNE AND his friends gave up on Roosevelt. It appeared that he didn't want to challenge Taft for the nomination and that he didn't share their central ideological belief in popular democracy. In January 1911, when they formed the National Progressive Republican League at Senator La Follette's home, their core principles included the Initiative, Referendum, and Recall, a federal corrupt practices act, and "the direct election of delegates to national conventions with opportunity for the voter to express his choice for President and Vice-President." Indeed, for many of those present, the "paramount purpose" of the reformers was to create direct presidential primaries.

The founding members of the National Progressive Republican League included almost the entire progressive movement: nine U.S. senators, six Republican governors, thirteen members of Congress, and a few lawyers, journalists, and activists, including Gifford Pinchot. The group selected Bourne as its president.

When TR refused to join them, the members began to attack him directly. "The ultra-radicals have been almost as bitter against me as against the reactionaries," he told Ted, Jr., in early January, explaining his reasons for staying clear of the fray. "Gifford Pinchot has joined the extremists." Pinchot intends "to try to nominate some progressive against Taft, and if that fails, to bolt and attempt to get up a third party. He believes that La Follette and Bourne will follow this course, which is possible."

The prospect of a third party was still too extreme a remedy for a life-long Republican, a man who, on more than one occasion, had managed to hold his nose and vote for the party's nominee in the past.

WITHOUT ANY HELP from TR, the National Progressive Republican League, led by La Follette and Bourne, began an aggressive national campaign. In some states, they were joined by Democrats with a similar commitment to direct democracy. During the spring and summer of 1911, the League helped to put direct presidential primaries on the ballot in several states, laws that allowed voters to declare their presidential preference while selecting delegates. There was a small roundup on page six of the *Washington Post* in mid-July which noted that "the presidential primary idea had its origins in Oregon but has been adopted in North Dakota, Wisconsin, Nebraska and New Jersey, all of which have presidential primary laws based on the Oregon law." But apart from the most aggressive backers in the progressive movement, very few political observers were paying close attention.

Having given up on TR, La Follette, on June 17, 1911, announced that he was running for President. A fire-breathing orator from the farms of Wisconsin, La Follette had built a reputation as a crusading three-term governor, fighting railroads and corporate greed. Along the way, he championed the public's role in government, creating the nation's first state primary law. Admirers called him "Fighting Bob" and "Battling Bob." By 1906, when he became a U.S. senator, his huge pompadour and sharp suits made him instantly recognizable as he fought to limit corporate power and concentration, and for laws to protect consumers and workers. If anyone symbolized and stood for progressive reforms, it was Bob La Follette.

La Follette and Roosevelt had known each other for more than twenty years. At one of their first meetings, Roosevelt and Henry Cabot Lodge joined Bob and Belle La Follette for a cup of coffee at a reception at the Agriculture Department. At the time, La Follette was a new member of Congress and TR was the Civil Service Commissioner. While making a dramatic point with characteristic animation, TR knocked a cup of coffee out of Belle's hand and onto the front of her white gown. Fifteen years later, when La Follette was elected to the Senate, he and Belle came to a reception in the White House. Roosevelt greeted them on the receiving line and cheerfully recalled that encounter. "When I wake up in the dark and think about that," Roosevelt laughed, "I positively blush."

Publicly, Roosevelt continued to have cordial relations with La Follette. In private, he considered La Follette's ideas dangerous, and La Follette had come to distrust him. Before running, La Follette sought Roosevelt's endorsement, without success. TR often asked La Follette to come visit him in New York. Somehow La Follette was never available.

WITH THE WIND at his back and TR on the sidelines, La Follette's presidential campaign began to gain a surprising degree of momentum. Men like Gifford Pinchot, who had been one of TR's strongest supporters, deserted Roosevelt and attacked him in public and in private settings. It was hard for TR to accept their perspective or their contempt. He continued to share his concerns with his son. "The wildeyed ultra-radicals do not support us because they think we have not gone far enough," he wrote Ted, Jr., that fall. "I am really sorry to say that good Gifford Pinchot . . . has been really offensive in his criticism to and of me."

By early October 1911, the progressive leaders thought that there would be enough primaries to offset the advantages of incumbency, quite possibly enough to beat Taft. On October 3, Amos Pinchot, Gifford's activist brother, told James Garfield that "the La Follette boom has had a tremendous response throughout the West, and . . . even here in New York City." He wanted all of the progressives to come out for La Follette immediately.

Garfield, who had served as TR's Secretary of the Interior, passed the word along to his former boss. The ultraradicals might have been unrealistic about La Follette's prospects, but it was hard to ignore their passion. If the Colonel didn't start to indicate that he might be willing to run, it could be too late. The progressives were planning to meet in Chicago in mid-October, and there was certain to be an effort to make La Follette the unanimous choice of the movement.

Garfield wanted to block that move.

ROOSEVELT'S MIND WAS elsewhere. On September 30, while TR and Edith were horseback riding with their seventeen-year-old son Archie, Edith's horse swerved, throwing her to the ground and knocking her out. For weeks, she was in terrible pain.

The Roosevelt family kept a lid on the story. "We have kept the accident out of the papers, and only a few people know how serious it is," he told Ted, Jr. "We have had a nerve specialist in for a consultation. He says that the accident has been very severe, but there is every reason to believe she will recover. . . . Two trained nurses are with her night and day, and Ethel is with her at intervals all the time. I am with her less often, but both last night and the night before she sent for me once or twice in the night to come in and rub her back or just be companionable. Sometimes I just sit quietly and hold her hand, and at other times she wants me to repeat poetry, but not as successfully as Ethel, for the poetry I know by heart is apt to be of a grandiose and warlike character, not especially fitting for soothing purposes in the sick room."

He was desperately worried about Edith, but he knew that he had to focus on the campaign before matters got out of hand.

Roosevelt asked Garfield to come to New York, where the two men had a long talk on October 10. TR agreed that it was time to speak plainly about what had to be done. In the meantime, he asked Garfield to try to block the stampede to La Follette in Chicago by suggesting that each state be free to select its own progressive delegates.

In Chicago, the halls were jammed with the leaders of the progressive movement, top political figures from around the country and powerful journalists such as the editor-in-chief of the Scripps newspaper chain. Everyone seemed convinced that Taft was on the ropes and that La Follette could win the Republican Party nomination. The virtually unanimous enthusiasm for La Follette made it impossible for Garfield to block an endorsement.

On October 18, the *Chicago Tribune* carried a front-page story with a headline saying that "National Leaders Open Fight Here for La Follette." The report was effusive. "United States Senator Robert M. La Follette's campaign for the Republican Nomination for President in 1912 was started in Illinois last evening with an enthusiastic mass meeting at Orchestra Hall. The meeting marked the end of the two day national conference of Republican progressives who will fight against the renomination of President Taft and follow the standard of the Wisconsin Senator. Cheers from a packed house greeted every mention of the name of La Follette." Other stories were equally effusive.

The *New York Times* front page story said that "Two hundred Progressive Republicans, in their first conference today, endorsed Senator Robert M. La Follette of Wisconsin and declared for a direct primary as a means for expression of a Presidential choice." The *New York Tribune* even said that James Garfield supported the endorsement of La Follette and "appeared to be expressing the views of Theodore Roosevelt who, it was feared, would oppose a declaration in favor of any individual."

In fact, Garfield was opposed to the convention's actions, but, as he wrote in his diary that night, he could not counter the overwhelming "sentiment of the people that L should be considered by the people as the Progressive leader. . . . If I had opposed [it] the supposition would be that . . . I represented T. R. and wished his or my own selection."

Reflecting the fever of the crowd, the ever-zealous Amos Pinchot predicted that even the southern officeholders would turn to La Follette. They will soon realize Taft can't win, he told a progressive friend, and they "will drop him like a hot potato and get their money on a winning horse."

Amazingly, by late October 1911, there were those who believed that the likely "winning horse" had become La Follette. And the means of his victory would be the presidential primary. As so often happens in politics, they were motivated by passion, not political realism.

If he wanted to enter the race with progressive support, Roosevelt had little time to lose.

Chapter Three

During the fall of 1911, as he witnessed La Follette's support expanding, Roosevelt edged his way from "no" to "maybe" to a still-secret "yes." He told friends that while he would not officially seek the nomination, he could not resist a genuine draft if it came from the people. With the help of a few secret operatives, Roosevelt started to take soundings, to plant the seeds for a "draft" and, wherever possible, to remove the ground from under his chief competitors.

Many of his old political friends and allies like Elihu Root were either neutral or with Taft. With the exception of Garfield, most of the ardent reformers were with La Follette. So Roosevelt assembled a diverse group of supporters that he later called "the Clan." The members were not "young lieutenants" of the kind that TR would describe a few months later in Judge Grant's living room; instead his early supporters were a collection of established political operatives such as William L. Ward and Ormsby McHarg, business leaders such as George Perkins and Frank Munsey, and a few special friends in the press, including John "Cal" O'Laughlin of the *Chicago Tribune* and Franklin Knox, a young publisher who also chaired the Michigan Republican Party.

The Clan included loyal friends and acolytes, men with a beef against Taft, men who thought that Roosevelt was the best hope for business, and men for whom ideology was secondary. Not one of those in the original group was from what TR sometimes called the progressives' "lunatic fringe." With the exception of Garfield, they were not devoted to the cause of popular democracy. Some, like William Ward, were political leaders who wanted to hold on to the power that they had accumulated and actively opposed primaries. Indeed, most of those in the Clan did not want Roosevelt to run in the primaries. They wanted to convince the party's leaders to join in an irresistible draft.

The men in the Clan began to garner support by arguing that Taft's policies were bad for business—and that La Follette's would be even worse. The antitrust case filed against United States Steel on October 26, 1911, accusing Roosevelt of naïvely capitulating to the Steel Barons, provided the Colonel with the perfect opening to expand on the argument, supplying a raft of powerful allies, a useful campaign theme, and a reason for a form of righteous indignation that would appeal to the business community.

The background was familiar to everyone on Wall Street. In November 1907, in the midst of a financial panic, J. P. Morgan had arranged for U.S. Steel to buy the Tennessee Coal, Iron & Railroad Company, one of its leading competitors. Corporate leaders Elbert Gary, the chairman of U. S. Steel, and Henry Frick, a member of the company's board, met in the White House with President Roosevelt to explain that the merger would help prevent a financial collapse. Based on their pleas, Roosevelt promised not to allow his justice department to file an antitrust case.

When Taft's Department of Justice filed just such a case four years later, the government's legal brief suggested that TR had approved the merger because he had been duped. "The President was not made fully acquainted with the state of affairs in New York relevant to the transactions as they existed," the brief stated. "If he had been fully advised he would have known that a desire to stop the panic was not the sole moving cause, but there was also the desire and purpose to acquire the control of a company that had recently assumed a position of potential competition of great significance."

The *New York Times* headline declared that "Roosevelt Was Deceived."

TR was furious. Of course, Taft knew nothing about that language, but TR still held him accountable. The charge was insulting and humiliating. It also provided fuel for those, including some of La Follette's supporters, who felt that as president Roosevelt had been much too cozy, perhaps scandalously cozy, with J. P. Morgan.

In mid-November, Roosevelt penned a major article for *The Outlook*, attacking Taft and presenting a new and important theory of industrial regulation and the control of trusts. Although Roosevelt had earned a reputation as a trustbuster, he had always believed that in some cases government regulation was preferable to the dissolution of large companies. He maintained that Taft had taken the crusade too far, arguing that his successor was too aggressive, that there were sometimes benefits to having large corporations, and that it was often better for the government to regulate such companies than to break them apart. Major segments of the business community immediately hailed the plan. Some even began to see TR as the new savior of business (and of their own businesses).

ONE OF THE named defendants in the Steel case was George W. Perkins, a director of U.S. Steel who was widely known as J. P. Morgan's "right hand man." In the summer of 1911, a congressional committee investigating the Tennessee Coal merger had asked both Roosevelt and Perkins to testify. Roosevelt did so, though he had deep reservations about responding to such a request. At first Perkins refused. When the committee threatened him with contempt, Perkins testified but used the occasion to lash out at the Sherman Antitrust Act itself. After the hearing, Perkins told a friend that he was losing interest in everything except the battle against the Sherman Act.

Perkins began to build a web of like-minded leaders—including Frank Munsey, known as a magazine and newspaper publisher but also widely believed to be the largest shareholder in U.S. Steel, who soon joined Perkins as the leading contributor to TR's campaign, and James Keeley, the powerful editor of the *Chicago Tribune*, who felt that the antitrust laws were stifling business. Keeley would shortly emerge as one of Roosevelt's most important supporters. Perkins told Roosevelt how much he appreciated his comments to the congressional committee and said that with the right kind of leadership they could get federal legislation changing the antitrust laws.

Roosevelt's article in *The Outlook* represented precisely the ideas that Perkins was encouraging. He made it clear that if TR wanted to run for President again, he would support him.

Before long, a great many reporters and political observers, and both President Taft and Senator La Follette, sincerely believed that TR's campaign was being funded by interests affiliated with U.S. Steel. On January 16, a front-page headline in the *Washington Post* said: "TRUST BOOMING TR—Steel Men Said to Be Backing Movement."

"It is not a campaign that originated with the progressive Republicans of the country," the *Post* said. "Practically every man conspicuously identified with it is a representative of big business." The piece went to list TR's major supporters.

Horace Taft was convinced that the reports were accurate. "As I have written to" my brother, Horace Taft told TR's top advisor, "it seems intolerable that the steel trust men are fighting tooth and nail for Roosevelt and that they expect to launch his boom and stampede the country. There is such outrageous hypocrisy in his posing as the popular idol and the unwilling victim of his own popularity when the steel trust is his chief backer and he himself is working night and day to get the nomination."

THE *OUTLOOK* ARTICLE gave Bill Ward the ammunition that he needed to solicit support for Roosevelt among leaders of the business community. Ward had personal credibility as a manufacturer (his company made nuts, bolts, and rivets) and political clout as the New York State representative on the Republican National Committee. By the first of December, Ward started to make the rounds of his friends in business and politics, asking them to support Roosevelt. He spread the word that he and others had concluded that Taft's tariff policies and aggressive enforcement of the antitrust laws were damaging the state's business interests.

On December 1, Ward visited Herbert Parsons, a New York lawyer, business leader, and former member of Congress to solicit his support. Parsons described the meeting to Taft. Ward, he reported, "stated that he had come to the conclusion" that the country's most important problems were "business difficulties; that Col. Roosevelt could be nominated for the Presidency, provided that he did not become a candidate; and that he, Ward, wanted me to join with him in being for the Col. Roosevelt's nomination." Parsons turned him down, explaining that he did not believe that any man should serve for more than two terms.

Ten days later, Ward served as Roosevelt's point man at the annual winter meeting of the Republican National Committee, where the party established the time and place for the national convention as well as the all-important rules that would govern the selection of delegates. The exact wording of those rules would be of crucial importance to the candidates.

As the delegates gathered, the *Boston Globe* described what it called "a well-defined movement in favor of the nomination of Col. Roosevelt." His supporters did not expect him to engage in a formal campaign, the paper explained. Instead they hoped that "his nomination would come through an outburst of enthusiasm at the convention itself."

The most important issue at the RNC meeting was a proposal advanced by Jonathan Bourne and the National Progressive Republican League to require that all delegates be selected in presidential primaries rather than at local and state conventions. Since TR did not plan to run in the primaries, observers predicted that Bourne's plan would be rejected thanks in large part to "the fear of friends of Col. Roosevelt that the primary system, if adopted at this time, might cut off the possibility of nominating the president for a second elective term."

Taft didn't want primaries either. Trying to influence the outcome of the deliberations, he hosted a sumptuous White House dinner for members of the committee. "There were more political schemes hatched, and died in hatching, than one usually sees in a dozen such dinners around Washington," Archie Butt observed. The night before, there had been rumors that a majority of the members of the committee wanted TR renominated. "The Roosevelt ghost stalked at every meeting," Butt said. Since Taft's political base in the South would rest on appointed officeholders, some of TR's supporters were lobbying the RNC to adopt a rule banning officeholders as delegates. Some of TR's friends from western states wanted all delegates to go to the convention without a binding commitment to any nominee, which would allow them to support TR when the "outburst of enthusiasm" grasped the convention floor.

With more than a little amusement, Butt watched the players at work at the White House dinner—calling it "an interesting game, almost like a faro bank room at Ostend"*—as "the schemers and planners" tried to win allies and commitments while the President, his brother Charley, and his private secretary Charles Hilles "kept all eyes and ears open to see that the enemy fort got no advantage." But the parties could agree on one issue: neither wanted to increase the number of primary states.

In what everyone knew to be a personal snub, Bill Ward declined to attend. The *New York Times* reported that Ward told the White House that he "isn't going out any more and was indisposed despite the fact that he was walking around the lobby of his hotel smoking a heavy, black cigar." Former governor Franklin Murphy of New Jersey remarked, "You know, Ward is delicate and can't stand the night air."

The next morning, the corridors of the Willard Hotel, where the RNC held its meeting, were filled with "an amazingly strong current of Roosevelt talk." There was widespread agreement that even if he did not seek the nomination he would accept it "if it were tendered to him."

---

* Like Monte Carlo, the casinos in Ostend, Belgium, were popular places for gambling.

The goal of his supporters, the *Baltimore Sun* reported, was "to leave matters sufficiently open to permit his candidacy at the psychological moment." That included limiting the impact of primary states. The press assumed that Ward was heading the Roosevelt cause. "Ward is for Roosevelt and is making no bones about it," the *New York Times* said. Ward planned to take an uninstructed delegation from New York to the convention, where he hoped that "when the uninstructed delegates begin to vote for Roosevelt to the certain wild cheers from the galleries they can carry it through with a rush."

Much of the RNC's time was devoted to writing the rules that would govern the selection of delegates, rules embodied in the document labeled "The Call for the National Convention." As the *New York Times* explained, "A National Convention is a law unto itself. Like other parliamentary bodies, it is the judge of the qualifications and election of its members." If there was a conflict between the Call of the Convention and state law, the Call would prevail. So the precise language of the Call was of the utmost importance.

As had been predicted, the most controversial issue involved the creation of presidential primaries. In mid-October, acting on behalf of the National Progressive Republican League, Jonathan Bourne had written to all of the RNC members asking them to require that every state hold a presidential primary, "giving every member of the party an opportunity to express his preference for party candidates for President and Vice-President." Working in league with the progressives, Gilson Gardner, a reporter with the powerful Scripps newspaper syndicate, sent a letter two weeks later to every member of the RNC, using the power of the press to reinforce Bourne's initiative. "Our newspaper syndicate," he said, wants to publish a statement "in our sixty-five papers" saying whether or not you support the plan.

At the RNC meeting, the Progressive Caucus was represented by Senator William Borah of Idaho, who asked that Bourne's proposal be included in the Call. None of the delegates supporting Taft or Roosevelt agreed. Taft's supporters argued that there should only be primaries in states where the state law had specifically created them—and that even then the state committees should be able to decide whether to use the new primary system to select delegates. Taft's view prevailed. "If a state committee wanted to have a popularity contest for moral effect," one of Taft's key supporters explained, "they can provide for a party primary." But the results would not be binding on the delegates.

Borah's motion obtained only seven votes. Every other member of the national committee, including Bill Ward and Roosevelt's other friends, supported limiting the number and power of presidential primaries.

Though the outcome was hardly a surprise, La Follette's supporters were furious. His office issued a statement complaining that "the Republican National Committee not only refused to let state committees hold presidential primaries if they so wished, but they went out of their way to affront the states which have made provisions for such primaries."

Ward kept Roosevelt informed of his efforts through private meetings and communiqués, developing tactics to keep the coordinated campaign a secret. As soon as he returned from the RNC meeting in Washington, he wrote to TR asking for a visit at the home of one of Roosevelt's friends since "it would not do for me to come to *The Outlook* office and if we should attempt to meet in any Hotel or Club, it might get in the newspapers, and just at this time I do not think that a meeting between you and myself would be a wise thing to be talked about."

Roosevelt asked a friend if he could use her house for "a political rendezvous."

"Bill Ward, the boss of Westchester, wants to see me somewhere not in *The Outlook* office, and I have told him to meet me at your house at 12 noon next Thursday," TR explained. "If we are in the way, I will then take him somewhere else."

WARD'S ARGUMENT THAT TR would be good for business resonated with Ormsby McHarg. A tough-as-nails native of South Dakota, McHarg had served in TR's Department of Justice—earning the President's plaudits for his aggressive investigation of a series of New Mexico land fraud cases—until he went after one of Roosevelt's friends. Roosevelt then promptly arranged to remove McHarg from the case.

Early in the Taft administration, McHarg served in the important and highly visible post of assistant secretary of commerce and labor, where he championed the views of business interests in the West who were horrified by the conservation policies that had first been championed by TR. Before long, he proved too outspoken for a government bureaucrat. McHarg was always blunt and colorful, good copy for reporters, but his candor finally got the best of him when he told the *Washington Post* that Gifford Pinchot's Forest Service—and perhaps former President Roosevelt himself—had used faulty and even deliberately false data to block development in the West. He called them "ultra-radical conservationists" and their allies in the Interior Department "liars." He labeled Pinchot himself "a trimmer." Some news accounts claimed that McHarg had criticized TR for "acting as if he were the Lord."

That was too much for Taft. He finally but reluctantly felt the need to fire McHarg, partly because of his implicit and perhaps direct criticisms of TR. "I believe we have nobody who has done harder work," Taft told the Secretary of Commerce and Labor, who was McHarg's supervisor. "But [McHarg] has been reported as saying things that [if he did say them] would certainly call for discipline on our part because they reflected seriously on my predecessor, Mr. Roosevelt, for whom I have the highest respect, and whose administration we are trying to follow, and whom it would be very deplorable for us in any way to criticize or hold up to public ridicule."

When he left government in late October 1909, McHarg was happy to return to private law practice in New York. With well-trimmed dark eyebrows, rimless glasses, and short gray hair that was often parted in the middle, he quickly became a part of the New York legal world. He was so fed up with TR that he told friends in the press that "he wants the Colonel eliminated as an influence in Republican Politics." In November, 1910, the *New York Herald* quoted him as calling TR "the most dangerous figure in public life in America."

With that background, McHarg might have seemed like an unlikely recruit to the Roosevelt express. But Bill Ward assured him that Roosevelt had changed since leaving office, saying that he had become much more sympathetic to business and that TR was alarmed by Taft's overly aggressive antitrust work. "The Colonel had changed his mind on some of these problems," Ward said. "He was particularly impressed by his talks with the German Kaiser. The Kaiser told him that he conferred honors on his great industrialists, while the Colonel had thought to send them to jail."

Ward told McHarg that Roosevelt would use radical talk on the campaign trail but that he should not believe it. "I just thought he was trying to out-devil La Follette," McHarg later explained. "Mr. Ward's explanation satisfied me."

So McHarg signed on to the campaign. According to his account, McHarg went to the RNC's winter meeting in Washington to "look the situation over." Following the meeting, McHarg recalled with what may have been a bit of an overstatement, "I took over the campaign quietly." Ward and Roosevelt kept his role quiet, he said. "We didn't want to make any noise about it because we wanted to feel out the sentiment of the country."

McHarg had gathered southern delegates for Taft in 1908 and led Taft's efforts in the Credentials Committee that year. Based on that experience, he traveled through the South seeking to drum up support for Roosevelt. Close observers suspected that he was trying to generate a political draft. As the *Atlanta Constitution* put it in mid-January, McHarg was building support for TR so that he can "yield to the pressing demands of his friends if the proper state of fervor can be superinduced by adroit political manipulation."

On several occasions over the next few months, Roosevelt would imply that he was unaware of McHarg's efforts. But in fact, McHarg reported directly to Roosevelt, holding personal meetings and sending regular updates. On January 8, he sent a full analysis directly to the Colonel, adding "if there is anything I can do for you call on me here at my office." He told TR how to reach him on the road and arranged to meet him again in person on January 12.

By January 19, McHarg had become bullish on TR's prospects in the South. "If we can win delegates from the south," he told TR, "Taft will be 'high and dry.'" Before long, he was telling TR that he was sure to win the delegates from Alabama thanks to the efforts of Judge Oscar Hundley, whom McHarg called "the first person to come out in the open for you in the South." Hundley ran "an aggressive, constructive campaign," McHarg reported, "and the result he has achieved in Alabama is marvelous. Single handedly, he has turned the state upside down." McHarg's optimism would prove to be misplaced, but TR may well have believed those reports.

Stories about McHarg's work appeared in a number of publications, but when reporters asked TR for a comment, he issued nondenial denials. "I have no time to discuss 'pipe dreams,'" he told the *New York Herald*. "There are some depths of tomfoolery to which I can't go."

The Taft campaign knew what McHarg was doing. They were getting their own reports from the field describing his visits to Hundley and others who seemed to have a special reason to like Roosevelt or oppose Taft.

McHarg and others are "laying mines throughout the country, to be exploded a little later," Taft's secretary explained. "A great many men here use a different figure of speech; they think the Colonel will not become a candidate unless there is a sweeping fire, and that these men are now busy making the preparations for that conflagration."

THE LEADING JOURNALIST on TR's secret team was John Callan "Cal" O'Laughlin. Before becoming a crack political reporter for the *Chicago Tribune*, O'Laughlin had served in TR's State Department and then as TR's secretary during his trip through Africa and Europe in 1909–1910. He published an account of those adventures called *From the Jungle Through Europe with Roosevelt*. With the support of his editor, James Keeley, who would soon emerge as one of Roosevelt's most important supporters, O'Laughlin agreed to serve as the Colonel's intelligence service, providing him with state-by-state status reports throughout December 1911, taking the temperature of the Catholic Church, and acting as Roosevelt's emissary to select journalists and political leaders.

By early January, Cal had won pledges of support from Senators William Borah of Idaho and Joseph Dixon of Montana. But he pleaded with TR to retain a distance from the insurgents. Cal hoped that Roosevelt would be drafted by a coalition that would include men from both factions of the party. "The Progressives will want you to take over their organization," he cautioned, "but I hope you will do nothing of the kind. . . . They are useful in muddying the waters, in making Taft impossible. It would be unwise for you to accept their support since it would offend the stand-pat element who are now willing to accept you."

O'Laughlin became convinced that Taft's supporters were monitoring his work. "I am afraid the Post office is opening my mail," he wrote. "Your letter dated January 11 reached me today unsealed. Won't you direct that envelopes be sealed with wax if their contents justify it?"

OF ALL THOSE on his secret team, no one was more zealous than Franklin Knox. A powerful five-foot-nine redhead from Grand Rapids, Michigan, Knox had come under Roosevelt's spell fourteen years earlier. Fresh out of Alma College, inflamed with passion for the Spanish-American War and America's efforts to help Cuba gain independence from Spain, he signed on to TR's famed Rough Rider brigade in Florida as it was about to leave for Cuba. He joined the diverse assemblage of 1,000 college men (many from Harvard), cowboys and westerners (Knox called them "rough and ready fellows") who were to become a fighting force once again in 1912. He was one of five men who joined TR in a deadly charge up Kettle Hill. Two of their comrades were killed and a bullet tore through Knox's hat. Knox grew to worship Roosevelt, and the Colonel knew that he could rely on him.

Back in Michigan, Knox began a career as a journalist, winning attention for an investigation of a Michigan quartermaster general who stole money by selling surplus army supplies at the end of the Spanish-American War. Before long, at the suggestion of Chase Osborn, a publisher and progressive political leader, he bought his own weekly paper in Sault Ste. Marie. Osborn quickly became his friend and patron. When Osborn ran for governor in 1910, he asked Knox to manage his successful campaign. When he won, Osborn asked Knox to chair Michigan's Republican Party. As a trusted friend and state party chair, Knox was in a unique position to develop support for Roosevelt.

Knox and TR developed an audacious strategy: they hoped to convince both Taft and La Follette to withdraw.

TAFT HAD BECOME a major liability for the Republican Party. At the 1910 midterm elections, the party had lost 57 seats in the House and 10 in the Senate, giving the Democratic Party control of the House and, when working in tandem with progressive Republicans, control of the Senate as well. The Democrats had also picked up several governorships, including those in New York, Connecticut, Rhode Island, Ohio, Massachusetts, and, for future developments most important, in New Jersey, where Woodrow Wilson had come into office. Moreover, the biggest defeats for the Republican Party were in states with old-line leaders, while most of those who were progressives were elected or reelected. Under the circumstances, the effort to convince conservative party leaders to remove Taft made sense. So long as TR did not threaten to join what he called "the lunatic fringe," the old guard bosses had reason to join his crusade.

Encouraged by Ward and Knox, a series of state party chairmen including Walter Brown, chair of the Republican Party in Taft's home state of Ohio, issued statements saying that Taft would be a major drag on the ticket. After a meeting with Roosevelt in Oyster Bay on December 11, just before the gathering of the Republican National Committee in Washington, Knox issued a statement of his own that had an unmistakable meaning for insiders.

"Many of the party leaders, including the national committeemen, hope that Taft will not insist [on running]," one newspaper reported. "They are beset with fears for their state and local tickets and for the Senatorships that are at stake in 1912. . . . They are making it evident that they would be greatly relieved if Mr. Taft would decline to become a candidate. Therein lies the hope of Roosevelt coming forward to save the situation. With Taft out of the way and the nomination spontaneously offered to Roosevelt, it is nominally believed that the Colonel could make the run. Mr. Knox's statement inferentially supports that."

Taft's close confidants understood the game. On December 20, a New York business leader told him that "the whole plan is to discourage you so as to cause you to decline to permit your name to go before the convention. If they could get such a confession of weakness from you, then the Colonel would go after the nomination and make the fight."

Knox proposed two strategies to get Taft out of the race. Neither involved the use of presidential primaries. First, he hoped to get a letter signed by fifteen to twenty state chairs that he would bring to Taft's attention to try to persuade him to withdraw. If that failed, Knox wanted the party chiefs to meet with Taft individually and in groups to tell him to get out of the race.

But Taft was made of much tougher stuff. Even though he weighed over 300 pounds, had a wonderfully jovial personality, and looked soft, he was prepared for a fight. In college, he had been Yale's heavyweight wrestling champion. As TR had told him three years earlier, he could be a terrific fighter when "the need arose." Taft was convinced that he could win the nomination. Even if La Follette and Roosevelt were to win some of the new primaries, the decisions embodied in the Call of the Convention that had just been adopted by the Republican National Committee ensured that most of the delegates would be selected in meetings and caucuses controlled by party insiders. His campaign had already started to gather support, using the power of incumbency, which would help him everywhere, particularly in the South, where the process would be dominated by federal officeholders who would be reluctant to alienate a sitting president. Moreover, he was not convinced by claims that he would hurt the party by running.

In any case, he told friends that if he could win the nomination he would be happy, even if he were to lose the general election.

ROOSEVELT'S EFFORTS TO UNDERMINE La Follette were more successful. But when combined with La Follette's other reasons for resenting TR, they also turned "Fighting Bob" into a bitter enemy, which would have consequences throughout the rest of the campaign. Less than a year later, La Follette wrote a lengthy account of the events as he recalled and understood them. They were the final chapters of a book that was originally intended to be a campaign biography. While laced with paranoia and bitterness as well as some questionable conjectures, a great many of the facts and assertions in his contemporaneous description are confirmed by documents to which he had no access at the time. Those documents show that TR was involved in at least one effort to undermine his campaign that La Follette almost certainly did not know about; moreover, La Follette probably did not know that TR was telling friends that La Follette had a dangerous temperament and would be an even worse president than Taft.

La Follette claimed that TR began to be interested in the race when Gilson Gardner, the reporter for the Scripps papers who had been taking soundings around the country on La Follette's behalf, went to Oyster Bay in October and described the campaign's progress. As a result of that meeting, La Follette said "it had suddenly dawned upon Roosevelt that Taft could be beaten."

Whatever the accuracy of that account, TR certainly had similar discussions in October with supporters such as James Garfield. Moreover, Gilson Gardner told La Follette that Roosevelt had become convinced that even if he were to lose the nomination in 1912, his "leadership of the Progressive movement would have become so established that you would be in the way in 1916." "Fighting Bob" may have been unrealistic about his prospects, but he had become an unwelcome nuisance. Partly to avoid having him as a competitor, TR arranged for his friends to hint that he might be interested after all, causing just enough confusion to place a major obstacle in La Follette's path.

George Miller of the *Detroit News* had been urging TR to run for more than a year. Now, using an off-the-record interview with William Borah, the progressive senator from Idaho, Miller wrote that a Republican member of Congress had told him that "Roosevelt will be nominated for President by the Republican Convention next year." Miller then described what he called "a very effective campaign going on all the time for Roosevelt, although it has no headquarters and no organization. The letters which are passing through the country from citizen to citizen and local leader to local leader are far more effective than any campaign that is going on. They are saying he is the one man we can nominate and elect. This is the kind of campaign which neither Col. Roosevelt nor anyone else can stop. You cannot stop a thing that seven out of ten men want to see go." Miller was so pleased with the piece that he sent a copy to Roosevelt.

As TR let it be known that he was moving closer to running, La Follette's campaign manager complained daily that his "work was being delayed and at important points brought to a standstill." Most of his old friends in the progressive movement began to consider deserting La Follette. They were attracted by the force of Roosevelt's personality and the greater plausibility of his candidacy. Thanks in part to the efforts of TR's supporters, La Follette's campaign, which had been gaining traction in October, had begun to lose momentum by late November.

But Knox and Osborn felt that La Follette needed at least one more push. "Fighting Bob" was scheduled to launch his formal campaign on New Year's Day in Lansing, Michigan, the state's capital city. The city's Progressive Club had asked Governor Osborn to give what would presumably be a warm introduction. After all, Osborn was the vice president of the Progressive Republican League, which had been launched in La Follette's living room almost exactly a year earlier. But on the night before the speech—on New Year's Eve, 1911—the *New York Times* reported that Osborn planned to denounce La Follette as "bad medicine" and ask him to quit the race in favor of TR.

Not wanting to be humiliated, La Follette skipped the Lansing rally. But Osborn appeared anyway and delivered a scathing attack in front of a largely hostile, pro–La Follette audience. Echoing Roosevelt's concerns, he called the senator "a potent agitator" who created "a condition of public intolerance." He then called on La Follette to "withdraw as a candidate, join me in asking President Taft to withdraw, and then permit the party" to "settle upon Theodore Roosevelt as a candidate for president." Throughout the first week of the year, Osborn's speech made headlines around the country.

Unknown to all but a very few insiders, Osborn's scathing remarks were part of a calculated, secret strategy. La Follette appeared to be "sweeping Michigan," Osborn told a friend a month later. "There was no doubt about it. I thought something drastic had to be done so I made my La Follette speech. That seems to have marked the turning point in La Follette's prospects."

Osborn sent the speech to TR along with a cover note. At lunch with Knox in Oyster Bay on January 6, TR called Osborn's Lansing speech "a brilliant stroke, the biggest thing pulled off in the campaign so far." When Knox proposed that other governors make similar speeches, TR "instantly and enthusiastically agreed." During the following weeks, as Roosevelt spread word of his availability for a draft, the strength oozed out of "Fighting Bob's" campaign.

By the time La Follette delivered a powerful speech in front of thousands of adoring supporters at Carnegie Hall on January 22, it was too late. Earlier that day, Amos Pinchot, acting on La Follette's behalf, met with TR at the University Club and asked him not to run. The Colonel refused to make any such promise. Roosevelt did not tell Amos that at that very moment Franklin Knox was crossing the country as his emissary, asking governors to sign an appeal for him to run, or that he and a group of his supporters had been spending the day working at his offices at *The Outlook* magazine, drafting his response to the "spontaneous" letter from the governors.

Amos and La Follette had dinner alone at the Plaza Hotel after the rally. When Amos described his visit with the Colonel, La Follette was furious. He felt that TR had been using him as a stalking horse, hoping to determine whether there was a true constituency for an effective challenge to the incumbent. But he said that he would continue to run even if Roosevelt entered the race because he was convinced that Roosevelt was not a true progressive. That encounter remained a vivid memory to Amos twenty years later. La Follette told him that "he considered TR a more or less unconscious instrument of Morgan and the Steel Trust and that he believed Gifford and I would someday discover that he had for years been tied hand and foot by Gary, Perkins and the other Steel Trust people."

By the end of January, the campaign to undermine La Follette had succeeded. He had been marginalized, outmaneuvered, and humiliated. Gifford Pinchot, who was wavering but still nominally in La Follette's camp, met with him in his living room—the room where the National Progressive Republican League had been launched—and told him that his strength had "sunk to a point" where it was in his own interest to withdraw. La Follette was hurt but adamant. He said that he would fight on alone even if he could only carry a single state.

Pinchot told the editor of the Scripps papers, Gilson Gardner's boss, that La Follette had become consumed by anger.

"The Senator has decided on war between the La Follette supporters and the Roosevelt supporters," Pinchot wrote on February 1.

> He is blinded by his irritation at Roosevelt's course, and hampered in his judgment by his nervous condition. He says, and this is perfectly true, that many of the Roosevelt supporters are not Progressives at all, but reactionaries trying to get on the bandwagon. And he fears that to these men and not the progressives

Roosevelt will recognize his obligation if he is elected. . . . I admit that Roosevelt, if elected, may not give as clear and strongly progressive an administration as La Follette would, but nevertheless, I do believe . . . he will be vastly more progressive and useful than Taft.

Some of La Follette's progressive supporters saw what was happening but felt helpless. Congressman William Kent of California, a charter member of the National Progressive Republican League, said Roosevelt was murdering La Follette and killing off the progressive movement. "If ever a man played a mean dog-in-the-manger game, Roosevelt is doing it at the present time," he told his mother. "He seems to me to be one of those great big, inhuman freaks that occur from time to time in the world's history, and not a blundering human being like the rest of us are."

ROOSEVELT'S TACTICS WERE taking a psychological as well as a political toll on La Follette. They added to his exhaustion from campaigning and his deep concern about his eleven-year-old daughter, Mary, who was about to have an operation to remove a tubercular gland near her jugular vein. The "hampered judgment" and "nervous condition" that Pinchot observed on February 1, contributed to La Follette's strange, self-destructive behavior at the Periodical Publishers' Association Dinner the following evening, on February 2, the night that his campaign imploded.

The Periodical Publishers' Association had some of the features of a trade association, fighting to keep postal rates low, and some of the characteristics of a political movement. Its annual dinners were grand affairs, held at lavish venues around the country, featuring leading writers, ambassadors, and political figures of the era, sometimes including the President. Speeches were often humorous, with a touch of the wit that characterized the Gridiron Club. Taft, for example, brought down the house in 1910 with remarks that mixed great humor with political commentary. TR was the group's guest of honor when the banquet was held at New York's Waldorf Astoria Hotel in 1911. So in the fall of 1911, when the association announced the lineup for the 1912 dinner in Philadelphia, the choices carried political implications. The honored guests for the banquet were to be Governor Woodrow Wilson of New Jersey, who was a candidate for the Democratic Party's nomination, and Senator Robert M. La Follette, who was seeking the Republican Party's nomination against the incumbent.

There were at least 625 people on hand. The organizers held a straw vote of the 93 members of the association who had come down from New York. They tallied 24 for Taft, 26 for TR, 7 for La Follette, 19 for Wilson, 2 for Eugene V. Debs—and a sprinkling of votes for editors such as William Allen White. The vote was anonymous, but a couple of guests put their names next to their ballots for La Follette—including famed muckraker Lincoln Steffens and Edwin Markham, the poet who was best known for "The Man with the Hoe." The room overflowed with those on every side of the spectrum and from every important part of the political landscape. Many of La Follette's most ardent supporters were on hand, including all of the progressive leaders in Congress and from along the eastern seaboard. It was an important and potentially receptive crowd.

Woodrow Wilson brought the house to its feet with a powerful commentary on the need for tariff reform. By the time La Follette reached the podium, it was after 10 P.M. He was carrying the text of a thoughtful and courageous dissertation on government, the economy, and the press.

The speech described the importance of journalism in a democracy, but warned that there had been a dramatic and dangerous change since the days of Horace Greeley, Charles A. Dana, and Joseph Medill. In the past few years, he wrote, "money power has gained control of our industry and government. It controls the newspaper press. The people know this. . . . the news is colored; so confidence in the newspaper as a newspaper is being undermined." But there were hopeful signs, too. The text celebrated "the power and influence and prosperity of weekly and monthly magazines," especially those set up in recent years by young men who "saw an unoccupied field and went out and built up great periodicals and magazines. They were free. . . . We entered on a new era."

The text ended with a word of caution to those courageous new owners and editors, including many who were in the room that night: it admonished them to remain vigilant and independent, because there were special interests who would, "sooner or later, reach out for the magazines." He predicted that there would be a new kind of peril—"the centralization of advertising that will in time seek to gag you."

The speech had flashes of brilliance that resonate today. La Follette was so proud of it—and so mortified by what happened next—that he printed the entire text as an appendix to his autobiography. But he never delivered the address as written.

What happened that evening became legend. In the days that followed, it was described by many of those who were there, perhaps most poignantly by William Allen White, who loved La Follette and believed that he would have become the best President of the era:

> For ten minutes or so, perhaps twenty, he read along fluently and well. Then he put his manuscript down for a moment to emphasize a point. The dinner guests noted that he wandered a lot and repeated himself. When he picked up his manuscript he had lost his place and read for five minutes or so paragraphs that he had already read. Then he laid it down again, and the second time he departed from his manuscript he began to lose control of his temper. He came out of his fury maudlin. . . . For nearly two hours, fumbling occasionally with his manuscript, he raged on and on, saying the same thing over and over at the top of his voice.

Owen Wister, the novelist, remembered that as people began to leave La Follette "shook his fist at them, saying 'There are some of the fellows I'm hitting. They don't want to hear about themselves.'" He had become incoherent. He was repeating himself. The toastmaster tried to stop him but in vain. He didn't end his talk until twelve-thirty, when he finally collapsed on the table.

The hall was practically empty. Amos Pinchot led La Follette out of the room. He was certain that La Follette's campaign was over. La Follette's campaign manager, Walter Houser, wanted him to withdraw, as did most of his supporters. Even though he refused to make a public announcement, his campaign seemed to be at an end.

But the La Follette obituaries would prove to be stunningly premature.

WHEN ROOSEVELT'S OFFICE released his formal announcement on the evening of Judge Grant's February 25 dinner party, it was framed as a response to a letter from seven Republican governors dated February 10, 1912. He told the public and friends, including those in Judge Grant's dining room, that it would have been cowardly to refuse the governors' plea, a case, he often repeated with bravado, of "il gran rifiuto," Dante's phrase for the moment when, at the gates of hell, a coward makes a great refusal. Based on the impassioned request of the governors, and with no concern for his own interests, he said that he could not refuse such a draft.

Roosevelt's words were more than a little disingenuous. He had been the instigator of the "draft." He had been trying to clear the field since early December, but even if La Follette could be marginalized, Taft was not going to withdraw. So in mid-January, Roosevelt decided that the best way to announce his willingness to run would be to respond to what would amount to a political draft in the form of a letter from the governors—a letter that Alice Roosevelt Longworth called "somewhat cooked," a letter that he would generate.

The letter was his idea. He suggested it to several of the governors on January 18 and then he wrote it. Starting on January 20, he sent Frank Knox on a cross-country trip to visit those governors who, based on the soundings of his advance agents like Cal O'Laughlin, seemed likely to respond favorably. Knox carried copies of the draft letter along with a personal note from TR to each governor, asking him to work with Knox, introducing him as "a former member of my regiment who is now chairman of the State Republican Committee of Michigan."

On January 22, as Knox was moving around the country, taking the draft letter to the governors for their signatures, and as La Follette was preparing to give his major address in Carnegie Hall, TR was in the offices of *The Outlook*, working on his response—the response that was ultimately distributed to the world on February 25, while Roosevelt was about to have dinner with Judge Grant.

One of the other editors at *The Outlook* kept a record of those meetings. According to his diary, Roosevelt suddenly had "an inspiration"— an idea to be included in his statement. He would "propose presidential primaries in order to be sure of popular demand."

To those in the room it was a masterstroke. The demand for primaries would immediately put TR at the forefront of the progressive movement and put Taft on the defensive. Equally important, in the eyes of some of his most progressive aides, it would give legitimacy to a third-party bid if he failed to win the Republican nomination.

Thus his formal response to the letter from the governors featured a paragraph insisting that the party adhere to "the genuine rule of the people."

"I hope that so far as possible the people may be given the chance, through direct primaries, to express their preference as to who shall be the nominee of the Republican Presidential Convention."

In mid-December, Roosevelt's emissaries at the Republican National Committee's meeting had helped to block the effort to require or at least encourage states to hold primaries. Now, for the first time, his response to the request by the governors put the Colonel at the forefront of the movement for popular government, providing the already widespread movement for political primaries with a new lightning bolt of energy.

———

TR'S NEWFOUND COMMITMENT to primaries required *The Outlook* to do a bit of fancy footwork. Reflecting Roosevelt's previous skepticism about popular government, and the concern that La Follette might be more likely than Roosevelt to win many, and possibly most, of any primaries, *The Outlook* had carried a cautionary editorial just two days earlier. "There is as yet no evidence to show that the Presidential primary will not be accompanied by certain disadvantages which might possibly outweigh its advantages," the magazine argued on January 20. "The experience of the states where it now exists may provide some interesting evidence on that question this year."

The following week, *The Outlook* reversed itself. It carried a ringing editorial endorsement of direct presidential primaries, calling for their adoption everywhere.

TR's statement even convinced Jonathan Bourne that he had "come out unconditionally for popular government principals." Bourne soon moved to Roosevelt's camp. But his endorsement carried a caveat.

At a meeting of two dozen of TR's supporters in Washington, Bourne stunned the group by declaring: "If we lose, we bolt." He still believed in a third party and now he thought that Roosevelt could lead it.

As usual, Bourne was a few months ahead of his colleagues. They couldn't imagine how Taft could win.

"We were all hypnotized by the clamoring voices across the land," William Allen White recalled. "We had forgotten about the mercenary southern delegates."

Chapter Four

William Allen White and his friends might have forgotten about the "mercenary southern delegates," but the members of the Clan, the men running and funding Roosevelt's fledgling campaign, had not. They knew that they were off to a late start in the South, where the Republican Party was, to a large extent, a fiction. By 1912, most blacks were disenfranchised and the Democratic Party had won every election since the end of Reconstruction. The Republican Party consisted primarily of those who had been appointed to office by the White House or wanted some form of support from the national government. Taft's campaign team had been hard at work in the region for months, using patronage and political favors to line up delegates before anyone else could enter the race.

At first, members of TR's campaign team were convinced that they could win at least some southern support. They hoped to find idealists or romantics who believed in his programs or in him. For those with more "mercenary" motives, Roosevelt's supporters had other arguments at their disposal. Some incumbent officeholders owed their job to Roosevelt. Others wanted to be in his corner in case he, rather than Taft, were to be selected as the party's nominee. In addition, there were scads of former Roosevelt appointees who had been removed by Taft, sometimes for his political friends, sometimes even for Democrats, men who were only too happy to find a way to get even.

As he charged around the region, Ormsby McHarg sent glowing reports from Alabama ("conditions in Alabama [are] more satisfactory than I had supposed they would be," he wrote Roosevelt on January 2) and from Georgia, where the Colonel could claim to be something of a native son. McHarg's claims may have been inflated, but TR wanted to believe them. He had always had a romantic affinity for the South. His mother was a Georgia belle, and she loved to tell her children about the daring exploits of her brother Irvine Bulloch and her half-brother James Dunwoody Bulloch. His uncles had served valiantly and famously in the Civil War, albeit on the Confederate side.

"From hearing of the feats performed by my Southern forefathers and kinfolk," Roosevelt wrote in his autobiography, "I felt a great admiration for men who were fearless and who could hold their own in the world, and I had a great desire to be like them."

Roosevelt began to think that in the general election he could win some states in the South and become a unifying force if he returned to power. But first he would have to win the Republican nomination, hopefully with the support of some delegates from the region. His campaign included several leaders with southern roots. Roosevelt's campaign manager, Senator Joseph Dixon of Montana, had close ties to his native state of North Carolina. Throughout the region, there were disgruntled business leaders who had been denied lucrative government contracts and countless disappointed office-seekers. Some men favored TR because they were enraged that Taft had selected a Democrat and former Confederate soldier as Chief Justice of the United States Supreme Court. They complained that he had chosen Democrats for important positions in his administration, including a Confederate war veteran from Tennessee as Secretary of War. What's more, two key southern state Republican Party chairs were close friends—Pearl Wight of Louisiana, who had worked closely with Roosevelt during his years as President, and Colonel Cecil Lyon of Texas, a political ally and bear-hunting companion.

But even with disgruntled business leaders and men like Wight and Lyon on his side, gaining the support of delegates from the South would soon prove to be a challenge. Wight immediately promised to join the crusade, pledging to "sink or swim with you." In a candid letter, though, he underlined the obstacles that they would confront in a region where almost every Republican owed his job or allegiance to the man in the White House.

"The power of public office and the weakness of office holders is so great that I doubt if either Col. Lyon in Texas or myself here can control these delegates," Wight told his friend ten days before his public announcement. "I know in the other Southern States that it is even more doubtful."

As was becoming evident everywhere, TR had only one hope. "If we can get the [Louisiana] State Central Committee to agree to primaries," Wight said, "I am sure we can beat them overwhelmingly." With Taft's tight control of the party, however, there was no realistic chance of creating any southern primaries.

Once they became convinced that TR couldn't win many southern delegates by the existing rules, his campaign team devised a complementary strategy: delegitimize the South's political base in the party. That approach had several virtues. By vilifying Taft's tactics in the South, TR could win sympathy in the North and lay the groundwork for a possible third-party bid based on the claim of a rigged process. More important, the campaign allowed Ormsby McHarg, who knew a great deal about such matters, to file credentials challenges against Taft's southern delegates as early and often as possible, allowing Roosevelt's publicity bureau to undermine a key element of the President's campaign strategy. Taft was trying to lock up the South's 246 delegates as quickly as possible so that he would look invincible to politicians and the press at the outset of the campaign. By filing challenges to most or all of them, no matter what the merits, TR convinced most newspapers to put those delegates into an undecided column, allowing his supporters to claim that the race was neck and neck.

Those flimsy and often bogus challenges worked for a while. But they also had an unforeseen and unfortunate consequence for the campaign. At the convention itself, they would undermine the legitimacy of TR's more plausible credentials challenges.

THE NEW MAGAZINES, run by progressives of all stripes, the powerful and influential weekly and monthly publications that La Follette had intended to celebrate in his disastrous speech in Philadelphia, offered the ideal vehicle for an exposé of southern political corruption. Those magazines—*McClure's, American Magazine, The Outlook, Collier's, Cosmopolitan, Hampton's, Everybody's, Pearson's, Review of Reviews,* and others—played a vital role in setting the stage for the progressive movement. They exposed corporate and government malfeasance at every level, created vivid portraits of those ground down by poverty or industrial injustice, presented new political theories, published fiction with a moral theme—and presented what one cogent observer called an "amazingly complete" portrait of the society.

Frank Munsey helped to invent the business model if not the political model of those journals. Like Henry Ford in the world of automobiles, he developed printing techniques allowing for mass production, mass distribution, and low costs: he believed in high volume and low margins. During the financial panic of 1893, Munsey's magazine business was almost bankrupt. At thirty-nine, with indebtedness of $100,000, his biographer wrote, he had "dropped into the abyss." In desperation, "with money gone and all signals red against him," Munsey slashed the price of *Munsey's Magazine* from 25 cents to 10 cents, so low that some distributors refused his business. His last-ditch gamble worked. By 1912, *Munsey's* was one of the most popular publications in the country. At a time when the nation's total population was about 92 million, *Munsey's Magazine* had a circulation of more than 700,000 people.

Unlike many of his publishing peers, Munsey had no interest in political causes. He was fascinated by the business rather than the editorial side of publishing. William Allen White famously quipped that he had "the morals of a green-goods grocer." "Munsey knew nothing about journalism as a craft," historian Henry Steele Commager observed; he "had no ascertainable policies beyond an uncritical attachment to the status quo, and recognized no responsibility to the newspaper profession or to the public. To him journalism was a business, not very different from the grocery enterprise in which he was so profitably engaged."

While other magazines of the era were exposing the excesses of capitalism in areas such as meatpacking and oil, and finding corruption in the corridors of power in local, state, and national governments, his biographer observed that *Munsey's* "crusaded not at all." Munsey "saw muckraking as an attack upon men of his own kind, whose philosophy he shared. . . . His magazines were redolent of reassuring description, devoid of muscular criticism."

Though indifferent or unsympathetic to many tenets of the progressives, Munsey joined Wall Street millionaire George W. Perkins as the Colonel's biggest funder and turned his publications over to the cause. Munsey and Perkins had been intimate friends since 1895. Though he was undoubtedly attracted to TR's power and buoyant personality, critics were convinced that Munsey was motivated by his business interests rather than by ideology. He was a major investor in several deals arranged by J. P. Morgan & Company including those made possible by the mergers that created the International Harvester Company and U.S. Steel.

Munsey started buying U.S. Steel stock in 1901 as it was being formed by the House of Morgan. By some accounts he became the company's largest shareholder; at one point his holdings in the company were valued at about $50 million. That amount would be equal to more than $1 billion today. As one economic historian noted, Munsey "owed that phenomenal amount to his friendship with Perkins." There was only "one subject upon which Munsey, the stock speculator, preached with apostolic fervor," Munsey's biographer observed, "the greatness of United States Steel, the grandeur of Morgan."

Munsey's biographer called his attachment to J. P. Morgan "excellent business, rotten journalism." His morals may have been those of a "green-goods grocer;" he may have had "no ascertainable policies beyond an uncritical attachment to the status quo;" but in 1912, Munsey's publications as well as his checkbook became an important part of Roosevelt's campaign. With its vast circulation, *Munsey's Magazine* could cause a stir and it did so by asking Judson Churchill Welliver to expose corrupt political practices in the South.

Jud Welliver was the ideal man for the job. He later gained fame as the nation's first White House speechwriter, working for Presidents Harding and Coolidge, leading a bipartisan group to use his name when they created what they called the Judson Welliver Society, which brings White House speechwriters together for uproarious dinners; still later he served as a publicist for the American Petroleum Institute and for Sun Oil. But in 1912 he was a first-rate investigative reporter, a full-blooded supporter of the progressive cause—and an invaluable ally for TR. His series of investigative pieces for *Hampton's Magazine* had led to congressional inquiries about the Sugar Trust and the Cotton industry; his reports on politics and the new reform movement—a group that he helped label as the "Insurgents"—had earned him national attention as an astute political observer.

While friendly with a great many reformers, including La Follette, Welliver was particularly close to Roosevelt. During TR's presidency, he had been a member of a group later described as "the charmed circle of Roosevelt favorites." TR even sent him abroad to make a survey and report on problems in the railroads and waterways of Europe.

By 1912, he was the chief political correspondent for Munsey's *Washington Times*, where he put his considerable skill and reputation into the service of the campaign. Roosevelt told Perkins that Welliver is "a most useful man under Mr. Munsey in getting our side presented through the newspapers." On January 2, 1912, while La Follette was still very much in the race, Welliver wrote a front-page story predicting that TR would run and that La Follette would withdraw. Along with Governor Osborn's speech in Michigan, the story helped to shift momentum from La Follette to Roosevelt.

One part journalist, one part activist-publicist, Welliver used his talents and Munsey's outlets to skewer the members of the Republican Party in the South who seemed likely to back Taft. His lead story for *Munsey's* February issue was immodestly called "A Vitally Illuminating Article on a Criminally Corrupt Condition in the Republican Party."

Welliver's basic thesis had been the core of northern complaints for years. Almost half of the delegates needed to control the Republican Convention and to choose the party's next presidential nominee would be selected by the political machines of eleven southern states. None of those states had cast an electoral vote for a Republican presidential candidate since 1876, after which the government withdrew the federal troops who had been protecting the rights of the newly freed slaves, thereby allowing for the creation of Jim Crow laws that reduced and ultimately marginalized the voting strength of blacks. At a constitutional convention in 1890, for example, Mississippi passed an amendment that imposed a $2 poll tax and that excluded any voter who could not read and interpret the state constitution to the satisfaction of the local registrar's office. The correct interpretation, of course, was subjective, giving immense power to local election officials. Some states required that voters own property worth at least $300. To protect poor white voters, some states created what they called a "grandfather clause" that permitted the registration of anyone whose father or grandfather had been registered before 1867, a condition few if any black voters could meet.

The impact of the voter suppression elements of the Jim Crow laws had accelerated during Roosevelt's seven and a half years in office. In Pearl Wight's Louisiana, for example, black registration dropped from 130,000 in 1898, three years before TR took office, to 5,300 in 1908, just before he left office.* By 1910 there were only 730 registered black voters in the state.

In 1912, it would take 540 votes to control the Republican Party's national convention—and 246 delegates would come from those eleven states, where they would be picked by what Welliver called "brokerage corporations dealing in Federal patronage." Using 1908 as an illustration, he went down the delegate list state by state, delegate by delegate, and showed that almost every delegate to the convention was on the federal payroll.

In an accompanying editorial, the editors called the situation "a wretched farce" that "should stir a revolt among Republican voters." If President Taft had a shred of dignity and good taste, it argued, he would refuse to rely on such delegates for his nomination.

Thanks to other publications in Roosevelt's camp, the article quickly caused a national sensation. The *Chicago Tribune*, for example, picked it up, reproducing almost the entire text.

THE ATTACK ON southern delegates was both ironic and disingenuous since few national political figures had done more to protect and use them than Theodore Roosevelt. By some accounts, he even owed his presidency to a compromise designed to preserve the South's power in the party.

---

* Here is how one contemporaneous commentary described the laws adopted in Louisiana. "Another intricate device to restrict Negro suffrage is found in the constitution of Louisiana, and some other southern states, known as the 'grandfather clause.' Restrictions requiring an elector either to be able to read and write, or else own property to the extent of $300, are followed, and apparently extended, by a provision that no male person who was on January 1, 1867, or prior thereto, entitled to vote, and no son or grandson of any such person, shall be denied the right to register and vote by reason of not possessing the educational or property qualifications prescribed by the constitution, provided he shall have resided in the state for five years next preceding his application for registration, and that he shall have been registered, by separate registry, prior to September 1, 1898, and no person shall be entitled to register under this section after that date." *The Survey*, Volume XXXIX, October, 1912–March, 1912.

Reformers had been trying to reduce the power of southern delegates for more than a decade. Based on a rule first adopted in 1888, the
number of delegates to the Republican National Convention allotted
to each state was based on the state's representation in the Electoral
College. Yet thanks to the Jim Crow voting laws, the post–Civil War,
post-Reconstruction South was solidly Democratic at every level of government. Welliver correctly pointed out that in 1908 Taft won almost
200,000 votes in Kansas, while he won fewer than 5,000 in Mississippi; yet each would be entitled to 20 delegates at the 1912 Republican
convention. He pointed out that "One Mississippi Republican has the
same representation as 45 Kansas Republicans."

At the Republican National Convention in 1900, some political leaders from the North tried to address the issue by reducing the
South's representation. Their motives were not entirely disinterested,
of course, since their own delegations would have gained additional
voting strength at the expense of southern losses. But many were also
motivated by the fact that blacks were being systematically disenfranchised. At the same time, a senator from New York was trying to reduce
the South's representation in Congress by taking seats from the eleven
southern states that had adopted constitutional amendments to exclude
black voters.

TR always managed to oppose those reform efforts. In 1900, by
some accounts, he was chosen as McKinley's vice presidential candidate as a result of a deal between McKinley's forces and the reformers.
Senator Matthew Quay of Pennsylvania offered an amendment that
year that would have sharply reduced the number of southern delegates
at the convention. McKinley's campaign manager was Senator Mar-
cus Hanna, who hated Roosevelt. But Hanna wanted to preserve the
South's voting power.

What's your price, he asked Quay.

"If you will nominate Roosevelt, I shall withdraw the resolution,"
Quay responded. "If you won't, I shall insist upon its coming to a vote,
and you know what will happen there."

So TR became McKinley's vice president and ascended to the presidency as the result of a deal that saved the voting power of the increasingly discriminatory southern states.

The reformers tried to reduce the number of southern delegates again in 1904. Once again Roosevelt, this time as the incumbent President who controlled the southern delegates' votes, quashed the reformers' demands. As one scholar explained: "He found that the southern delegates were too immediately useful to sacrifice."

IN 1908, ROOSEVELT needed the southern votes to assure that his handpicked successor, William Howard Taft, would be nominated. But unlike 1900 and 1904, when a convention vote on southern representation had been shelved, a coalition of forces was determined to bring a motion to the floor. Some champions of the resolution were reformers; some simply hoped to increase the voting power of their states; others, in a diverse group called "the Allies," hoped that they could use the vote to stop the Roosevelt-Taft steamroller as it moved toward victory.

The dilution motion was introduced as a minority report on behalf of seventeen states from the Rules Committee. Supporters handed out sheets of paper containing a table that showed the impact on each state. Alabama would drop from 22 delegates to 6; Louisiana from 18 to 5; Texas from 36 to 9. Northern states would have their representation increased substantially.

As the votes came in, it seemed that every northern state would support the resolution. The *New York Tribune* called it "one of the most determined efforts in history to bring about a change." If the Allies won, the *Washington Post* reported, they might be able to block Taft's nomination.

Once again, Roosevelt opposed the dilution of votes from the South. "I object strongly to the proposal to put in the platform the plan about cutting down Southern representation because of the suppression of the negro vote," he told friends in New York. Delegates from the South, including black delegates who were among the most important beneficiaries of the status quo, were outraged by the impact such a rule would have. But delegates from the North, for a mixture of idealistic and self-interested reasons, supported the resolution.

There were powerful interests and powerful arguments on both sides and the outcome seemed uncertain. Former congressman (and future senator) James E. Watson, an influential delegate from Indiana, described what happened next.

"Along toward evening," he recalled, "a friend of President Roosevelt brought a message from him to me, one that he was showing to various persons in the convention, in which Roosevelt said that this resolution was but a ruse on the part of the 'Allies' to wrest certain southern delegates from Taft, and that it must not be adopted under any circumstances."

There was silence on the floor as the vote was counted. Every northern state voted for the resolution. Every southern state opposed it. Delegates from the west were split. Not counting the 46 delegates from Taft's home state of Ohio, there were 463 votes in favor and 468 opposed. If Ohio lined up with the other northern states, the resolution would pass.

But Taft and Roosevelt's managers had made clear what was at stake. In a dramatic move, almost all of the delegates from Ohio voted against the resolution. It was defeated 506 to 471.

Roosevelt's message "determined the contest," according to Watson.

But for Roosevelt, there was a bitter irony. As Watson noted in his memoir, "had that resolution passed in 1908, Taft would not have been nominated in 1912, and Roosevelt would have been, for the delegates from the southern states made possible Taft's re-nomination in the latter contest and assured Teddy's defeat."

Chapter Five

B y waiting until February 25, 1912, to announce his candidacy, Roosevelt allowed Taft to have a significant head start. Taft had spent
the past year building a huge lead in delegates from states where there
were no presidential primaries, particularly in the South, where White
House patronage, rather than cotton, was the political king. To buy
time, McHarg was filing challenges at every turn that were designed
to limit Taft's claims of inevitability. Roosevelt's managers also tried
to rally popular support by making a series of impressive, if mislead-
ing, claims. They said that the Taft campaign was collapsing in the
South, "gleefully" distributing telegrams from supporters such as Pearl
Wight of Louisiana. They pointed out that delegates from some southern states had been chosen before the start of the year, in violation of
the Call of the Republican Convention that had been adopted in mid-
December. As a result, they said that those delegates, who favored Taft,
should not be seated.

But the Colonel knew the truth. His incoming mail was full of cautionary messages. As Pearl Wight had advised, his only real hope in
Louisiana was to create a primary there, and the same could be said
for other states in and outside of the South. Unfortunately, by late February, Bourne, La Follette, and the National Progressive Republican
League had been able to create only a handful of presidential primaries.

Roosevelt had almost no chance of winning enough delegates unless he could convince more states to hold primaries.

George Perkins and a few other wealthy supporters agreed to pony up $100,000 to kick things off, enabling TR to expand and enrich his political team and to recruit Senator Joseph Dixon of Montana to replace McHarg as campaign manager in late February. Brought up as a Quaker and abolitionist in Snow Camp, North Carolina, in the years following the Civil War, Dixon spoke with a gentle southern drawl. He moved to Montana in 1891, inspired in part by Theodore Roosevelt's accounts of the West in *The Century Magazine*, becoming a senator in 1907. Unlike the often abrasive McHarg, Dixon was what one TR operative called "a great smoother" who "can stroke the ruffled feelings of an angry man with a more delicate touch than I ever saw."

Dixon promptly asked *New York Times* reporter Oscar King (O. K.) Davis, who had covered Roosevelt's 1910 speaking tour in the West, to sign on as the campaign's secretary. With La Follette apparently out of the race as a result of the fiasco at the Periodical Publishers' Association dinner, Dixon and Davis were joined by Gifford Pinchot and other reformers who had defected from La Follette's faltering campaign. One of the most energetic new recruits was Medill McCormick whose family owned the powerful *Chicago Tribune*. In Washington, McCormick led a "publicity bureau" that churned out stories and press releases drafted by a few talented working journalists, including the ever-reliable Cal O'Laughlin of the *Chicago Tribune*. The reporters served as "objective" journalists by day and campaign advisors and publicists by night.

The publicity bureau translated the demand for direct presidential primaries into a powerful political and public relations issue. They released statement after statement demanding that primaries be instituted everywhere, keeping their candidate on the front pages of every paper in the country—and putting Taft on the defensive. Soon their demands became a drumbeat.

Using language composed by O'Laughlin and Davis, Dixon dared the President to face the voters.

"I hereby challenge you to a test by means of primaries in every state in the union," Dixon wrote Taft's campaign manager, Rep. William B. McKinley of Illinois, on March 5. Dixon knew that McKinley wouldn't take the bait.

The letter generated national headlines and precipitated follow-up stories in every state. The account in the *New York Times*, where O. K. Davis was still employed, said that "the primary question is the most troublesome thing the Taft managers have to meet." It was particularly effective in Illinois, where Taft was sure to control the delegation unless the legislature created a primary. As Davis later recalled, O'Laughlin's "*Chicago Tribune* took the matter up with the utmost energy."

During the weeks that followed, Roosevelt's friends in the press were unrelenting. Mark Sullivan, the idealistic young associate editor of *Collier's* who went on to great fame as the author of a series of colorful works of history called *Our Times*, wrote an editorial on the subject almost every issue.

TR's managers had an early success in Massachusetts, where their efforts led the state legislature to adopt a primary bill on March 11. Roosevelt used that victory to call on Taft to support similar efforts to create "the preferential primary in Michigan, Illinois, Maryland, the District Columbia and New York." He knew, of course, that Taft would do everything in his power to oppose such legislation.

Dixon and the press office were determined "to have something doing every minute," O'Laughlin boasted. Attacking the incumbent at every turn, they called him fat, incompetent, and corrupt.

Taft gave them plenty of ammunition. In mid-February, just before Roosevelt's formal announcement, the President created a firestorm by withdrawing the nomination of two customs officers and six postmasters in North Carolina who had announced their support for TR. Roosevelt charged that the President had "put the offices on the auction block." Dixon called it "flagrant prostitution." The customs officer episode provided a case study in the power and corrupting influence of patronage.

Roosevelt's team knew how to keep the pot boiling. At Dixon's behest, Kansas senator Joseph Bristow seized on the North Carolina episode. He introduced a resolution calling for a congressional inquiry into Taft's efforts to put pressure on southern postmasters. There were similar reports from other southern states, including Alabama. Papers around the country ran front-page articles. O'Laughlin told TR that the press coverage showed that his campaign was "in great shape" but emphasized the need to continue to generate negative stories, to "keep on the offensive." McHarg, who took credit for the Bristow resolution, told TR that it was "a drop in the bucket compared to what can be shown."

TAFT'S CAMPAIGN MANAGERS knew the stakes—and how to play the game. In state after state, they blocked legislation that would create primaries. They even stymied the effort to create a primary in Michigan, where TR's supporters included that state's Republican Party chair, Frank Knox, and Republican governor Chase Osborn.

In other states during early March, Taft's team found ways to keep control. As TR's supporters saw it, the President was rigging the process and circumventing the will of the people as expressed in local primaries and local conventions. Some states that did not have direct presidential primaries allowed people to vote for delegates to district conventions. Though TR's name was not on such ballots, his supporters often managed to field competing slates of delegates who would be in his camp. In the Fifth District of Missouri, for example, Roosevelt's supporters won a primary to select delegates to the district convention by an overwhelming vote. But Taft's operatives controlled the district's party apparatus. The New York Times reported that they "declared the primary vote illegal, held a rump convention consisting of 35 appointed delegates," and proceeded to elect two Taft supporters as delegates to the national convention in Chicago.

Frank Knox smelled a conspiracy. Taft's tactics in the Fifth District of Missouri illustrated the potential uses of raw political power. Knox was convinced that Taft's forces planned to use the Credentials Committee at the national convention, which they were likely to control, to win the nomination by hook or by crook. Very likely by crook. In a dispatch from the road, Knox informed Roosevelt that Taft's campaign manager "has told his friends not to worry about the outcome [of individual contests], that he has control of the national committee, and that enough seats will be contested to permit the fight to be won in the Credentials Committee."

Roosevelt's campaign team saw foul play everywhere. Knowing that he needed secrecy as manager of the campaign, Senator Dixon started to send his most sensitive messages in code. Roosevelt expressed his frustration in letter after letter. "The action of our opponents in Missouri in sending those fake contesting delegations is the kind of position they are desirous of taking," he told the owner of the *Kansas City Star*, one of the few newspaper publishers who was on his side. "It is literally as Medill McCormick said, 'if they cannot murder the progressive movement, they wish to see the Republican Party commit suicide.'"

TO HAVE ANY chance of winning, TR's campaign concluded that they would have to resort to tactics that seemed a bit more acceptable in the still slightly "wild west" than in the drawing rooms of New York and Massachusetts. They were prepared to be every bit as ruthless as Taft.

In one of the campaign's early success stories, the Roosevelt forces won most of the delegates from Oklahoma by using what might be called "Rough Rider" tactics. Here is how Frank Knox described the scene to TR:

> Our fellows put up a great fight lasting all day and until four in the morning. One man dropped dead and two or three were carried out unconscious. The state chairman, Harris, a Taft man, was told if he tried to put over any crooked deals from the chair that he wouldn't get out of the hall alive. Feelings ran so high that gun-play was expected. Indeed, I am told that one of

Roosevelt's men stood behind Harris with his hand on his gun ready for an emergency.

But with the exception of Oklahoma and a few other states, Taft's people were dominating the ground game, sometimes by effective political tactics, often by extraordinary means. They were determined to lock up as many delegates as possible before TR's troops could get their boots on.

WITH THE CAMPAIGN going against TR in so many states, the North Dakota presidential primary, scheduled for March 19, took on special importance for Roosevelt. It would be the country's first-ever statewide direct presidential primary.

TR's supporters stressed that "no effort should be spared to make the decision . . . overwhelming."

But in early March, there had been an unexpected complication. Robert La Follette, so recently taken for dead, entered the North Dakota primary race. And he did so with a vengeance.

La Follette knew that he could not win the Republican Party nomination. But he was so angry at TR's tactics, so contemptuous of his opportunistic support of progressive principles, so convinced that he should have been the party's standard bearer—and perhaps so furious at those who had deserted his campaign—that he was determined to deny Roosevelt the nomination. TR had spent months as a landowner and cowboy in the Badlands of North Dakota and popularized his experiences in books that captured the imagination of schoolboys in the East. But as a true son of the upper Middle West, La Follette had an enormous following in the state.

Progressives in the state overwhelmingly supported La Follette. In desperation, Roosevelt accepted the support of North Dakota's conservative faction, putting his effort in the hands of a group that La Follette called "an unholy alliance of enthusiasts and stand-patters."

Traveling the West as emissary for his one-time regiment leader,

Frank Knox began to worry about the facts on the ground. He sent daily reports directly to the Colonel, the man he sometimes called "the big chief." In a disingenuous effort to invigorate the slightly discouraged troops, Knox told reporters that Roosevelt was headed for a clear victory in North Dakota. But in his state-by-state rundown on March 11, he told TR that the campaign there was in deep trouble.

Roosevelt read the letter with alarm. He answered it the day it arrived. He knew that his enemies in the press would have a field day if he were to lose the first primary to La Follette—even if he came in second, ahead of Taft.

"It will be a misfortune if we do not carry North Dakota," TR told Knox. "The East will construe it not as a defeat for Mr. Taft but as a defeat for me."

OUT IN CALIFORNIA, Hiram Johnson did not want to believe what he was reading in the papers. After La Follette's breakdown at the publishers' dinner, Governor Johnson and some but not all of his insurgent colleagues had switched to Roosevelt. With La Follette back in the race, he felt that he was fighting a battle on two fronts.

Many of the stories he was reading were deeply discouraging, but Johnson hoped that the news reports were inaccurate, the product of the political bias of the owners and reporters on the right who favored Taft, or of those on the left who supported La Follette. He told Amos Pinchot that it was difficult "to obtain accurate information here on the eastern situation. We are dependent, of course, upon press dispatches, and the Associated Press is prejudiced against our side, while the United Press [which had a warm spot for La Follette] apparently is not taking as kindly to Col. Roosevelt as we had hoped. I should greatly appreciate it if you would write to me concerning recent developments and what you hope for New York State. The dispatches that have come to us recently . . . are all to the effect that Taft will carry it overwhelmingly and that the Colonel will not exceed fourteen delegates. . . ."

Governor Johnson ended on an ominous note. "If La Follette shall carry North Dakota, as seems likely, and Taft shall have seventy-five out of ninety delegates from New York, the effect upon the country at large will be difficult to overcome."

Roosevelt knew that he had to do something. He decided to bring his leading supporters together for what he called "a gathering of the Clan."

FROM THE DAY that he decided to be a candidate, TR had believed that he could stay above the fray, let his campaign team do most of the political work, and, most important, avoid barnstorming around the country making speeches. He dreaded the travel, the trains, the strain on his voice. For several years, he had complained to friends and family about the difficulty of speaking and the exhaustion of long trips. "I have six weeks of grey horror before me when I go to see Ted in San Francisco," he had written his friend Arthur Lee a year earlier, on the eve of the trip that included a visit to his son as well as a series of speeches, most notably his "New Nationalism" address in Kansas. "I will have to make a speech-making tour thither and back. However, thank fortune! I think that with this tour my troubles of that kind are at an end, and I will never again have to go on a similar trip."

Since presidential primaries were a new phenomenon, it had not occurred to TR that he would have to engage in retail campaigning. For as long as humanly possible, he resisted demands that he deliver more than a few select speeches. But his supporters around the country knew that the campaign was floundering and pleaded with TR to take his message around the nation. "It is your duty to your country-men to actively and publicly and aggressively defend the great cause of equal opportunity and equal human rights for all men," Kansas governor Walter Stubbs said in an urgent wire. Stubbs had witnessed the power of Roosevelt's speech at Osawatomie less than two years earlier. "An appeal from you to every American citizen who loves his country would change a million inactive supporters of yours into a fighting army that would be absolutely irresistible."

TR did not want to go out on the stump. "I do not think it would be wise for me to follow such a course," he told Dixon. But with his campaign foundering, he knew that he had to do something "to stabilize the ship."

ON MARCH 15, the Clan gathered at the home of Mrs. J. West Roosevelt, the widow of TR's cousin, for a session that lasted all night and well into the morning. The Colonel had been using his cousin's home as a pied-à-terre while she spent the winter in Miami. The group consisted of practical men such as William Ward, who had been put in charge of the campaign in New York; Joseph Dixon, who came up from Washington; Governors Herbert Hadley of Missouri and W. E. Glasscock of West Virginia; Henry L. Stoddard, Roosevelt's close friend who owned and edited the *New York Evening Mail*; and the campaign's most important financial backers, George Perkins and Frank Munsey. Not one of those at the meeting came from the most progressive wing of the party. Even though some of those that TR had earlier called "ultra-radicals," men like the Pinchot brothers, were now on his team, not one was a charter member of "the Clan."

Though the campaign denied it, the *New York Times* correctly surmised that TR had "become alarmed, feeling that he was not receiving the support in some of the Western States that he had been promised." While some members of the Clan expressed total confidence in the efforts that were underway, TR trusted what he was hearing in his daily letters from Frank Knox, in the pleas that were coming from Governor Stubbs, and in the increasingly concerned missives from Hiram Johnson. It was clear to him that his campaign needed to be reset and reenergized.

To retune the effort, he wanted Ormsby McHarg to play a bigger role and to create more delegate challenges in southern states. Even if such challenges were trumped up, they would undermine the public force of Taft's claim to a solid South.

According to Stoddard's account, the most powerful men in the campaign and, other than TR, certainly the most powerful in the room, were Frank Munsey, George Perkins, and William Ward. Munsey and Perkins didn't like McHarg. Since he had worked for Taft and then bitterly and publicly denounced TR before returning to the fold, they doubted his tactics and his motives. They called him "a soldier of fortune." He was also far too independent, outspoken, and insensitive for them.

McHarg was convinced that TR needed to win at least some of the 246 delegates from the South. Dixon disagreed. McHarg thought Dixon was naïve and criticized his leadership, accusing him of "flubdubbing around," saying that he and his publicity bureau were "satisfying themselves by issuing vitriolic bulletins hoping to stir the animals up" but that all they were doing, in fact, was "warming up their little coterie around the headquarters."

In a somewhat unofficial capacity, McHarg had been working for TR from the earliest phases of the campaign. TR had kept his involvement off of the official grid, partly to avoid a direct fight with his wealthiest supporters. He had selected Dixon rather than McHarg as his campaign manager. But when Munsey and Perkins tried to eliminate McHarg entirely, Ward came to his defense with a powerful threat.

"You two will get McHarg back in the campaign, or I will get out," Ward announced.

After hours of debate, Roosevelt agreed that McHarg should have an important and official role. Newspaper stories the next morning incorrectly reported that McHarg was now running the campaign. The *New York Times* headline said that McHarg was "In Control of the Colonel's Forces." TR was forced to issue a statement later that day, in time for the afternoon papers, explaining that Dixon was still in charge.

Still seeking a degree of plausible deniability about McHarg's work in the South, Roosevelt gave a statement to the press that was more than a bit disingenuous.

If Dixon is still in charge of the campaign, a reporter asked, "How does this leave McHarg?"

"I haven't seen McHarg," Roosevelt told reporters. "Mr. McHarg worked for Mr. Ward. I think it was Mr. Ward. I don't know anything about Mr. McHarg. I don't know what he has been doing."

In fact, Roosevelt had continued to correspond with McHarg on a regular basis. Only a few days earlier, he had engaged in an extensive exchange of letters with McHarg, complimenting him on his work in the South, and telling him to share some of his most explosive findings with one of his aides.

As a result of the meeting of the Clan, McHarg's role was now both enhanced and official. He knew how politicians thought and how conventions worked and that in politics, where perceptions can be enormously important, it would be essential to let political leaders think that TR had a good chance of winning. Otherwise, whatever their personal preferences, the party bosses would line up with Taft. TR agreed to give McHarg the authority to create delegate challenges in every southern state. Whether warranted or not, he would generate such challenges "for psychological effect." They would reduce the number of delegates that the press would attribute to Taft, thereby influencing the opinions of politicians and others who wanted to be on the winning side. It was a campaign tactic that seemed essential at the time but created major problems for Roosevelt at the convention.

Taft's campaign claimed that it already had 127 delegates in its corner. Dixon denied it. He told the press that the actual number was only 63.

After the meeting with the Clan, a reporter asked TR if he believed Dixon's delegate count.

"I not only believe it," he told reporters on March 16. "I know it."

But in fact, he did not believe or know it. His campaign was losing ground every day. He had little chance of winning either of the first two primaries. La Follette seemed certain to win North Dakota on March 19, and Taft was likely to get most of the delegates from New York a week later. His enemies in the press would have a field day. They would claim that the contest was effectively finished. Politicians who were undecided would desert him and his third-term crusade might even become a joke, a subject of derision.

The campaign needed a jolt of energy. As Governor Stubbs insisted, Roosevelt had to take to the campaign trail himself. Much as he hated the thought of campaigning, TR told the Clan that he would agree to become a full-on candidate once again. On March 19, La Follette won the North Dakota primary. As TR had predicted, the front-page *New York Times* headline focused on his loss, not on Taft or even La Follette. It said: "Beat Roosevelt in North Dakota."

But with his exquisite sense of political theater, Roosevelt arranged to deliver a dramatic speech on March 20, one that would drown out the negative news from North Dakota.

Chapter Six

O n March 20, 1912, Carnegie Hall was filled to capacity. Only two months earlier, Robert La Follette had delivered a powerful address to an overflow crowd of cheering supporters in the same venue. On that evening in January, La Follette had been introduced by Gifford Pinchot, and he had shared a late dinner with Gifford's brother, Amos. Now the Pinchot brothers were with TR. Notwithstanding La Follette's dramatic primary victory in North Dakota a day earlier, the Pinchots were among the more than 3,000 people crammed into the lavish main hall to hear what the press was calling Roosevelt's first speech of the campaign.

The balcony was filled with activists and social workers while the main floor glittered with men and women in evening dress. Another crowd of Roosevelt supporters filled the Carnegie Lyceum, a smaller theater and recital hall, and as many as 5,000 others, who could not gain admission, stood cheering in the street. The main floor had the excitement and flavor of opening night of the opera season. Frank Munsey had reserved 14 boxes. George Perkins was there with a party of friends. Edith Roosevelt, just back from her trip to Latin America, joined a family box, providing public support for her husband's return to politics.

When Roosevelt bounded onto the stage, the building exploded with wild cheers. "Teddy, O! Teddy," people shouted, waving handkerchiefs and hats from the galleries.

Standing on the raised platform, Roosevelt waved his hand, asking his admirers to take their seats. But a shout came from the back of the hall, and most of those in the crowd jumped back to their feet and cheered for another two minutes.

Roosevelt had been working on his speech for more than a week. Some of his closest advisors urged him to stress his conservative, probusiness credentials. They were trying, in part, to offset the impact of the proposal for the recall of judicial decisions in his Columbus speech, which had sent tremors through the business world, including many of his staunchest supporters. "All your friends and the committee here unanimously and strongly urge that your Carnegie Hall address be mainly a charter of business prosperity," his former Secretary of the Navy wired from Chicago. The treasurer of Roosevelt's New York campaign pleaded for such a statement: "If a strong chord of sympathy can be struck in your Carnegie Hall address with the aims of those who are working conservatively to develop large business enterprises on the basis of the square deal, I think it would do more for our cause between now and election time than any other subject which could be discussed there." TR's treasurer sat in a private box, hoping that Roosevelt would heed his advice.

But thanks to La Follette's return to the race, with the front pages of the papers that day featuring the results from North Dakota, a probusiness speech was impossible. Strange and unlikely as it seemed, La Follette was back in the campaign and in a position to attract some of the progressive voters and contributors who would otherwise have supported Roosevelt by default. "La Follette is a wonder," a Roosevelt admirer told the press. "What other man on earth could collapse as he did, not only physically but politically, and come back as he has done? I think Roosevelt has to reckon with him even more than with Taft."

Roosevelt had darker fears. He began to envision a La Follette-Taft alliance. "La Follette is really for Taft if he can't get it himself," he told John Bass, who had managed his campaign in North Dakota.

His speech had to strike a balance between Taft and La Follette, to show that he alone was the candidate of "steady, wise progress." But he knew that he had to stress progress more than steadiness and wisdom. Whether out of conviction, political necessity, or both, Roosevelt was determined to use the Carnegie Hall speech to win the support of progressives who might defect (or return) to La Follette, to land a blow for progressive principles, to continue his new fight for political primaries, and to explain and reinforce his Columbus speech calling for a public right to recall judicial decisions. He wanted the speech to inspire his supporters in the galleries rather than those in the box seats—and to invigorate his campaign forces in the West.

"The great fundamental issue now before the Republican Party and before our people can be stated briefly," he began. "It is: Are the American people fit to govern themselves, to rule themselves, to control themselves? I believe they are. My opponents do not." The crowd started to cheer.

With those words, he set the tone and the text of his campaign. He called his speech "The Right of the People to Rule." Though he had the capacity to bring an audience to its feet and to stir passions in ways that some of his friends found frightening, he delivered most of the speech in careful, almost scholarly tones. Nevertheless, the crowd cheered and applauded, punctuating his arguments, as he read the speech, throwing each page of his typewritten text to the floor as he completed it.

With his clipped enunciation of each point, he made the case for direct presidential primaries:

> "I believe the majority of the plain people of the United States will, day in and day out, make fewer mistakes in governing themselves than any smaller class or body of men, no matter what their training, will make in trying to govern them. I believe, again, that the American people are, as a whole, capable of self-control and of learning by their mistakes. Our opponents pay lip-loyalty to this doctrine; but they show their real beliefs by the way

in which they champion every device to make the nominal rule of the people a sham."

He attacked Taft's use of patronage and the power of incumbency and political bosses to control the delegate selection process.

"It is a small minority that is to-day using our convention system to defeat the will of a majority of the people in the choice of delegates to the Chicago Convention."

He presented his argument for the cause of social justice:

"We are today suffering from the tyranny of minorities. It is a small minority that is grabbing our coal-deposits, our water-powers, and our harbor fronts. A small minority is battening on the sale of adulterated foods and drugs. It is a small minority that lies behind monopolies and trusts. It is a small minority that stands behind the present law of master and servant, the sweat-shops, and the whole calendar of social and industrial injustice."

Roosevelt devoted much of the text to a thoughtful and careful explanation (or defense) of his belief in the public's right to recall certain judicial decisions. His words, crafted in large part by three brilliant young lawyers, were almost academic; with their help, he had refined and narrowed the scope of his proposal. While appealing to progressives, he wanted to convince more conservative listeners that his plan had substance, that it would not apply to federal courts, and that it would not undermine the role of an independent judiciary.

As he neared the end of his address, TR started to pace back and forth on the platform, turning up the pitch and the passion as he explained his reasons for running, his deep-seated belief that he and he alone could save the nation from radicalism on either end of the political spectrum, from the "unreasonable conservatism" championed by those who supported Taft, if not by Taft himself; and perhaps even more dangerous, from the "unreasonable radicalism" of La Follette.

"I am not leading this fight as a matter of aesthetic pleasure," he explained. "I am leading because somebody must lead, or else the fight would not be made at all. I prefer to work with moderate, rational conservatives, provided only that they do in good faith strive forward toward the light. But when they halt and turn their backs to the light, and sit with the scorners on the seats of reaction, then I must part company with them. We the people cannot turn back. Our aim must be steady, wise progress.

"It would be well if our people would study the history of a sister republic. All the woes of France for a century and a quarter have been due to the folly of her people in splitting into the two camps of unreasonable conservatism and unreasonable radicalism. . . . With convulsion and oscillation from one extreme to another, with alternations of violent radicalism and violent Bourbonism, the French people went through misery toward a shattered goal. May we profit by the experiences of our brother republicans across the water, and go forward steadily, avoiding all wild extremes. May our ultra-conservatives remember that the rule of the Bourbons brought on the Revolution, and may our would-be revolutionaries remember that no Bourbon was ever such a dangerous enemy of the people and of freedom as the professed friend of both, Robespierre. There is no danger of a revolution in this country; but there is grave discontent and unrest, and in order to remove them there is need of all the wisdom and probity and deep-seated faith in and purpose to uplift humanity we have at our command."[*]

---

[*] He continually returned to this theme in private correspondence, using the analogy of the French Revolution and warning, for example, that if Taft were to win "the powers of pillage [he will] have gained a respite" that would be followed by "extremists of the other type . . . and we shall suffer at the hands of these fifth monarchy men quite as much as we suffered at the hands of the reactionaries." TR to Arthur Hamilton Lee, March 21, 1912, Morison. Also see TR to John St. Loe Strachey, March 26, 1912, Morison.

His final words brought the reformers in the galleries to their feet.

"Friends," he concluded, "our task as Americans is to strive for social and industrial justice, achieved through the genuine rule of the people. . . . In order to succeed we need leaders of inspired idealism, leaders to whom are granted great visions, who dream greatly and strive to make their dreams come true; who can kindle the people with the fire from their own burning souls. The leader for the time being, whoever he may be, is but an instrument, to be used until broken and then to be cast aside; and if he is worth his salt he will care no more when he is broken than a soldier cares when he is sent where his life is forfeit in order that the victory may be won. In the long fight for righteousness the watchword for all of us is spend and be spent. It is of little matter whether any one man fails or succeeds; but the cause shall not fail, for it is the cause of mankind."

The audience erupted with applause.

ROOSEVELT'S WORDS ENERGIZED progressives everywhere. Telegrams poured in. Scripps reporter Gilson Gardner called it "the best speech you ever made." But while TR knew that the speech had been a triumph for those in the hall and for progressives everywhere, he felt despondent.

He kept focusing on negative news reports, the perceived incompetence or at least inexperience of his campaign organization, and on the alienation of former friends. The conservative press hated the speech. To them, the claim that he was prepared to sacrifice himself to save the country from radical leadership seemed like self-interested sophistry. The *New York Times* commented on the speech by calling him "a reckless maligner of the American people" who is "incapable of accurate statement." Roosevelt was furious. He felt that the New York papers "deliberately inverted the truth."

Despite the Carnegie Hall speech, all the momentum seemed to be with Taft. Roosevelt was surrounded by opportunistic pols, politically inexperienced idealists, and strangers. He missed his longtime allies who were now either neutral or with the President.

"At present I am very much alone here," he confided to one of his close friends who was watching events from England. Apologizing for his "pessimistic outpourings," TR said that "the odds are about four to one against me." He could win a popular vote, he said, "but there is not a popular vote, and the big politicians and the financiers, and such influences as the ultramontane Catholics . . . will probably control" the process.

He warned another English friend that if he were to lose, America will alternate "between reaction on behalf of sordid money interests" as represented by Taft, and "violent and foolish radicalism" as represented by La Follette, "who is half a zealot and half a self-seeking demagogue."

TR had good reasons for his pessimism, as a confidential letter to Frank Harper, Roosevelt's private secretary, explained. The letter, which itemized many of the concerns about the competence of the campaign team and the decisions they had been making, came from Jerry Matthews, a reporter for the *New York Sun*, who had turned down repeated requests to serve as the campaign's press secretary but had offered to be of use wherever possible. To be sure that his comments remained confidential, Matthews deliberately sent the letter to Harper at his home address in New Jersey rather than to his office in New York. It reads like an epitaph.

"I am very sorry that the outlook appears so unfavorable," Matthews wrote. "Our friends talked too much and too loudly, and gave too little attention to organization. They waited at least six weeks too long." He said he had told TR's friends for weeks that they did not have an efficient organization "and they have not [got] one now. Some of the men at headquarters in Washington are apparently as confident as ever, but I am not. It looks to me like a tragedy to take a great name that is a national asset, and is today the best capital that the progressive Republican movement has, and permit it to be made a subject of derision, through mismanagement of politicians, but that is what is occurring.

"I warned our friends at headquarters that they ought to give attention to North Dakota the very first thing they did, but I do not believe any special attention was given to it until too late. The effect of the results has been bad. I told our friends that they could not afford to lose the first state in which a legalized primary was held, in view of the stress we have laid on the primary as a means for expressing the overwhelming popular sentiment for Roosevelt. They seemed to think, until within a very few days before the election, that they had a comparatively easy victory."

"Senator Dixon is an excellent politician. He is doing his very best, but he is surrounded by a lot of volunteers who are inexperienced as politicians, however good they may be as reformers and writers. . . .

"The men who are trying to nominate Mr. Taft admit that he cannot be elected. They are trained politicians, and are looking beyond the immediate result. They expect to get control of the party machinery. They believe that a Democratic administration will succeed the present administration, and that one of its incidental results will be a great [financial] panic, a thing which is likely to occur within a few years under any political conditions. From such conditions, they expect to see much human suffering ensue as the result of enforced idleness, due to industrial depression. They believe that the industrial workers of the country will be chastened by adversity until they will be willing to accept a reactionary for President in 1916."

If he wanted to have any chance at all, Roosevelt knew that he had to start winning. Hiram Johnson continued to warn him that the campaign would be over if he couldn't win in New York on March 26. But Roosevelt knew that he had an inexperienced organization and that the rules that governed the primary process in New York were stacked against him.

THANKS IN PART to support from both Roosevelt and Taft during the 1910 campaign, New York State had agreed to hold its first-ever primary election, and thanks to a law adopted by the legislature in 1911, the ballot would also include a direct presidential primary vote for delegates to the national convention. The new law was exceptionally confusing, as the Republican Party's leaders acknowledged even before TR entered the race. Moreover, there were a great many races and a great many parties on the ballot—from the state assembly to the presidency—making the ballot intolerably long and easily susceptible to ridicule.

The law was deliberately tilted toward the preferences of the party's leaders. Each county committee had the right to nominate candidates to run in the state's congressional districts. The Republican Party's designated nominees appeared on the ballot beneath an eagle. In Westchester County, where Bill Ward held sway, those candidates were sure to favor Roosevelt. But virtually every other county committee favored Taft. The Roosevelt forces had to nominate delegates across the state. TR's candidates appeared beneath a black square—which symbolized the "square deal," Roosevelt's longtime campaign slogan. In addition, the law provided for four at-large candidates to be selected at the state convention. As a result, the Roosevelt forces had to find candidates to run as delegates at the state convention. Even for a former governor and president, finding, fielding, and publicizing the progressive team proved to be a formidable task.

TR's supporters tried without success to amend the presidential primary law to make it more fair and more favorable. On March 8, the Colonel's nephew, state assemblyman Theodore Douglas Robinson, introduced a bill providing for a statewide vote for the presidential candidate that would have required all delegates, no matter their personal preference, to vote for the man who won the most votes in the statewide contest. His bill was quickly defeated by a combination of old guard Republicans and a united Democratic Party. "There is no more demand for this bill than there is for a mad dog," Democratic minority leader Al Smith quipped.

Frank Munsey and George Perkins made sure that the Colonel had a substantial war chest for New York State. In addition to the money that they were pouring into the national campaign, they each contributed $15,000 to be spent in Manhattan and they helped to raise another $30,000.

President Taft could see only one explanation for their largesse: the role that U.S. Steel had been playing since October 1911, when his Department of Justice had filed the antitrust complaint. "Men conspicuous in the Steel Corporation and the Steel Pool are furnishing the money and the organizing ability," he complained, stressing what he deemed the irony in the situation. "Letting the people rule is letting the Steel Trust rule."

Each side accused the other of fraud. The leader of the New York County Committee claimed to have proof that Roosevelt's supporters planned to import phantom voters from one district to vote for Roosevelt in another district by using the names of people who had moved out of the district since the last election. Roosevelt's supporters made similar claims. There was probably some truth to the charges on both sides. Years later, O. K. Davis, one of the Colonel's most important insiders, described how one of TR's lieutenants stole money from the Taft camp in order to fund more poll workers. Both groups hired private detectives.

On the eve of the election, Roosevelt made a last-ditch plea for support, speaking at six meetings in New York City. To show how absurd the primary process had become, he started each meeting by unfurling a fourteen-foot-long ballot that was to be used in the 23rd Assembly District. The ballot included votes for every level of government.

"Our opponents have made the primary ballot law so long that the people can't express their views," he said, provoking a mixture of laughter and applause.

The biggest crowd of the night—more than 3,000 people—greeted him at the New Star Casino, where he received a tremendous round of applause when he was introduced by Oscar Straus, the former Secretary of Commerce. After warming up the audience by unfurling the fourteen-foot ballot, Roosevelt proceeded to tweak the President.

"I saw a letter from the President today," he said, "expressing his pleasure that all Republican voters would be allowed to vote."

Roosevelt had great fun with the word *"allowed,"* giving it special emphasis in a falsetto voice. The line had brought laughter at each of his previous stops.

"It's not enough that you're *'allowed'* to vote," he continued. "It's your *right to vote.*"

The response had been the same all night. But this time, as the laughter and applause subsided, a woman stood up in the back of the room.

"How about the women and their *right to vote,*" she asked?

News stories said that her voice used precisely the same falsetto tone that Roosevelt had used to ridicule Taft.

When the woman stood up, some people recognized her as Maud Malone, the petite, fiery, Irish-born librarian and founder of a division of the National Women's Suffrage League. At twenty-six, with her brown hair drawn back over her temples, she seemed a bit like a schoolgirl. But reporters knew that she had been disrupting political meetings for years and was at the extreme edge of the suffrage movement.

Throughout the audience, people yelled at her and asked the organizers to throw her out. But Roosevelt, who did not know anything about his questioner, insisted that she be allowed to stay in the hall.

"Let that woman alone. Don't put your hands on her."

He moved to the front of the platform and almost reached out to her. "I will answer your question, Madam," he said with a combination of chivalry and condescension. "But you must be silent after I have finished. I have asked repeatedly that you women be allowed to vote to determine whether you want to vote."

"That's no answer," she said, remaining standing.

Roosevelt, who had told her not to talk back, was stunned.

"It's the best answer you will get," he said. "I am not here to debate women's suffrage with you."

"Mr. Roosevelt, you want women to have babies but not the right to vote."

The platform party was in disarray. Roosevelt's supporters rushed around the stage, asking her to take her seat. With what may have been a touch of mockery, the band started to play a popular new Irving Berlin song called "Take a Little Tip from Father." When the band paused, Maud Malone shouted again.

"Mister Roosevelt, have women a right to vote?" she persisted.

Pointing a finger at her, Oscar Straus told her to sit down. But she remained standing.

"Let me handle this," Roosevelt said. He shouted at her to sit down, but it was hard to hear anything above the din.

"This is no square deal, Mr. Roosevelt," she shouted when she could be heard.

"Madam, after this exhibition tonight, I feel that I am justified in saying that I have more respect for women than you do." With that, he sat down.

Finally, after fourteen minutes, a security guard grabbed her arm and guided her toward the door.

As she left, Roosevelt returned to the podium. The noise was so deafening that he could hardly be heard.

"Be quiet all of you," he shouted, shaking his fist and asking to be allowed to finish. "It's probably a put up job on the part of our opposition."

In fact, Maud Malone was an equal-opportunity disrupter. She went after conservatives and liberals alike. Three years earlier, she had dramatically disrupted a speech by Otto Bannard, Taft's friend who was then running for mayor. But TR, with good reason, had begun to see conspiracies everywhere.

AT 5 P.M. the next day, TR rushed through the huge waiting room at Pennsylvania Station accompanied by Frank Harper, his private secretary, and Medill McCormick, former head of the *Chicago Tribune*, who had become his chief of publicity. They were headed for campaign appearances in the Middle West, starting in Chicago. The polls in New York would be open for several more hours, but TR was already deeply concerned. Before he could board his private car, attached to the Chicago Limited, a pack of reporters—five of whom would be traveling in another car of the train—stopped him and asked for his comments on the New York primary.

"The behavior of the New York County political machine workers has been scandalous," the Colonel said. "I have just received word that our poll watchers have been thrown out of the polling places." The polls were still open but TR complained that "so far the mayor and the police have refused to help."

Other than that, he said that he would not have any further comment until the next morning.

Roosevelt went to bed at 10 P.M. but Harper and McCormick continued to work as the train sped toward Chicago, fielding telegrams throughout the night. A day earlier, speaking as TR's campaign manager, Joseph Dixon had predicted that Roosevelt would win a majority of the delegates in New York and promised that he would have a big win in Indiana, which was holding its convention that evening. But Roosevelt, Harper, and McCormick knew better. Dixon was continuing to mislead the press, the campaign's supporters, and perhaps himself. In fact, the prospects in both states seemed grim.

Just after midnight, O. K. Davis, who was handling the campaign's press operation out of TR's New York headquarters, sent a wire to Harper on the train saying that the early returns did not look favorable. Davis said that he would arrange to have a statement about the "farcical primaries" wired to the campaign press operation at Crestline, Ohio, to be handed out to the wire reporters on the train when they woke up in the morning.

Messages kept arriving as Roosevelt slept. Dixon sent a telegram at 12:21 A.M. charging "utter fraud" in New York. But he thought that he saw a silver lining in the results. He was convinced that Roosevelt could put the results to good effect in Illinois. He urged him to use "the outrageous specific incidents as the text of your speeches [in Chicago] tomorrow, not glittering generalities but case after case of actual concrete facts. The effect on the Illinois legislature and the publicity that will be given to your utterances throughout the country should carry tremendous weight."

Dixon offered chapter and verse of fraudulent behavior. "In more than one half of the city, the ballots did not arrive at the polling places for two hours after the opening of the polls. . . . In two congressional districts the names of the Roosevelt delegates were not on the ballots at all. It was an entire breakdown of the election machinery. In several districts, the regular election inspectors were removed by the county organization just as the polls opened. . . . half the districts were without ballots until eight o'clock."

The campaign's New York City chairman, who had served briefly as a Roosevelt appointee on the U.S. Court of Appeals for the District of Columbia, wired that the "primary election in this city [is] not only a farce but a criminal misuse of power and dastardly robbery of people's rights."

For the press, the campaign's leaders released a statement saying that they planned to ask New York's Democratic governor to order a new election; otherwise, they promised to challenge the results at the Republican Party convention in June.

For once the White House had some good election news. They were winning in New York and in an important if less publicized election in Indiana. Shortly after midnight, President Taft called to congratulate the head of the party in New York. His campaign chair happily issued a triumphant statement.

"Republicans do not need to be reminded of the slogan which has been a guidepost in politics," he said wryly. "As New York and Indiana go, so goes the nation."

At 12:35 a *New York Times* reporter convinced a porter to take him to Roosevelt's car, where he tried to wake the Colonel to get his reactions to the results. But Harper, who was standing guard, refused to allow it.

Roosevelt would need all of the rest that he could get before arriving in Chicago.

———

ROOSEVELT'S FIRST STOP the next morning, en route to Chicago, was in Fort Wayne, Indiana. By then he knew the results in that state, where a highly contentious state convention awarded all four delegates-at-large to Taft. The accounts from TR's supporters claimed that the proceedings in Indiana had been as corrupt as those in New York.

Both campaigns claimed to have won a majority of the delegates to the Indiana state convention. The outcome depended on control of 128 delegates from Indianapolis. Working for Roosevelt, former senator Albert Beveridge had organized a surprisingly effective campaign that stunned the regulars.

Taft's national committeeman from Indiana confessed "utter amazement at the way the Roosevelt sentiment has come to the front here since the Colonel's announcement. [His supporters] just seem to have arisen out of the grass and the bushes and to have overrun everything and everybody," he said. The "common individual" was attracted to "the lion-hunting, swashbuckling, gallery-playing gentleman from Oyster Bay." Only a series of political promises could keep people in line. "I have had to make some promises and have not hesitated to do so, since I recognize the importance of accomplishing results, and I must ask of course that the administration redeem these for me," Taft's Indiana state leader told the White House.

TR's friends in Indiana were convinced that Taft's supporters had "fixed the Evansville and Indianapolis districts" and practiced "the most outrageous and infamous frauds."

Taft's partisans controlled the state credentials committee and gave all 128 delegates from Indianapolis to the President. When William Wood, the committee chair, stood up to read the majority report at the state convention, Roosevelt's boosters climbed onto their chairs and shouted "Roosevelt" and "Keep still, Wood!"

"This isn't a mob," Wood shouted back. "I will read this report if I have to stay here until August."

Infuriated, Roosevelt's supporters went to the back of the room, nominated their own slate, and announced that they would seek justice at the national convention in June.

Dixon's wire to Harper on the train reported that "Indiana is seething with indignation and outrage such as has not been seen since Civil War days."

The press treated the results in New York and Indiana as decisive. The *Times* headline reported that "Taft Gets Indiana; Roosevelt Men Bolt."

The front-page headlines about New York were devastating. The *Washington Post* declared that there had been a "Roosevelt Rout in New York." "Taft Snows Colonel Under," the *New York Times* trumpeted. "Col. Roosevelt met one of the most decisive defeats in his career last night as a result of the first test of the new primary law," the first paragraph said. "In every congressional district in the greater city where he made a fight his delegates were snowed completely under."

The *New York Evening Post* was especially cruel. "The events of last week reduce Mr. Roosevelt's candidacy to the absurd," it said. "It can no longer be pretended that he has a ghost of a chance to get a majority in the Convention. The mathematics of the situation are fatal to him. With New York against him, with Indiana against him, with Colorado four to one against him, without a delegate from Iowa or Wisconsin, where is he to turn? The plain fact is that little is left of his campaign but anger, wrath, malice, and all uncharitableness. His managers shout 'fraud' and 'larceny.' He himself cries 'farce' and 'outrage.' To such wild charges and to rump conventions and 'contests' in every possible district, the glorious Roosevelt candidacy has now come down. It was going to sweep the country; it is, in fact, everywhere making a showing which is pitiful and humiliating."

TO SOME OF the most important insurgents, including California Governor Hiram Johnson, the New York and Indiana results were devastating.

"The result in North Dakota has given a fictitious turn to the campaign," Hiram Johnson wrote to one of TR's strongest supporters. "While the election ought to have been recorded as a tremendous blow to Taft, it has been taken as an indication generally of the tremendous strength of La Follette and a defeat for Roosevelt. Following this, have come the results in Indiana and New York. However these results were obtained, the ordinary individual looks simply at the fact that Taft, apparently, has been victorious."

TR had always loved a good, righteous fight.

Now he had one.

Chapter Seven

Dixon hoped that Roosevelt's visit to the Middle West would give the campaign a new beginning. With invaluable support from Roosevelt's backers, the Illinois legislature appeared to be on the verge of adopting a law to create a presidential primary to be held on April 9. If his team could get the law passed and if TR could then win the Illinois primary and follow up with quick victories later that same week at the convention in Michigan and the primary in Pennsylvania, the momentum would shift. TR might even become unstoppable. Despite primary losses in North Dakota and New York, and a probable victory by La Follette in the Wisconsin primary scheduled to take place on April 2, a landslide in Illinois with its sixty-eight delegates would ignite the campaign, validate the primary process, and invigorate dispirited supporters. Responding to Hiram Johnson's heartfelt concerns, O'Laughlin promised that victories in Illinois and Michigan would soon turn things around.

But first Roosevelt's supporters needed to convince the Illinois legislature to put the presidential primary on the state's April 9 ballot. A vote for local candidates was already set for that date. In mid-November, Medill McCormick, who had been the *Chicago Tribune's* publisher but was identified in the paper's news story simply as "a manager of the La Follette campaign," wrote to Republican governor

Charles Deneen asking him to make legislation creating a presidential primary a priority.

Since it would require a two-thirds vote of the legislature to add a presidential primary to the April 9 ballot, the effort was a long shot. "Primary Plans Doomed to Fail" a *Tribune* headline predicted. In view of the two-thirds requirement, the paper said that "the plans went to smash." Some Democrats, including Woodrow Wilson's supporters in the state, came out for the law, but the Taft-oriented Republican Editorial Association adopted a resolution denouncing the proposal, calling primaries "a rich candidate's advantage and not a poor one's opportunity."

In early January, the *Chicago Tribune* began an editorial campaign to support the reform. On January 7, 1912, the paper's lead editorial declared: "Put Roosevelt's Name on the Ballot." The editorial the next day insisted that every state with a primary should put TR's name on the ballot. In addition to New York, at that point there were six such states: New Jersey, Wisconsin, Nebraska, North Dakota, California, and Oregon. As soon as TR announced that he would be a candidate and wanted states to create primaries, the effort in Illinois picked up steam. When opponents objected that the primary would cost extra money, TR's supporters said that they would provide private financing to cover the costs. "I personally will guarantee whatever extra expense may be incurred," Chauncey Dewey, the chair of Roosevelt's Illinois campaign, announced.

To bring pressure on the legislature, the *Tribune* developed a creative campaign, contacting every member of the state House and Senate, asking where they stood on the issue. In a March 21 editorial with the headline "Smoke Them Out," the paper said, "The names of the men who will not give the state this extension of suffrage should be known." On March 21, 22, 23, 24, and 25, as the results of its survey came in, the *Tribune* ran front-page articles listing the names of supporters and opponents. Editorially, it said that the results showed that the measure would pass if the governor would call a special session of the legislature.

On March 25, Governor Deneen called a special session to consider the proposal. The legislature did not vote the next day, however, because enough members stayed away to prevent the formation of a quorum that could act. The *Tribune* continued to run front-page stories and editorials on March 26 and 27. Finally, on March 28, at 2 A.M. the Illinois Senate passed the law creating a presidential primary to be held on April 9. The state's House of Representatives passed the bill later that morning. With less than two weeks to spare, Illinois created a presidential primary.

HUGE CROWDS GREETED Roosevelt's train when it pulled into Chicago's Union Station at 2 P.M. A high-level greeting committee headed by Chauncey Dewey met him on the platform.

Observers reported that by the time he arrived the former President was furious about the results the day before. The *Tribune* said he was "mad clear through." With a bit of prompting by the *Tribune*, so were tens of thousands of citizens. In a front-page headline, the paper called the New York primary "Probably Illegal." As he started his first campaigning outside of New York, crowds lined sidewalks from the train station to the Congress Hotel, cheering him on, calling Roosevelt's name as he passed.

As soon as he settled into his suite, the Colonel tore up the "dispassionate" speech that he had written about the regulation of business. Calling in a series of stenographers, he dictated a new one that the *Chicago Tribune* proudly proclaimed did not have "a weasel word in it."

That night TR addressed the largest political meeting ever held in America's second-largest city. An overflow crowd of 4,300 people filled the Auditorium Theatre while another 10,000 people stood outside the hall. Some supporters gathered in designated overflow areas; others tried to break their way into the theater. The throng bellowed their approval as he delivered a "fighting speech," providing details of his opponent's "fraud and trickery" and calling the New York primary "not just a farce but a criminal farce."

"If the politicians by trickery invert the will of the people," he thundered; "if they cheat the people, you may depend on it that I will have a great deal to say—and I will not hesitate a minute to say it." His cause was now the peoples' cause.

On his way back to Union Station late that night, crowds again lined the route, shouting "Teddy, Teddy, hurrah for Teddy." It had been an exhilarating day. He was ready at last for an exhausting itinerary that included appearances in Missouri on March 28, in Iowa and Minnesota on March 29, and in Detroit and Chicago (again) on March 30, before he returned to New York on March 31.

By 11:45 P.M., when his train left for St. Louis, Roosevelt felt tired but exhilarated. He knew that he had an enormous national audience for his message of reform.

SUDDENLY, ROOSEVELT WAS on fire. Stimulated by adoring crowds and true believers, invigorated by the conviction that he was fighting liars and crooks, energized by themes of social justice and true democracy, he seemed to become young again on the campaign trail. The old man who dreaded long days and nights on the road kept adding speeches to his schedule and new states to his itinerary. He believed in his cause and in himself.

As his train sped from town to town in the Middle West, Roosevelt addressed passionate crowds everywhere he went: in six speeches in the rain-drenched streets of St. Louis; in Iowa and Minnesota, where he talked from the back of his train as he passed through small towns on his way to St. Paul; in St. Paul, where he entered an auditorium in an automobile that was flying a dozen American flags; in cities across Michigan, where he addressed the throngs that surrounded the platform of his private railroad car. Speaking from the balcony of his hotel in Detroit, he told a huge crowd that government corruption underlined the need for more popular democracy; returning to Chicago for an hour, he attended a lunch organized by Medill McCormick and met with progressive supporters; back in New York, he attacked Taft again—and again.

His typically extensive and diverse reading list for the trip included books that fed his passion, his belief in the righteousness of his cause. He spent evenings inhaling a batch of current novels that included Stewart Edward White's *Conjurer's House: A Romance of the Free Forest*, the story of a free trader in the Northwest who was captured and sentenced through the power of the Hudson's Bay Company, and Robert Louis Stevenson's *Pavilion on the Links*, a short story involving a crooked banker, his daughter, and Italian revolutionaries whose money was stolen by the banker.

Even La Follette's victory in Wisconsin on April 2 couldn't deter him. He continued to make speech after speech, to issue blast after blast, until the sound of his campaign drowned out all memory of La Follette's success. Back on the trail after a brief stop in New York, he delivered fifteen speeches in Kentucky on April 3, focusing on the nation's outcasts. "We fight to make this country a better place to live in for those who have been harshly treated by fate."

Returning to Illinois later that week, he rushed from city to city, giving speeches everywhere, "thundering his disapproval" of corruption to 7,000 people in the state armory. He ended his Illinois campaign in Springfield with a sustained tribute to Lincoln, visiting the martyred President's pew in the Presbyterian Church, his home, and his tomb in the company of one of Lincoln's few surviving associates.

Before leaving Illinois to campaign in Pennsylvania, which would hold a primary a week later, Roosevelt delivered a powerful parting shot.

"Lincoln declared this to be a government of the people, by the people, and for the people," Roosevelt roared. "But President Taft is in favor of government of the privileged class and for the bosses."

CAMPAIGNING BEFORE LARGE audiences everywhere, issuing fresh allegations of fraud and corruption by the Taft campaign, Roosevelt's comments became so sharp that Taft's supporters and some reporters concluded that Roosevelt intended to form a new party if he felt—or could plausibly argue—that his nomination had been stolen.

"Colonel Talks Bolt," the *Washington Post* said in a front-page headline. That was also the private conclusion of Taft's campaign team. "Believed here that Roosevelt managers are preparing to bolt the Chicago Convention," Taft's campaign manager told a colleague.

A prominent Chicago banker spelled out his concerns in a letter that proved remarkably prescient. "Roosevelt managers are framing up a case upon which they may withdraw from the National Convention and run him as the candidate of a new party," he told Taft's secretary, Charles Hilles. "I have been apprehensive from the beginning that Roosevelt's candidacy would end in an attempt to organize and lead a new party and I am confirmed in that opinion by daily developments."

The banker was convinced that TR's supporters had always intended to bolt and were only seeking an excuse. "It is no secret that the original plan of [Gifford] Pinchot and [James] Garfield was to organize a new party. They are fanatics, self-centered and eager to be founders of a new party. These men have already demonstrated their influence over Roosevelt. . . . His blood is hot and he is working himself into a more unreasoning frenzy every day. . . . The question now is will he have enough votes in the Convention to make such a movement respectable. It would be ridiculous for him to bolt with only a handful of delegates."

In order to have enough delegates to gain the Republican nomination—or, at the very least, to justify forming a new party—Roosevelt had to start by winning in Illinois.

TR IS "BESIDE himself with rage," Taft told his brother Charley, calling him "temperamentally irresponsible"—or worse. "He has become so violent," Taft said, "that some people fear he is losing his reason. Others say he is drinking, but I do not think so." Taft felt that his former dear friend had been distorting everything, especially about the New York primary. "Roosevelt really seems . . . to have lost all control."

"The conduct of the Colonel is certainly that of a desperate man who stops at nothing," Taft wrote a noted Harvard Law School professor.

For much of the country, Roosevelt's tone had gone way over the top. "Mr. Roosevelt hits out wildly like a man dazed by the heavy blows he has received," the reform-oriented *Nation* magazine reported. "All semblance of restraint or dignity he long since cast to the winds and his violence of language, his recklessness of assertion, his apparent inability to reason coherently, make of him a spectacle disturbing to his friends and mortifying to the country . . . there appears the almost insane hatred of Mr. Taft. . . ."

All of that might be forgotten, or at least excused, if Roosevelt could win the Illinois primary, putting him back in the race. But many close observers thought Illinois looked like a long shot. The *Washington Post* reported that TR was losing support in Illinois with Taft ahead in fifteen of twenty-five districts. "In Illinois there has been a drift away from Roosevelt and to Mr. Taft," the *Post* reported. "There seems to be little doubt in the estimation of those with whom correspondents conferred that Mr. Taft will cover a majority of the districts."

AND THEN A miracle happened. Roosevelt swept Illinois.

The results were so striking—and such a departure—that it became the dividing line for Roosevelt supporters. Those who were with him before April 9 called themselves the "Before April 9th men." The campaign welcomed those who joined later. But they knew who had really been with them from the start.

Roosevelt didn't just win. It was overwhelming. The headlines in the *New York Times* were typical of those around the country.

ROOSEVELT WINS

IN ILLINOIS BY

2 TO 1 OVER TAFT

Landslide for the Colonel at
Primary—Carries Chicago
By 30,000

In his first primary victory, TR won 61 percent of the vote. He won every county and earned all of the state's 68 delegates. Overnight, he passed La Follette, whose combined total from victories in North Dakota and Wisconsin was 36 delegates, and he convinced many of the skeptics that he had a chance. The resounding results in Illinois also added credibility to his claim that Taft's supporters had been cooking the books in other states. "In light of the Illinois vote," Medill McCormick told reporters, "no honest and straight thinking man can believe that the results in New York City were representative of anything but political brigandage, which by brutal and dishonest methods deprived the people of the right to nominate."

If anything, the campaign's internal memos were even more bullish.

"I fully believed, and I do now, that the whole result of our fight hinged upon the result of the Illinois campaign," an exuberant Amos Pinchot wrote Medill upon hearing the good news. "Today flags in Wall Street are all at half-mast, the New York papers are editorially shocked into silence, something terrible has happened and they do not know what or why. As soon as I can get up to town, I am going to make for the University Club and go round with an 'I Told You So' sandwich sign upon my person."

"The news this morning from Chicago literally paralyzed the enemy," Dixon wired former senator Albert Beveridge, who had led the losing campaign in Indiana. "As certain as fate, it is the fatal blow and the Taft boom collapses! Indiana made the sacrifice in delivering the first assault—and Illinois has swept the field. There may be a few quivering of the limbs before the undertaker is called, but the fatal dose has certainly been administered. You can hardly conceive the changed atmosphere in Washington today. They are groggy and dazed!"

The presidential primary appeared poised to prove that a challenger, or at least a charismatic challenger with a national following, an important newspaper in its corner, a powerful message, and some very wealthy supporters, could retake the White House.

TR's supporters were convinced that they would deliver two more powerful punches in rapid succession. They seemed likely to win convincingly at the Michigan state convention on April 11, where he could count on the support of Governor Chase Osborn and state party chair Franklin Knox, and in the Pennsylvania primary two days later.

IN RETROSPECT, the Illinois election represented the first decisive presidential primary victory in history. Taft had won in New York and La Follette had won in North Dakota and Wisconsin. But none of those races had turned the tide of the campaign. The Illinois vote showed, for the first time, how a primary victory can change a campaign's momentum.

How did it happen? Any winning political effort has a thousand authors, but some can claim a higher word count than others. The most important force behind Roosevelt's Illinois miracle was the *Chicago Tribune*, and the most important force behind the *Chicago Tribune* was its English-born editor, James Keeley. Keeley provided the effort with secret but indispensable leadership and funding. He led the paper into a level of political engagement that might seem unethical or even illegal a century later but seemed heroic to Roosevelt and his supporters at the time.

In order to maintain the appearance of journalistic independence, Keeley deliberately worked behind the scenes. The greeting committee that met Roosevelt at Chicago's Union Station on March 27, for example, was led by Chauncey Dewey, the chair of the Roosevelt organization in Illinois and the man who had offered to fund any extra costs created by a presidential primary. In some respects, Dewey had a lot in common with Roosevelt as a derring-do cowboy rancher and big-city political force. Earlier in his career, Dewey had spent years running his father's 200,000-acre spread in Kansas, where he was sometimes called "the handsomest cowboy in Kansas." He left the state in 1904 following a sensational six-week murder trial in which he was accused of killing three men in a shoot-out. He moved to Chicago and became a political fixture, sometimes called "a machine boss," in the city's Second Ward. Partisans claimed that he had decided to support Roosevelt because Taft refused to appoint him to a variety of public offices. As the public face of the Roosevelt campaign in Illinois, Dewey also led the committee that sat with the candidate on the stage at the Auditorium Theatre.

Unknown to all but a very few insiders, however, Dewey was taking his orders from Keeley, the *Tribune's* absolute leader. Keeley had transformed Roosevelt's cause into a personal and professional crusade.

Most people assumed that the *Tribune's* interest in Roosevelt had been inspired by thirty-five-year-old Medill McCormick, the handsome oldest son of the paper's controlling family. Medill headed TR's publicity bureau in Washington, D.C., often served as the campaign's spokesman, and was at Roosevelt's side as he traveled from New York to Chicago on the night after the New York primary. People tended to treat him as the paper's publisher, but Medill had, in fact, left the company two years earlier to save his sanity and his sobriety. Like many wealthy scions of the era, Medill had entered politics and would later become a United States senator. Having shifted his allegiance from La Follette to Roosevelt in late January, Medill was TR's publicity director and friend, but he was no longer running the *Tribune*.

Talented, brilliant, and driven, a graduate of the exclusive Groton School and Yale University, Medill married the equally impressive Ruth Hanna in 1903 at a wedding ceremony hijacked by the arrival of two uninvited guests: President Theodore Roosevelt and his jaunty daughter, Alice. Ruth's father, Senator Mark Hanna, was Roosevelt's archrival. Nevertheless, Alice was thrust into the bridal party. She and Ruth Hanna quickly became intimate friends.

His life seemed charmed, but in fact Medill was possessed by demons. Working his way up the well-greased corporate ladder, he covered the police beat, reported from China and the Philippines, and ascended to the corporate suite in less than a decade. But every few years he would descend into bouts of depression—riddled with a disease that would probably now be identified as bipolar disorder. Today doctors might treat him with medication, but Medill sought relief in alcoholic binges. He would leave the paper for months and, prodded by his ambitious and self-centered mother, seek help. At her urging, in late 1908 he went to Vienna, where he became an early patient of Carl Jung.

Jung later described the case in a few candid letters, in unpublished interviews that he called "protocols," and in a book where he concealed his patient's name. When Medill had another relapse in 1910, Jung met him in New York and became convinced that the source of the problem was the pressure of the paper and the connection that it forced Medill to have with his "power devil" mother. Without consulting his patient, Jung sent a letter to the *Tribune* directors calling Medill a hopeless alcoholic who could not be trusted to run the paper.

In April 1910, the board allowed Medill to take an unlimited leave without pay. It installed his younger brother, Robert ("Bertie") McCormick, as president. But Bertie had a full-time job as the reform-minded president of the Chicago Sanitation District, so the board gave almost dictatorial power to Keeley.

Keeley told a congressional committee in July 1911, that "my power is absolute." A bit incredulous, one of the committee members asked about Medill McCormick, who most people thought was still in charge. But Keeley set them straight. McCormick had been replaced, he said. "I repeat. My authority is absolute."

A "cigar-chomping, ambulance chasing, newshound straight out of *The Front Page*," Keeley used his power on Roosevelt's behalf. He believed in stunts, scoops, and what he called "personal service" journalism. Keeley told an audience at Notre Dame University that a great paper "not only informs and instructs its readers but is of service"; such a paper "commands attention, gets circulation and also holds its readers after it gets them." His paper offered health advice and led crusades for women's suffrage, against vice, and against government corruption and corporate greed. The crusade to create a presidential primary in Illinois fit that mold.

His biographer reports that Keeley was often described as ruthless. If so, he was ruthless with a purpose. After hundreds of children along with their parents perished in a blaze that consumed the Iroquois Theater during a matinee performance of *Mr. Bluebeard* on December 30, 1903, the *Tribune* gave a face to the tragedy, describing the fire's victims, often including their pictures, names, and addresses.

"I wish the *Tribune* would let up for a while on the rich malefactors and tell some wholesome truths about those foreign born murderers and anarchists," one of the older members of the McCormick family complained with only a touch of irony.

In late 1911, Cal O'Laughlin, the *Tribune* reporter who was moonlighting for TR, introduced the Colonel to his editor. It was love at first sight. Keeley was already working with George Perkins, who was to become Roosevelt's strongest financial backer. Although his paper's news stories scalded leaders of industry on a regular basis, Keeley had become convinced that antitrust laws were stifling business.

Since TR was still publicly denying that he intended to run, when O'Laughlin urged the Colonel to meet with Keeley, he assured him that "Keeley is safe and can be talked to openly, though not to the extent of revealing everything." Keeley met with TR in New York in the first week of January and signed on at once. The paper's editorial calling for the state to put TR on the primary ballot followed that meeting. Keeley immediately asked O'Laughlin for a list of Roosevelt's supporters who could be mobilized. Two weeks later—at a time when Medill McCormick still professed to be supporting La Follette—Keeley organized a lunch at Chicago's Union League Club, where a group of the city's business leaders launched the Roosevelt National Committee. The committee promised "to centralize and crystallize the demand that Colonel Roosevelt be the Republican Party standard bearer." That story, which was carried by papers around the nation, galvanized Roosevelt's supporters everywhere.

Keeley kept his role hidden. When the committee members' names were published in a front-page article in the *Tribune*, Keeley's name was nowhere to be found. Somewhat disingenuously, the committee members told the press that there had been no contact with TR himself.

During the weeks that followed, Keeley directed the campaign in Illinois, keeping TR informed through a stream of messages, some to TR, others directed to the candidate through O'Laughlin. He often exerted his leadership through Chauncey Dewey, who assured Roosevelt that he was "acting under Mr. James Keeley's directions as you advised."

"Tell Keeley that there are few things I value more than having a chance to know him," Roosevelt wrote O'Laughlin. Small wonder. By the time the candidate arrived in Illinois, Keeley's paper was running the crusade to create a presidential primary, and he had agreed to have the *Tribune* pick up the tab for almost every aspect of the Colonel's visit.

We "will expect you to make arrangements to have Roosevelt private car and press car escort," TR's traveling secretary wired Keeley in the abbreviated language used in telegrams. "Will expect you to provide transportation for Roosevelt party from Chicago as far as Pittsburgh. Mr. Roosevelt insists that he must remain for the entire trip in private car now occupied by him. Please wire confirmation."

Equally important, Keeley had orchestrated one of his famous crusades—this one to create a statewide presidential primary. Thanks in significant measure to the work of Keeley and the *Tribune*, Roosevelt could claim a landslide victory in a large and very important state.

AFTER ILLINOIS the Taft forces might have been left "groggy and dazed," as Dixon claimed, but even if Roosevelt could repeat his electoral success everywhere, which was far from clear, there were not enough delegates at stake in primaries to win the nomination. He had to win some conventions, too.

An excellent place to start was Michigan, with a high-profile, high-stakes convention set to take place two days after Illinois, on April 11.

Chapter Eight

T R had every reason to believe that he would win most or all of the delegates chosen by the Michigan State Convention. He had the unwavering support of Governor Chase Osborn, Republican state party chair Franklin Knox, and temporary state convention chair Truman Newberry of Detroit, his former Secretary of the Navy, whom Knox had installed in the convention's key leadership position. But Michigan quickly demonstrated that in the wake of the Illinois primary, Taft's forces were not about to concede.

For all of his loyalty to Roosevelt, Frank Knox was less useful as a political operator than as an acolyte. Speeding around the country on Roosevelt's behalf, Knox had been neglecting matters in his home state. In his memoir, Roosevelt's press secretary called Knox an inefficient "greenhorn" who was "so certain of winning all the delegates from his state" that he spent time in hopeless places like Colorado while paying "little or no attention to organization work at home."

In addition to his desire to help TR in the hinterlands, Knox had left the state for another reason, one that ultimately helped to undermine Roosevelt's campaign in Michigan. On January 21, while Knox was going from state to state on Roosevelt's behalf, asking governors to sign the letter imploring him to run, Governor Osborn announced that he intended to dismiss Michigan's tax commissioner, Robert Shields, for using his office to intimidate political opponents. Shields quickly retaliated by releasing a letter that Knox had written in late 1909, while organizing Osborn's gubernatorial effort. Writing on behalf of "Chase and I," the letter asked Shields to raise $20,000 for Osborn's campaign.

Overnight, the "Chase and I" letter became a sensation and an embarrassment. After a few weeks of delay and indecision, Knox finally apologized to Shields, but he was haunted by the experience. He explained his feelings in a series of letters to Osborn's secretary, saying that he was plunging into "almost ceaseless work" for the campaign "as an escape from deadly self-introspection and condemnation." He told her that he planned to take a major role in helping TR "chiefly because it gives me a graceful opportunity to get out of the state chairmanship and thus be a burden no longer." Osborn wouldn't allow him to resign as the chair of the party. But Knox left the state for long stretches of time to avoid seeing his "enemies."

With Knox out on the road, Shields found a way to get even. He decided to organize an internal Republican Party coup. By the time Knox saw what was happening, it was too late.

On the morning after the Illinois primary, Knox sent Roosevelt an ominous telegram from Bay City, Michigan, where the delegates were starting to gather.

"Taft forces in desperation over Illinois defeat are going to any length to steal convention tomorrow," Knox warned.

Without consulting the state committee, Knox had installed Truman Newberry as the temporary chair of the convention, where he could make sure to give TR a fair deal—or more. But in a surprise move, Shields and Taft's other supporters responded by calling a special meeting of the state committee to replace Newberry. Worse yet, the committee replaced him with Shields.

The temporary chair had the power to decide which of two opposing delegations from Detroit should be seated. Newberry would have seated the delegation that supported TR. But with Shields in the chair, the committee seated Taft's delegates instead.

"Illegal meeting of state central committee attempted to oust New-berry today and to seat contesting delegation [from Detroit] tomorrow," Knox wired the Colonel. He asked TR to send a telegram to Newberry to "stiffen him up."

Either Knox didn't understand how dire things had become, or he didn't want Roosevelt to think that he had mismanaged the state. Unre-alistically, he told the Big Chief that "We are all ready for them and will carry things through to the ditch and back."

WHEN HE RECEIVED the telegram from Knox, TR was in Pennsylva-nia, crossing the state by train, in the midst of what a reporter called "the liveliest day of his campaign so far." His traveling entourage was packed with supporters, such as a priest from Wilkes-Barre who had become TR's close friend during the coal miners' strike a decade earlier, and Owen Wister, the novelist who had been TR's Harvard classmate, a Philadelphian who had gained renown as the author of *The Virginian.*

Wister described the scene as TR worked in his stateroom, filled with papers and secretaries. "The train rolled on and at the stations along its course crowds to the right of us, crowds to the left of us vol-leyed and thundered. They demanded the buzz saw—a look at him, a word from him. He gave it: often busting out of his busy seclusion and back into it again, all in a breath. The energy, the action, the ham-mered words, the blaze of genial jocund power, the prompt and mar-velous application of some special sentence to some special place." Recounting the scene twenty years later, Wister said "I can call it noth-ing but gigantic."

"We knocked them over the ropes in Illinois," Roosevelt repeated at every stop, straining his voice in shouting to overflowing crowds in Johnstown, Altoona, Harrisburg, and Lancaster, and using the kind of boxing metaphor that he loved. "I want to see them take the count in Pennsylvania."

When he arrived in Philadelphia, four hundred policemen were lining the streets to keep back crowds that packed the route from the train station to the hotel. The streets were almost impassable.

Crowds jammed the Metropolitan Opera House an hour before Roosevelt arrived and thousands more pressed at the doors from outside, begging for admission. In a passionate address, TR called for social and industrial justice, attacked the champions of special privilege, and claimed that Taft and his supporters were "trying to permit our government to be twisted away from its original purposes" and to become "a government by corporations."

Between stops, TR returned to his role as the campaign's commander-in-chief, issuing orders in two telegrams to Truman Newberry in Michigan.

"Both your wires received," Newberry replied. "An illegally called meeting of State Committee has unseated me as temporary chairman and violated all our state convention precedents by making a temporary roll call including Taft contested delegates" from Detroit.

"We are all fighting mad," Newberry assured the Colonel, "and are going through for a touchdown without flinching."

THOSE WHO WERE following events in Michigan knew there would be a battle for control of the forces at the National Guard Armory on Thursday morning. The national press was on hand. Coming two days after the Illinois primary, the results were sure to be vitally important— and dramatic. Editors seeking exciting copy got their wish. Front-page headlines around the country the next day described a "Delegates Riot" with "Soldiers in Hall." The *New York Times* told readers that a "Republican Riot Splits Michigan."

Both sides claimed the right to control the proceedings. The Taft forces insisted that Frank Knox had acted improperly by installing Newberry as the temporary chair without a vote of the State Central Committee and in giving him the unilateral power to decide on credentials challenges. They were convinced that Newberry would decide for Roosevelt's delegates in all of the challenges, many of which were of dubious lineage. With a majority of members of the committee favoring Taft—or wanting to get even with Knox and Osborn—they decided that both Knox and Newberry should be replaced.

On Wednesday night, the party's secretary, Paul King, called an emergency meeting of the State Committee. Knox declared the meeting illegal and boycotted the session, but it took place anyway. With Knox's nemesis Robert Shields in the chair, the State Committee elected Taft supporters to chair the party and the state convention, and they voted to seat Taft delegates from the hotly contested areas of Detroit and Battle Creek.

Knox refused to accept the results of the Wednesday night vote. He insisted that he alone had the power to issue credentials. The next morning, he issued white tickets for Roosevelt supporters and ordered that they be admitted. Acting pursuant to the decisions of the State Committee, however, state party secretary Paul King issued red tickets for Taft supporters.

When the Armory opened at noon on Thursday, it was surrounded by more than 1,800 angry men. Delegates and competing delegates demanded to be admitted. Hundreds of officers from rival law enforcement agencies, each allied with one of the factions, held them back. There were local and state police, private detectives, and Company B of the Michigan National Guard. The sergeant at arms, who apparently favored Taft, announced that he would admit those with red credentials. A few hundred Roosevelt delegates were admitted but hundreds of others were held at bay.

Furious Roosevelt supporters tried to force their way in. "Six fat policemen hurried them back while the Sergeant at arms stationed himself at the front door to examine tickets," the *Baltimore Sun* reported. But the efforts of the sergeant at arms were in vain. Hundreds of Roosevelt men made their way into the building through side doors, windows, the basement and by climbing over the transoms.

But no one could find Roosevelt's delegates from Detroit. Taking different trains, the Taft and Roosevelt delegations from Detroit left for

Bay City late Wednesday night. Somehow the Michigan Central Railroad's train carrying 200 Roosevelt delegates ran into difficulty and arrived at 2 P.M., five hours late. When the convention started, only Taft's delegates from Detroit were present. Roosevelt's backers were certain of foul play.

Strangely, Truman Newberry refused to try to enforce his claim to be the temporary chair. Despite his promise not to "flinch," he watched the events from across the street, "resting on a doorstep as a spectator."

Inside, the convention hall was ringed by scores of police, militiamen, sergeants at arms, and several dozen burly guards from the Sugar Trust who had been sent to help Taft's friends. "The Taft machine put a bunch of 50 or 60 strongmen with revolvers and clubs in the convention hall to bar our Roosevelt delegates," Dixon told Hiram Johnson, trying to explain the day's events. "The Mayor of Bay City called on Governor Osborn for protection. The governor ordered out troops" to try to bring order to the proceeding.

Frank Knox and Paul King sat at tables on opposite sides of the stage. Each claimed the right to serve as chair; each shouted at the top of his lungs, trying to call the convention to order as hundreds of supporters and opponents cheered and jeered. No one could be heard. No one could claim control.

As the crowd continued to yell, Judge W. D. Gordon of Midland, a fifty-two-year-old Roosevelt delegate and former Speaker of the Michigan House of Representatives, jumped up on the platform. Moments later, John Cremer, a former reporter from Detroit who was working for Taft's faction, jumped on the stage and threw Judge Gordon off. Gordon landed on the press tables at the front of the hall and then fell to the ground, hitting his head, which resulted in permanent injuries.

There was pandemonium. Delegates supporting each candidate—along with friends of Gordon and Cremer—rushed to the front and started a brawl. Roosevelt's supporters were certain that Cremer had hurt Gordon intentionally. As the fight became more serious, the guards around the hall—some of them police, others representing the Sugar Trust—used their clubs to restore order. Both Frank Knox and Paul King, still trying to command events from the stage, continued to shout out calls for the convention to come to order, but neither could be heard above the din.

Finally, Robert Shields mounted the stage and shouted out a motion nominating a Taft ally as temporary chairman. Knowing they were outnumbered and would be defeated in any vote, Roosevelt's supporters finally moved to a corner of the room, where they held a rump convention naming their own delegates to the national convention.

It was clear that the fight over the Michigan delegates would have to be decided by the national convention in Chicago. Unfortunately, Knox forgot to designate a secretary to take minutes of their proceedings—which made their case in Chicago, whatever its merits, virtually unwinnable.

Governor Chase Osborn, sidelined by a serious foot injury, was so outraged that he joined those asking Roosevelt to consider forming a third party.

"I wish you and Dixon would take it up with Colonel Roosevelt," he told Knox a few days after the Bay City fiasco. "He ought to run for President this year whether he runs on the Republican ticket or not. That is the way I look at it now."

In fact, Knox had created part of the problem himself. "Almost all of this was precipitated by your letter to Shields," Osborn told Knox. But he praised his protégé for making "a great fight up at Bay City" despite the fact that "the brewers and the mines and the Taft rollers were all against you."

After Michigan, Roosevelt and his supporters had more reason for their fury; more reason to claim that Taft's forces were stealing the election; and more reason to start planning to leave the Republican Party if TR did not get the nomination.

But events the next day gave them reason to doubt that such a move would be necessary.

ON A GLORIOUS spring day, the people of Pennsylvania provided the Colonel with another bruising electoral triumph. Exuberant *Chicago Tribune* headline writers called the Pennsylvania results an "avalanche" that left "Taft Backers Stunned." A bit less predictably, the generally anti-Roosevelt *New York Times* called the vote "sweeping," and "a crushing defeat."

Even Roosevelt's own supporters were amazed by the results. They knew that TR had some strong allies—including many aligned with the Steel Trust, which was an important industry in the state—but they were sure that Taft would benefit from the support of the regular Republican organization, headed by United States Senator Boise Penrose, the state's most powerful "party boss." "The significance of the Roosevelt victory can be realized," the *Times* said, by the fact that Senator Penrose, "for the first time in a generation," would now lose his position as the party's chair and national committeeman.

Thanks to overwhelming support in Pittsburgh and in the coal regions, where he captured nearly 80 percent of the vote, the Colonel won more than two-thirds of the popular vote and 64 of the 76 delegates at stake. The results exceeded the campaign's own internal predictions. Notes started to pour into headquarters predicting that Roosevelt's victory was now inevitable. Even Hiram Johnson was impressed.

Combined with the results in Illinois, the Pennsylvania primary changed the entire political landscape. Despite reverses in New York, Indiana and Michigan, the Roosevelt team could taste victory. During the next couple of weeks the campaign expected to win primaries in Nebraska and Oregon. They were confident that if they could win the Massachusetts primary on April 30, the fight for the party's nomination would effectively be over.

THE RESULTS IN Pennsylvania shocked the President. If Roosevelt felt wronged, so did he. Taft poured his feelings into a remarkable letter to his brother Horace. He had been personally as well as politically hurt by all of the attacks. They did not seem honorable.

"It is true that I have had the bosses with me," he said. But so did Roosevelt. "In Pennsylvania, William Flinn, one of the most notorious of political bosses and contractors, who made a shameless political contract with [Richard R.] Quay which found the light of publicity, put up a very large fund and expects to be one of the beneficiaries of Roosevelt's success." Quay's father, Senator Matthew Quay, had been one of the nation's most powerful "bosses" until his death in 1904. Taft was convinced that the son, one of Roosevelt's most important supporters in the Keystone State, was no better than the father. In fact, they had both been indicted for corruption a decade earlier in a case that alleged that Richard R. Quay, who was then the state's treasurer, had used the state's treasury for personal gain.

Association with such bosses "when it is by and for Roosevelt has nothing evil in it," Taft complained with a combination of irony and bitterness. "It is only when they support me that bosses are wicked. Considering the use which Roosevelt made of bosses in the past, one would think the hypocrisy of such attacks would be seen, but not in the case of a popular idol."

The fact that the Colonel retained the support of reformers while benefiting from the support of political bosses was bad enough. Even worse, Taft and his community of supporters took the link between Roosevelt and the Steel Trust in Pennsylvania as an article of faith. Taft's managers were certain that the campaign's leading funders were people who wanted the antitrust case against U.S. Steel to be dropped. Their beliefs were effectively articulated by Taft's personal secretary, Charles D. Hilles, who played a key role in the contest and went on to chair the Republican National Committee. "The allies of the Steel Corporation in Western Pennsylvania furnished unlimited sums of money to our antagonists and the cooperation of men of organizing ability," Hilles complained.

———

AFTER PENNSYLVANIA, TAFT was reeling. In the boxing metaphors that were so popular, he was leaning against the ropes in a protective crouch, gloves up, stoically letting Roosevelt hit him again and again. The strategy wasn't working. While it suited his own temperament and won plaudits from his friends from Yale and the Ivy League, he looked weak and defenseless to those in the working class who formed the majority of voters in the primaries.

"As a rule, the Professional and business men are with the president and we are pleased that he is receiving the blows of the opposition with Christian fortitude," Hilles told Taft's brother, preparing him for what was to come. But Taft's appeals to the laboring classes are not succeeding, he explained. "It seems difficult to hold our ground by peaceful measures." According to Hilles, some Roosevelt supporters were appealing to the fears of anti-Catholic workers by claiming that Taft planned to establish close relations with the Vatican.

"The situation is very critical," Hilles said. "We are not so much disturbed at the loss of the delegates in Illinois and Pennsylvania, as we are at the underlying causes. It seems very probable that the use of money to an unprecedented extent, and the circulation of disquieting rumors as to the President's relations with the Roman Catholic Church, and the unrest of the inflamed laboring classes may rob us of West Virginia and Massachusetts. If we cannot check the reverses before Massachusetts is reached, I very much fear a stampede."

The Nation magazine, which had dismissed Roosevelt's attacks as desperate ravings only two weeks earlier, told readers that Pennsylvania's primary vote had brought "President Taft's re-nomination into grave doubt." Combined with Illinois, it had "impaired the President's political prestige" and turned "the psychology of the campaign against the President."

"If Mr. Taft is to save the situation for himself," the editors said, "he must now go out and fight Roosevelt—openly and directly as the latter is fighting him. If the President has any ammunition in reserve, let him use it at once. . . . If the President will do that fearlessly, he may yet turn the tide of battle in his favor."

Taft agreed. He felt unfairly attacked and righteous about his cause—including the sanctity of the judiciary. He refused to give up. "It may be that Illinois and Pennsylvania will cause a stampede and [that TR] will carry Massachusetts against me on April 30th and enough other states to nominate him," he told his brother.

But he wasn't a quitter:

> I shall not withdraw under any conditions. I represent a cause that would make it cowardly for me to withdraw now. It seems to me that I am the only hope against radicalism and demagogy, and that even if I go down to defeat [in the general election], it is my duty to secure the nomination, if I can, under the rules that the Republican party convention has established, in spite of all threats to bolt or establish a third party. It is of the utmost importance that such a nucleus as our present party organization constitutes, should be held and controlled, for the maintenance of true constitutional principles.

He thought it quite possible that the Democratic Party nominee (which he expected to be House Speaker Champ Clark) would win the election if Roosevelt formed a third party. But Taft expected that the Republicans would win four years later, and he wanted to make sure that at that point the Republican leadership would "not be Rooseveltian and wildly radical."

When he wrote that letter, Taft apparently still wanted to conduct a gentlemanly campaign. "I do not expect to make any personal attacks on Roosevelt," he said. But within days, Taft had changed his mind. After being pummeled for so long, and concluding that he had no choice but to answer in kind, Taft finally had his "fighting blood up," as the *Chicago Tribune* put it.

"If Mr. Taft had his way, he would not engage in personalities," the paper reported. "But his advisers have been begging and pleading with him to do so. They want him to mash the colonel to a pulp."

As it happened, Taft had plenty of ammunition in reserve. Undignified as it seemed for a sitting president to engage in political campaigns, Taft decided to fight back—to attack TR in ways that he found deeply distasteful, to make charges and to release letters and documents that could be embarrassing to his one-time friend and mentor—starting with material that he would use in the campaign in Massachusetts.

"President Taft will yield to the urgent appeals of his friends and start to fight Col. Theodore Roosevelt with his own weapons," the *Washington Post* reported.

From now on, the *Post* said, "there is to be war to the knife."

THERE WAS ONE man who might have tried to prevent a bloody fight between the once great friends. Both of them loved Archie Butt, the military aide who had served them so faithfully. After years of hard work and pressure, Archie was exhausted. Friends noticed that he had lost at least twenty pounds in the past few months. Taft's physician warned that if he did not get some rest, Butt was likely to suffer a complete collapse. His roommate and close friend planned a trip to Italy in early March that would combine relaxation with business and include a private meeting with Pope Pius X.

Butt was at dinner with Taft on February 25, the night that TR announced that he was running. The announcement arrived at 7:30, just as the family was entering the dining room. Taft read Roosevelt's statement to the group. It was painful, stronger than the President had expected.

"He could not have made it stronger," Taft said. "It will be a rallying cry to the Progressives of the country and to the discontented."

Butt stayed awake all night, debating the wisdom of going, feeling that "the President will need every *intime* near at hand now." He could see that Taft hated to see him go. Butt felt "like a quitter." Though he was "very tired and really need[ed] a rest," he canceled his reservations early the next morning. But Taft insisted that Archie take a restful holiday so that Butt wouldn't "break down just when he needs me most."

On March 2, Butt and his roommate sailed for Europe on the S.S. *Berlin*, planning to return long before the campaign was over.

There was a great deal of speculation and debate about the purpose of Butt's trip. He met with the Vatican's Secretary of State on March 18 and with Pope Pius X three days later. On March 21, the *New York Times* reported that Butt had gone to Rome to meet with the Pope, carrying a letter designed to help Taft in the campaign. "According to some reports that are, of course, without verification," the paper said, "Major Butt's visit was connected with the attitude that American Catholics will take in the next Presidential election."

The Roosevelt campaign seized on such stories for its own purposes. TR's supporters told anti-Catholic audiences in Pennsylvania that Archie Butt had gone to Rome "to open diplomatic negotiations with the Vatican." In fact, there had been no such discussions.

On the day after the Illinois primary, Butt boarded a spectacular new vessel in Southampton, England. Tragically, that boat was the *Titanic*. On April 14, as the candidates were fighting for every vote in the Pennsylvania primary, the *Titanic* struck an iceberg in the Atlantic, creating the deadliest peacetime maritime disaster in history. For more than a week the world stood still as people around the world tried to absorb the news.

Archie Butt died that night, bringing heartache to both Roosevelt and Taft. His heroic efforts to save women and children on the Titanic became the stuff of legend.

Chapter Nine

The next major primary, to be held in Massachusetts on April 30, would be crucial, perhaps even decisive. Roosevelt had lost the first three primaries—to La Follette in North Dakota and Wisconsin and to Taft in New York. By early April, he looked like a certain loser. But then his overwhelming victories in Illinois on April 9 and in Pennsylvania a week later turned the story on its head. A few days later, he won primaries in Nebraska and Oregon. By taking advantage of the new presidential primary process, the campaign had turned the tide. As George Perkins noted, "After a tremendous battle to get primaries in some of the States, we succeeded in Illinois, Pennsylvania and Nebraska . . . [delivering] one 'solar-plexus' after another to the Taft cause."

In ways that the original crusaders for reform might not have anticipated, Roosevelt's primary winning streak was also having a dramatic impact on delegates selected by the old rules. In some states, especially in the South, delegates in Taft's corner were starting to consider defecting. "Reports from the South tell of unrest among the Taft minions in that section," Atlanta attorney Churchill Goree told Hilles. "Persistent rumors to the effect that the men who have been instrumental in organizing the federal officeholders are ready to desert the administration appear to be well documented."

The southern delegations were almost entirely selected and controlled by federal officeholders, and in order to keep their jobs those men wanted to go with the winner as much as they wanted to please the incumbent. "The federal office holding clique, always having a predilection for the band-wagon, has already sensed the defeat of Mr. Taft in the Chicago Convention and are only waiting for the opportune moment to throw off the machine yoke," Goree warned.

Roosevelt's campaign manager sent a telegram boasting that "the Taft house is falling down." Dixon told Hiram Johnson about missives showing that "Southern delegates, who were selected and instructed at early conventions on the assurance that Roosevelt was not to be a candidate, are resenting being misled and preparing to get in line with the overwhelming sentiment of the Republican Northern States."

It became an article of faith that the defections would become overwhelming if TR could win in Massachusetts. "The desertion of Taft delegates in the south to Roosevelt marks the turning of the tide," Frank Knox wrote Chase Osborn, "and may mean the beginning of a landslide. If we should carry Massachusetts on the 30th, Taft's goose is cooked."

The creation of a presidential primary in Massachusetts had been one of the earliest achievements of Roosevelt's forces. On March 2, the White House told reporters that "Massachusetts will send a solid delegation" and said that 137 members of the state's lower chamber were for Taft compared to 6 who were for TR. A day later, Governor Stubbs of Kansas told a rally of 2,000 Massachusetts progressives that "A great, free people ought to have a right to vote for the nomination of a candidate for the highest office in the land." TR's state leader, Matthew Hale, a member of the Boston City Council and former Roosevelt family tutor, called on the state legislature to create a presidential primary, threatening to run candidates against anyone who opposed it. Taft's forces, led by Senator Murray Crane, tried to block the new law, using whatever tools they could. But they were outmatched and outmaneuvered.

To take effect in time for the election, a primary law had to be adopted by March 12. It seemed certain to fail until March 11, a day

before the deadline, when two state senators who had initially opposed
the law changed sides. One of those senators explained that he actually opposed the direct election of delegates but had become convinced
that the public favored it. "Elect all by Direct Vote," the *Boston Globe*
headline declared. "Roosevelt Supporters Claim Victory over Machine."

After the losses in Illinois and Pennsylvania, the Bay State had
become Taft's final line of defense. Unseemly as it might be, he would
have to campaign in person. "It is necessary to go to Massachusetts,"
Hilles explained to Horace Taft. "If we lose in the primaries there, there
will be danger of a stampede." He was particularly concerned about
holding on to the President's men in the South. Hilles blamed the possible defections on corrupt practices as well as on the natural desire of
officeholders to go with the winner. But the result was the same. "Our
adversaries are spending money like drunken sailors, and the conversion to Roosevelt of Taft-instructed delegations in the South, who need
the money, must be checked by a showing of our strength in the northern States."

If he was going to have any chance of carrying Massachusetts, Taft
would have to go on the offensive.

TAFT HAD AT least one powerful weapon in his arsenal: Roosevelt's
decision not to bring an antitrust case against the International Harvester Company in 1907. The facts of the case could probably have been
interpreted in several ways, and normally the judicial and judicious Taft
would have been careful to present all sides. But with his fighting blood
up, he agreed to allow documents to be released in a way that made
Roosevelt look weak at best and corrupt at worst, a servant of the rich
and powerful who could be influenced by enormous campaign contributions. The story also reinforced the most sinister interpretations of
what had happened in the case of U.S. Steel and of Roosevelt's relationship with the campaign's chief financial supporter, George Perkins.

International Harvester had been created in 1902 when J. P. Morgan
& Company, sometimes known simply as Morgan, arranged a spec-

tacular merger of the McCormick Harvesting Machine Company, the Deering Harvester Company, and three smaller companies. In order to avoid a fight over control of the new entity, the companies' owners and managers agreed to give control to Morgan. The entire deal was engineered by Perkins, who was at the time a Morgan partner and a close associate of the firm's famous leader, John Pierpont Morgan, the man who dominated America's corporate finance sector at the turn of the century. As historian Ron Chernow noted, the merger put Perkins "in Pierpont's league." It also provided him with a $3 million fee (which today would be equal to about $80 million) and a seat on the company's powerful board. He had been forced to resign from the New York Life Insurance Company as a result of charges of making "illegal campaign contributions and falsifying records related to the sale of railroad securities"—charges that were later dropped—but Perkins built his reputation and became rich and powerful, thanks in large part to his role in creating International Harvester.

During Roosevelt's years in office, as Chernow explained in his magisterial study, while the President sometimes seemed to include the company among what he called "the malefactors of great wealth," the administration was very generous to Morgan, giving it enormous power in financing the construction of the Panama Canal. J. P. Morgan & Company had been one of the most generous benefactors to his 1904 reelection campaign, contributing $150,000. Chernow called Roosevelt and Morgan "secret blood brothers."

By 1912, George Perkins had retired from J. P. Morgan, but he was still a member of the Harvester board. As one of Theodore Roosevelt's largest financial supporters, he was also a fat target for anyone who wanted to debunk Roosevelt's populist rhetoric.

The Taft campaign wanted to show—or to leave the impression— that Roosevelt had been and would be the handmaiden of big business, corrupted by campaign contributions from Perkins and the Morgan interests. As exhibit A, on April 24, 1912, the administration released a series of documents that explained how Perkins had convinced Roosevelt not to file an antitrust suit against International Harvester in 1907. The documents showed his warm personal and political relationship with Perkins and Morgan and implied a possible connection between Roosevelt's decision and Morgan's $150,000 campaign contribution (which would today be equal to about $4 million) just three years earlier.

The Harvester story had already been injected into the campaign in early March by Senator La Follette. Farmers in North Dakota were incensed by the high price of the company's products. Populists in the state argued that the company should be broken up to create competition and lower prices. La Follette claimed that Roosevelt's Department of Justice had been planning to file an antitrust suit against Harvester until Perkins went directly to the President and convinced him to intervene.

"We are going to carry North Dakota for La Follette," Senator Asle Gronna said with a twinkle in his eye. "We have to buy harvesters in North Dakota."

But the Harvester matter did not become a major national story until April 24 when the Department of Justice released letters that seemed to prove that La Follette's charges had been true. Formally, the letters were sent in response to a request from Congress, but it was widely assumed that the decision to release them, as well as the timing, was dictated by the Taft campaign and the President's decision to start using what political ammunition he had at his disposal.

The first letter was dated August 22, 1907. Writing to Attorney General Charles Bonaparte from his home in Oyster Bay, Roosevelt said that "George W. Perkins of the International Harvester Company has just called on me and submitted to me certain papers, of which I enclose copies." Based on those documents, and his conversation with Perkins, Roosevelt told Bonaparte: "Please don't file the suit until I hear from you." Roosevelt said that the case was being investigated by the Bureau of Corporations and that the Justice Department should wait for its report before acting.

In a letter to Roosevelt a month later, Herbert Knox Smith, the commissioner of the Bureau of Corporations, recommended against bringing an antitrust case against Harvester. The letter seemed to contain evidence of a clear threat. Smith said that Perkins had made it crystal clear "that after all the endeavors of this company and the other Morgan interests to uphold the policies of the administration . . . if the company was going to be attacked in a purely technical case, the interests he represented were 'going to fight.'"

Under the circumstances, Smith urged Roosevelt to drop the case. "It is a very practical question whether it is well to throw away now the great influence of the so-called Morgan interests which up to this time have supported the advanced policies of this administration . . . and to place them generally in opposition. I believe Mr. Perkins's statement that his interest would necessarily be driven into active opposition was a sincere one."

Arguing that there is a difference between "good and bad" trusts, Smith urged Roosevelt to tell the Department of Justice not to file an antitrust suit against International Harvester.

FOR THE FIRST time in the campaign, Taft's forces were taking the initiative, setting the tone of the debate. For several days, Roosevelt and his team scrambled to find a way to answer the charges. He and his current and former top aides exchanged a series of telegrams trying to gather material and to prepare a response. Not having a good answer to the substantive charges, they made a number of ad hominem attacks, arguing that Perkins had given money to Taft in 1908 and claiming that Taft had been in a meeting where the case was discussed and where he had never raised an objection.

The attack on Roosevelt's ethics, and particularly the suggestion that he had made political decisions in return for huge campaign contributions, fed into a narrative that had dogged him for years. During the 1904 campaign, the press and his opponents in the Democratic Party criticized Roosevelt for accepting hundreds of thousands of dollars from trusts such as U.S. Steel, General Electric, and International Harvester, as well as from the superrich barons of industry—not just from J. P. Morgan but also from Edward H. Harriman of the Union Pacific Railroad and Henry C. Frick of U.S. Steel. Those men, their companies, and their friends contributed more than $2 million to Roosevelt's campaign. Roosevelt said that he saw no conflict of interest as long as his contributors believed in the principles of the Republican Party; he accepted contributions "without any kind of promise, express or implied."

In some respects, that argument was valid and understandable. As one study explained, TR's rich contributors "supported Roosevelt because they preferred an 'unpredictable head of a predictable party' in power rather than the 'predictable head of an unpredictable party.'" But ethicists have always worried that huge campaign contributions can have a more subtle corrupting influence, even on people of principle, leading them to support positions that nicely coincide with the interests of their funders.

As Doris Kearns Goodwin notes in *Bully Pulpit*, there were those who suggested more insidious motives. Some critics claimed that Roosevelt's administration was using the Bureau of Corporations to blackmail companies into supporting him, threatening prosecution unless the company agreed to make a large contribution to the presidential campaign. On October 24, 1904, Alton Parker, the Democratic presidential candidate, gave a speech arguing that "political contributions by corporations and trusts mean corruption." Directing a series of questions at Roosevelt, he asked "Why do corporations and trusts subscribe to political campaigns? What would a trust think of a party which, after accepting from the trust a campaign contribution of $500,000, should permit the party's representatives in office to take actions inimical to the trust?" In words that could have applied directly to Roosevelt's decision not to prosecute International Harvester three years later, he charged that large contributors such as Morgan and International Harvester "have enjoyed favors contributed either directly by statute or indirectly by the non-prosecution of violations of law."

After winning the 1904 campaign, Roosevelt proposed legislation to bar companies from contributing to candidates. That proposal became law in 1907. Nothing in the new law, however, limited personal contributions by supporters such as George Perkins and Frank Munsey.

No documents have come to light that prove that in blocking prosecution of the Harvester case Roosevelt acted out of a venal motive. It seems more likely that he had become convinced—or had convinced himself—that there really were good and bad trusts and that Harvester truly was a good trust with Morgan as a good owner. His views may have been influenced by his relationship with Perkins and the knowledge that Morgan and Perkins were huge political benefactors. But the nexus between their support and his actions would be very difficult, if not impossible, to prove. Indeed, on some level he may even have denied it to himself. For that reason, many campaign finance laws historically have created limits on the level of contributions based on the *appearance* of a conflict of interest. There is deemed to be a risk that contributions at a certain level could be perceived by the public as corrupt and so undermine the vitality of our democracy. The Supreme Court found that argument a valid concern in its 1976 *Buckley v. Valeo* ruling but found it somewhat less persuasive thirty-four years later in *Citizens United v. FEC* and then in 2014 in *McCutcheon v. FEC*.

Nevertheless, there is good reason to think that at least one of TR's policy decisions in the campaign of 1912 was, in fact, directly influenced by the level of Perkins's financial support. When he ultimately left the Republican Party and created his own new Progressive, or Bull Moose, Party, Roosevelt proudly presided over the writing of an innovative platform filled with exciting new ideas about such issues as social justice and the role of women in society. Famed social reformer Jane Addams told a reporter that the platform "contains all of the things I have been fighting for for more than a decade." But people who cared about trustbusting were far less pleased.

Although he is little known today, few Progressive Era figures exemplified the movement's ideals better than Charles McCarthy. Working in an obscure Wisconsin office called the Legislative Reference Library, McCarthy became the visionary behind "The Wisconsin Idea," a staunch proponent of "evidence-based policy making," and a behind-the-scenes architect of many of the Progressive Era's legislative initiatives. He was recruited by the new party to help draft its platform, which was released on August 7, 1912. Five days later, McCarthy wrote a private memorandum to his own files describing the way in which some of the strongest ideas had been scuttled by Roosevelt as the result of pressure from George Perkins.

Toward the end of the platform committee's work, McCarthy wrote, "we began to hear that certain men were not pleased with the radicalism of the platform and finally we were called before Colonel Roosevelt" in one of the rooms in TR's hotel suite. "Mr. Perkins came in, said something to Mr. Roosevelt, and Mr. Roosevelt then said, 'Where is it George, point it out.'

"Perkins waved his hand and said, 'All through it,' and went out of the room. Mr. Roosevelt then said to us in substance: 'Next to Mr. Dixon, Mr. Perkins has made this movement in this country possible. He has furnished so much money that when the campaign expense account is published he will be damned and I will be damned in this country. Now gentlemen, I wish that you could, if possible, fix up these little things in this platform to which Mr. Perkins objects."

Perkins's primary concern was a section of the draft platform that called for strengthening the Sherman Antitrust Act. It was, of course, the issue that had attracted Perkins to the Roosevelt campaign in the first place, after Taft's Department of Justice filed its antitrust case against U.S. Steel.

McCarthy wasn't taking it. "Mr. Roosevelt, he said, I came from Wisconsin. I came down here to do what the people of the country want, not what Mr. Perkins wants." Other members of the drafting committee including Gifford Pinchot sided with McCarthy.

But Perkins felt so strongly about the issue that he threatened to leave the campaign unless the language was amended. Ultimately, Roosevelt sided with Perkins, according to McCarthy, and stripped out the section of the draft platform that called for strengthening the Sherman Antitrust law.

TAFT'S ATTACKS ON Roosevelt's role in the International Harvester case were reinforced by an unlikely ally: Massachusetts Congressman Augustus "Gussie" Gardner, the son-in-law of Roosevelt's close friend Henry Cabot Lodge. Gardner and Lodge were almost members of the Roosevelt family. Alice Roosevelt Longworth said that she "saw Gussie Gardner daily" and considered him "one of our best and oldest friends." Press accounts had suggested that they would be leaders of TR's presidential campaign. But Roosevelt's proposal for the recall of judicial decisions had made such support impossible.

Lodge promised to remain neutral, but Gardner did not, and by the time of the Massachusetts primary, he had decided that he had to come out for Taft—and to do so without equivocation. On April 16, feeling that Taft lacked outspoken supporters to plead his case, Gardner challenged Roosevelt to a debate. Roosevelt declined the invitation, saying there was "no reason for my holding a joint debate with you." Gardner repeated the challenge three days later. This time he made his telegram more specific. "You have told the public that President Taft has alienated your respect by his subservience to great interests. I deny it. President Taft has instituted proceedings against all the great offenders. He has made no exceptions on account of expediency. Can you say as much? I charge you with making exceptions for your favorites, sometimes under the allegation of technicalities, sometimes for reasons unknown."

Gardner's charges mirrored the claims made eight years earlier by Alton Parker and Roosevelt's critics in the press. But this time the charges were hurled by a member of his own party, someone who saw his daughter daily, and the son-in-law of one of his oldest friends. Gardner sent a telegram to Roosevelt challenging him to make public the internal deliberations over the Harvester case, which, he said, "show that the Morgan interests always favored your administration."

"It was particularly hard when one's dearest friends were on the other side," Alice Longworth recalled, "and especially when they were resourceful fighters. Gussie Gardner was one of those."

For the first time, the Roosevelt campaign was playing defense. TR sent a torrent of telegrams to current and former aides asking for their recollections and for copies of materials in their files. He told his secretary to "get ready today and tomorrow copies of all correspondence between me and President Taft since I have come back. All of it. Also copies of all correspondence between myself and Herbert Knox Smith about the Harvester Trust and Mellen Steamship line and any other subject. And all correspondence with Mr. Charles J. Bonaparte on same matter. Meet me at the train tomorrow afternoon with these copies."

His supporters told him that it was time to abide by his old axiom: "When you hit, hit hard."

"Frenzied and shameful fight being made against you here," Senator Beveridge wired TR from Massachusetts, where he was acting as a campaign surrogate. "Nevertheless, I feel sure you will carry Massachusetts overwhelmingly. It needs only your final appeal to burn opposition up when you come. Should you see fit to do so, you are justified if you strike and spare not."

Taft was getting the same advice, with friends calling on him to "mash the colonel to a pulp."

WHEN HE ARRIVED in the Bay State on Thursday, April 25, Taft seemed truly energized for the first time in the campaign. "After remaining silent for weeks under the repeated attacks of Col. Roosevelt, President Taft came into Massachusetts today and returned the fire," the *New York Times* reported. Wearing a black sack coat and a waistcoat and pair of light-colored striped trousers, he traveled throughout the state giving more than a dozen speeches, accusing Roosevelt of dishonesty and of abandoning the concept of the "square deal," quoting from the correspondence on the Harvester case, and waving a gray cap at the crowd from the back of his private train. "It wrenches my soul" to have to attack "an old and dear friend, Theodore Roosevelt, but he has made so many charges against me that I must respond. I deny those charges. I deny all of them. I do not want to fight Theodore Roosevelt but then sometimes a man in a corner fights. I am going to fight."

As the day wore on, Taft grew increasingly aggressive. After a while, his speeches "split the colonel wide open," the *Washington Post* reported "and exposed the works to view. . . . Everywhere his words created a profound sensation."

Wherever he went, large crowds greeted him, cheering for "our next President." The platform and streets were packed with people when Taft's train arrived in Springfield at just after noon, and they continued to flock around his private railcar along the route as the train stopped briefly in village after village. He gave speeches at Worcester, Natick, and South Framingham. He closed the day at what the press called "a monster meeting" in the Boston Arena, with a crowd estimated at 9,000 people, and then at an overflow meeting at Symphony Hall. With marchers from his summer home in Beverly, Massachusetts, and from the Taft Club at Harvard, songs and cheers filled the Arena's great hall. His message was clear. The *Post's* banner headline read, "President Accuses Predecessor of Double Dealing."

Taft's appearances had an impact, but Roosevelt was set to respond the next day, coming to the state for two days of speeches to be delivered with all of the anger, ammunition, and fiery rhetoric that he possessed.

Taft couldn't leave the field to his opponent; he had finally joined the battle; and there was too much at stake not to return. Before he left the state, his staff announced that the President would be back in Massachusetts on Monday, the day before the primary.

WHEN ROOSEVELT CHARGED into the state the next day, he was on the defensive but also on fire. This was political warfare at last. For two days, on the weekend before the primary, Roosevelt had the state—and the press and the imagination of the public—to himself. Newspaper headlines captured the flavor of his rhetoric. The *Atlanta Constitution*: "Crooked: So Roosevelt Styles Attack Made by Taft; Declares That President Has Violated Every Canon of Ordinary Decency"; the *Boston Globe*: "Roosevelt Hurls Savage Answer to Taft's Attack: Astounding Hypocrisy"; the *Chicago Tribune*: "Roosevelt in Scathing Terms Denies Charges of President: Accuses Taft of Breaking Pledge to People"; the *Hartford Courant*: "Roosevelt Accuses Taft of Grossest and Most Astounding Hypocrisy: Venomous Attack on the President's Fitness for Office."

Taft had made some good arguments and delivered some good lines, but fundamentally he had the temperament of a judge, not a fighter. Roosevelt was a warrior dressed for battle. He did not need to answer Taft's arguments directly; his strategy was to hit and hit hard; to regain the initiative. He created a level of political frenzy that subsumed the issues.

People believed what they wanted to believe. Responding to the documents showing that he had ordered that the case against International Harvester be dismissed, Roosevelt claimed that Taft had been in the cabinet meeting when the case was discussed and had not objected to Roosevelt's decision. He released a telegram from James Garfield, who had been his Secretary of the Interior, supporting his assertion. A day later, Taft released a statement backed by documents showing that he could not have been at such meetings. The meetings would have to have been held between August 22, 1907, when Perkins visited TR in Oyster Bay, and September 24, 1907, when Roosevelt decided not to prosecute the case. As Taft proved, he had been away from Washington from August 18 until December 20, first on a speaking trip through the West and then on a trip to the Philippines. Two other members of TR's cabinet, Secretary of State Elihu Root and Secretary of Agriculture James Wilson, issued statements agreeing with Taft and saying that he had never been in such meetings. But for most people, the whirl of charges and countercharges, of telegrams and dates, was too complex to analyze. As Cal O'Laughlin wrote in the *Chicago Tribune*, the "conflict of evidence probably will puzzle the public" and be too complicated "to straighten out."

The Colonel's campaign had become more than political combat—it was now political theater, a carnival that built public excitement wherever he went. Overjoyed reporters treated his arrival in Boston as a heroic sporting event. When Taft spoke to 9,000 people in the Boston Arena, he brought the crowd to its feet. When Roosevelt spoke to an equally large crowd—with others lining the streets, causing a near riot trying to get in—his admirers danced in the aisles.

"No Castilian toreador was ever received with more frenzied shouts of joy in a Spanish bull ring than was Col. Roosevelt in the Arena last evening," *Boston Globe* reporter (and later arts critic) A. J. Philpott reported. "He was received as great popular idols are received, as Jim Jeffries was received when he stepped into the prize ring at Reno, as great gladiators were received in the days of the Roman Coliseum in the days of Caesars, as William Jennings Bryan was received when he hurled his 'cross of gold' speech at the Democratic Convention in 1896."

If Philpott's account was overblown, so was the reaction he was describing. "It was a tumult, a hysterical shout, that greeted the colonel the moment he stepped on the platform which was roped like a prize ring," the article continued. "Men and women—9,000 of them—stood up on chairs, shrieked, waved hats, flags, papers, waved their arms, as they shouted and shouted. And the colonel, standing at the front of the roped ring, smiled through it all."

His young state campaign manager, Arthur Hill, who had been at the first dinner at Judge Grant's home, became part of the show.

"Arthur D. Hill was so tickled he danced for glee," Philpott wrote. "Just outside the press gallery he danced to a ragtime tune. Some of the other Roosevelt enthusiasts felt like doing something so they just yelled. As 'Alexander's Ragtime Band' was struck up—the audience caught on and helped with the chorus. Arthur D. Hill led a force of messenger boys near the press seats during the song. He was the musical director of the evening."

SINCE THIS WAS the state's first presidential primary, and the ballot was extremely complicated, it was hard to predict the outcome. Some observers projected that Taft would win "by a scant margin." Oddsmakers put his chances at ten to seven based largely on his superior organization and its ability to get its voters to the polls. The Colonel's managers confidently predicted victory. After all, he had been winning everywhere else.

Roosevelt was a bit less certain. "I am a better warrior than prophet," he said with a grin. Recognizing the uncertainty of the results, "he said continually that he believed he could win the nomination without the aid of Massachusetts."

Everyone agreed that Roosevelt might be able to win without Massachusetts, but that Taft could not. Taft had to win. "Even the President's closest friends fear that if he shows weakness in the Bay State primary his defeat will be as certain as anything in politics can be," the *Baltimore Sun* reported. "If, on the other hand, a majority of the Massachusetts delegates are instructed for the President, confidence will be restored in the campaign and the nomination of Colonel Roosevelt on the first ballot will be prevented."

For the first time, papers went public with stories about the possible defections in the South that had been worrying Taft's managers. Taft had gained 32 delegates during the week to 8 for Roosevelt, but insiders understood that those victories could be illusory. The *Washington Post* said that delegates from South Carolina and Virginia were talking of "flopping." "If Theodore Roosevelt looms up as a likely winner, the 'black and tan' delegates from South Carolina will climb on his bandwagon," it reported. "Roosevelt managers say these rumors are the forerunner of a wholesale desertion from the Taft ranks of delegates from the South."

Publicly, Taft's managers asserted that there was no fear whatever that there would be desertions. But privately Taft's team had become convinced that Massachusetts was vital and that even then they could only win through "a very ugly fight."

There was one important Boston voting bloc in Taft's camp that tended to be overlooked by most observers: the African-American community. Though he had no love for Taft, William Monroe Trotter, the crusading black editor-publisher of the *Guardian* newspaper, hated Roosevelt. In a series of articles and editorials, he told his readers that Roosevelt had seemed somewhat friendly to blacks during his first term, most famously by inviting Booker T. Washington to dine in the White House. But Trotter argued that after he was elected in 1904, TR changed his tune. "In his second administration he went over to the South," Trotter insisted. "He did absolutely nothing for us, and everything against us, including Brownsville."

Like many other Americans, Trotter was outraged by Roosevelt's decision in 1906 to give a dishonorable discharge to 167 black soldiers who had been charged with killing a white bartender and wounding a police officer in Brownsville, Texas. The Brownsville case became a national cause célèbre, with TR's critics pointing to the fact that military commanders insisted that the soldiers had been in their barracks all night and claiming that the evidence used against the soldiers, including spent shell casings, had been planted. The episode became a lasting stain on Roosevelt's reputation.

As Secretary of War, Taft was responsible for executing Roosevelt's order. He was out of town when the President acted but tried to delay the decision once he returned. He urged that at the very least the men be given the benefit of an honorable discharge. But TR was adamant. He made it clear that "the order in question will in no way be rescinded or modified." Under the circumstances, Taft felt obliged to discharge the soldiers. As a result, the stain of Brownsville covered him as well as the man who had made the decision.

"Only his innermost circle was privy to Taft's continuing anxiety,"

Doris Kearns Goodwin concluded. "Privately, Taft continued to believe that had he been present in Washington during the Brownsville incident, he might have prevented the President from issuing the draconian order."

Although Trotter was not privy to Taft's backstage efforts to prevent an injustice, he still thought that he was preferable to Roosevelt. "The issue of all race-loyal is to oppose the third term nomination of the lyncher of our Colored soldiers," he told his readers.

ON MONDAY, APRIL 29, Taft returned to Massachusetts, creating what reporters correctly called "an occurrence absolutely unique in the history of the Union—a President of the United States and ex-President, each in a special train and attended by political supporters and a crowd of newspapermen, canvassing the state for the votes of the people, and not for an election to the presidency but merely in an effort to secure the nomination of one of the great political parties." Many observers called it the bitterest fight since the scandal-ridden election of 1884 when Democratic candidate Grover Cleveland, who had fathered a child out of wedlock, defeated James G. Blaine, who was plagued by a series of public corruption charges.

During a grueling twelve-hour day interrupted by rain at several stops, Taft spoke to crowds that the *New York Times* estimated at 500,000 people in more than a dozen rallies, including at least 50,000 in New Bedford alone. His voice had practically given out, and he had difficulty making himself heard.

Taft complained of Roosevelt's misrepresentations, of instances where the Colonel had put words into his mouth, and that, still worse, "he's got a lot of people to believe it."

"No man has a right to misrepresent another to get himself in office," he shouted at one point. "Condemn me if you will, but condemn me by other witnesses than Theodore Roosevelt."

"My former friend Roosevelt likes to appropriate Abraham Lincoln all to himself," he continued as the audience laughed and applauded.

"But I ask you good people of Lowell if you think Lincoln would have treated an opponent, much less a friend, the way he treated me."

"No, no, no," people in the audience shouted back.

But when someone in the crowd shouted that "Roosevelt is a liar," Taft stopped him. "That isn't in my vocabulary," he said. "My experience on the bench has taught me the value of words and one of the most unsafe things to do is to go further than the facts."

Roosevelt says all the bosses are supporting me, Taft said. "I deny it." But Roosevelt and I are alike in one respect. "When we are running for office, we don't examine the clothes or the hair or the previous condition of anybody who tenders his support."

The crowds were filled with his admirers, but he hated the process. "I should not be here and I am very sorry I have to be here," he said at every stop. He did not think that a sitting president should be compelled to engage in a war of personalities over a presidential nomination. For the first time, he called for a constitutional amendment extending the term in office from four to either six or eight years and making the President ineligible for reelection.

Some editorial writers were equally offended by the process. The campaign itself was providing another reason to doubt the benefits of the new system. The *New York Times* called it "Party Suicide by Primary" and said it was "a first rate device for splitting a party wide open and inviting defeat on Election Day. It is as if an army before engaging the enemy should divide into two portions and fight a terrific battle, one half against the other. . . . The hatreds and passions are too deep to be soon allayed." After such a bitter fight, the paper said, it would be almost impossible for the party to come back together in the general election. The old system may have been open to objection, it argued, "but for any electorate save one confined within the walls of an insane asylum, its advantages over this Massachusetts plan are obvious."

CROSSING THE STATE simultaneously in his own train, Roosevelt remained the warrior. He started campaigning at 8 a.m., marching through roaring crowds to board his train at North Station in Boston, and he ended the day with a triumphant final speech at the Majestic Theater in Pittsfield, which was packed far beyond capacity, with 2,000 admirers inside the hall while an even larger number of supporters stood outside in the rain. On the train between twenty stops for speeches, he received telegrams throughout the day quoting excerpts from the speeches that Taft was delivering and at each stop he answered Taft's charges and added some fresh complaints of his own. He continued the war of words and personalities, calling the President the handmaiden of corrupt leaders and lustily attacking "Mr. Taft's policy of flabby indecision and of helpless acquiescence in the wrongdoing of the crooked boss and crooked financier."

Reporters noted a change in his tone. Perhaps because he was being forced to answer a steady stream of charges being directed his way, Roosevelt's appearances lacked some of the bite and passion that had become his hallmark. "People seemed to expect something more sensational in the way of a speech than the colonel had to hand out, and he cooled rather than wakened their ardor," one reporter noted. Much of his time was spent answering Taft. By the time he finished, the crowd's response "wasn't the hero-worshiping which greeted him when he entered."

Late that night, both Taft and Roosevelt left the state, now truly bitter enemies but knowing that they had made their respective cases as well as possible and that the vote the next day could prove to be decisive.

WHEN THE RETURNS started to come in late Tuesday night, the Roosevelt camp was jubilant. "Massachusetts has ended what Illinois began," O'Laughlin wrote in the *Chicago Tribune*. "The victory of Col. Roosevelt in that state is conceded by Taft politicians to be the final blow to the president's candidacy." The paper's headline said, "Bay State Vote Taft Waterloo."

The Colonel's campaign headquarters issued the following statement: "The returns from Massachusetts show that without any question Mr. Taft's candidacy is at an end. At this hour, it looks as if Roosevelt has swept the state and will elect the eight delegates at large from 8,000 to 12,000 votes and will carry twenty-four or twenty-six of the twenty-eight delegates elected by congressional districts."

In Washington, D.C., Senator Dixon declared victory. "The result in Massachusetts settles the Taft candidacy beyond and to the exclusion of any doubt," he wrote. "Barometer readings of the sentiment of the Republican voters from the Atlantic to the Pacific coast tell one unbroken story. Wherever the Republican voters have been given an opportunity to express their sentiment, as in Massachusetts, Pennsylvania, Illinois, Nebraska, and Oregon, it has been one unbroken line of Roosevelt victories. . . . The Republican states of the North have spoken. Roosevelt will be nominated at Chicago on the first ballot and will be elected in November by the biggest majority ever given a political campaign."

At home in Oyster Bay, "The Colonel was almost too happy to talk," the *New York Times* reported. Shaking hands with friends and reporters, he called the result "the most astounding thing in American politics."

"If Mr. Taft had swept Massachusetts, he might have won the nomination by steam roller methods," Roosevelt said. "But without Massachusetts, he cannot win it even with the steam roller method."

When the candidates went to bed that night, it seemed certain that Roosevelt would be nominated by the Republican Party.

But the next morning, after all of his electoral setbacks, Taft could claim a miracle of his own.

Chapter Ten

At the dawn of the twentieth century, and in the first year of presidential primary voting, it was difficult to count votes on a primary election night. But in Massachusetts there was another phenomenon that is unique to presidential primaries and remains an issue in some states to this day. The ballot provided for both a preferential vote for President and for a separate vote for eight at-large delegates. When the dust finally cleared, in what one reporter called "a strange tangle in the primary result," the candidates learned that Taft had won the preferential vote for President by 3,655 votes, whereas the at-large delegates who favored TR had won by 8,245 votes. As a result, the eight at-large delegates were TR men even though a narrow majority of voters had expressed a preference for Taft.

In what seemed to be an unusually principled move for such a bitter campaign, the Colonel announced that he would instruct his at-large delegates to vote for Taft. The *Boston Globe* said that TR had taken "an entirely correct position" since "the preferential vote should control the delegation at large." An editorial by the pro-Roosevelt *Chicago Tribune* hailed the Colonel's position as "a consistent application of the principle he and his supporters are fighting for throughout the country," to "Let the people rule."

A day after declaring that Roosevelt was certain to be the party's nominee, Cal O'Laughlin told his readers that "the revised returns from Massachusetts place a different complexion on the Republican nomination situation. President Taft still remains in the running." For those keeping score, Roosevelt had won four primary victories (in Illinois, Pennsylvania, Oregon, and Nebraska); La Follette had won two (in North Dakota and Wisconsin); and Taft had won two (in New York and Massachusetts). Five primaries remained.

Four crucial primaries were scheduled for May, starting with Maryland with 16 delegates on May 6, followed by California with 26 delegates on May 14, then by Taft's home state of Ohio on May 21 with 48 delegates, and finally by New Jersey with 28 delegates on May 28. The final primary was set for June 4 when South Dakota's 10 delegates would be chosen.

In some respects, though, the most important battles were about to be waged in southern states like Louisiana, with 20 delegates, and Texas, with 40, which did not have primaries and never voted for Republican candidates for President. The fight for delegates from Texas would last all month, but the state's crucial precinct conventions were set for May 4; Louisiana's process was set to start on May 14. In both states, a large number of the precinct voters were federal employees or contractors and their friends and families who were interested in preserving their jobs or contracts and thus could be influenced by implicit or explicit threats and promises from the White House. On the other hand, they wanted to keep their jobs and contracts in the next administration, too, and therefore wanted to be sure to side with the likely party nominee. The stronger TR looked in the primaries, the more likely they were to support him instead of Taft.

For much of the campaign, some of Roosevelt's managers expected to win both states. In spite of the power of the incumbent, the challenger had important assets. In Texas, TR had the support of Cecil Lyon, heir to a lumber business, rancher, and longtime friend who had joined the President on a colorful expedition that Roosevelt described in "A Wolf Hunt in Oklahoma," published by *Scribner's Magazine* in

1905. In Louisiana, he had the backing of Pearl Wight, who "amassed a fortune in the South American fruit trade, shipbuilding, railroading and banking" after moving from Maine to New Orleans in 1866, during Reconstruction. Both men were Republican Party leaders and members of the National Committee who had served as the party's "referee" for both President Roosevelt and President Taft in selecting postmasters and doling out other federal patronage. As a result, they had tremendous leverage in selecting the delegates to national conventions.

They had something else in common. Both were leaders of the lily-white faction of the Republican Party in their states. For more than a decade, they had led the effort to exclude blacks from the voting rolls and from the Republican Party.

When it became clear that Roosevelt might win delegates in Texas and Louisiana, Taft's managers fought back with every tool at their disposal. In Texas, Taft named Houston businessman Henry Frederick MacGregor to replace Cecil Lyon as state party chair. MacGregor, who had been a member of the integrated "black and tan" faction of the party, immediately took charge, seeking to eliminate any lasting influence that Lyon might have. He told the postmasters, who all owed their jobs to the White House, to "take hold of the campaign at once and get Taft Republicans to the polls." One of his lieutenants told supporters to "organize your county, appoint precinct chairmen for the purpose of going into the convention when called and capture them [the conventions]. If you cannot capture them, withdraw and hold a convention and elect delegates to the County Convention, contesting the others, and from County Convention to State Convention on the same lines. Capture if you can, but do not be captured."

In Louisiana, Taft found ways to keep the support of the men he had appointed to office even though they had been recommended by Pearl Wight. He won the backing of the powerful sugar interests by threatening to eliminate the protective tariff on imported sugar if the sugar interests didn't support him.

"I have never had to fight the kind of opposition that has come up,"

Wight told Roosevelt's campaign manager; "first from the office hold-ers, every one of whom had been recommended by me for their place, next from the most powerful combination in the state fearing that the duties on sugar would be interfered with. . . . It makes the fight, at times, very disagreeable and sometimes depressing."

In both states, Roosevelt aligned his campaign with what were known as the "lily-white" factions of the party, while Taft, out of convic-tion or opportunism (or both), tried to rally the support of those few blacks who still had the power to participate in party affairs. Speaking for the Taft campaign, Charles Hilles told Booker T. Washington that "in Texas and Louisiana it is our action that has made it possible for the colored people to have representation and recognition. Cecil Lyon had eliminated the colored people from the Republican Party in Texas, and we are making a strong appeal to them. Pearl Wight had eliminated them from the Party in Louisiana, and it is because of the action of our friends in giving them proportionate recognition on the State commit-tee that we are having opposition in that state."

Taft seemed likely to get all or almost all of the delegates from both states before the Colonel crushed him in the Illinois and Pennsylvania primaries. Now his campaign faced a new reality. "Until the elections in Illinois and Pennsylvania, everything was coming our way fast," Taft's Texas state leader wrote Hilles. "The effect of these elections has been to make our situation more uncertain. The danger is that the postmasters and the machinery are so closely connected that if it looked like it was doubtful that [Taft] would receive the nomination, the effect would be of a negative character on the primaries and the county elections." But "if Massachusetts goes alright," he said, "I shall feel that we will make enough showing by May 4th, the date of our primaries, to get back to where we were."

Thanks to the Bay State primary and to hardball tactics that might not have seemed to suit his judicial character, Taft still had a good chance of securing the support of most of the delegates from the South. The Taft campaign came up with a particularly inventive approach in Mississippi, one that would bear fruit at the Chicago convention six weeks later. Their white state leaders, Postmaster Michael J. Mulvihill of Vicksburg and National Committeeman Lonzo B. Moseley of Jackson, were convinced that Roosevelt's supporters were trying to bribe some of the black delegates who were pledged to Taft. On April 27, Moseley and Mulvihill sent a memo to Hilles reporting that one of the black delegates "stated that the Roosevelt people have offered to pay the expense of his campaign for election as a delegate and his expenses at the State Convention, an amount that he estimates at slightly under four hundred dollars." Moseley and Mulvihill proposed that the Taft campaign use such offers to Taft's advantage throughout the South.

"The right persons in each State should advise separately each colored delegate to take any money that is offered by the Roosevelt people, report the fact immediately to his advisor, and then vote in the convention for the President," Moseley and Mulvihill wrote. "Heretofore it has been an ordinary occurrence for the Negro to sell his vote; but usually when he has sold it he has delivered the goods. The novelty of the present suggestion is that it opens a channel of confidence between the delegate and the head of the delegation which will result in keeping you posted as to what attempts are being made to seal the delegates by corruption, and it will check the delegate from delivering the vote he has sold." They said they were "convinced it is a situation you will have to face at Chicago, therefore all the information you can get in advance may not be amiss."

As one illustration of what they had in mind, the memo described a man named "A. Buckley, colored, poor man, editor of a little country paper; needs money but is a high class man . . . [who] might be one of the men that could be induced to take money from the opposition and still vote for the President."

The Moseley-Mulvihill strategy ultimately had an important impact at both the Republican National Convention in June and TR's Progressive Party Convention in August.

To solidify his flank in the former Confederate states, Taft left on what reporters called his "southern trip" on April 30, to reassure wavering delegates and to give speeches in Augusta and Savannah, Georgia. At the same time, his campaign hired detectives to follow Ormsby McHarg. They called McHarg "the official contest attorney" since he was organizing delegate challenges in as many southern states as possible. Suspecting that McHarg was using illegal means to achieve his goals, bribing delegates where needed, Taft's managers wanted to be able to expose his tactics at the national convention.

HAVING LOST IN Massachusetts, albeit narrowly, Roosevelt knew that he needed to win all of the other primaries. "The personal fight between Roosevelt and Taft is now transferred to Maryland," the *New York Times* reported.

Before TR announced his candidacy on February 25, a Democratic state senator named Frank Harper had introduced a bill to create a primary in Maryland. His bill, in the words of the *Baltimore Sun*, was "sleeping in the Senate Committee on Elections where it has been reposing for several weeks." With a La Follette–Taft fight looming, and the possibility of Roosevelt entering as well, the *Sun* reported, "Democrats are rallying to support the bill" because they expected the "primary fight to be far more bitter among Republicans than Democrats." In contrast, the Republicans in the Maryland Senate were in Taft's corner and opposed Harper's bill—until TR formally entered the race. Starting in early March, Roosevelt's forces led an aggressive campaign to adopt a primary.

When the Taft campaign finally accepted Harper's legislation in late March, Roosevelt's supporters hailed it as another great victory. "Maryland has followed the example of Illinois and has provided presidential preference primaries for the pending campaign," O'Laughlin triumphantly told readers of the *Chicago Tribune*. "Thus the movement to permit voters directly to name the candidate they desire as the nominee of their party is spreading to all parts of the country."

TR spent Friday and Saturday campaigning in Maryland, on a whirl-
wind tour that included a major speech and outdoor rally at the Lyric
Theatre in Baltimore on Friday night where 500 young supporters carried torches that illuminated the stage. He was in top form, attacking
Taft as the tool of the bosses, loved only by corrupt or self-interested
federal officeholders.

"I ask you, the people of Maryland, to speak at the primaries on Monday so that the boss and the great sinister influence which lies behind
the boss shall realize that there is another state where the people rule
themselves," he thundered to tumultuous applause. "This fight has
just begun." He concluded his campaigning in Maryland the following
night with what the press called "a monster mass meeting" in Cumber-
land, where he was "at his best, the lecturer, special pleader, preacher
and fiery denunciator."

But the Taft campaign was giving no ground. Convinced that his
speeches in Massachusetts had helped him win his narrow victory,
they arranged for the President to spend a full day campaigning
in Maryland on Saturday, May 4, where he could speak to crowds
around the state and "reply to any new attacks" by Roosevelt. With
Roosevelt still in the state, Saturday became what the *New York
Times* described as "an exhibition of National politics such as it has
never seen before."

All day the men slugged it out in speeches across the state, landing blows in each appearance. At every stop, Taft accused Roosevelt of
hypocrisy and of caving in to pressure from George Perkins and J. P.
Morgan in the International Harvester case. Meanwhile, his surrogates
went after Roosevelt with every unsavory argument that they could
find, even claiming that TR had undermined the work of the Food and
Drug Administration.

"I am a man of peace," Taft shouted at Hyattsville, "and I don't want
to fight. But when I do fight, I hit hard." And then in an unfortunate
turn of phrase, he added: "Even a rat in a corner will fight." Roosevelt-
leaning political cartoonists had a field day with that remark.

BY THE TIME the candidates left the state, observers considered the outcome too close to call. To some experts, it appeared that the black vote could be decisive, since it represented almost 35 percent of the registered voters in the state. In some counties, blacks accounted for more than half of the eligible electorate. "Much Depends on Negro Vote," the *Baltimore Sun* intoned. In some of the state's southern and eastern counties, blacks were likely to constitute a majority of the Republican vote. In Caroline County, the *Sun* reported, "the fight revolves around negro preachers who are evangelizing the county for Taft and Roosevelt."

For some months, Dixon had known that the black vote could be the key to victory in several states. He listed Kansas, New York, Massachusetts, and Maryland as "pivotal states" where the "negro vote holds the balance of power," noting that Republicans typically could count on blacks to deliver "23,000 votes in Ohio, 15,000 in Indiana, 22,000 in Illinois, 48,000 in Maryland, 13,000 in West Virginia, 13,000 in New Jersey, 28,000 in New York, 34,000 in Missouri, and 6,000 in Delaware."

The stakes for black voters in Maryland were particularly high. If Dixon's numbers were correct, there were more black voters in Maryland than in any other state. For several years, some leaders of the Democratic Party had been attempting to create Jim Crow laws that would disenfranchise blacks in Maryland in the same way that they had been disenfranchised elsewhere in the South. While he had been resoundingly criticized for failing to appoint black officeholders in the South, Taft had been a steadfast opponent of efforts to change Maryland's election law. When changes in the law were proposed in 1908 and 1909, Taft condemned them as "vicious," a "gross injustice," and "a violation of the spirit of the 15th Amendment." Noting these statements, the pro-Taft, black-owned *Chicago Defender* argued that "as long as William Howard Taft is president, no law will be spread in the federal statute books curtailing the rights and privileges" of black voters.

Roosevelt courted black voters, too. After his speech to "a Lily-White affair" at the Lyric Theatre on Friday night, Roosevelt spoke at the Metropolitan Methodist Episcopal Church. He told the black crowd that all white men should live by the golden rule and should try to make all of their fellow citizens "prosperous, happy and law-abiding."

TR had a special request for his audience.

"I want to enlist your support to prevent any bribery at the polls next Monday. There is reason to believe that unscrupulous white men will try to bribe you in the interest of our opponent. If there is such a thing as putting in the penitentiary such white men, I will do all I can to help. If I find any man attempting to bribe on my side, I will put him in the penitentiary just as quick as anyone else." His comments may have been sincere, but they proved ironic if not hypocritical in view of events to come.

Money flooded into the state on both sides for turn-out-the-vote efforts on Election Day, by some estimates as much as $30,000 for Baltimore alone. (That sum would be worth about $750,000 today.)

As the votes were still being counted, Taft's campaign issued a statement accusing the former President of buying votes.

"In Prince George's County," they said, "Roosevelt money in large amounts was poured into the county. Large rolls of small bills, accompanied by checks to be used if needed, were sent out from Washington on Sunday, a well-known leader in the district having voluntarily exhibited such a roll in Washington Sunday afternoon."

TR's supporters issued an immediate response: "Every one of these statements is a deliberate, willful lie."

When the returns came in late Monday night, Roosevelt swept Baltimore with the kind of enthusiastic landslide that he had achieved in Illinois and Pennsylvania. But by winning the vote in every county on the state's Eastern Shore, Taft seemed to have pulled even or perhaps slightly ahead. Under Maryland's primary law, which Taft's supporters claimed would work to their advantage, voters elected delegates from each county and sent them to a state convention. Delegates were required to vote for the presidential candidate who won the most votes in the county.

The early returns were a tie. The morning papers on May 7 gave each candidate 63 delegates. The outcome would come down to the result in tiny Howard County, which had three delegates.

In his autobiography, Roosevelt's press spokesman, O. K. Davis, describes what happened next.

According to Davis, TR's Maryland state chairman did not think Howard County was important. It had only three votes and blacks were dominant. But two young black men visited national campaign manager Joseph Dixon and asked for the chance to create an all-black slate and to organize the district. The black delegates said they were for TR "because he is more favorable to the colored race." Dixon gave them a little money and they reported directly to him.

On the eve of the vote, the *Baltimore Sun* said that "it looks as if the Taft delegates will carry Howard County." But the paper noted that there could be an upset since "the negroes will support Roosevelt and three negroes are named as delegates [on Roosevelt's slate]."

As the votes from the counties on the Eastern Shore came in, and "one county after another kept reporting for Taft," Davis recalled, Dixon was so dejected that he went into his private office, lay down, and refused to see anyone. It seemed that TR had been defeated again. After losing Massachusetts, he could not afford to be rejected by the voters in Maryland.

But when the results from Howard County finally came in, it turned out that the white farmers in the rural district hadn't voted. The *Sun* called it "a victory for the colored Republicans over the White Republicans." Despite frantic efforts to get them to the polls, most of the white electorate spent the day planting corn. Of those who voted in Howard County, 75 percent were black. TR carried the county by 80 votes. Thanks to a few young blacks who took the initiative in a rural county, Roosevelt had won Maryland by a razor-thin margin.

But there was a caveat. While the new state law required that all 16 of the state's votes go to the winning candidate on the first ballot, the delegates themselves would be free to vote as they pleased on every other issue facing the convention. Taft's campaign managers had shrewdly managed to place many of their own men in the state's delegation to Chicago. They immediately predicted that while they would vote for TR's nomination as required by the new law, at least 8 of Maryland's delegates would be with Taft on other crucial issues, such as credential challenges and the selection of the chair of the convention.

THE BIGGEST PRIZE in the West was California, which would send 26 delegates to the convention. Thanks to the triumph of progressives during the previous two years, it had also become a national symbol, the hotbed of new progressive thought, led by Hiram Johnson. A reform-minded governor elected in 1910, Johnson had successfully championed a series of reforms in 1911 that included the initiative, referendum, and recall, as well as women's suffrage.

In some respects, the progressive movement's hold on the state still seemed fragile. For decades the Southern Pacific Railroad and its vaunted Political Bureau had dominated California's politics. With vast resources at its disposal, one historian explained, the Southern Pacific Railroad Political Bureau's "sole raison d'etre was to ensure that the company would not have to pay its share of the tax burden, would escape state and local regulation, and could expand its system unhampered by outside influence." Partly to challenge the railroad's power, a statewide group of reformers, including many leaders of smaller businesses, professionals, and journalists formed the Lincoln-Roosevelt League. Reform forces won a major victory by electing the mayor and City Council of Los Angeles on December 7, 1909. "We have met the enemy and they are ours," one leading California reformer wrote Senator La Follette after the election that December. "We put the Southern Pacific push to rout—horse foot and dragoons."

Thanks to a series of spectacular graft trials that implicated much of the city's political leadership, reformers were making national head-lines for their work in San Francisco. At first the trials were handled by Francis J. Heney. A true son of the wild west, Heney had killed a man in self-defense in Arizona Territory. He was a lawyer who gained national fame when Theodore Roosevelt's attorney general brought him on board as a special prosecutor in a series of corruption and bribery cases known as the Oregon Land Fraud Trials. Speculators and timber companies had illegally obtained large portions of the public land with the assistance of public officials. Heney and his team indicted most of Oregon's congressional delegation, including a Republican senator who had represented Oregon for over twenty years.

In 1906, with TR's approval, Heney moved to San Francisco as a special prosecutor in charge of a series of headline-grabbing cases against leaders of the business and political establishment who had been charged with public corruption. On November 13, 1907, during a recess in the court proceedings, a prospective juror shot Heney in the head. The wounds were so serious that papers ran premature obituar-ies praising him for his work and his martyrdom. With Heney in the hospital, Hiram Johnson, one of the other prosecutors, took over his cases. Johnson quickly proved to be every bit as colorful and effective as Heney.

Looking for someone to run for governor, the Lincoln-Roosevelt League considered Heney, who had recovered from his wounds. But as Johnson's biographer notes, Heney's "ruthless conduct of the graft prosecution revealed explosive capacities" that led many to consider him "a little too radical for the good of the movement." So they turned to Johnson, who proved to be an exceptionally able and colorful cam-paigner and an effective orator who stuck to a single indelible slogan: "Kick the Southern Pacific out of politics." Ringing a cowbell for atten-tion, Johnson campaigned throughout the state, including in rural areas where large farmers and ranchers were furious about what they deemed exorbitant freight rates.

As soon as he was elected, Johnson announced that he had an agenda that extended far beyond railroad rates. "In some form or another," he said in his Inaugural Address, "nearly every government problem that involves the health and happiness or the prosperity of the State has arisen because some private interest has intervened or has sought for its own gain to exploit either the resources or the politics of the state." During his first year in office, he successfully championed most of the progressive agenda, including laws controlling railroad rates, establishing an eight-hour day for women, providing protection for child laborers, and establishing employer liability and workers' compensation. He created a Conservation Commission to suggest steps the state should take to protect its resources and, most notably, championed landmark laws designed, in his words, to "return the government to the people" such as the initiative, referendum, and recall.

Overnight, Hiram Johnson became the progressive movement's West Coast darling, and California became a model for the nation.

THE STATE REPRESENTED a particularly tempting target for TR's campaign for another reason. Even though the "Call" of the convention that was adopted by the Republican National Committee on December 12, 1911, required each state to select two delegates in each congressional district as well as a few through a statewide process, California had drafted a law that allowed all delegates to be selected in a novel winner-take-all statewide primary.

Due to what Hiram Johnson called a "bug" inserted in the party rules by the old machine, as a practical matter he had the power to select the entire delegation by himself. But since he and his allies were so deeply committed to popular democracy, he backed the legislation calling for a primary; and he did so with the blessings of Roosevelt, who was not yet a candidate.

As an excellent lawyer, however, Johnson worried that the proposed winner-take-all primary system might present problems. Since TR was not yet in the race, he directed his question to the campaign of Robert La Follette, the progressive candidate that he expected to support.

"The preferential primary law about to be passed by our legislature contemplates election of all delegates to National Convention at large," he wired La Follette's campaign manager on December 13. "Under the Call issued by National Committee would this prevent seating of our delegates?"

Later that day, he sent a similar message to La Follette himself. "This morning at conference of progressives' sentiment was unanimous not to change our law, notwithstanding yesterday's Call of National Committee," he said. "Will the Call prevent seating our delegates in case of success?"

The state's decision to ignore the Call of the Convention was to prove fateful in the months ahead.

When the state adopted the winner-take-all primary in mid-December, Johnson was supporting La Follette. A few weeks later, once he learned that TR planned to run, he switched his loyalty to Roosevelt. The internal battle among the state's progressive forces quickly became incredibly complex and troubling, as George Mowry explained in *The California Progressives*.

Hiram Johnson and two of his California colleagues—William Kent and Francis Heney—had been in La Follette's living room in January 1911, where they had helped him to found the National Progressive Republican League. Many of the California progressives signed on with La Follette when he announced his candidacy that summer, but Johnson kept waiting, pleading with the Colonel to run. Much as he admired La Follette (who, unlike the Colonel, had publicly supported his candidacy a year earlier), he doubted that La Follette could defeat Taft. But Roosevelt continued to resist, saying that he was certain that he would be defeated. "I would not feel that I had a right to object to being sacrificed if it were necessary to sacrifice me," TR told Johnson on October 27. "But I do feel very strongly that I ought not to be asked to cut my own throat." Reluctantly, and with severe doubts, Johnson joined his fellow reformers and signed on to the La Follette campaign.

In mid-January, Johnson was presented with a dilemma when TR told him that he was beginning to reconsider. While composing letters to some friendly governors asking them to "draft" him, Roosevelt asked Johnson to "come East to consult on the political situation." The men had lunch on February 2. Believing that La Follette's was a lost cause, Johnson started to conspire with Roosevelt while ostensibly backing La Follette. He wired his closest progressive friends that TR was planning to be an active candidate.

When La Follette imploded at the magazine publishers' dinner that same night, it offered Johnson an excuse to change his allegiance. But by then he had a new set of concerns: Roosevelt had started to listen to too many conservatives. He "did not like the people who were heading the new movement," Mowry wrote. "They were not his kind of people." Roosevelt regained Johnson's confidence later that month with his controversial speech in Columbus, Ohio, calling for the recall of judicial decisions.

Not all of the California reformers were prepared to abandon La Follette. Many still believed in "Fighting Bob" and didn't trust TR. Feelings were so intense that Johnson started to engage in a correspondence that, in Mowry's words, "took on the air of the best international spy novels. Messages were broken in half and each part sent in code." He was eager to declare himself, Mowry wrote, but "reluctant to initiate California's swing to Roosevelt."

When Johnson finally declared for TR on February 19, just before Roosevelt's public announcement, he did not carry all of the state's progressives with him. Johnson told Congressman Will Kent, who planned to stay with La Follette, that he was "taking the wrong road to martyrdom." Nor did he convince E. W. Scripps, whose reformist newspapers were an important force in the state. Scripps was furious when Johnson switched allegiance. "I will hardly be able to forgive Governor Johnson," he wrote to one of his reporters.

Scripps considered TR "half a loaf." "I am inclined to believe that the majority of the people would rather have a sick La Follette for a leader than a robust Roosevelt."

Roosevelt's progressive allies tried to win his support, but Scripps was intransigent and La Follette refused to give up. After winning the primaries in North Dakota on March 19 and Wisconsin on April 2, La Follette decided to plant his flag in California. He made plans to be there for almost a full month, from April 19 until the election on May 14, practically moving to the state. With the support of the Scripps papers and some reformers, he may have thought that he had a chance of winning. Others had a darker view of his motives.

Whether paranoid or insightful, Johnson became convinced that the La Follette and Taft forces were colluding, "We have discovered that in some instances La Follette's petitions were circulated by Taft men, and paid for with Taft money," he told one friend. Taft certainly expected that La Follette's presence in the race would hurt Roosevelt. La Follette may have hoped that Taft would win or he may have thought that Taft and TR would split the vote, offering him a chance to squeak through.

Taft had the support of the conservative establishment, including several newspapers. In a three-way race, anything could happen—particularly with the unpredictable effect of women who could vote in California for the first time.

Johnson saw enemies everywhere. He called California "the scene of the bitterest fight in the union today, made so by La Follette." He wired Dixon at TR's headquarters that La Follette "is coming to California with the avowed purpose of destroying what the progressives have done and taking the state from us and . . . insists that we are all traitors and have sold out to the interests and that all of those who have left him are scoundrels and thieves."

"We have a much more difficult fight in California than I anticipated," he told one of his friends. "I don't like the situation . . . [because of] the division among our own people." The press was claiming that "every man who left La Follette [for Roosevelt] was bought by the interests, particularly by the Steel Trust."

"There is in the state, I find, considerable sympathy for La Follette," Johnson complained. His adherents are saying that "he was deserted in his time of need by those who should have stood by him; that Roosevelt stabbed him in the back; that he alone had made the struggle; and that Roosevelt is seeking at the last moment to reap the benefit."

"The old machine, which we whipped, has never been dead," he told O'Laughlin. "Every crooked newspaper in the State, and, unfortunately, there are many of them, is playing up La Follette and saying that he was 'stabbed in the back' and 'deserted when on a sick bed.'"

"The result," he wrote, "is very uncertain."

Johnson was as concerned about the primary's impact on the reform movement that he was leading in California as about what it would mean for TR. "Every rat in the state, should we be defeated in the coming presidential preference primary, will be out of his hole," he wrote. If Taft's supporters were to win the primary, he feared that they would then have the power "to undo what we have done in this state."

Meanwhile, La Follette and his surrogate campaigners were making their case everywhere. Speaking in the Bay Area on May 8, one of his law partners called Roosevelt an "artful dodger." He pointed out that La Follette, unlike TR, had been an early supporter of women's suffrage. He quoted from an article by TR which said that "where women do not want the vote, it should not be forced upon them," and which called the suffrage movement "much less important than many other reforms." He also quoted from speeches and articles in which TR had opposed the creation of direct presidential primaries and that showed that TR had been inconsistent on hot issues such as the tariff.

On the same day, another La Follette surrogate pointed out that TR had opposed putting a provision for the recall of elected officers into the state constitution in Arizona but favored it in California.

Unlike "Fighting Bob," La Follette's surrogates charged, Roosevelt could not be trusted.

When voters went to the polls in California on May 14, Johnson remained far from confident. But the election turned out to be a triumph. Roosevelt carried the statewide election by a landslide with a margin of more than 75,000 votes, giving him all of the delegates in the statewide, winner-take-all primary. With 18 percent of the vote, La Follette came in a distant third.

Taft won only one congressional district in California. But that district would be a source of continuing controversy, since the state's winner-take-all primary violated the Call of the Republican National Committee, which required that delegates be selected by congressional district.

Chapter Eleven

B y mid-May, most of Roosevelt's supporters were confident that he would win the nomination and the election. His overwhelming victory in California on May 14 seemed to make victory inevitable. In a telegram congratulating Governor Johnson for his "magnificent victory," Frank Munsey, who was devoting the resources of his publishing company as well as his own considerable bank account to the effort, said that "TR now has enough votes to be sure of the nomination." Telegrams and letters from friends, flatterers, idealists, and hard-nosed politicians flooded into his office and his home in Oyster Bay proclaiming that the fight had been won.

Overnight, the advent of primaries had changed politics—seemingly forever. "The Roosevelt candidacy has more than justified itself already in the impetus which he has given to the demand for the direct primary as a means of selecting presidential delegates," one noted reformer wrote in an analysis that proved to be a bit too optimistic. "He has put the finishing blow to the old convention system as we know it."

In that first year of political primaries, in the intoxicating aftermath of California, it seemed for a moment that the popular will would be forceful enough to overcome the power of conventional leaders, of the officeholders and "party bosses." That theory was soon put to the test.

Roosevelt proclaimed that he now had almost enough votes to win.

Based on the news from California, he announced that he already had 501 of the 540 delegates needed to win on the first ballot. Members of his inner circle were glowing. "Things are looking very good," one of TR's assistants told Frank Knox. "If Ohio and New Jersey follow the excellent lead of California, the Taft people will be literally wiped off the political landscape."

Taft's managers disputed the numbers, saying that TR had only 309 delegates and that Taft already had 520. They called Roosevelt's claim "ludicrous," pointing out that his own campaign manager only claimed to have 419 delegates. The truth was probably somewhere in between, but Roosevelt had good reason to believe his own propaganda. He had rekindled the imagination and reclaimed the support of millions of voters. After his triumph in California, the Ohio primary, to be held a week later, took on special significance. Taft imprudently told reporters that "the vote in Ohio, my home state, much to my gratification, will be the decisive one and will settle the question of the nomination."

Taft's prediction proved to be far off the mark. On May 21, 1912, TR won Ohio easily, carrying 32 of the state's 42 district delegates. Even if Taft could win the nomination without Ohio, as he assured his friends, the Buckeye State's results were humiliating. A headline in the *New York Times* captured the mood in the President's camp. "Taft Men in Gloom: Ohio Result Revives Talk of Compromise Candidate."

Talk of a compromise candidate was, indeed, in the air. Neither Roosevelt nor his leading supporters, however, had any interest in anointing someone else. Why should they? He was the popular choice of the Republican electorate. He, not some theoretical compromise candidate, had won the primaries. What would it say about the people's right to rule if the party handed the nomination to someone who had not campaigned in any states or won any primaries?

What's more, after California and Ohio, the campaign was on a roll. Roosevelt's team had every reason to think that he would win the remaining primaries in New Jersey and South Dakota as well.

To those caught up in the excitement of the democratic cause, TR's selection now seemed both right and inevitable. In speech after speech, Roosevelt used the same line, always earning cheers from the crowd.

"Some of our opponents are saying that neither Mr. Taft nor myself should be nominated at Chicago," he roared. "I will name the compromise candidate: he will be myself."

After Ohio, Roosevelt's campaign manager told the press that the campaign for the nomination was over.

"There is no further room for doubt," Joseph Dixon told reporters. "On last Thursday at Cleveland, Mr. Taft in his speech said: 'The vote in Ohio, my home state, will be the decisive one and will settle the question of the nomination.' Ohio has spoken. . . . Roosevelt will be re-nominated on the first ballot at Chicago and elected in November by the biggest majority ever given a presidential candidate. This is the end of the contest."

The Colonel's supporters around the country were convinced that the battle was over. After reading about the Ohio results, Governor Stubbs told Roosevelt, "It was the greatest victory of them all and I think settles the contest."

For months there had been rumors that Roosevelt's supporters would leave the convention and start a third party. Campaigning in Ohio, Taft made such charges a part of his stump speech. "The arrogance of his statement that he is the Republican Party finds no parallel in history," Taft joked, "save in the famous words of Louis XIV who said "The State: I am it." But after Ohio, there were reports, perhaps planted by Roosevelt's allies, that some of Taft's supporters were so sure of, and so concerned about, a Roosevelt victory at the convention that they were considering forming a third party themselves. The *New York Times* said that Senator Elihu Root was talking to Senate colleagues about the advisability of such an option.

Publicly, TR proclaimed that his nomination was now inevitable. After going through several hundred telegrams, he happily told the press that "the result in Ohio has settled the contest."

Adding to the appearance of inevitability, he swept the New Jersey primary on May 28, winning all of the state's 28 delegates, and he then won all of South Dakota's 10 delegates in a primary on June 4, the last day of the preconvention season. After New Jersey, Roosevelt's friends told him that Taft's supporters were in "a pitiable state of 'blue funk'" and getting ready to desert the Taft ship. Progressive leaders had become convinced that there would be what they called "a complete surrender."

"The fight is won," Cal O'Laughlin wired TR. "It is an overwhelming victory for the people and I congratulate them as well as you."

Unlike many of his supporters, however, Roosevelt was a seasoned politician who knew that only a minority, albeit a fairly large minority, of the delegates had been chosen in primaries. He knew the power of the forces arrayed against him. In some respects, the battle for the nomination had only begun.

"How soon after you get the nomination do you expect to begin campaigning?" someone asked him after his triumph in New Jersey.

Roosevelt "made a comical grimace and shook his fist in mock severity at his interrogator."

"In the course of long experience as a hunter," Roosevelt said, "I have learned never to divide the bearskin until the bear is dead."

And as Roosevelt's supporters would soon learn: even after losing most of the primaries, Taft was far from dead.

THE *NEW YORK TRIBUNE*, long a major force in the Republican Party, and an editorial supporter of Taft, provided what may have been the most reliable count of the candidates' delegate strength. During May, it reported a remarkable increase in delegates pledged to Roosevelt, while Taft was only inching ahead. When the month started, Taft had a huge lead. By early June, his lead had evaporated.

On May 5, just after the Massachusetts primary, the *Tribune* said that Taft had 410 delegates to Roosevelt's 251.

On May 12, after the Maryland primary, the *Tribune* estimated that Taft had 418 delegates while TR had 297. It listed 36 for La Follette, 10 for Iowa senator Albert B. Cummins who was running as a favorite son with support from many of his home-state delegates, and 39 as uncommitted or unassigned.

A week later, on May 19, after the California primary, and counting delegates from Minnesota and North Carolina, the *Tribune* reported that 425 delegates were reliably for Taft and 397 for Roosevelt—a jump of 100 delegates in one week for the challenger. The *Tribune* still counted 36 for La Follette and 10 for Senator Cummins, but the paper put another 40 of the delegates chosen during the previous week in an "unassigned" column since there were competing slates from Washington State, with 14 delegates, and from large parts of Texas and Arkansas. During the next few weeks, those unassigned delegates would become crucial.

At the end of May, following the vote in Ohio, the *Tribune* said the race had become a virtual tie with 435 for Taft and 430 for Roosevelt.

On June 2, following the New Jersey primary, the *Tribune* said that Roosevelt was ahead with 458 delegates compared with 439 for Taft. But by then there were 110 "unassigned" delegates. As long as he could control the convention machinery, the *Tribune* concluded, Taft would be awarded most or all of those contests and so win the nomination.

In the final tabulation before the convention, after Roosevelt won all 10 delegates in the June 4 primary in South Dakota, the *Tribune* noted that TR was ahead 469 to 454. During the month following the Massachusetts primary, by the *Tribune's* count, Taft had picked up 44 delegates while Roosevelt had added 218. It was easy to understand why Roosevelt's supporters were jubilant.

Still, the *Tribune* predicted that Taft would win the nomination, albeit narrowly. It expected Taft to be awarded 85 of the 106 slots that by their analysis remained unassigned or uncommitted, places where there were serious challenges. If correct, that would give the President 539 delegates on the first ballot—exactly one short of the number needed. There were still 36 delegates pledged to La Follette and 10 pledged to Senator Cummins. Assuming that he could pick up all of the 21 unassigned delegates that the *Tribune*'s analysis was not awarding to Taft, TR would go to the convention with a realistic hope of having 490 delegates, leaving him 50 delegates short of the number needed for the nomination.

Looking at those figures, TR knew that he needed to pick up at least 50 and possibly as many as 70 delegates to get the nomination. It had become clear that the fight in the national committee—which was to start deliberations that same day—would be decisive.

ON JUNE 5, 1912, the attention of political observers turned to Chicago. The campaign managers for both candidates arrived in town to start preparing for the convention and preconvention skirmishes. East Coast leaders traveled west by train on a special car attached to the Twentieth Century Limited; reporters dubbed it the "Harmony Special," with space divided between supporters of each candidate. The campaigns also established headquarters in the same hotel, the Congress, with Joseph Dixon managing the effort for Roosevelt and Taft's managed by Illinois congressman William B. McKinley, who was not related to the late president. Many of their key operatives who arrived that week were those who would be responsible for making the case for the delegates whose credentials were still contested, including those delegates the *Tribune* was calling "unassigned." Charles Dix of Ohio would take the lead for Taft and Ormsby McHarg of New York for Roosevelt.

When TR's campaign team arrived at the hotel from the train, a dozen local supporters greeted them by singing a parody of a song of the era called "They Gotta Quit Kickin' My Dawg Around," with the words: "You bet they ain't a-kickin' Teddy's dawg around."

For a time, Roosevelt's managers believed that they would be able to control the national committee. After all, many of the members had supported him only four years earlier. In April, William L. Ward, the national committeeman from New York, told friends that he was "traveling around the country rounding up other national committeemen for the Colonel." According to an account in the pro-Roosevelt *North*

American newspaper of Philadelphia, Ward was confident that he could get 29 of the 53 national committee members to support Roosevelt—or at least to oppose Taft. With control of the committee, Ward expected to be able to have a friendly political leader selected as the temporary chair of the convention. The temporary chair would then name the Credentials Committee, and the Credentials Committee would vote favorably on Roosevelt's delegate challenges.

As one Roosevelt supporter explained, "Taft loses and Roosevelt wins by virtue of the anti-Taft majority in the National Committee."

Presumably, this was a strategy that Ward and Ormsby McHarg were pursuing in mid-March, at the time of the all-night session where Ward prevented George Perkins from removing McHarg from the campaign. "You will observe," the source told the *North American*, "that the same man who had charge of the fight for the seating of Taft delegates in the convention of 1908 will make the same fight for Roosevelt this year. That's Ormsby McHarg."

As a means of controlling the convention, Ward's plan made sense. The national committee would select the temporary chair of the convention who, in turn, would select the Credentials Committee. The national committee would also make the first round of decisions about the delegate challenges. The Credentials Committee might simply decide to adopt its recommendations. In addition, the temporary chair would preside at the convention until a permanent chair was elected. If the contest proved to be close, the candidate who controlled the national committee could very well be able to determine the outcome of the battle.

But Ward's strategy, in fact, had failed. He had not been able to convince enough committee members to go his way. Taft, not Roosevelt, had a majority of the committee members, and a decisive majority at that.

The battle for control of the convention quickly became a toxic brew of public appeals, name-calling, legal strategy, backstage intrigue, political maneuvering, threats, and bribery. The primaries and state convention phase of the nominating process was over and, as Cal O'Laughlin told his readers on June 6, "The fight has now reached a point where political strategy and manipulation is expected to count." When it came to political strategy and manipulation, it was soon evident that in addition to having a majority of members on the national committee, Taft's forces were tougher and more experienced. Their ranks were filled with veterans who knew the rules and knew how to make backroom deals. Roosevelt had some seasoned and cynical veterans like Ward and McHarg, but they were outvoted and outmaneuvered. On both a personal and professional level, he deeply missed having the support of old friends and political veterans like Elihu Root, Henry Stimson, and Henry Cabot Lodge.

With the RNC's first vote, Taft's supporters demonstrated that they controlled 38 of the national committee's 53 members, thus putting Roosevelt's men in what one headline called "A Hopeless Minority." The vote, on an attempt to increase press access to the proceedings, showed where the committeemen stood. It also proved that delegates who were obliged to cast their ballots for Roosevelt from some states where he had won the primary, including Illinois and Maryland, would support Taft on a range of procedural issues.

Cal O'Laughlin provided a daily chronicle of the proceedings. By now he was wearing three hats. He was the *Chicago Tribune*'s chief political reporter; a close TR ally, supporter, and operative; and, at the convention, he attended and participated in some of the meetings of the Republican National Committee with a proxy from Sidney Bieber of the District of Columbia. Since the convention was in Chicago, O'Laughlin could be sure that everyone of importance would read his stories, which regularly appeared on page 1 of the *Chicago Tribune*.

His story on June 7 described the situation as seen from the inside of the Roosevelt camp. "The first step to overturn the rule of the people through the wiles of the politicians was taken by the Taft forces at the meeting of the Republican national committee in the Coliseum yesterday," he wrote. "Politics was played by master hands at the game, and every point that could be scored was scored heavily."

In a crucial early decision, Victor Rosewater, a Taft ally, was selected to head the national committee, with all of the power that came with the job. Rosewater, the editor of the *Omaha Bee* and a founder of the American Jewish Committee, was already the acting chair of the national committee, but for a moment it seemed that he might be displaced. He had been defeated for reelection to the national committee in the Nebraska primary a few weeks earlier by an insurgent named Robert Beecher Howell. Howell claimed that he and not Rosewater should represent Nebraska on the committee during the convention. His claim had a certain logic for those who felt that the convention should represent the popular will. But party rules as well as sheer political power were against him. Under the existing rules, Rosewater's term was scheduled to continue until the end of the convention. Howell's challenge never even came up for a vote.

THE WARD-MCHARG STRATEGY failed in other respects, too. The Roosevelt campaign had filed challenges to 254 of the seats assigned to Taft. Many of those challenges, particularly those filed in the South by McHarg, were widely believed to be bogus. They were so frivolous that the *Tribune* did not count them as "unassigned" in their totals. As McHarg told a congressional committee a year later, he arranged for local lawyers to file challenges to some 200 delegates, whether the challenge had merit or not. After all, there was always something to protest. As soon as a state held its primary or convention, McHarg would cry "fraud."

McHarg had a political strategy. As Rosewater explained in his memoir, the Taft managers wanted to roll up as many delegates as possible early in the year, particularly those in the South, before Roosevelt had a chance to organize his campaign. McHarg wanted to block the force of that strategy. Whatever the merits of the challenges, McHarg hoped they would bolster the spirits of supporters around the country; slow down Taft's early march toward the nomination; and, at the very least, create some confusion with the press and the public about the number of delegates firmly committed to Taft. At first that strategy may have made sense, but by the time of the convention it had clearly backfired; it had come to resemble the famed parable of the boy who cried wolf. Even Cal O'Laughlin told his *Chicago Tribune* readers that "the contests against the Taft delegates have been largely technical or without justification" and "should have been decided in favor of the Taft forces."

McHarg's worthless challenges had the effect of calling into question the more legitimate claims being made by other challengers. After spending several days looking into all of the cases, the Taft-controlled national committee ultimately and unsurprisingly voted to seat virtually all of the delegates pledged to the President. McHarg then said that the real fight would be in the Credentials Committee, but to many observers that goal seemed unrealistic, partly because of his own hodgepodge of challenges.

"There is not the slightest chance that the committee on credentials, which has been composed in large part of the very men whom McHarg has tried to browbeat and who assert that he has grossly insulted them, will reverse the action of the national committee," the *New York Tribune* said. "That is the reason the Roosevelt leaders are so dejected." In some conventions, the Credentials Committee can prove to be decisive. But in 1912, with Taft's forces in full control, the Credentials Committee held only one day of meetings, at which it decided to ratify all of the national committee's decisions.

George Perkins, who had never liked McHarg and had tried to have him removed from the campaign months earlier, was among TR's dejected—and angry—leaders. He sent a scathing note to the Colonel.

"As I have repeatedly said, we cannot overestimate the damage that McHarg has done the cause, and the Committee is very much incensed," Perkins wrote. "He has put our own people in the position where they were honor bound to vote against cases that the public had been given to understand were going to be good cases." If this continues, "I think the result will be exceedingly unhappy from every point of view—the least of which will be the very unfortunate impression built up in the public mind."

One major newspaper called McHarg's credentials challenges "too preposterous for consideration by anybody outside an insane asylum." McHarg's frivolous challenges were calling every other case into question.

ULTIMATELY, THE ROOSEVELT campaign decided to contest 72 delegates. Over the years there has been speculation about how and why the campaign settled on that number. One possible answer was supplied by Nicholas Murray Butler, the president of Columbia University and a strong Taft supporter. Butler claimed that he ran into TR's convention floor manager, Governor Hadley of Missouri, on a train to Boston about a year after the convention and asked, "How did you arrive at that precise number?"

"I will tell you how that came about," Hadley said. "After the National Committee adjourned, some of us made up our minds that there were twenty-eight seats which should have gone to Roosevelt delegates." Hadley was chosen to present their conclusion to the Colonel.

"Twenty-eight!" Roosevelt exploded. "Twenty-eight! Why if you got the whole lot it wouldn't change the result or give you control of the convention. You must make it at least a hundred. Contest at least a hundred seats."

According to Butler's account, Hadley laughed as he concluded his story. He couldn't find 100 seats to contest, but he thought he could make a colorable case for 72.

Some scholars have concluded that TR had a strong argument in cases involving 30 to 50 delegates. If he could win 50 contested delegates, he might still need up to an additional 20 to go over the top. TR hoped that he could either convince some delegates to change sides or, despite the bad blood between the two progressive candidates, win the support of some of the 36 delegates who were pledged to La Follette and/or the 10 who were pledged to Cummins. At the very least, he hoped to prevent Taft from winning the nomination on the first ballot. If the fight continued into later ballots, there was no telling what might happen.

Each delegate contest was different, but the contests shared many of the same themes. The rival camps made arguments that energized their base. In many of the cases not brought by McHarg's friends in the South, each side of the argument made a certain amount of sense. As a result, the decisions really came down to which side had more raw power, enough votes to carry the day. The contests in Texas and Washington State were particularly hard-fought.

In Texas, TR's friend Cecil Lyon had used his influence as national committeeman and patronage distributor to build a base of support and to create a lily-white party. He attacked President Taft's supporters for trying to enfranchise black voters. "You haven't met a man here today whom you couldn't take to the dining room with you," he proudly told the party's executive committee when arguing for his slate. "If you want to go back to the old conditions, Cecil Lyon will not go with you."

Taft's managers, led by his newly installed Texas party chair, Henry F. MacGregor, assisted by Joseph Kealing of Indiana, proved surprisingly adept at using every argument and means of persuasion. William McDonald, Taft's leading black supporter, said that most of the state's 245 counties, those that supported Lyon and Roosevelt, were "inhabited chiefly by prairie dogs." He said that "all of the populated counties," where there were black residents, "are strongly for Taft."

"In preference to the negro voters, who support Taft," he said, Colonel Lyon had built his base by "favoring Democrats—Democrats."

Lyon was equally forceful. When it was his turn to respond, he went over to McDonald and "thrusting his fist almost against the delegate's face, charged him with having bolted from the party organization."

Before the convention started, Roosevelt expected to be awarded all 40 of the delegates from Texas. As late as June 9, TR thought that he would win half of the delegates from Texas and Washington State. On June 15, Cal O'Laughlin told readers that "owing to the personal strength with the committeemen of Cecil Lyon, in the Texas case the Taft managers are fearful they will not be able to command a majority."

When the national committee awarded all but six of the contested Texas seats to Taft, Roosevelt and his supporters were furious. Francis Heney, speaking for TR's forces, accused the Republican National Committee of "Mexicanizing America."

"This is more than plain stealing," he said. "This is treason."

But historian Lewis L. Gould, who made an extensive study of the contest, concluded that "MacGregor and Kealing beat Lyon at his own game on his home ground with his own weapons. In this contest to see who was the better practitioner of the legal piracy called Republican politics in the South, Taft had outstolen Roosevelt."

THE BATTLE OVER the 14 contested delegates from Washington State, which both camps counted in the totals that they were giving to the press, illustrates the competing narratives. Campaigning in Ohio, Roosevelt said that "the most scandalous thing our opponents have recently tried and failed is to steal the delegates in Washington State." Based on the accounts that he was reading, and seeing events from the perspective of his campaign, his anger was justified. Some historians have argued that TR probably should have won the delegates from Washington. But Taft's forces had a decent argument as well.

According to some press accounts, and to reports from his men on the ground, Roosevelt was far ahead in delegates going into the state convention, which was to be held in Aberdeen, a gritty harbor town in the western part of the state. The streets were lined with saloons and featured a red-light district that flourished thanks to the lumber camps on the outskirts of the town. The town had been selected for the convention partly because earlier in the year the City Council and local police had proved that they could handle unruly protesters in a battle with union organizers from the International Workers of the World.

A fight over the delegation from Seattle and King County dominated the Aberdeen convention. Both camps claimed to represent the county's 121 votes. Each side's argument had some merit. One slate, which favored Roosevelt, had been elected overwhelmingly in an "advisory primary." The primary had been created, or "called," by Thomas Morphine, the chair of the King County Central Committee, who supported Roosevelt and was backed by the 250-member County Committee. But a majority of the county's Taft-dominated Executive Committee refused to authorize the primary. The President's backers in the county argued that under state law the Executive Committee, and not the County Committee or the committee chair, controlled the process. They said that the primary was illegal and boycotted the vote. Naturally, TR won the vote overwhelmingly. He and his supporters said that he had won the primary and deserved to have his delegates seated. Claiming that they were playing by the rules, however, the Taft-dominated King County Executive Committee named a slate of 121 delegates pledged to Taft.

On May 14, the day before the Aberdeen convention, the state's Taft-dominated Credentials Committee decided to seat all 121 of Taft's delegates. Their decision may or may not have been based on a correct reading of the law, but they had a colorable argument. At an 11 A.M. meeting with representatives from both camps, Governor Marion Hay tried to work out a compromise, to no avail. The rest of what happened that day combined theater with political organizing. By mid-May, having witnessed events in Michigan and elsewhere, both sides knew what tactics the other would use. Each was hoping to create a strong case for the national convention and for the press and public opinion.

The convention was called for 2 P.M. The Executive Committee created special badges and said that they could only be given to delegates who had been selected by the Credentials Committee. Taft's supporters arrived at the Grand Theater with their badges long before 2 P.M. They arranged for twenty-five armed guards to lock the doors and to prevent anyone without a proper badge from entering. When Roosevelt's delegates from King County tried to enter the theater, the police allegedly threw some of them down the steps.

Roosevelt's supporters had already arranged for an alternative site for a counterconvention. Saying that they had been unjustly unseated and abused, TR's forces held the counterconvention in the Knights of Pythias Hall and named their own slate of 14 delegates to go to the national convention in Chicago, pledged to TR. Meanwhile, the pro-Taft convention, meeting with no TR backers in the room, named a 14-member delegation to go to the national convention, all pledged to renominate the President.

Both sides claimed foul play. Ormsby McHarg, who was in charge of the challenges, sent a letter to TR on May 29 saying "the efforts on the part of the people opposing you in Washington are the most brazen I have encountered in the whole campaign. No wonder the people in states subjected to such un-American treatment are demanding primaries." Nevertheless, McHarg said he was confident that Roosevelt's slate would win in the Credentials Committee, and TR may have believed that assurance.

Taft's supporters were equally adamant. "Every effort was made for harmony, but without success," wrote Taft's postmaster in Everett, Washington, who had been sending updates to the national campaign headquarters throughout the spring. He said that the President was legally entitled to the delegates from Seattle and from the Aberdeen convention. "A Rump Convention was held by the supporters of Col. Roosevelt, but they cannot have any legal standing with the National Committee. The Roosevelt supporters have declared war and will carry the battle to the polls."

Reaction in the press divided along partisan lines. The frequently pro-Taft *New York Times* said in an editorial that Taft was entitled to the delegates from Washington. It blamed the disturbances on Roosevelt and attacked him for his consistently incendiary comments. TR's supporters in Aberdeen "raised a great disturbance in the hall, interfered with the proceedings, and laid the basis for another contest without a particle of right or reason to justify their conduct," the *Times* said. "The Taft forces controlled the convention, but refusing to submit to majority rule, the Roosevelt delegates went to another hall. It is very evident that . . . the Colonel or his friends are attempting to take by disorderly methods the property of another."

WHILE THE REPUBLICAN National Committee was considering the delegate challenges, the TR camp made an important announcement. On June 12, after a two-hour meeting in Oyster Bay, Judge Ben Lindsey of Denver told the press that he had managed "to persuade the Colonel to announce that he was in favor of woman suffrage." By 1912, women had won the right to vote in six western states: Wyoming, Utah, Washington State, Colorado, Idaho, and California. The women's suffrage movement was pressing for a constitutional amendment to allow women to vote everywhere, but up until Judge Lindsey's announcement, both Roosevelt and Taft had argued that the decision should be left up to each state.

"He was induced to take this definitive stand by what the women voters have done" on behalf of progressive causes and candidates in "Colorado, Washington, California and other western states," Lindsey said. "Colonel Roosevelt told me that he was convinced from this record of the advantage to the country to be gained by placing the ballot in the hands of women." As a result, TR now agreed that the Republican platform should include a plank calling for a constitutional amendment to give all women the vote.

Some progressives welcomed his conversion. "We won't look a gift horse in the mouth," the chair of the Woman Suffrage Party said. "Even if Mr. Roosevelt had his own purposes in announcing himself for suffrage, we don't care. We welcome anybody who comes out for us and don't question whether he came willingly or was forced to it."

Others did care about Roosevelt's sincerity, contending that he was only motivated by the fact that women would be voting for President for the first time that fall. The *New York Times* reminded readers that TR had been heckled by Miss Maud Malone only a few weeks earlier. A number of leaders of the suffrage movement thought his conversion was offensively opportunistic. "He thinks he can fool the women, but he cannot for they are not so easily fooled," one leader of the Equal Suf-frage League told the *New York Tribune*.

"He is nothing but a faker," Ellen La Motte told the press. "Roosevelt is merely after votes. He sees six good suffrage states which would give him a million women's votes." La Motte was a cousin of wealthy industrialist Alfred I. du Pont who grew up in his home before attend-ing Johns Hopkins Hospital Training School for nurses and becoming a specialist in treating tuberculosis. She and other women cited TR's articles in *The Outlook* where he had dismissed the importance of the issue. "Now he thinks he is caught in a forked stick and there is noth-ing sincere in his latest stance," La Motte said.

Grace Raymond, the secretary of the Woman Suffrage Party, Bureau of Brooklyn, sent a letter to TR complaining that his new support for women's suffrage "is received by the women suffragists of the State of New York with much indifference owing to your former apparent antagonism to the movement."

But while he was a latecomer to the cause, many reformers con-cluded that TR's position was preferable to Taft, who continued to argue that the decision should be left to each state and continued to oppose a constitutional amendment.

THE REPUBLICAN NATIONAL Committee met for more than a week, from Thursday, June 6, to Friday, June 14. When the dust settled, TR could claim 19 additional delegates, leaving his campaign at least 40 to 50 short of the number it needed. Equally important, it now seemed that Taft would probably have enough delegates to win the nomination on the first ballot.

Looking at the standings at the end of the committee's deliberations, Cal O'Laughlin told his readers that by his calculation Taft now had 536 delegates, which would leave him four votes short of a first-ballot win; TR had 496, which meant that he would need 44 more delegates; and La Follette and Cummins had 36 and 10 delegates respectively.

On the morning of Sunday, June 16, famed reporter Samuel G.

Blythe, who had come to the convention to provide commentary for the *New York Tribune*, started his first column with these words: "The great basic truth concerning the political situation in Chicago, the one fact about which the whole convention revolves, is one very simple truth. This is it: No man in this city, nor any man of this hemisphere, or the other one, knows, absolutely, who will be nominated by the convention that meets next Tuesday."

There was only one man who possibly could turn the tide. Breaking all tradition, Theodore Roosevelt decided to go to Chicago to take charge of the campaign.

Chapter Twelve

E very fiber in his body told Roosevelt to go to Chicago: his love of adventure, adulation, and action; his belief in the righteousness of his cause; his anger at the men whom he felt were stealing the election, not just from him but from the public's will as expressed in the primaries; his crusading zeal; his passion for a good fight; the chance to "hit and hit hard"; and his unique ability to act as his own publicist, to create sensational headlines and a compelling narrative. Alice Roosevelt once said, "My father always wanted to be the bride at every wedding, the corpse at every funeral, and the baby at every christening." The Republican Convention was certain to be the biggest party of the year. How could he resist?

And there was something else. The convention could become the crucible for his rebirth—or it could become the funeral for the cause he now championed, for the people working at his side, and for his own remarkable career. It could be the moment he envisioned when he said it was the responsibility of every man to "spend and be spent."

His friends had a chilling foreboding, convinced that the old guard, who had come to regard TR as a dangerous radical and a threat to their interests, would stop at nothing to prevent his victory. No one presented that view in words that were better phrased, more stark, and perhaps more paranoid, than Brooks Adams. Adams was a notable figure, the great-grandson of one president, grandson of another, and the brother of famed historian Henry Adams, who had been a part of Roosevelt's circle in Washington, D.C. Brooks Adams was an important member of a family that was as close to an aristocracy as the young nation had produced. A lawyer by training, he was widely considered eccentric, arrogant, gruff, and even a crank. But he had become a significant economic historian who worried about the effect of the quest for wealth, and ultimately greed, on a range of American values and morals. He knew TR well and, as the historian Daniel Aaron put it, had "urged his friend to seek a third term and save the country."

At the end of May, two days after the New Jersey primary seemed to have placed the nomination in Roosevelt's grasp, at a time when so many of the candidate's friends were rejoicing, Adams wrote a passionate, cautionary letter on stationary from the family's "Old House" home in Quincy, Massachusetts. He warned TR about both his enemies and his friends and pleaded with him to take personal control of his campaign at the convention. It was a powerful missive.

"This is a revolution and revolutionists must succeed at their peril," Adams cautioned. "You must win. You can take no chances. Your weakness is the lack of cohesion of your army. You have no officers. . . . Without you, your following is a mob . . . you know better than I what [your enemy] is capable of. It, at least, has no scruples. It is not *bosses* that you are fighting, but the special vested interests who retain the bosses. . . ."

Speaking as one classically trained, Harvard-educated historian to another, Adams put his concerns in a context that both could understand. "Call it what you will; empire, dictatorship, republic, or anything else, we have the same problem which Caesar had in Rome when he suppressed the plundering gangs of senators led by Brutus, who murdered him for it. We must have a power strong enough to make all interests equal before the law, or we must dissolve in chaos. All these special interests are now banded against you at Chicago and they are capable of anything, including murder, if you give them the chance which Caesar gave to Brutus. Therefore, be on hand and lead your men yourself. Trust no lieutenant."

Adams blamed TR for handing the presidency to Taft four years earlier. Now he concluded with these words: "I appeal to you to let no scruple interfere again, for if we lose now we shall never have another chance. . . . Ignore conventional scruples. If you are absolutely certain of your nomination on the first ballot—well and good. If not go and lead your men, else when too late you may have the reflections which Napoleon had when he let Ney lead his guard at Waterloo."

At breakfast on Friday morning, Roosevelt announced to his family that they were headed for Chicago. As proposed by Brooks Adams— and in conversations with most of his advisors, culminating in a three-hour evening phone call with Bill Flinn of Pennsylvania—he was going directly into battle to lead his men. It was a break from tradition, but tradition be damned. The *New York Evening Mail*, which was edited by his friend and supporter Henry Stoddard, gave him some cover for breaking precedent with a seven-column banner editorial on the top of the front page. It said: "We now demand of him, in the name of a majority of Republicans in the Republican states of the North, that he assume personal direction of the struggle there against the theft of a presidential nomination."

One reason for the decision, the Colonel told his family, was evidence that their home phones were being tapped. Knowing that tapping was a risk, the campaign had set up a telegraph wire between his Oyster Bay home and his new campaign headquarters at the Congress Hotel in Chicago, since such wires were more difficult to tap. But he still had to use the phones.

"It appears there has been a leak in the private phone to Chicago," he told nineteen-year-old Nick Roosevelt, a cousin in his junior year at Harvard who was staying with the family. Nick, who went on to become a distinguished diplomat and foreign correspondent, started keeping a diary for posterity.

"I am taking Ferrero and Herodotus with me to amuse myself," TR shouted to Nick while running up to pack, "and get my mind off the business in Chicago."

At 5:30 P.M. a passel of friends and family, after eluding hundreds of supporters who surrounded the station, boarded the Lake Shore Limited headed for Chicago. By the time they reached Chicago at 4 P.M. the following day, it was, in some respects, too late. The Republican National Committee had concluded its work, giving all but 19 of the contested delegates to Taft.

But Roosevelt was not the least discouraged. With his overwhelming sense of optimism, excitement in the face of battle, and righteous belief in himself and his cause, Roosevelt believed the words of Cal O'Laughlin, who exuded optimism when he jumped on the train in South Bend early Saturday afternoon. Greeted with "much joy" by the family, and especially by TR, Cal rode the rest of the way on the train with the exuberant entourage. Cal had agreed to serve as Roosevelt's private secretary were he to regain the White House.

"I had heard so much of him and expected a rather negative person to whom for some reason Cousin Theodore had taken a fancy," Nick wrote in his diary. "But he proved to be exceedingly attractive, quite young—about 30—and of a most active mind. The kind of person you can't forget."

Like most of the others in the inner circle, Cal had all but given up on most of the credentials challenges, or given up on using them as anything other than a public relations foil. The campaign would register every possible claim, some legitimate, some less so, saying that they were entitled to more than 70 additional delegates, and that the Taft forces and the bosses that they followed were a bunch of thieves and crooks. While sitting in the back car of the train, Cal gave a list of the "stolen delegates" to TR along with an explanation of the reasons for challenging each one. But that part of the strategy was largely a cover for their real plans.

"If necessary," Nick reported, "'roughhouse tactics' would be used to terrorize them." As a last resort, TR was prepared to walk out of the convention and create a new party. However, if they were going to leave the convention, their effort "must appear regular and unboltlike."

But they actually had another plan, another approach to victory.

Cal told the group that "a panic has struck the Taft forces" since it now seemed that scores of Taft's delegates from the South would defect.

"All the news was of the best," Nick Roosevelt recorded in his diary. "TR was bubbling over with cheerfulness."

"I think—and I really mean this seriously," TR told his family, "I really think that there never has been before a campaign waged on such high principles." While that statement may have been sincere, it was to prove ironic in view of the tactics that his campaign planned to employ in pursuit of the nomination.

STARTING IN EARLY June, spokesmen for Roosevelt's campaign had been openly predicting that dozens and perhaps scores of delegates from the South would switch sides—or "flop," in the argot of the era. After spending a day meeting with TR and Dixon in Sagamore Hill, Medill McCormick told the *Washington Post* that TR would have 614 votes on the first ballot.

"Where do you expect to get them?" an incredulous reporter asked.

"The Southern delegates will flop to him," McCormick said. "When I was in Washington the other day, the negro delegates from the south came and offered to vote for Mr. Roosevelt. We looked them up and found they had been instructed for Mr. Taft. One of them replied, 'Of course we are instructed for Mr. Taft, for we could not have got elected if we had not been for the President. But Mr. Roosevelt can have us on the first ballot if he wants us.'"

There had been rumors and promises of such defections for weeks, but the first public announcement of a "flop" took place on the day that TR arrived in Chicago. And it was flavored with the hint of scandal.

For several days, the Taft campaign had been making as yet unsubstantiated claims that Roosevelt's men had "tried to bribe two Taft delegates from the south." Taft's managers were holding in reserve the information that had been gained during the past six weeks as the result of the plan suggested by Moseley and Mulvihill of Mississippi. They had been collecting specific information about the less than savory entreaties by Roosevelt's agents, or those claiming to be his agents. But as TR traveled to Chicago, his campaign leveled the first documented charge of such conduct, claiming that Taft, not Roosevelt, was offering such bribes.

On Friday, as TR and his group were headed west by train, his campaign released a letter as their exhibit A. It came from Charles Banks, a successful banker and businessman from Mississippi, thought to be one of the wealthiest black men in the region. The letter was addressed to Taft's campaign manager, William B. McKinley.

The Banks letter immediately became a national sensation, quoted in full by the scandal-hungry press. It was in every newspaper on Saturday afternoon when TR's train arrived at the station, where he was mobbed by supporters.

"The bribery charges that have been bandied about between the Taft and Roosevelt camps for the past three or four days, none of them backed by evidence, have at last culminated in a tangible indictment," the *New York Times* reported. In his letter to McKinley, Banks enclosed $1,000 "placed in my hands at your suggestion." The letter implied that the Taft campaign had given him the money in an effort to bribe him, to keep him from changing his allegiance.

With the outraged tone of a man who felt that he had been treated unfairly, Banks admitted that he was supporting Roosevelt, but said that he had switched sides because of his dissatisfaction with the administration's decision not to appoint blacks to office in the South—concerns that he had discussed with President Taft as early as April 1909—and his belief that Roosevelt would improve on that record. "The insinuation that I can be or have been bought are known to be untrue and unfounded by no one better than those connected with your campaign as well as those of four years ago," Banks wrote. "I have never asked any of you for one cent and never applied for an office." After all, he was wealthy already.

"A man worth $75,000 or $100,000 in his own right," Banks told the Taft forces, "and with hundreds of people in his employ either as tenants, wage hands, clerks, &c, and whose credit runs up into the thousands, is not apt to allow you, or any set of men, to buy him with a few hundred dollars."

McKinley replied later that day, saying that he did not deny giving the money to Banks, but offering what seemed to be a fairly innocent explanation.

"Yes, I gave Banks the money for traveling expenses" to be shared with other delegates, he said the next day. "It amounted to $1,000. He returned $800, with the explanation that the other $200 represented $100 apiece given to two delegates who had failed to return it. These two, by a strange coincidence, are the only two Roosevelt men in the delegation besides Banks himself."

The story launched a narrative that would play out over the next few days. "This case and the general talk of the bribery of Southern negro delegates make an analysis of the negro vote in the convention worthy of study," the *New York Times* said. "The hopes of the Roosevelt managers for controlling the convention rest today more strongly than anything else on their hopes of winning over enough of the Taft negro delegates from the South to make up the deficit that still separates them from a majority. Along with the negroes go a few white men from the South but it is the negro votes they have set out to capture."

The *Times* went on to explain that there were 57 black delegates from the South and that "the Roosevelt men claim fifty of these on the first ballot." (Commentators offered different numbers, but most said there were 68 black delegates, possibly including alternates.) Roosevelt campaign leaders were pointing to 38 black votes that they said would come from Louisiana, Georgia, and Mississippi. "That explains the fear the Taft managers experienced early in the campaign," the *Times* observed, "and the credence that Col. Roosevelt's leaders gave to the claims of Ormsby McHarg."

But the paper offered a cautionary note. It accurately pointed out that the southern black delegates at the 1912 convention were "for the most part a different crowd from those usually sent to conventions." Like Charles Banks, most were "large property holders, bankers, insurance men and merchants. A great number are lawyers with large practices among their own people, and nearly all of them own the land on which they live." The paper proceeded to list the names and occupations of the men from each of the southern states. They were not, it concluded, men whose votes were for sale.

Another *New York Times* story the same day described the black delegates in terms that were less flattering, or at least much less enlightened. "If this proportion is kept up throughout the announcements expected tomorrow," it said, "Theodore Roosevelt will owe his nomination, provided he gets it, to the impecunious negroes of the South." The standard definition of "impecunious," of course, is penniless or having little money. That description of the delegates to the 1912 convention was false and offensive. It infuriated some who read it.

Roscoe Simmons immediately wrote an angry letter to the paper's editor listing several of the black delegates and highlighting their accomplishments, starting with the men from Mississippi: Charles Banks, "a born leader"; Wesley Crayton, described by the *Times* as a farmer who was "poor as a church mouse" actually owned a large liquor shipping business in Vicksburg and "lives in a mansion"; Perry Howard is "a brilliant Jackson lawyer and banker"; and Daniel Gary is a planter and a former college professor.

Simmons was a famed black orator, born in Mississippi, related by marriage to Booker T. Washington, who had become well known in the North thanks in part to time spent living with family friends such as Medill McCormick and Senator Mark Hanna. One contemporaneous article said that "with nothing behind him except truth and his amazing genius, this man at thirty-five years is the ambassador of 12,000,000, the wisest champion his Race has ever had and his country's foremost orator."

Having known and campaigned for TR in the past, and admiring him deeply, Simmons had become the chairman of the Roosevelt Colored County Committee in the New York State primary. In early June, he sent a note to TR saying that "I have spent considerable time getting in touch with the men in the South . . . [and] have succeeded in reaching many of the delegates, the majority of whom are for you, though they may have been sent up on a Taft platform. Most of my correspondence is, of course, confidential, but I have taken the liberty to write Mr. Ward at Chicago about the men, more than twenty-five of them, with whom I have communicated. Many of them are quite willing to deal with Mr. Ward in getting themselves straight before the people, but no one else." Having helped to organize black support for Roosevelt in the South, he wanted to be sure that people understood that their motives were high-minded.

"Do you ask why colored men are for Theodore Roosevelt?" Simmons stated rhetorically in his letter to the *New York Times*. "I will answer. They are for Roosevelt because he embodies the principles of the Republican Party, and because Mr. Taft, who is against them, is the embodiment of all that the Republican does not represent. Further, they are opposed to Mr. Taft and favorable to Mr. Roosevelt because they are unwilling to allow the Republican Party in the South to become a cotton-stringed bow for Democratic fiddlers."

The quest for black delegates continued at a mass rally on Saturday night where Roosevelt's supporters begged black delegates to break their pledge to Taft because TR would be so much better for the issues that affected them directly. Rev. Reverdy C. Ransom, the fiery pastor of the Bethel A.M.E. Church of New York City, who had just been named editor of the powerful *A.M.E. Review*, ignited a crowd of more than 1,000 people at Chicago's black-owned Pekin Theater by telling them that Taft had been "untrue to his oath of office and a traitor to the race." A black lawyer from Virginia asked everyone in the crowd to circulate a petition. "We will implore every one of these men who have come up from the land of darkness with the power in their hands to nominate Theodore Roosevelt," he said. Another speaker said that the failure to nominate Roosevelt would mean putting the Negro in the South back forty years.

To those who objected to breaking their instructions, the owner of the *Kansas City Sun* brought the crowd to its feet when he said that Lincoln "broke his instructions when he freed the slaves" and that when the black delegates broke their instructions to vote for Roosevelt they would be "voting for a man who would free the negro from class bondage."

With a sixteen-piece orchestra, the Pekin Theater had become a launch pad for black jazz. The audience members joined in a rollicking new ragtime campaign song that played off of a profound Christian message. "He's coming back," they sang. "Yes he's coming back to the White House from Oyster Bay."

THE STORY OF the fight for defectors, most of whom were black delegates from the South, continued to generate headlines on Sunday, June 16. While Roosevelt spent the morning in church, his campaign started to release a series of carefully timed announcements. First it reported that Timothy Woodruff of New York, who had served as TR's lieutenant governor, was deserting Taft to join his old colleague; then it released the names of five delegates from Georgia who planned to defect (including one white delegate); and then, an hour later, Senator Dixon's office released the names of five defecting black delegates from Mississippi. The campaign said that it would announce the names of additional defectors from Louisiana on Monday.

A reporter asked when Senator Dixon would make his announcement about Louisiana. "That's not a fair question," Dixon said with a smile. "Come around tomorrow morning."

The *New York Times* observed that "the Roosevelt leaders are working very shrewdly in handing out their claims of recruits, timing them carefully so as to impress the delegates with the idea that the stream is running steadily in the Colonel's direction." For the first time, Taft's managers were beginning to have doubts. By some accounts, their own internal reports showed Taft with a margin of only 2 delegates.

But the narrative of defecting black delegates soon began to sour. On Monday, the 28-member Georgia delegation held a boisterous meeting filled with harsh words and physical threats. As Paul Casdorph explained in his careful study of race in the Progressive Era, the black delegates had been alienated by "the organization of numerous Roosevelt clubs open to white voters only in Georgia [which] left little doubt that the Negro would be barred from party councils should TR win the nomination at Chicago."

Moreover, as Casdorph notes, "the charges that they were defecting or were for sale infuriated the black delegates." In fact, the delegates had been resisting inducements from various sources. For example, Roosevelt's supporters apparently offered a bribe to at least one of the delegates from Georgia, Henry Lincoln Johnson, a graduate of the University of Michigan Law School whose wife, Georgia Douglas Johnson, later became a celebrated poet and playwright. Johnson remained a voter in Georgia, but the couple had moved to Washington, D.C., in 1910 when President Taft named Johnson to the powerful post of recorder of deeds. Johnson later told his friends and family that Perry Howard of Mississippi told him that the Roosevelt campaign could make him "independently wealthy" and "secure his family forever." But Johnson refused, because he had promised his support to Taft.

When the Georgia delegation's meeting ended, all 12 black delegates announced that they intended to stick with Taft. The *Atlanta Independent*, a black paper that strongly supported Taft, reported that although they were offered "long green and gold coins," every one of the 12 black delegates "stood the test and obeyed the mandate of their constituency."

Roosevelt's strongest southern state was Mississippi, where it appeared that he would hold on to the support of Charles Banks, Perry Howard, and at least two if not three other black delegates. But it was the day before the convention was to open, and as the day wore on, the Roosevelt campaign did not seem to have any new supporters and there was no evidence of defecting black delegates from Louisiana. An affidavit released by the Taft headquarters late Sunday evening may contain the reason. It was signed by F. H. Cook of Vidalia, Louisiana, pastor of the Zion Methodist Church, editor of a local paper, and cashier of the Sons and Daughters bank. He said that a man from Colorado, after ascertaining that he was a delegate, "said to me that if you will come over with the T. R. crowd, here is a thousand dollars, which of course I refused, and at the same time he had the money in his hand and attempted to count it out for me. I make this sworn statement because it has been going the rounds by some responsible person that I had agreed to sell out. All of which is utterly false upon its face."

A number of newspapers had ceased to believe that enough delegates would defect to change the convention's outcome. "One of the striking developments of the week here has been the complete failure of the long-heralded 'bolting Taft delegates from the South' to develop as support for Col. Roosevelt," the *New York Times* wrote. "Ever since it became apparent that the President would get practically solid delegations from nearly all the Southern States, Senator Dixon has insisted that many of these delegates, after taking their seats as supporters of Mr. Taft, would throw their votes to the Colonel. The assertion was made as loudly as the Senator's claims for his Southern contests. It now looks as if the bolting Taft delegates are about as mythical as the contests were flimsy." Dixon's claims "have simmered down to a bare eleven delegates."

Still, Roosevelt was not about to give up. On Monday night he made a personal appeal to the black community, speaking to what the *Chicago Defender* called "a vast throng" at the Bethel A.M.E. Church, where Rev. Ransom again led what amounted to a political rally, warming up the crowd with a rousing speech called "A Nation's Duty to Its Black Citizens." Ransom cautioned that "whoever will be the nominee, it will not bring us the political millennium." But he called Taft "an enemy of progress." We "have nothing to hope for in him," he said. "Now is the time for [us] to turn Insurgent and insist on the nomination of the man who will give us the square deal."

Arriving shortly after 10:30 P.M., TR delivered a powerful speech against graft—and a powerful appeal for the votes of black delegates. Many of those in the crowd knew that his remarkable career had started as an anticorruption reform legislator, a civil service commissioner who crusaded for ethics reform, and a crime-busting police commissioner. "My interest in politics," he reminded the crowd, "has been and still is a moral interest. I hope the time will come when the people won't use the word 'politician' and 'graft' in the same breath."

"Any man who sells his vote, and especially a Negro, demeans not only himself but his race. . . . The Negro who sells his vote, no matter whom he sells it to, does an injustice to the entire Negro race. Certain white men are at work trying to buy off the Negro delegates from the south. The white man who buys such a vote is lower than the Negro who sells it. If he can be found, I shall do my best to have him punished.

"I like the Negro race," he concluded. "I remember the regiments that fought beside my own [in Cuba], and remember what work they accomplished. There is a great deal to be done for the race, and I am actively interested in the uplift of the Negro. I do not think Mr. Taft is."

With his excellent sources in the campaign and the press, Roosevelt probably knew while he was speaking that the papers the next morning would say that it was his campaign, rather than Taft's, that was trying to bribe black delegates.

THAT SAME NIGHT, while Roosevelt appealed to the men at the Bethel A.M.E. Church, a huge pro-Taft event filled Chicago's Institutional A.M.E. Church to capacity. "The speakers spoke in glowing terms of his splendid administration," the *Chicago Defender* reported. Sergeant Mingo Sanders and Corporal James H. Ballard, two of the black men dishonorably discharged at Brownsville, had been campaigning around the country for Taft, always stressing the villainy of TR's decision in Brownsville. They repeated their denunciation of the former President. J. C. Napier, register of the U.S. Treasury, said that "President Taft has proved himself to be the true friend of the colored people. . . . His stand on the question of disenfranchising the Negro twice prevented such an occurrence in Maryland, where the Democrats attempted to accomplish it."

In an editorial endorsing Taft, the editors of the *Chicago Defender* accused Roosevelt of using "a mere jingle of words, linguistic pyrotechnic to catch the thoughtless and emotional." By contrast, "in those matters peculiarly affecting and appealing to the members of our own race," the paper said that Taft "has seemed to be moved by a feeling, when occasion called for it, to treat and recommend for our encouragement and welfare, the considerations due us."

ON TUESDAY, AS the convention opened, the *New York Times* front-page banner headline said:

TAFT MEN SAY THEY'LL WIN TODAY
AND THAT COL. ROOSEVELT WILL BOLT

Negroes Tell of Bribes to Beat Taft

The paper quoted three affidavits that made quite specific charges of attempted bribery by the Roosevelt camp. The first of the claims was from Rev. James W. Shumpert, the presiding elder of the Methodist Episcopal Church in Meridian, Mississippi. It was aimed directly at Charles Banks.

"On Thursday, June 13," Rev. Shumpert's affidavit said, "Charles Banks, a delegate from Mississippi, came to where I was staying in Chicago. He asked everybody to leave except me. He began by asking if I had ever seen a thousand-dollar bill. He then put his hand in his pocket and brought out a big roll of bills. The outside bill was one of the denomination of $1,000. It was the first I had ever seen. The roll of bills were nearly all gold certificates."

"He then wanted to know how much I would ask to go with him and support Mr. Roosevelt," Rev. Shumpert's affidavit continued. "I told him that I would not be bought; that I had not come to Chicago to sell myself. He then said that all, or a majority of the delegates were going to Roosevelt, who would be nominated, and that Mr. Roosevelt would make him the referee in Mississippi in connection with all federal offices. I repeated that I would not be a party to any such a transaction and then excused myself."

Another affidavit came from A. Buckley, the man described in the Moseley-Mulvihill memo as a "poor man, editor of a little county paper" who "needs money but is a high class man" who "might be one of the men that could be induced to take money from the opposition and still vote for the President." In his affidavit, Buckley said that on June 14, Charles Banks offered him "$100 cash, another $100 on the first day of the convention, and a third installment of $100 on the second day of the convention. Mr. Banks pulled out a roll of green-backs and said, 'I have the money and will give you $100 now.'" Buckley said that on the following day, June 15, Dr. Sidney Redmond of Jackson had made a similar offer.

A third affidavit, from an alternate delegate named D. W. Sherrod, made similar charges.

By the time the convention opened on Tuesday morning, it had become clear that the southern strategy was unlikely to succeed. With a somewhat triumphant tone, the New York Times wrote: "Yesterday [Sunday] was a Roosevelt day. Today [Monday] was a Taft day. The carefully planned scheme of the Roosevelt managers to spring announcements of changes from Taft to Roosevelt, which they had intended to make the big feature of the day before the convention, was suddenly checkmated, and in the checkmating a noble scheme of bunko came to light. The Southern delegates who had been collected for weeks past into the desertion column were won over by false pretenses. . . . It now turns out that the Roosevelt managers made them believe their bread was buttered on the top side, when it was really buttered elsewhere."

It is unclear how much Roosevelt knew about any efforts to bribe the black delegates. In view of his strong aversion to graft and his repeated attacks on the claim of bribery by Taft's forces, it is certainly possible that his managers shielded him from knowledge of their tactics, or that any such efforts were being made by supporters who were engaging in a bit of freelance work. There is no doubt, however, that such efforts were being made in his name. In his draft memoir, Nick Roosevelt describes a conversation with Lindon W. Bates, Jr., a young former New York State assemblyman and leader of TR's efforts in the state.

"Lindon Bates wanted Charlie [Curtis] and myself to get into an auto and go to a certain hospital in which lies a Taft negro delegate, hurt in an accident." The delegate was A. M. Fluker of Georgia, who was in St. Luke's Hospital, having broken three ribs earlier in the day in a train accident. "By paying for his dues, and giving him an auto ride," Nick said, "we could probably, with some careful talk, win him over to our side. I could see us 'sticking pins into his feet,' as the manager called it, and 'buying' a delegate for the old man. I was much tempted to do it, but it being very late, I retired to bed."

Taft's managers were particularly worried about efforts to change the loyalty of members of the Credentials Committee, which would rule on the delegate disputes. Taft had a margin of 32 to 21 votes, but a shift of 6 of those delegates would give Roosevelt control. Hilles warned Taft that two District of Columbia delegates, Aaron Bradshaw and Calvin Chase, had been offered $5,000 each by the TR camp to "desert" Taft and go to TR. He said that Bill Flinn, Walter Brown, Frank Knox, and Dick Quay were "the practical men at the bargain counter."

The bars and hotel lobbies were filled with rumors about efforts on both sides to court and even detain the black delegates. The Taft forces were certainly worried that the delegates pledged to their candidate would be convinced to defect—whether by appeals to their reason or appeals to their pocketbook. By some accounts, the Taft machine was keeping as many delegates as possible under lock and key.

A colorful account in the *American Magazine*, purportedly written by political humorist Finley Peter Dunne, illustrates the not-so-fanciful claims that were flying everywhere. The *American Magazine* had become a leading journal since it was purchased by refugees from *McClure's*, including the editor, John Phillips, William Allen White, and famed muckraking journalists Ray Stannard Baker, Ida Tarbell, and Lincoln Steffens. The magazine's articles by Ray Stannard Baker, later collected in *Following the Color Line*, were among the first by a mainstream publication to describe the life of black Americans and focus on America's racial divide.

"The Taft managers took no chances on the negro delegates getting away from them and encountering temptation from the Roosevelt people," the magazine reported. "Usually, the Negro delegates are prominent figures at ante-convention gatherings. But at Chicago it was almost impossible to find a Negro delegate on Monday night preceding the opening of the convention. They were actually under lock and key. One bunch of fourteen was held in a Pullman car in Ohio and only rushed up on the morning of the opening day in time to vote for Mr. Root for temporary chairman. Others were detained in rooms at the hotels until their leaders marched them up to the convention hall." A cartoon accompanying the story showed rifle-carrying guards in business suits escorting a group of well-dressed black delegates. The caption read: "The Free and Independent Colored Delegates en route to the convention hall."

"'What will you do if they try to break away in the convention,'" a Taft leader was asked.

"'They won't dare to,'" he said. "'The police would throw them out.'"

A few weeks later, Samuel Blythe penned what some considered the definitive early account of the events in Chicago. When it appeared, Joseph Dixon, who had a unique view of events as TR's campaign manager, wrote his wife that "it is not far from the truth." One of Frank Munsey's editors called Blythe "the mounted police of literature, with his guns trained on pretense."

"The struggle was to get the colored brother for Roosevelt against the effort to keep him in line for Taft," Blythe wrote. "In reality, the nomination of the candidate for President, by a party that had been in power—except for eight years—since 1860, was determined by a handful of negro delegates and a handful of white delegates from states that cast no Republican votes."

By the time the convention opened, that struggle—TR's only remotely plausible way of getting the nomination—seemed to be over.

Theodore Roosevelt and William Howard Taft, the friend and colleague he considered the most loveable man he knew, pictured here at Taft's 1909 inauguration.

TR and his son Kermit in Africa on a year-long safari that began immediately after TR left office.

Many of TR's friends grew disenchanted with Taft when he fired Gifford Pinchot, Roosevelt's friend and conservation partner, as the nation's chief forester.

President Taft protects Secretary Ballinger as Roosevelt lurks behind Chief Forester Pinchot

Although TR sounded like a candidate on a nationwide tour in 1910 promoting what he called the "New Nationalism," he refused to agree to challenge Taft.

By the summer of 1911, the insurgent wing of the Republican Party had given up on TR and began to give their support to Wisconsin Senator Robert La Follette, who announced that he would challenge Taft for the Republican nomination in 1912.

Senator Jonathan Bourne created Direct Presidential Primaries in 1910 in Oregon. Such primaries seemed to offer a means to challenge Taft, but by late 1911, only a few states had adopted them.

In late 1911, TR secretly decided that he wanted to challenge Taft. His early effort was organized, in part, by Ormsby McHarg, a conservative lawyer and political operative.

TR asked Franklin Knox, who had been one of his "Rough Riders" in Cuba, to go around the country asking governors to sign a letter "drafting" him to run — in a process that TR's daughter Alice called "somewhat cooked."

Roosevelt's two largest financial supporters, financier George Perkins and publisher Frank Munsey, were furious when Taft's Justice Department filed an antitrust suit against U.S. Steel, leading Taft and many other observers to conclude that TR's campaign was being funded and partly run by U.S. Steel.

While many corporate leaders and newspaper publishers hated him, Roosevelt had scores of friends in the working press. Here he is with reporters at his home on Long Island.

TR's campaign theme, included on buttons and banners, was "Let the People Rule."

In his first major speech of the campaign at Carnegie Hall in March 1912, TR insisted that the great issue of the day was "The Right of the People to Rule."

Maud Malone heckled Roosevelt for not supporting universal suffrage for women.

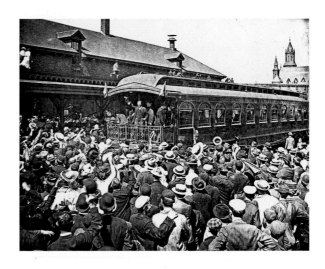

After TR won primaries in Illinois and Pennsylvania, he and Taft fought a bitter campaign in Massachusetts, leveling vicious charges at every stop.

At first it seemed that TR had won again in Massachusetts, but late returns allowed Taft to claim a narrow victory.

By the time the Republican Convention opened in Chicago on June 18, 1912, TR had won most of the delegates selected in primaries, though Taft controlled most of the other delegates thanks to his influence with party leaders and office holders.

The boisterous California delegates, convinced that Taft had stolen the nomination, were anxious to walk out of the convention and create a new party.

In a last-ditch effort to win the Republican nomination, TR tried to convince the black delegates from the south to defect and support him instead of Taft, providing fodder for cartoonists and prompting charges of attempted bribery on both sides.

The Free and Independent Colored Delegates enroute to the convention hall

Lawyer Perry Howard was one of several black delegates who defected to support TR. When TR's supporters left the convention to start the Bull Moose Party, men like Howard were with them.

Leaders of the new party in the states of the Deep South said that only whites could participate, but blacks who had supported him asked TR to allow them to be seated at the Progressive Party convention in Chicago.

When TR addressed the Progressive Party convention, he said that blacks were welcome from other states but none would be allowed from the Deep South.

TR finally embraced women's suffrage in June 1912, gaining the support of reformers including Jane Addams (right), though she was reluctant to accept his decision to exclude blacks.

DISCARDING THE ACE

Theodore Roosevelt's negro policy affords Robert Minor the opportunity for a characteristic expression of his art.

Many of Roosevelt's strongest white and black supporters were disillusioned and furious at his decision to exclude black delegates, feeling that he had abandoned his promise to "let the people rule."

Chapter Thirteen

For anyone who understood politics, power, and the parliamentary realities of nominating conventions, the outcome should have been clear by the time the 1912 Republican Convention opened on Tuesday morning, June 18. Sam Blythe had provided *Saturday Evening Post* readers with an excellent briefing six weeks earlier. "Taft will win," he wrote, "because the men who control the convention, control the machinery, are for him." They were for him "solely to perpetuate themselves in the control of the machinery. They expect Taft to be beaten in November but they want to retain the organization for future use." Blythe then explained their strategy:

> The temporary roll of the convention will be for Taft, unless the old-line politicians lose their cunning. With any sort of intelligent political work Taft should have a clear majority of the temporary roll. Then the situation becomes easy. The delegates of the temporary roll call will select a credentials committee, to which will be referred such contests as have been held to be meritorious by the national committee. Then the question resolves itself into a situation where a lot of delegates vote whether they themselves shall remain on the roll and become the permanent delegates to the convention, or shall vote to unseat themselves.

Roosevelt's core campaign staff agreed with Blythe's assessment. They knew that they were now fighting for public opinion. One way or another, it seemed preordained that they would create a new party, or walk out of the convention and claim to be the true representatives of the Republican Party. Thanks to the primaries, they had a strong case to make: After all, TR had won the popular vote against Taft overwhelmingly. It seemed clear that he would have won hundreds of additional delegates if the public had been allowed to participate in the selection process everywhere. What's more, he had a clear majority of the delegates from states outside of what were often derided as the "rotten boroughs" of the old Confederacy, delegates chosen from areas where no Republican candidate could ever win an election. Outside of the delegates from those eleven states, Taft had about 300 delegates in his corner, whereas TR had at least 450.

In the view of his millions of supporters, Roosevelt was the legitimate nominee. If the people really were allowed to rule, TR would be the Republican Party choice. But his campaign team needed to use the convention to make their case as effectively as possible, to make sure that the general public would agree.

Once the temporary roll had been chosen, and the chance of finding enough defecting delegates evaporated, the only real issue was how and when to leave the convention. "It being perfectly clear to all of us at Chicago that the National Committee had determined to steal the convention," O. K. Davis recalled in his memoir, "it was a matter of supreme importance to make the record so plain that the theft would be entirely obvious all over the country." As the senior press advisor for the campaign, Davis had a front-row view of the deliberations.

Inside TR's reform ranks, there was a bitter fight over tactics. One faction, led by Hiram Johnson and his idealistic, irrepressible, and rowdy group of California delegates, wanted to leave the convention before it even started. They felt that the entire event was a transparent fraud, that the delegates had clearly been stolen, and that the public would be with them if they refused to participate. Indeed, they were convinced that "it would add strength to the Roosevelt movement if the Progressive forces refused to enter the convention at all, basing their course upon the actions of the National Committee." The other faction wanted to make their case to the convention and the world. Roosevelt was in the latter camp. As a superb publicist as well as the candidate, a lifelong Republican, and a former president, he felt that "it was of the utmost importance to make the record perfectly clear, all the way up to the point where the theft of the seventy-two delegates had been irrevocably confirmed."

While a majority of the progressive leaders were on his side, Roosevelt had what O. K. Davis called "an extremely difficult situation" since the Californians kept trying to leave the convention as quickly as possible. "Governor Johnson and some of his friends were eager to fight and it couldn't begin too soon for them," Davis remembered. "They argued for it vigorously, and not only in the conferences."

Insiders knew that the convention itself—the fight over the temporary roll, over the permanent chairmanship, even over the credentials challenges—was theater, for effect, for public consumption. They expected to lose the credentials challenges. Roosevelt planned to bolt, but not until he had made every effort to prove that the process was rigged.

Roosevelt may have had one other reason for staying in the convention for as long as possible. In his memoir, famed *New York Times* reporter Arthur Krock describes a conversation between George Miller, one of Roosevelt's favorite reporters, and TR. Miller asked the Colonel why he was staying in Chicago; why not walk out at once? "I intend to stay to see that Mr. Taft is nominated," Roosevelt replied.

Henry Pringle, who wrote important biographies of both Roosevelt and Taft, concluded that TR meant that he needed to stay in the convention to make sure that the delegates would not turn to a compromise candidate. If TR had walked out at that point, the convention might have named Missouri governor Herbert Hadley or Supreme Court justice and former New York governor Charles Evans Hughes as the candidate, making it much harder for TR to create a new party because the Republican candidate would be a reformer.

Setting the tone for the first day, O'Laughlin wrote a front-page article designed to help Roosevelt claim the public and parliamentary high ground. The headline said it all: "Battle Today Means Reform or New Party."

ON TUESDAY, IN the first hours of the convention, the reformers lost a crucial procedural fight. It was a fight that insiders knew they would lose yet wanted to lose well, so that, in the process, they would win friends for the cause of a new party.

As chairman of the Republican National Committee, Victor Rosewater called the proceedings to order at noon. He was a small man with a weak voice, especially hard to hear in an era before effective sound amplification. After an opening prayer, the secretary of the Republican Party read the official "Call for the Convention." The Call represented the law that would govern the selection of delegates.

As adopted by the Republican National Committee the previous December, the Call provided that where there were contesting delegations from a district, the secretary of the national committee shall submit the claims "to the whole Committee for a decision as to which delegates reported shall be placed on the temporary roll of the Convention." The party's rules thus allowed the national committee, which Taft controlled, to select the delegates to be placed on the temporary roll. The men on the temporary roll would, in turn, be able to select the temporary chairman and to vote on any credentials challenges.

As a result of the weeklong deliberations of the national committee in which President Taft had won virtually every contest over disputed delegates, no one could doubt that Taft would control a majority of those on the temporary roll. Therefore, it seemed inevitable that Taft's forces would be able to control the convention itself. However, Roosevelt's managers had one clever, long-shot strategy, or one creative public relations stunt, to present to the convention and the world. It was also a strategy that pitted Hiram Johnson's hotheads against TR's proceduralists.

A month earlier, Roosevelt had selected Governor Herbert Hadley of Missouri as his floor manager. As the convention started, and by prearrangement with Rosewater, Hadley made a point of order and delivered an eloquent speech arguing that no delegate whose selection had been challenged should have a right to be seated, even as part of the temporary roll of delegates, until there had been a vote of the full convention on which delegates to seat. As what he called precedents, he cited the case of the 1864 convention that had nominated Abraham Lincoln for his second term as well as the case of the convention of 1884. Based on those precedents, he said, only the delegates that were clearly entitled to be seated—those that had not been challenged—should be able to participate in the vote. The delegates who had not been challenged would then hear the majority report from the national committee, issued by the 37-member pro-Taft majority, which would offer one list of delegates to be seated, a list that included what Hadley described as 72 "names placed on the roll that were not honestly elected"; and then they would hear the minority report, issued by the 15 pro-Roosevelt members of the national committee, which would propose the substitution of the names of 72 delegates who, in Hadley's words, "have been elected by the honest votes of the Republican voters in the different States and Congressional districts."

"As long as we do not fairly meet and frankly discuss and honestly decide this question," Hadley proclaimed, "any man who goes out from this Convention with a nomination secured by the votes of those men will bear a tainted nomination, and will neither deserve nor receive the support of the American people."

There were shouts of approval throughout Hadley's speech, and by the time he ended, he had become a matinee idol. William Allen White called him "slim and lithe as a movie actor." There was not "a politically minded school boy" in America, according to a story a decade later in *Time* magazine, who did not know his name. Within hours, there was a buzz at the convention, with the press and reformers spreading his name as a possible compromise candidate.

Everyone understood what was at stake. The number of delegates on Hadley's list, specifically approved by TR, was the number needed to control the convention without relying on any support from delegates pledged to La Follette or Cummins. If the 72 delegates whose seats were being challenged could not vote on the legitimacy of their own seats, the Roosevelt forces would have a working majority. The convention would then vote for the 72 delegates named in the minority report and TR would gain control of the convention. It was a clever parliamentary trick, or public relations gambit; it sounded reasonable; but no one expected the Taft forces to agree.

Taft had practical reasons for opposing Hadley's motion, but he had a good procedural argument as well. If Hadley's motion had been accepted, it would have enabled any candidate to "game" the system by challenging enough delegates to control the convention, no matter how flimsy the claim, as long as there were a few members of the national committee on his side. A reasonable if also imperfect compromise would be to prevent each delegate from voting on his own case, or even on the cases of those in his delegation, but to allow all other challenged delegates to vote. Such a compromise, however, would unquestionably leave Taft in control.

Having permitted Hadley to make his case, and to win the hearts of reformers around the nation, Chairman Rosewater predictably issued a lengthy ruling discussing and rejecting Hadley's arguments and holding that Governor Hadley's resolution was out of order.

While his motion was as much theater as practical politics, Hadley did not allow the performance to go to the final act, the act envisioned by the more radical members of Hiram Johnson's California delegation and the others in the "bolt now" camp. Ten years later, California journalist and reformer Chester Rowell provided an insider's memory of the events. He said that Roosevelt's camp knew that Rosewater, after letting Hadley speak, would certainly rule that his motion was out of order. At that point, the Californians wanted Hadley to appeal to the floor, to shout his appeal to the galleries and through the galleries and the press to the American public.

For some time, there had been rumors that Roosevelt intended to flood the convention bleachers with rough-and-ready supporters with strong lungs and strong arms who would yell out their demand that he be selected—and who might even use force. This would be the signal for the kind of "roughhouse tactics" that Nick Roosevelt had heard his cousin discuss with Cal O'Laughlin; tactics designed to "terrorize them."

Rowell expected Hadley's appeal to result in a huge demonstration that could only be stopped by the police who were patrolling every inch of the hall. And the police were literally everywhere. "Not since the Haymarket Riot have so many members of this fine body of constabulary been gathered in one place," the slightly cheeky *American Magazine* account observed. "In spite of the disclaimers published in the papers, it is impossible not to get the impression that the Chicago police force dominated the convention and nominated Mr. Taft for President. They were in the galleries; they patrolled the aisles and mingled with the delegates, scrutinizing them with the familiar expression they wear when elbowing through a crowd of hoodlums and trying to 'spot' those who are 'liable to start something'; in the passageways there were scores of them, actually, and this is no exaggeration, crouched along the walls ready to spring with club and pistol in hand upon this historical deliberative assemblage."

At that point, once the police had attacked the Roosevelt boosters, and perhaps done so rather brutally, in front of the world's press, the strategy called for TR's supporters to walk out of the hall and hold their own convention, claiming to be the true Republican Party. It was the kind of tactic that they had used, and used effectively, at conventions in Michigan, Washington State, and elsewhere.

The plan was then to have two Republican candidates and to claim that TR was the only legitimate nominee, the clear choice of voters who had been given the chance to express themselves, not the handpicked choice of the bosses and special interests whose will was enforced by the police rather than by the rule of law. They hoped that most states would allow TR to run as the official nominee of the Republican Party. "He would have stood a better chance of election under those circumstances," Rowell said, "than as the nominee of a third party."

In a letter to Henry Haskell, the editor of the *Kansas City Star*, Hadley confirmed Rowell's memory of the events but added a few details of his own. Up to the last moment, Hadley said, he had intended to shout out a voice appeal to the delegates. He expected Rosewater to allow him to do so, an impression he had gained from Rosewater at a meeting the night before and from the secretary of the national committee earlier that day. But when Rosewater did not allow him to make such an appeal, Hadley made an on-the-spot decision not to go over Rosewater's head.

Hadley's decision infuriated many of the most aggressive members of the progressive caucus. Remembering events a decade later, Hadley said that he did not want, to "resort to rough stuff, which was favored by less than half of the so-called Roosevelt delegates (for some were instructed for Roosevelt who were not for him) and in which, through arrangements Fred Upham had made with the Chicago police, they would have been badly worsted."

There were some who could never forgive Hadley for his caution. After the convention, Hiram Johnson berated "the timid and shrinking" men who had viewed "with such horror" his proposal to seize control of the convention by force.

AS ROSEWATER'S ROLE as the temporary chair of the convention demonstrated, the choice of a permanent chair would be crucial. The chair would have the power to make vital parliamentary rulings that could be virtually impossible to overturn. Months earlier, before TR entered the race, Taft and the national committee had wisely selected Elihu Root for that role, knowing of his reputation for fairness and judgment. There was no doubt that he had impeccable credentials. A brilliant lawyer, with powerful corporate clients, he also had been the United States attorney for the Southern District of New York. Roosevelt had once called Root "a man of singularly keen intellect . . . possessing great tact in judgment . . . entirely fearless in standing up for the right." When thinking about candidates to succeed him in office, he told friends that Root was his first choice and that he would make a splendid president. He had been TR's secretary of war and secretary of state before becoming a senator from New York. Moreover, he had chaired the 1904 Republican Convention—at Roosevelt's request. Root was not a man who could easily be dismissed as a tool of the special interests.

Hadley warned TR not to challenge Root as temporary chairman. "If we should oppose the election of Senator Root as Temporary Chairman and should fail," he cautioned, "it would be taken as an indication that the Taft forces were in control of the convention and would weaken your chances of nomination. I think there are a number of delegates who are instructed for you who are probably in favor of the nomination of either President Taft or someone else who would vote for Senator Root as against anybody who might be a candidate against him."

Nevertheless, most of TR's inner circle insisted on challenging Root. The role of the chair was simply too important to ignore. Moreover, this was really all about a public relations effort to show that the convention had been rigged. If they did not dispute the choice of a chair, it would be much harder to claim that his rulings, at least some of which were certain to go against them, were unfair. So after briefly suggesting that he would not object to Root as the convention chair, on June 4 the Colonel offered as strong a case as he could comfortably make against Root's selection.

"In the past, Mr. Root has rendered distinguished service," TR said. "But in this contest, Mr. Root has ranged himself against the men who stand for progressive principles. . . . He is put forward by the bosses and the representatives of special privilege. . . . It is the duty of every progressive Republican to oppose the selection as temporary chairman at Chicago of any man put forward in the interests of the supporters of Mr. Taft in this contest."

In an effort to garner a few La Follette delegates for their candidate as permanent chair, the Roosevelt forces shrewdly nominated Francis McGovern, the governor of La Follette's home state of Wisconsin for the post.

The vote was agonizingly close. Root won by a razor-thin margin with 558 votes, 18 more than Taft would need to win the nomination. (McGovern had 501 votes, and a smattering of delegates voted for other candidates.) Some observers argued that Root's numbers overstated the strength that Taft would have once the actual presidential balloting began. Root's total included the votes of at least 22 delegates selected in primary states where the law required them to vote for TR when the presidential balloting began, a group of men who actually supported Taft and had been put on the delegation by Taft supporters with the understanding that they could vote with him on procedural issues, such as the selection of the permanent chair. The vote counters listed 22 such delegates: 7 from Illinois, 8 from Maryland, 4 from Pennsylvania, and 3 from Oregon.

Some Roosevelt supporters claimed that he still had a good chance. Convinced that 22 of the men who supported Root for chair were pledged to vote for TR on the first ballot, Cal O'Laughlin assured Nick that the vote had gone just as they had expected. "He said we would surely win," Nick wrote in his diary that night.

The banner headline in the *Boston Globe* the next day reflected and fed that optimism. "Root Victory Shows Taft in Minority," it said. "He cannot hold all Root's votes for Chairman." Other papers carried reports that emboldened Roosevelt supporters and may have concerned Taft. "Today's proceedings in the Republican National Convention demonstrate one thing clearly," the *New York Times* said. "So far as the nomination for President is concerned, this situation is up in the air."

Of course, the reporters wanted it to be a horse race, if only to sell papers. Even if Taft had only 540 votes, the minimum needed to win,

Roosevelt had fewer than 500. He would have to find more than 40 votes somewhere. La Follette, who controlled 36 votes, was inalterably opposed to Roosevelt, and it was not clear that TR could pick up the 10 delegates that were pledged to Senator Cummins. To win, Roosevelt would need to pick up more than 40 of the votes pledged to Taft. That was the reason the campaign continued to insist on "purging the role" of the 72 "stolen" delegates. If the nomination were to go to a second or third ballot, and delegates were free to leave their first choice, or the choice that they were obliged to support under state law, both Roosevelt and Taft would lose some of the men pledged to them. Under some state laws, the delegates were selected in a process that was separate from the primary, and the primary results were only legally binding for the first ballot. Thus, Roosevelt would lose those delegates from Ohio and Maryland who really favored Taft, but Taft would lose some delegates from Massachusetts who really favored Roosevelt.

With the race so close, there was an obvious third option. The convention could turn to a compromise candidate. But as that option became more widely discussed, and as a particular name began to emerge, Roosevelt became increasingly intransigent. Selecting someone who had not even run in the primaries would make a farce of the notion of letting the people rule. What's more, most of his energy was now devoted to creating a third party.

Still, the sound of compromise was in the air. After his performance on Tuesday, the name on everyone's lips was Herbert Hadley.

LATE TUESDAY NIGHT, according to Stanley Washburn's oral history, twenty-eight men met in Roosevelt's headquarters at the Congress Hotel. The son of a former senator from Minnesota, Washburn later gained fame as a war correspondent, explorer, and author. "TR stood absolutely silent while his leaders were making speeches," Washburn recalled. "The last to address the faithful 28 was Hadley who climbed onto a chair and made a stirring speech for Roosevelt which was greeted with profound applause. Just in front of him stood the Colonel with Hiram Johnson on one side and Arthur Hill [the Boston lawyer who had been with Roosevelt from the start], on the other. It was a very hot night and the speaker mopped his brow, nodding appreciation to the beaming audience."

Though short and stout, with rimmed glasses and hair parted in the middle, Johnson was an outstanding orator with piercing blue eyes and a fighting jaw. He was convinced that Hadley planned to double cross TR.

"When the din of applause had subsided," Washburn said, "'Hiram Johnson raised his hand and with one little fat finger pointing at the speaker said, 'Governor, I want to ask you a question.'

"'Certainly Governor Johnson.'

"'What are you going to do when the convention meets at noon tomorrow? I know, you know, every man in this room knows that they are going to steal the nomination from Theodore Roosevelt. What I want to know is this. Are you going to get up with California, Minnesota, Pennsylvania, and Ohio, and walk out of the hall and nominate this man?' Then he put his arm on Roosevelt's shoulder.

"The governor of Missouri replied, 'They would not dare to steal our delegates.'

"The governor of California said bluntly, 'They are going to do it, and what are you going to do? Are you going to lead your delegation out of the hall?'

"A deadly silence fell on the room, every man tense with expectation.

"After a long hesitation, Hadley replied, 'If this happens, which is impossible, I shall have to be guided by the situation of that moment.' There was no applause this time and silence fell again.

"Hiram turned to the room, and putting his hand on Roosevelt's sleeve said in a deep melodious voice, 'This man is being assassinated in the house of friends.'

"Hadley then got down off the chair. Everyone drew away; no one spoke to him; and he very quietly walked out of the room."

Washburn concluded his description of the scene as follows. "Though

I had had a lot of political experience before, this was quite the most dramatic episode I had ever witnessed."

HADLEY SET THE delegates on fire again on Wednesday afternoon. As soon as Chairman Root called the meeting to order, Hadley made a motion to "purge the temporary roll" and to substitute the list of delegates that he had presented on Tuesday. This time, taking account of Hiram Johnson's blistering criticism, he alluded to the decision not to resort to the threat of force.

"We could have forcibly insisted on calling the roll on the motion" yesterday, he said, "and we could have forcibly taken control. Instead, we waited patiently until today." The huge audience listened carefully as he made his case. "It may be true that there are many persons who do not agree with us that Theodore Roosevelt should be our candidate for President, but there can be no difference of opinion that his voice today is the greatest of the western world."

For the next three hours, delegates took to their feet to present arguments for and against Hadley's motion. When the debate ended at 3 P.M., voices throughout the hall demanded that Hadley return to the rostrum. When he appeared, "both floor and galleries were on their feet, whistling, cheering, yelling, pounding their chairs and stomping their feet." People threw hats in the air and one black delegate raised an umbrella and lifted it high above his head. In one far corner, Governor Stubbs of Kansas waved his arms wildly as delegations from New Jersey and Hadley's home state of Missouri began to march around the hall carrying their home state banners. As the Roosevelt delegates "yelled themselves hoarse," delegates from California, Nebraska, and Kansas joined the parade through the huge hall. Then Oklahoma and Pennsylvania fell in line.

A delegate from Pennsylvania ran to the front of the stage with a megaphone and shouted, "Hadley, the next president. Three cheers." While the crowd roared, the sergeant-at-arms led the Hadley booster off the stage.

As the demonstration grew in size and excitement, it "started a running fire of talk on the convention floor to make him the compromise candidate for President," the *Baltimore Sun* reported. Senator Root occasionally pounded the table for order but made no serious attempt to stop it.

Some of TR's supporters in the galleries who felt that they should have been seated as delegates got into the act.

"I am a regularly chosen delegate from Mississippi," a challenge delegate shouted to all who could hear. It was Willis Mollison, a black lawyer from Vicksburg who had not been seated by the credentials committee. "The man who holds my seat has no more right to it than a pickpocket his to the pocketbook he picks."

Not everyone in the hall caught the Hadley fever. Alice Roosevelt Longworth, sitting near the press stand, was clearly not pleased, convinced that the opposition had a hand in the demonstration. It seemed that the Republican Party had a new hero—and that it might have a new candidate.

Then suddenly, after the Hadley demonstration had gone on for almost an hour, an attractive young woman in white, sitting in the galleries, stood up and unfurled a huge lithograph of Roosevelt. While waving the picture with one hand, she waved a handkerchief in the other. As she waved, the delegates on the floor looked up at her and started to cheer, and she used her handkerchief to blow kisses back at them. Instantly, the Hadley demonstration turned into a Roosevelt demonstration with the focus on the young woman who was soon identified as Mrs. W. A. Davis of Chicago. Delegates started to cheer for Teddy and for Mrs. Davis. They brought her down to the floor and "she came marching up the main aisle with her face flushed and her eyes blazing with excitement. As she marched she turned her face to each delegation and called on them to cheer, and each response rocked the building."

The delegates then lifted her over the press seats and onto the stage. Delegates from California took their huge California bear and waved it over her head. While holding the picture of TR, she tried to give a speech with what the *New York Times* called "that remarkable voice of hers" that was "audible over the din."

The demonstration went on for forty minutes until Senator Root finally brought it to an end. By that time people had moved back from Hadley to their true hero, TR.

Hadley's motion to "purge the roll" was, of course, certain to fail. Taft's floor leader and Hadley's counterpart was former congressman James Watson of Indiana. On behalf of Taft's supporters, Watson moved to send the motion to the Credentials Committee. The final vote showed 564 in favor of Taft—a gain of 6 votes for the Taft forces from the battle over the permanent chair.

TR SPENT WEDNESDAY afternoon at his hotel, in the main reception room of his spacious headquarters, surrounded by friends, family, political aides, and the press, following the proceedings in the convention hall through telephone and wire reports. Messengers ran in and out with dispatches from his lieutenants on the convention floor, describing the Hadley demonstration. From time to time TR read a few lines to the reporters.

"The cheering for Hadley has now lasted twenty minutes," he read with a laugh. "That's right. There is nothing too good for him. He is splendid. He deserves it."

Then a note came in describing the lady in white. Laughing again, he read the press one report saying that "girls carrying Teddy bears were carried on the platform" and another that said it was a good thing that it was once again a Roosevelt convention.

As "buoyant and cheerful as ever," according to press accounts, TR told the assembled reporters that he hoped that Hadley would serve as Vice President on his ticket. But he also made it clear that he was inalterably opposed to a compromise candidate, any candidate, even Hadley. Maybe especially Hadley. If any of his supporters moved over to Taft or to a compromise candidate, he said, he would organize candidates to challenge them in their home states and districts.

While he did not let the reporters know his true feelings, TR was furious with Hadley. He suspected that some of Taft's floor managers were trying to force both camps to turn to Hadley as a compromise candidate, replacing Roosevelt. In fact, that was exactly what Taft's floor manager had in mind that afternoon. Whether Hadley knew it or not, Watson wanted the convention to turn to him.

Watson had not trusted Roosevelt since his speech in Columbus championing the recall of judicial decisions. He liked Taft but was certain that he would be defeated in the general election, particularly if TR ran on a third-party ticket. But he felt a certain midwestern kinship with Hadley and thought that he had a chance to force Roosevelt out of the race and to win. "If I were picking a presidential candidate off of a tree, as if I were picking an apple, I would not choose Governor Hadley," Watson told a group of insiders in the Taft ranks during the convention, "but if I were choosing a man whom I think could be elected this fall, I would choose him." Among other virtues, he said, "he is Roosevelt's floor leader in this convention and the Colonel could not possibly turn his back on him."

"I persisted in my idea of nominating Hadley," Watson later recalled, and so on that Wednesday afternoon he "arranged a coup to give Hadley a boost." He laid the groundwork for the moment when the convention exploded for Hadley. When the demonstration ended, Watson went to Frank Kellogg of Minnesota, an important Roosevelt supporter, and suggested that they back Hadley as a compromise candidate. Later that night, he took his idea to New York congressman Lucius Littauer. According to Watson's account, both Kellogg and Littauer took the idea to TR, who was receptive at first but then consulted his leading supporters, who angrily rejected any notion of compromise. Most of his supporters were so furious that, as Watson recalled events that night, they "immediately landed on Hadley and abused him for betraying Roosevelt, some going so far as to charge that he had all the time been playing the middle-of-the-road game in order to attract the nomination to himself."

ALICE LONGWORTH CALLED Wednesday a "night of rumors." In Roosevelt's five-room hotel headquarters, a fight raged on between two factions. On one side were men that the *New York Times* called "hotheads," like Hiram Johnson and Gifford Pinchot, who were "crying for war to the death" and who wanted to walk out immediately. On the other side were "the cool heads," more practical men like Governors Hadley and Stubbs, and Senator Borah, leaders of the progressive faction of the Republican Party who had been with Roosevelt from the first but did not want to leave the party, or at least not until they had made a better case for such drastic action. Even Senator Bourne, who had been the instigator of the primary process and who, months earlier, had urged the progressives to be prepared to bolt, felt it necessary to stay within the party.

"The Roosevelt camp has gradually divided into two groups," a delegate from New Jersey told the *Washington Post*. "One group is satisfied to beat Taft, and have a moderately progressive candidate nominated," he said. "The second group believes that the setting aside of Roosevelt after he has carried the primaries would in itself be a victory for the reactionaries and stand-patters."

William Allen White explained that the leaders who were most involved in politics in their home state—he listed "Stubbs, Bristow, Allen of Kansas, Gov. Aldrich of Nebraska; Hadley of Missouri; Glasscock of West Virginia; the men from the Dakotas and Minnesota; Gov. Deneen of Illinois"—wanted to "make the nomination regular" since they controlled the Republican organizations in their states and had organizations that were as progressive as any new party would be. They didn't want to rock the boat. By contrast, he said, men like Garfield, Pinchot, Medill McCormick, Beveridge, and most of the New Englanders didn't control their party organization at home and "felt that they would do better fighting outside the party." White concluded that "these two classes of men represented the extremes in the colonel's councils."

Hadley had begun to believe that many of Roosevelt's leaders were doing "almost as much" to defeat TR as the Taft leaders. He had become convinced that most of them did not want Roosevelt nominated by the convention at all. Echoing the comments that others had made to the press during the convention, he wrote a revealing note to a friend almost a decade later. "Heney, Beveridge, Pinchot, Perkins, Munsey, and most of those who were out of the Republican organization in their respective states, wanted Roosevelt defeated with grievances so that a new party, of which they would be the leaders, would be brought into existence," he said. The "defeated with grievances" group seemed to have Roosevelt's ear. By contrast, "men like Stubbs, White, Allen, Borah and others who could still work through and with their Republican organizations in their respective states, wanted to win."

As a practical matter, winning was probably out of the question. But it was too early to bolt. Roosevelt wanted to form a new party, but he needed to bring as many people with him as possible, and he also had to have a principled way to explain his reasons for not encouraging or even allowing the convention to turn to a compromise candidate, some other progressive, someone such as Hadley.

Late Wednesday evening, William Allen White was at Roosevelt's headquarters, where Senator Beveridge was standing on a chair orating to the crowd in the large Florentine Room. Roosevelt called White into one of the inner rooms.

"What do you know about Hadley, really," TR asked.

White explained that they were "dear and beloved friends." He told TR about Hadley's capacity for student poker and recalled how he had been suspended in his senior year for harmless student activity and still graduated with honors. White could hear Beveridge holding forth in the main room and the late-night crowds outside the window, down on Michigan Avenue, talking, chanting, and singing songs celebrating Teddy. "The tension and strife about the place, the slowly mounting fever, was all but crackling our blood," White recalled.

Roosevelt chuckled as White described some of Hadley's youthful escapades.

Roosevelt's feelings seemed to soften. He then told White that he was going to see Hadley in a few minutes. "They want to compromise on Hadley," he said. "I can take Hadley, but they must purge the roll of the convention first." Roosevelt knew, of course, that the Taft forces would never agree to that ultimatum.

White then told Roosevelt that while only a few people knew it, Hadley had been stricken with tuberculosis. He was going down to the floor of the convention, managing Roosevelt's troops, with a temperature of 101, 102, and, at the climax, 103 degrees. "Roosevelt cried for a moment, shocked and pained by the tragedy of it," White said. White made it clear that, whatever rumors were in the air, Hadley had no intention of running for President.

When he arrived at TR's headquarters, Hadley started the meeting by saying that he did not want to be nominated for reasons with which "I assume you are familiar." But according to Hadley's account, he told Roosevelt that he should consent to the nomination of a compromise candidate such as Justice Charles Evans Hughes or Iowa Senator Albert Cummins.

Roosevelt said that he would prefer Hadley to either of them but that in any case he would not consent to any compromise candidate unless the convention agreed to "purge the rolls" and replace the 72 delegates who had been seated through fraud.

TO BRIDGE THE differences between his supporters, Roosevelt convened a meeting in the Florentine Room on Thursday with delegates from every state. Some wanted to leave at once; some wanted to stay. Ultimately, TR forced them to agree to two resolutions that would keep them in the convention for the moment but provide a clear basis to walk out of the convention on Friday or Saturday. They decided that (1) they would only take part in the convention if the "72 delegates to which we are entitled were seated"; and (2) "if the convention declined to seat the delegates fraudulently unseated, the Roosevelt delegates would decline to be bound by the action of the convention." His supporters had unanimously agreed to stay in the convention for the moment, Roosevelt explained, but they reserved the right to leave if the disputed delegates were not seated.

"Any man nominated by this convention as now composed," Roosevelt told the press on Thursday afternoon, "will not be tolerated by the Roosevelt delegates." That would include Taft, of course, but it would also preclude the nomination of a compromise candidate.

"If the honestly elected majority choose to inaugurate a movement to nominate me as a progressive candidate on a progressive platform, and if in such event the general feeling among the progressives favors my being nominated," he announced, "I will accept."

On Friday morning, the fourth day of the convention, Cal O'Laughlin's front page story in the *Chicago Tribune* carried a headline that set the stage for the Roosevelt forces:

ISSUE TODAY:

PURGE ROLL

OR NEW PARTY

———————

If Delegates Indorse

Larceny Roosevelt

Men Will Sit Mute

———————

Colonel Still in Race

———————

Should Stolen Votes Nominate

Then New Convention
Will Be Called

Roosevelt was acting on principle—on principles necessitated by the advent of political primaries, O'Laughlin said. Any other course would "cheat the Republican voters of the primary states of realization of their express will. The colonel entered the fight for principle. He proposes to continue it. That principle is the rule of the people."

ON FRIDAY AFTERNOON, the credentials fight finally came to the floor of the convention. At 4 P.M., Governor Hadley announced that the Roosevelt forces planned to challenge the seating of only three delegations: California, Texas, and Washington State. Those states represented their strongest cases. But they also illustrated the peculiarities of the laws that govern nominating conventions and the ways in which reasonable delegates who have political motives can disagree on the proper resolution of delegate challenges.

The starting point for the organization of a political convention is the Call to Convention, an invitation from the national party to state parties asking them to convene and to select a presidential nominee. The Call provides the legal framework for the convention. As adopted by the Republican National Committee in December 1911, the Call was very specific in certain respects. It said that the national convention would include a specified number of delegates at large from each state as well as "two delegates from each congressional district." Furthermore, it said, "The Congressional District delegates shall be elected by conventions called by the Republican Congressional Committee in each district" and that "in no state shall an election be so held as to prevent the delegates from any Congressional District and their alternates from being selected by the Republican electors of that district."

To Elihu Root, who was an excellent lawyer, the Call served as the law of the convention, even where there was a conflict with state law. Several court decisions over the years have agreed with him. They have ruled that political parties "enjoy a constitutionally protected right of political association under the First Amendment" that allows them to set their own rules and to enforce those rules even when they are in conflict with state law. The U.S. Supreme Court has ruled that, since those rights are protected by the First Amendment, "courts may not interfere on the ground that they view a particular expression as unwise or irrational." That interpretation of the Constitution gives political parties enormous freedom to determine the laws that will guide them and to determine which delegates to seat.

THE FIRST SERIOUS challenge to reach the floor of the convention on Friday afternoon came from California. Under the leadership of Hiram Johnson's progressives, California had adopted a winner-take-all presidential primary law. Since Roosevelt won the statewide primary by more than 75,000 votes, Johnson argued that Roosevelt was entitled to all 26 of the state's delegates. But Taft had bested Roosevelt, albeit narrowly, in the state's Fourth Congressional District. Based on the state's law, California's secretary of state certified all 26 Roosevelt delegates. But based on the Call of the Convention, which required states to allow each congressional district to select its delegates, the Republican National Committee put the names of Taft's delegates from the Fourth Congressional District on the temporary roll of the convention. The majority report of the Credentials Committee agreed to seat the two Taft delegates, but Roosevelt's supporters on the committee issued a dissent. It was the legal problem that Hiram Johnson had anticipated in December when the RNC adopted the Call and the state decided to ignore the language in the Call and to create a winner-take-all primary.

When the California case came to the floor of the convention, Governor Hadley moved to substitute the minority report and to seat

Roosevelt's delegates from the Fourth District. Francis J. Heney, the brilliant San Francisco prosecutor who was also a leading "hot head," rose to speak.

"Mr. Chairman and gentlemen of the Convention, the question involved in this case is one which goes to the very root of self-government. It involves directly the question whether or not the people of a sovereign state of this nation are entitled to decide for themselves how they shall select their delegates to the National Convention."

Taft agreed to abide by those laws when he entered the state's primary, he thundered. But "now he crawls out of his promise and robs the state of her rightful representatives." There was deafening applause from the Roosevelt supporters in the hall. Heney said that California had passed a series of reforms to free itself from political bondage, "which is startling to distinguished gentlemen like the chairman of this convention."

Root looked sternly at Heney and Taft's delegates shouted in anger. A Taft supporter from Pennsylvania rose to say that Heney's remarks were out of order. Root said that Heney's comments were not out of order—yet.

"If Taft accepts these two votes, he will be guilty of treason against the law," Heney shouted in concluding his statement.

As the whole floor exploded in cheers and boos, Governor Johnson rose to speak. "The question today," he said, "is shall the people rule?"

"Yes, yes, let the people rule," came the thunderous response from a thousand throats, the *Chicago Tribune* reported.

"The revolution is on and the progressives are sure to triumph," Johnson continued. The Roosevelt delegations exploded. Every man jumped to his feet in a demonstration that went on for several minutes.

When he could be heard again, Johnson waved a telegram in the air and said it was the one that Taft had sent to the California secretary of state, entering the primary and promising to abide by the state's laws.

Having agreed to live by those rules, he said, Taft should not now be allowed to defy them.

The roll call on the California challenge provided the closest vote of the convention. Some men changed sides, and a few men abstained. "The Colonel's followers were crazy with joy, while the opposition began to get nervous," the *New York Times* reported. "The California delegation cheered every flop to the echo. The last switch came with Hawaii. Its six votes were thrown solidly for California and pandemonium reigned for five minutes."

Each side had reason for hope—and for bitter resentment. Most damaging, 6 delegates from Illinois who were pledged to Roosevelt as a result of the Illinois primary voted against seating the pro-Roosevelt men from California. Those six votes determined the outcome. The next morning, the *Chicago Tribune* listed their names as well as the results of the primary votes in the districts where they had been elected. In the Ninth District, for example, which was represented at the convention by Taft supporter Fred W. Upham, the vote was 6,798 for TR and 4,134 for Taft. Though pledged to vote for Roo-sevelt for President, Upham and the other five delegates were legally, if perhaps not morally, free to vote as they wished on credentials challenges.

On the final tally, Taft had 542 votes—only 2 more than he needed to prevail. The *Tribune* speculated that the vote on delegates from Washington State the next day would be another cliff-hanger, but in fact the vote on the delegates from California took the remaining air out of the Roosevelt balloon. "Everyone recognized that if Roosevelt could not win in this contest, he could not win in any of the others, and that Taft would be nominated," one of his advisors recalled.

As soon as the outcome was clear, Mrs. Roosevelt, who had been watching from the gallery, left the hall.

Hiram Johnson had won the crowd, and to this date many observers have concluded that he had the better case. But in fact, as he himself had feared six months earlier when he sent a telegram to La Follette expressing concern about the conflict between the requirements of the

Republican National Committee's Call and the state's winner-take-all primary, the law was on Taft's side. In the century since that first credentials battle, the Supreme Court has made it clear that where there is a conflict between a national party rule and a state law, the party rule prevails.

"The State of California had no business to pass such a law," Root later said. The rule laid down by the Call to the Convention was legally controlling. "I don't know if it is the best rule, but it was the rule under which they were elected even though there may be a better rule."

ROOSEVELT AND HIS advisors knew that they were unlikely to win any of the other challenges. After the proceedings in the convention hall ended for the day, TR held court at the Congress Hotel. Except for a brief drive to a bookstore hours earlier, he had been there all afternoon, receiving guests, talking strategy, and reading bulletins from the floor. Some of the visitors, including a few staunch supporters, such as Senator Borah, delivered sobering news. Much as they loved him and agreed with his substantive positions, they were not prepared to join him in forming a new party. Others promised to be with him to the end. Most visitors refused to be quoted. "I do not care to get between quotation marks tonight," Governor Deneen of Illinois told the *Washington Post*.

Asked by the press for a comment, Roosevelt offered a pithy phrase that drew on his years ranching, riding, and hunting in the West. "Out in the short grass country," he said, "we used to do things and talk afterwards. That is what I intend to do."

He continued to meet with his advisors late into the evening. Word had already leaked that his managers had arranged space at Orchestra Hall for a meeting the following night. But if he planned to bolt, as so many advisors had urged for so long, there were endless practical questions to be settled. Would it be a new party, or would he—indeed, could he still—claim to represent the true Republican Party? To most of TR's intimate supporters, it had become clear that they would need to create a new party, which had been the goal for many of them from the start. Even so, should they walk out of the convention and simply announce that TR was running as the candidate of the new party—or should they hold a new convention of their own at a later date with delegates elected from all of the states? The group decided that in order to build a grassroots organization in every state, to expand their base and to bring Democrats into the process, they would have to announce that the new party would have its own delegate selection process and that it would meet in a convention six weeks later. In theory, the voters and delegates would even have the option of selecting a candidate other than Roosevelt.

There was one other very practical matter to consider. It would cost a fortune to create a new party overnight. How could they afford to move ahead with a national campaign and the costs of a second convention? The *New York Times* presented the issue in stark terms. "One very embarrassing feature of the new party situation," the paper wrote, "is the enormous cost of getting such a movement going. Some Roosevelt financial backers who have spent their money like water to promote his boom as a candidate for the regular Republican nomination are unwilling to throw any of their money after the large amounts they have provided to no apparent purpose."

But two of the men in the hotel room with Roosevelt were so rich that they could, on their own, assure much of the funding for the campaign. In an era before Congress had imposed any limitations on spending by individuals, they could contribute as much as they wanted and as much as they could. After spending time huddled in a corner, considering all of the options, at 2 A.M. George Perkins and Frank Munsey came to Roosevelt with a promise. Amos Pinchot described the scene twenty years later.

Each man placed a hand on one of Roosevelt's shoulders. "Colonel," they said, "we will see you through." Munsey then added this promise. "My fortune, my magazines and my newspapers are with you."

Having made the final decision to walk out of the convention and create a new party, the progressive leaders had to determine the best way to make an exit the following day. Those in the room included Hiram Johnson and Francis Heney of California, Henry J. Allen and William Allen White of Kansas, Gifford Pinchot, James Garfield, Senator Borah, Governor Deneen of Illinois, and Governor Hadley. The Californians didn't want to return to the convention the next day, but Roosevelt said that they had to follow the best possible procedural course: to sit through the remaining credentials challenges, which they were certain to lose, and then, right before the final report was issued, make a statement of conscience on behalf of the progressive forces. After that, they would remain in their seats as delegates but not vote on the selection of the nominee. They would say they were "Present but not voting."

As Roosevelt already expected, much as they admired and supported him, Senator Borah and Governors Deneen and Hadley could not accept his terms. They said that they would remain in the Republican Party and cast their votes for Roosevelt.

With no bitterness, TR turned to Henry J. Allen of Kansas, the colorful editor of the *Wichita Beacon,* who had been championing his candidacy since early 1910. Since Hadley would be remaining in the party, Roosevelt said, "I am going to ask Mr. Allen to deliver the valedictory of the Progressives to the convention if the Taft managers decide to grant us that privilege."

EVEN AT THAT late hour, thousands of supporters were still gathered out on Michigan Avenue, calling for him to give them a word, a sign. Finally, TR raised a hotel window and shouted to the crowd below.

"My friends," he called out, "my hat is in the ring and will be in stronger than ever."

The crowd pleaded for him to continue, but TR lowered the window and returned to the meeting. He would have plenty of time to announce his plans the next day.

Chapter Fourteen

The mood at the convention on Saturday morning was almost giddy, a spring break between seasons of intense battle.

Everyone knew the outcome. "Delegates in Rollicking Mood," a *Boston Globe* headline proclaimed. Taft was sure to be nominated, vindicating the planning, hard work, and political hardball of his supporters and proving to his opponents that what they deemed political theft could work. For the men TR had once called "ultra-radicals" and for delegates from states like California who had always wanted a new party, the moment was almost exhilarating. They had fun jeering at what they called "the steamroller," shouting out "toot toot" and "choo choo" and "all aboard" at every opportunity. Even the people in the gallery got in on the act. Every time Chairman Root announced that "the ayes have it," a spectator high in the stands blew two short blasts on a mechanical whistle.

The day was less exhilarating for TR's supporters who felt obliged to stay in the party, men like Senator Borah and even Governor Hadley, who saw trouble on the horizon. But nothing that would happen on the floor really mattered. The delegates were free to have fun with each other and with the leaders of the factions.

"Theodore Roosevelt is out," the *New York Tribune* reported. "To use his own vernacular, he has been knocked clear over the ropes. The vote of the convention on the decision of the Credentials Committee on the California contest decided it. When Colonel Roosevelt heard the result, he threw up his hands."

But of course TR did not throw his hands up in defeat. He thrust them in the air in defiance, greeting visitors and working at his hotel while the delegates spent one last day at the convention hall.

Starting at 9 A.M., the final challenges reached the floor of the convention. Since Taft's leaders had proved that they controlled the convention, the outcome was inevitable. Nevertheless, TR was determined to let the convention rule on two final cases before formally announcing his decision, hoping to put a spotlight on Washington State and Texas. In Washington State the Roosevelt forces were on the side of political reform and popular democracy; in Texas, however, they were aligned with longtime state party boss Cecil Lyon and supported Lyon's successful effort to exclude black voters from the electorate.

On the convention floor, each side repeated the arguments that it had made over the past weeks in the hearings held by the Republican National Committee and then by the Credentials Committee, but this time they were playing to the huge, contentious crowd in the Coliseum and, through the press, to the American electorate. Both sides agreed that the outcome in Washington State depended on the composition of the 121-member delegation to the state convention from King County, which included Seattle. Taft's delegates had been selected by the party's leaders with little public input; Roosevelt's had been elected in a primary.

Representing Taft, Maurice Galvin of Kentucky argued that the primary in King County was both illegal and illegitimate. The state law did not provide for primaries, he said, and the county's Executive Committee, which was legally vested with the power to select delegates, had chosen a pro-Taft slate. The primary had been called by the County Committee, not the Executive Committee, after the County Chairman, who favored Roosevelt, "illegally and intentionally packed the [County Committee] meeting with 131 men who had not been elected as members of the county committee and who had no right to participate in the meeting." As a result, Taft's supporters boycotted the "so-called primaries" and of 100,000 qualified voters only 6,900 people participated.

Herbert Halbert of Minnesota responded for the Roosevelt supporters, arguing that the King County primary had been legal and binding. Roosevelt had won overwhelmingly, by a vote of 6,400 to 500. If those delegates had been awarded to him instead of Taft, he would easily have won the delegates selected at the state convention.

"The Republican Party can stand defeat with honor," he concluded to great applause. "But it can never stand defeat with dishonor."

Each side had a point; each had a dollop of truth and a teaspoon of legality.

When James Watson moved the adoption of the majority report, "bedlam broke loose on the floor" with shouts from every part of the room.

"Toot, toot; choo choo; choo choo; toot toot."

"What about the speed limit," someone cried out.

"Sand the track, Watson, you're slipping."

As Root leaned on his gavel, smiling amid the chaos, a Pennsylvania delegate shouted out, "More gasoline! More gasoline!"

Near the rear of the hall, a crowd started to sing "Nearer My God to Thee"—as passengers had done on the *Titanic* as it was sinking into the Atlantic Ocean only two months earlier. Others followed with a chorus of "John Brown's Body."

When Chairman Root called the question on the Washington State challenge at around 11:45, a delegate from Mississippi rose to object.

"I rise to make a point of order," he said. It was Perry Howard, the prominent black lawyer from Jackson. A week earlier, TR had considered asking him to give one of his seconding speeches.

"The gentleman will state his point of order," Root said coolly.

"The point of order is that the steam roller is exceeding the speed limit," Howard said. There were gales of laughter and cheers and hoots.

Root's response fit right in with the mood. "The Chair is ready to rule upon the point of order," he said. "The point of order is sustained.

The justification is that we have some hope of getting home for Sunday." On the floor and in the galleries, people on both sides of the party laughed and cheered.

Everyone knew that this was also very serious business, but to the surprise of many of those in the hall, Roosevelt's managers did not ask for a roll call. Taft's delegates from Washington State were seated on a voice vote.

During a break, while waiting to take up the next case, the crowd started to sing "Merrily We Roll Along." As the intermission continued, a band singer in the balcony sang a chorus of "Moonlight Bay." The crowd cheered wildly and asked her to sing it again, which she did to another round of cheering.

The intermission continued for more than ninety minutes as the hall filled with rumors, all false but all juicy, of possible compromise candidates and a surprise choice for Vice President. Finally, at 1:30, Elihu Root called the convention back to order. He announced that the Credentials Committee, by unanimous consent, had agreed to abandon all of the remaining challenges with the exception of Texas.

Since the outcome was clear, Hiram Johnson walked out of the hall, saying that he would not continue to participate in the proceedings or feel bound by the convention's actions. He released a statement announcing that he had instructed the rest of the California delegation to stay in the hall in deference to the wishes of Colonel Roosevelt.

The convention finally took up the Texas case at 2:15. Taft's side, with Cecil Lyon as a foil, felt that it had the moral high ground. Using many of the same arguments that had been advanced a few days earlier in front of the national committee, Thomas Devine said that "the issue in Texas is whether the sentiment of the majority of Republicans in the State should prevail, or whether the boss-ridden machine should be sustained." Devine had just been named national committeeman from Colorado.

Devine charged that Cecil Lyon had used his power as national committeeman and patronage distributor in Texas to build a base of support, extract payments from those he placed in office, and to create a lily-white party by purging the rolls of black voters. He held up a copy of a postcard that Lyon had sent to voters "raising the lily white issue and stating that the time has come when voters need to decide whether the Negro or the white man was to rule in the state of Texas." While the pro-Roosevelt delegation was lily-white, the Taft supporters included black delegates such as William McDonald.

Devine pointed out that during the past sixteen years, mostly under Cecil Lyon's rule, the Republican vote in Texas had dropped from 141,000 in 1896 to 26,000 in 1910. Much of the loss was the result of disenfranchising blacks.

Devine had one more charge to hurl at Roosevelt and his reformers who wanted to seat Lyon and his men. "The Lyon machine," he said, "is made up largely of postmasters and other federal officials or their relations and is entirely run for selfish purposes." It was precisely the charge that Roosevelt's supporters were flinging at Taft's delegations elsewhere.

Speaking for Roosevelt, John Sullivan of Ohio argued that Lyon's faction had played by the rules in selecting its delegates and that they deserved to be seated. What's more, he attacked a number of those on Taft's slate, including men he claimed were really Democrats.

The merits of the arguments didn't matter, of course, since Taft clearly had the votes on the floor of the convention as he had in the committees. After a voice vote on the Texas cases, the Roosevelt forces allowed the convention to adopt the roll of delegates and alternates to the permanent convention. They knew that a great many of them would be leaving the hall later that night.

WHILE HIS SUPPORTERS were going through the charade in the convention hall, Roosevelt spent the day at the Congress Hotel, greeting visitors, making plans for the event that was to take place at Orchestra Hall later that night and making arrangements for his new party. He was leaving the party that had been his political home for his entire adult life. For many people, such a split would have been painful. Nevertheless, reporters claimed that he was in a jovial mood. After lunch, he even found time to go for a car ride with Edith.

He could delegate a lot of decisions, but some needed his personal attention. For the evening rally, who would be admitted, who would speak, in what order? What remarks should he make? Was this to be a nominating convention or were they simply announcing the formation of a new party that would hold a nominating convention to take place at a later date? Who would control the new party? Who would manage it? Would Senator Dixon continue to be the leader? How would the platform be formulated? Was it a branch of the Republican Party or truly a new party? If it was a new party, what role would there be for elected Republican leaders such as the progressive governors who had asked him to run? Could they participate as Republicans or would they have to leave the party? How about the presidential electors? Some states had already named the electors for the Republican Party in their states. Would voters in those states be allowed to vote for those electors or would each state have to create a new party with new electors? How about Democrats? What role would they have in the new party? Might TR even consider a Democratic Party running mate? How about La Follette? What if he decided that he should be the nominee of the new party? Would that be allowed? Would there be an open selection process? The number of problems to be addressed was dizzying.

But as he was talking with visitors that Saturday morning, trying to keep them in his camp, and meeting with his advisors making arrangements for the new party, TR learned that he might still have a chance to be the Republican Party's nominee.

Two days later, as he was headed back by train to Oyster Bay, he described the scene to a reporter with the Associated Press. Roosevelt said that on that morning "a number of Southern delegates sent word to him that if he would enter the fight in the convention again, they would assure him enough votes to win."

Roosevelt "sent back word that he would agree only if thirty of the delegates would pledge themselves in writing that they would join with the Roosevelt delegates, start all over again, elect a new Temporary Chairman, and purge the convention of the seventy-two delegates he declares were fraudulently seated by the National Committee."

TR told the AP that 19 of the southern delegates agreed to his proposition, but that he could not get the votes of the 30 that he demanded, so the plan fell through. He refused to give the reporter the names of the men who had offered to switch.

Taft's campaign immediately dismissed Roosevelt's story as ridiculous and called it "another attempt to paint himself as a hero." But there is reason to believe that something of the kind did take place. Since Roosevelt met with an intermediary rather than the delegates themselves, he may, in some respects, have been misled or there may have been a misunderstanding. But he probably was told that some or all of the delegates offering to defect were black.

Frank Munsey's biographer says that at the very last moment an "offer of a block of votes sufficient to sway the outcome was brought to Munsey, the broker being a Southern Republican lawyer of experience in such deals." Although he did not name the lawyer, he was almost certainly white.

The source for the story was Stuart Oliver, the general manager of Munsey's paper in Baltimore.

> "I was present when the proposal was laid before Munsey," Oliver said. "I have no doubt whatever that the votes would have been delivered if paid for. The price was two hundred thousand cash.
>
> That sum would have purchased enough votes to allow a twenty-per-cent margin of safety; one out of five could have gone back on his bargain and still the result would stand. Some votes were offered as low as $400, some as high as $3,000, and on the latter, $100 was to be paid down at once, the remainder after the votes were cast.

He refused, of course," said Oliver. "He didn't make a scene or become indignant. He simply told the go-between that he wasn't interested and wouldn't pay a cent for any man's vote."

Amos Pinchot describes a somewhat similar episode in his *History of the Progressive Party* that could throw light on the events that took place that week.

Pinchot recalled being "summoned to George Perkins' room" one morning. When Pinchot arrived, he found Perkins on the telephone. The speaker on the other end of the line was doing most of the talking. Perkins, Pinchot said, had been put in charge of the delegates from the South "and especially the colored brethren." Pinchot watched the conversation as Perkins became more and more agitated and then angry and incredulous and finally disgusted. "Perkins denounced the speaker at the other end of the wire with considerable vigor, but on second thought opened the door to further parley by stating that he could not discuss such a matter on the telephone and a decision could be made only after a discussion with the parties whom he did not name."

When he got off the phone, Perkins described the purpose of the call. "The body of Negro delegates, whose loyalty to the Colonel had been won in the usual manner," Pinchot wrote, "had taken advantage of the critical situation in which the Roosevelt delegates found themselves to raise their figures." The man on the phone had explained that the delegates loved Roosevelt, but they loved Taft, too.

As Pinchot understood it, Perkins had already paid the black delegates to defect to Roosevelt. The payments were to be made in two installments—one of which had already been paid, the other of which would be due once they cast their ballots. Now the delegates were saying that they wanted to stay with Taft, perhaps because they believed in Taft, perhaps because they were trying to induce Perkins to make a higher bid. Equally infuriating to Perkins, apparently they intended to keep the money that they had already been paid by the Colonel's camp. He had been outbid and outsmarted.

In fact, the delegates may have been following the script proposed to Hilles in late April, suggesting that "the right persons in each State should advise separately each colored delegate to take any money that is offered by the Roosevelt people, report the fact immediately to his advisor, and then vote in the convention for the President."

Perkins was furious. He described the demands as "shameful and humiliating." But he was still planning to try to make a new offer. He told Pinchot that "politics being what they were, there was perhaps nothing to do but to play the game."

Pinchot was convinced that the Roosevelt campaign's hunt for black delegates, with all of its unsavory elements, was being orchestrated by the campaign manager, Joseph Dixon. Every day during the convention, Roosevelt's top advisors gathered around a mahogany table in the front room of his hotel suite. It was clear that they would lose the credentials challenges. Unless they could win some of the delegates pledged to La Follette or Cummins, which seemed very unlikely, they would be at least 50 delegates short. Nevertheless, Dixon was always confident that TR would prevail, "a conviction which under the circumstances was hard to account for," Amos said.

At each meeting, in a deep calm voice, Dixon would say: "Gentlemen, as surely as we are sitting here, Colonel Roosevelt will have enough delegates to nominate him. I will not go into particulars, but you may rest assured that Theodore Roosevelt will be the nominee of the Republican Party at this convention."

At the time, Pinchot was more perplexed than comforted. But when he learned that Perkins had been bribing or attempting to bribe delegates, and hoped to continue to do so with greater success, Pinchot concluded that it was on those efforts that "Dixon in the darkest hours was building the otherwise inexplicable hopes he was communicating to us."

In all likelihood, Dixon and his colleagues, knowing of Roosevelt's strong moralistic views on such matters, shielded him from the details of their efforts. Certainly, Amos did not share what he had learned. "I never told Roosevelt about this strange little backwater in the river of righteousness on which the progressive craft was sailing so gallantly," he said, "and I doubt that he ever knew of it."

By the time the story reached TR, it had probably assumed an entirely different hue. He may have been led to believe that it was Taft's minions and the black delegates who were engaged in such tawdry behavior, not his own campaign. As a result, the stories that reached him had a profound impact on his view of the venality of the man in the White House, and on what he came to believe were the corrupt black delegates from the South.

AT 3 P.M., back in the convention hall, the list of delegates was adopted by voice vote, and Elihu Root was promptly installed as permanent chair—to what the *New York Times* called "a deafening noise of cheers, whistling, booing, and other signs of approval and disapproval." When the demonstration ended, Root asked the delegates for unanimous consent to allow "our Republican brother," Henry J. Allen of Kansas, to make a statement to the convention on behalf of Colonel Roosevelt. Of course, Henry Allen did not intend to remain a Republican brother for much longer.

"Mr. Chairman," Allen began, "in a convention where the minority report always sounds louder than the majority report, it is a great thing to have unanimous consent on anything." He asked for ten minutes of "quiet attention . . . while I present the attitude of the progressives of this Convention." After that, he said, "I pledge to you that no effort will be made during the remainder of the convention to put any sand in the gasoline or to do any mischief whatsoever to your sparkplug."

He did not have much luck with his request for "quiet attention." When Allen said that he wanted to begin by reading "a statement that has just been placed in my hand from the Honorable Theodore Roosevelt," the crowd exploded. "With the mention of Roosevelt's name bedlam broke loose," the *Chicago Tribune* reported, "with progressives leaping to their chairs and cheering like mad, waving canes, hats, fans, and cavorting about" with "exuberant enthusiasm."

"We want Teddy, we want Teddy" came "a cry from a thousand throats. The storm of cheers rose and fell in deafening waves." Then the delegates started to march around the hall, led by the men from California, carrying state banners above their heads, "yelling like maniacs." Finally, the procession "ran into a squad of police in the rear of the hall." They were dispersed, but "the cheering, flag waving and whistling went on unabated."

When Root finally restored order after twenty minutes, Allen began to read a statement from Roosevelt that was certain to be incendiary.

"The convention has now declined to purge the roll of the fraudulent delegates placed thereon by the defunct National Committee," the statement began, "and the majority which endorsed this fraud was made a majority only because it included the fraudulent delegates themselves."

Many of the "fraudulent delegates" in the hall started to shout out in anger.

"As a result," Allen continued, "the convention is in no proper sense any longer a real Republican Convention representing the real Republican Party."

When Allen paused, James Wadsworth of New York called out a request for him to read the rest of Roosevelt's words. They were all filled with invective.

"The convention as now composed has no claim to represent the voters of the Republican Party. It represents nothing but fraud in overriding the will of the rank and file of the party. Any man nominated by the Convention as now constituted would be merely the beneficiary of this successful fraud."

By this point everyone on the floor was yelling.

"If a man doesn't know when he is dead, his friends ought to tell him," a Taft delegate shouted.

Allen tried to continue.

"I am going on," he said. "What I have to say represents the sentiment of the majority of the Roosevelt voters."

Ignoring cries of "no, no" and "sit down," Allen continued.

"The Roosevelt delegates feel that they can no longer share in the responsibility for the acts of the Convention."

"That's good," people shouted.

Allen proceeded to list his bill of particulars against the outcome in state after state in a speech that William Allen White called "a masterpiece of ironic sarcasm"—attacking the convention's treatment of the challengers including the two delegates from California and the men from Washington State.

Roosevelt's supporters roared their approval. Taft's delegates shouted, "Get out" and "Sit down." A delegate from New Hampshire called for Root to use his powers as chair to throw Allen out of the hall. But Allen was just warming up.

"We will not join you in saying to the home state of Abraham Lincoln that the 150,000 majority with which you defeated Mr. Taft and his managers in Illinois was overruled by those very managers with the consent of those who have arrogated powers never intended to be theirs."

The shouting continued—and so did Allen. "When Theodore Roosevelt left the White House four years ago he left you an overwhelming majority in both branches of Congress; he left you an overwhelming majority in all the Republican States."

By now there was so much disruption that Root called on the police to start to eject people from the hall. One reporter counted at least three fistfights on the floor. Kermit Roosevelt, who was sitting with the delegation from Maine as a sergeant-at-arms, told his diary that a "Montana man clawed up a Florida delegate."

"We have pleaded with you for five days," Allen concluded at last. "We fight no more. We plead no longer. We shall sit in protest and the people who sent us here shall judge us."

To a chorus of cheers and boos, Allen left the podium—and formally ended Roosevelt's campaign for the Republican nomination.

At 9:28 that night, William Howard Taft was renominated by what remained of the Republican Party—with the support of 561 delegates, a narrow margin of 21 votes. A great many of Roosevelt's supporters had left the hall.

An hour later, Theodore Roosevelt and his supporters arrived in Orchestra Hall to launch a new party.

Chapter Fifteen

When the 1912 Republican convention adjourned after Taft's nomination at 9:30 P.M. on Saturday, June 22, 150 of the credentialed delegates marched the short distance from the Coliseum to Orchestra Hall. They were led by the joyous men from California, happy to be free of the old regime at last and waving their huge state banner. They entered the hall at 10 P.M. Hiram Johnson, who had left the convention hours earlier, led them to the stage as the audience "cheered wildly." Orchestra Hall was already filled to the breaking point. "The crowd of people wanting to get into the hall extended for blocks in a line four deep," the Associated Press reported. "Thousands failed to get in the building."

As other delegations entered, the crowd sang patriotic tunes and recreated the sounds of the steamroller that had echoed from the rafters of the Coliseum only hours earlier. Many of those who had been with him in his campaign for the Republican nomination, including Borah and Hadley, stayed away. But other marquee supporters were there: George Perkins, Frank Munsey, Senator Dixon, Frank Knox, Governor Stubbs, James Garfield, the Pinchot brothers, and Medill and R. R. McCormick. People cheered the New Jersey delegation and then shouted out their support for Cecil Lyon of Texas as he made his way down the aisle. Those with credentials from the Republican Convention joined scores of others who had been denied seats at the Republican Party table, men committed to TR who had been selected in various states but had lost their credentials challenges at the Republican Convention.

They were all there in common cause, as part of a crusade, determined to launch a new party that would be free to advocate the most advanced ideas of the era, to fight for social and industrial justice, suffrage for women, and better pay and better conditions for workers. Capping off the evening, Theodore Roosevelt entered at 11:30 P.M. to thunderous applause and delivered a powerful address that ended with the memorable words "We Stand at Armageddon and We Battle for the Lord."

THE BIRACIAL GROUP that entered the hall from Mississippi that night included those who had been given credentials by the Republican Party and those who had not. There was Perry Howard, who had memorably objected to the proceeding on the Washington State case earlier that day with the tongue-in-cheek claim that the steamroller was moving too fast. Howard was a successful lawyer who had a graduate degree in mathematics from Fisk University and a law degree from DePaul University in Chicago. He was joined by the banker and entrepreneur Charles Banks from Mound Bayou. Though Banks and other black delegates had been tainted by charges of bribery earlier in the week, he had a national reputation for his work in helping to build an all-black community that was so successful that TR had visited it on October 22, 1907, during a tour of the South and had singled it out for several paragraphs of praise in a speech a year later. Banks's black-owned cotton oil mill, with funding from northern investors that included Sears, Roebuck chairman Julius Rosenwald, was scheduled to have a grand opening that November. The group also included Willis Mollison from Vicksburg, one of the challenge delegates rejected by the Republican Convention earlier that day, a former teacher and newspaper editor who had become one of the most successful black lawyers in the state. There were white members of the group as well, including Frank S. Swalm, the owner of a drugstore in Brookhaven.

The *Chicago Tribune* ran an AP account of the evening showing that the men had already been hard at work. It said that "The Mississippi Roosevelt delegates entered the hall fresh from a meeting in their headquarters, and announced the election of S. D. Redmond of Jackson as the first national committeeman of the new party."

Redmond was a physician who had earned his M.D. with honors at Illinois Medical College in 1897 and a law degree at Illinois College of Law. He did postgraduate work at Harvard Medical School in 1905–1906 at the age of thirty-four. After founding and serving as president of the Mississippi Medical and Surgical Association, Redmond had become a successful lawyer and business executive. As the president of the American Trust & Savings Bank, one of two black banks in Jackson, and an investor in real estate, he was one of the richest black men in the South.

Redmond had come to Chicago as part of the delegation set up by the Roosevelt forces to challenge Taft's slate of delegates. Like Willis Mollison and Frank Swalm, he had lost his credentials challenge a few hours earlier. But now he was in the hall with the new party, standing at Armageddon, marching and singing and praying for the Colonel.

Roosevelt knew Dr. Redmond and some of the other men personally. In May, Redmond sent a letter warning TR that "Many of the Federal officeholders of this State are now busy intimidating many of your supporters with threats of indictment and dire calamity should they give evidence in your favor" and enclosing a memo suggesting the most effective way to make his case in Mississippi. In mid-June, TR had asked Redmond for his advice about the most appropriate "colored man to second my nomination." Redmond suggested his brother-in-law, Perry Howard. Redmond and Howard were part of the state's highly educated black elite. Their wives were sisters, two of the three daughters of Hiram Revels, the first black United States senator from Mississippi.

"From what you say," Roosevelt replied, "I should think that Mr. Howard would be peculiarly fit" to give the seconding speech.

Having been elected national committeeman by the defecting delegates, and having a relationship with the former President, Redmond felt empowered to create the new party in Mississippi. He and Perry Howard and TR's other supporters in Chicago announced that the state's new party would hold a convention in late July to select a biracial slate of delegates to go to the Progressive Party's formal nominating convention in Chicago in early August.

TR's black supporters returned home the next day expecting to be an important part of the new party. But to their amazement, they were soon told that they would not even be allowed to join it. What followed provides a somewhat different perspective on Roosevelt's professed belief in the right of the people to rule.

ON JUNE 21, the day that TR gave up on the Republican nomination, and the day before the pro-Roosevelt faction of delegates and challengers from Mississippi walked out of the Republican Convention with Roosevelt and selected Dr. Redmond as their leader, Gordon S. Orme sent a telegram to John M. Parker that suggested the rules for the months that followed. Orme was a leading rice dealer and the owner of the Empire Rice Mill in New Orleans.

"If Roosevelt would form a new party with a plank stating this is a white man's party, colored or Mongolian races can come in for commercial or educational purposes only, all laborers excluded, the right of franchise limited to Caucasian race," Orme wrote Parker, "he could carry every Southern and Pacific coast state besides labor vote and probably entire country." Orme sent identical telegrams to some of Roosevelt's other close friends in the South.

Parker was a Democrat who had been born in Mississippi and lived there before moving to Louisiana, where he became a leader of that state's cotton trade. Four years later, he would run as the Progressive Party's candidate for Vice President, and eight years later he would become the governor of Louisiana. Roosevelt and Parker had been friends for at least a decade. They had been companions on what became known as the Great Mississippi Bear Hunt in late 1902, where TR famously refused to shoot a bear that had been tied to an oak tree by a helpful guide who wanted to give him an easy shot. Roosevelt felt that shooting a bear in that condition would be unsportsmanlike. When that episode became the subject of a cartoon in the *Washington Post* the next day, it inspired two toy store owners to create the immensely popular stuffed toy that they called the "Teddy Bear."

Parker immediately agreed with Orme's proposal, and after very little internal debate the Roosevelt camp decided to approve the Parker Plan for the South.

"Our idea is to have no Negro delegates from any southern state," TR's twenty-four-year-old son Ted assured Parker a month later.

Ted had moved from San Francisco to New York earlier that year to accept a job as a bond salesman. Ted, his wife, and their baby daughter Grace were living with his parents in Oyster Bay. In his spare time, he had been helping his father's campaign. It seems likely that his letter reflected his father's views and that he was speaking for his father as well as the campaign when he referred to "our idea."

"We recognize that practically it would be impossible to work with the best elements of the community if they were on the delegation, and that they represent the very worst type of citizen of the south," he told Parker. "They are absolutely venal in every way, and the majority have no intelligence at all."

Ted may not have known much about the delegates, that his father's strongest black supporters included business leaders, lawyers, physicians and poets. He also may not have known that many had supported Roosevelt at some personal risk to their careers since Taft was still in power and his faction of the party remained important to southern blacks. But his father knew many of the black leaders personally and presumably knew that the group included a Harvard-educated doctor whose advice he had solicited for the best person to second his nomination; a successful lawyer whom TR had called "peculiarly fit" to give a seconding speech on his behalf; and a businessman whose work in Mound Bayou TR had touted a few years earlier and whose latest venture was financed by the chairman of Sears, Roebuck.

Roosevelt did not adopt the Parker Plan in its entirety. Parker also pushed for a plank making it clear that the new party was designed for whites only. The former President was not prepared to go that far. Black votes would be needed in the North. For political reasons, Ted explained, his father did not want to put "a white man's plank" into the party platform.

Ted later became a strong civil rights advocate. But in June 1912, he was working for a party that would need white votes in the South and black votes in the North. So, speaking on behalf of his father's campaign, he assured Parker that we do "wish it understood that our party in the South will be purely a white party."

ON JULY 24, Roosevelt sent O. K. Davis to the South to explain the policy to the leaders of the new Progressive Party in all but two southern states. However, Ted told Parker that Davis would not be going "to either Louisiana or Mississippi, as I knew you would attend to them."

Attend to them, he did. Parker had already called his friend Benjamin Franklin Fridge in Mississippi and told him how he wanted matters handled in that state. Unlike the black leaders, most of whom had earned multiple degrees, Fridge considered himself "an uneducated man." "My father," he once explained, "was not able to send me to school." He was the son of a Confederate veteran of the Civil War who had been held in prison under the watch of black guards at Ship Island, Louisiana. Contemporaneous accounts described Fridge as a staunch Democrat, successful business leader, and the father of the state's adjutant-general. He agreed with most of the positions of the Progressive Party and, having admired TR ever since he "straddled his horse to organize the Rough Riders," was pleased to sign up for the cause. When Parker told Fridge to make it clear that the party in Mississippi was to be lily-white, he did as he was told.

Following Parker's instructions, Fridge issued a call for the convention in Mississippi and sent out a notice inviting "all white citizens of Mississippi" to participate in the selection of delegates. To accompany the notice, he issued a statement, presumably pursuant to Parker's instructions, stating, "This is strictly a white man's party, the movement is led by white men, and we expect only white men in our organization." Papers throughout the state carried the message. A huge headline in the *Jackson Daily News* announced: "COL. ROOSEVELT THROWS NEGRO LEADERS OVERBOARD —Progressive Party Will Be Launched in Mississippi as a White Man's Organization."

Redmond, Howard, and the other black leaders were stunned. Having burned their bridges with the leaders of the Republican Party in the state and with President Taft and his political team, their options were limited. They were determined to become a part of the party that quickly became known as the Bull Moose Party after TR told a reporter that he felt as strong as a Bull Moose. They were convinced, or claimed to be convinced, that there must be some mistake, that Fridge did not speak for TR, that Roosevelt could not have intended that they be excluded from the party. They were skillful political operators; to survive and even thrive in the world of business, law, medicine and politics in Mississippi, they had learned to move nimbly in the face of challenges from segments of both the black and white communities. Perry Howard quickly devised a strategy designed to make it as difficult as possible for Roosevelt's supporters to follow through on the Parker plan.

Howard sent a letter to Dixon, who was managing the Bull Moose campaign, in his Senate office. "Please indicate whether or not we shall be accepted as delegates in the coming National Convention of the Progressives. The Call [issued by Fridge] and press comment would indicate that we are to be ignored. Surely this cannot be true in view of the great sacrifice which some of us made in order to stand by the Colonel."

In a passage designed to show that he was a man of means, not seeking any funding, Howard asked Dixon to "please wire me at my expense as to the method of procedure and what we might expect by way of admission into the Convention."

"I am sure that your high sense of honor will not allow us to be humiliated," he concluded, "and I stand upon yours and the Colonel's assurance that we would receive a square deal."

Without answering Howard directly, Dixon's administrative assistant wired back saying that the new party had to represent "a new deal from the beginning." It could not be simply an offshoot of the "old Republican organizations" he said. Instead, it would have to be clear that it would represent "both the old Republican and Democratic Parties."

The state was abuzz with rumors saying that the Redmond-Howard group had been summarily dismissed—"excommunicated," as some put it, a bit gleefully, with much too much schadenfreude for the would-be Bull Moosers. The black and white Republicans who had stayed in the party in Chicago supporting Taft had a field day, making fun of those who had defected to Roosevelt. As one paper reported, "the regular Republican leaders, and the colored brethren who have kept within the party are in high glee over the throw-down."

The press, which was largely identified with the Democratic Party, made fun of the black progressives at every turn. The *Vicksburg Evening Post* said that "unless they can attach themselves to the new party organization" the Redmond-Howard faction would be "out of the political game for good. . . . They are kicking up a rumpus for the sole and only purpose of preventing their complete elimination from political affairs."

"The most terribly tragic aspect of the whole matter," the *Jackson Daily News* wrote, "is that the change of plans will prevent about forty or fifty well-dressed Mississippi negroes from attending the Bull Moose convention in Chicago on August 5 and living for a week or so at the expense of the Harvester Trust and other financial easy marks who are putting up the costs for the formation of the third party."

The black leaders fought back, denying that they were out of the party. Redmond wrote a letter to the *Vicksburg Evening Post* rebutting the claim that he had been told "to cancel our Call." He blamed at least part of the misinformation on "our opponents among the old faction" who "are so anxious to read us out of the third party and have us break with its leaders that they are willing to perform the job for us, mislead the press on our attitude, and as good as say to us, 'if you will not break with those gentlemen, we will break for you.'"

To reaffirm their role, Redmond, Howard, Mollison, and Banks formed a biracial group and announced that that they would be holding caucuses around the state on July 27 to send representatives to a statewide convention in Jackson on July 31 to select a slate of Progressive delegates. They added some of the most impressive blacks in the state, including Samuel Beadle, a successful Jackson lawyer and poet whose poems are included in poetry collections to this day; William A. Attaway, president of the Delta Penny Savings Bank of Indianola; and William P. Harrison, a successful pharmacist from Vicksburg.

Their announcement was designed to address any possible objection to their role, except for objections based on their color. They said that the convention and new party would welcome people of all races. They made it clear that they did not expect or want the party or the delegation to be controlled by blacks; they only wanted to have a chance to participate. They welcomed Democrats, including Fridge. Indeed, the statement said that they "would have no objection to Mr. Fridge taking the lead in this movement, nor anyone else who bases his party creed upon the enduring constitution rather than upon the sinking sand of race and color."

"No one," they said, "has or will have cause to fear the old bugabear of negro domination."

The Redmond-Howard group insisted that Roosevelt could never have intended to have an all-white party. The Fridge effort was clearly based on a misunderstanding. "In view of the conferences held with Colonel Roosevelt and Senator Dixon since the convention adjourned, in which we were positively assured of a square deal," they said, "we are forced to believe that the promoters of the 'Lily Whites' call are laboring under the wrong impression as to the scope and plan of the progressive movement and that the leaders of this great movement have never had in mind the disenfranchisement of any class of people because of color only."

There was a "fairly large" crowd on hand on July 31 when the Redmond-Howard faction held its state convention. Willis Mollison was selected as the chair and delivered a powerful address. "There is no place for any new party in Mississippi which violates the pledge of that foremost American, Theodore Roosevelt, that every man shall have a 'square deal,'" he said. "We do not wish to do violence to the memory of the immortal Lincoln whose blood nurtured the tree of the Black man's liberty. Colonel Roosevelt loves to liken himself to the martyred statesman. . . . I do not believe his mighty arm, which a few short weeks ago was around the black man's neck in entreaty and benediction, will be raised so soon to strike this black man down. He must do it before I can believe him weak enough or wicked enough to do this deed."

Presumably Redmond, Howard, Banks, and Mollison believed that TR had been informed about, if not directly involved in, the effort to bribe black delegates. It was one thing to hear about such efforts from men like McHarg and Bill Ward. But if Perkins and Dixon were involved, as Amos Pinchot asserted, how could TR not have known?

Mollison's speech also contained a not-so-subtle threat. Everyone in politics knew that there were several northern states where the black vote would be important if not decisive. "It will be a blunder worse than a crime for the Progressives to throw away the certain vote in Illinois and Ohio," Mollison said, "for the will-o-the-wisp in Mississippi and Louisiana."

The Redmond-Howard convention selected a biracial delegation to go to the Progressive Convention, half white and half black, with white businessman Frank S. Swalm as its chair. They named an all-white slate of presidential electors, however, in order to make it more likely that whites would vote for TR when they went to the polls in the fall.

The white press covered the biracial convention in some detail, though many observers regarded it as a stunt, a form of political theater. The only convention that really mattered was the one called by Fridge, which met briefly in Jackson the next day, on August 1. That meeting was attended by "several Jackson admirers of Roosevelt" and about "fifty out of town delegates." After brief comments from Fridge and others, the group elected an all-white slate. The *Vicksburg Evening Post* reported that Fridge "did not seem to be the least bit worried about the negro politicians who recently held their convention here and seemed to take them as a joke."

Fridge immediately sent a telegram to Dixon, who was already in Chicago. "We had a very fine convention today. Twenty delegates selected. All white. I hope everything will be satisfactory."

In fact, though, Fridge was far from sure about the outcome in Chicago. He was new to national politics and did not know any of the players. He had put his reputation on the line for a cause that he believed in but with ground rules for participation that had been created by others. His friends followed him to the train station the next day, pleading with him to reconsider.

"You will never be seated," they told him. "Don't you go up there." He was certain to return home with his tail between his legs.

Both groups of delegates left by train for Chicago on August 2, each worrying about being humiliated, each hoping to be seated at the Progressive Convention.

ROOSEVELT FINALLY EXPLAINED his views on the seating of the southern delegates on August 1 in a carefully scripted letter to Julian Harris of Georgia, a writer, editor, and personal friend who was most famously known as the son of Joel Chandler Harris, author of the Uncle Remus stories. There was a "particular fitness" in sending the letter to "the son of the man whose work made all Americans his debtors," Roosevelt said, whose writing "showed a deep and most kindly interest in the welfare of the negro." Harris had also been chosen to represent Georgia on the Bull Moose Party's national committee.

As with most of his important documents, TR had sent the letter to a few trusted advisors for their comments. O. K. Davis urged him to strike out some words that might seem to suggest that he planned to exclude black delegates because he was "sore at the result of the Chicago convention." Any such language might be distorted for propaganda purposes by the "venal negro leaders," Dixon warned. "These unscrupulous hounds might use it as a basis of justification for their false assertion."

The Colonel's letter to Julian Harris was released to the press on August 2 as the competing delegations from Mississippi were heading by train to Chicago. At the same time, competing delegations that included blacks were on their way to the convention from Alabama, Florida, and Georgia, three other states where the Progressive Party had enforced an all-white policy.

TR's letter to Julian Harris made national headlines the next day. As he did so often, Roosevelt described his views as taking a middle ground, in this case between those in the North who "insist that we get from the South colored Delegates to the National Progressive Convention," and those from the South who "ask that I declare the new party shall be a white man's party." TR said that he was not "able to agree to either proposal." In states where there was a sizable black population and black vote—such as Rhode Island, Maryland, New York, Indiana, Ohio, Illinois, New Jersey, and Pennsylvania—the party would "bring the best colored men into the movement on the same terms as the white man." But in the South, where the number of black voters had become "negligible," they would have to develop a different policy.

Those reading the document closely could find several strands of the Colonel's reasoning, including a review of the failure of the Republican Party in the South and what to some seemed an idealistic view of a new Progressive Party led by "the best white men in the South, men of justice and vision as well as of strength and leadership." Roosevelt was thinking of men like John Parker and Julian Harris himself, men who are "sincerely desirous of doing justice to the colored man . . .

securing him just treatment before the law; white men who set their faces sternly against lynch law and mob violence and attack all such abuses as peonage." Such men could never come to power in the South in a party "based primarily upon the negro vote and under negro leadership or the leadership of white men who derive their power solely from negroes."

"I earnestly believe that by appealing to the best white men in the South," Roosevelt wrote, "and by frankly putting the movement in their hands from the outset, we shall create a situation by which the colored men of the South will ultimately get justice." That strand of the letter drew positive comments from some Roosevelt supporters. "If the people have the soberness to follow such wise suggestions, it would be the means of laying the foundation of an advanced civilization and for the future happiness of the nation," one admirer wrote from Atlanta.

Despite the warning from O. K. Davis, however, the letter revealed Roosevelt's searing anger at the events in Chicago, anger that may have been fueled by largely inaccurate reports presented to him by supporters and lieutenants who did not want to offend his moral sensibilities by sharing the details of their own unsavory efforts to secure the support of black delegates who had promised to vote for Taft. "In the Convention at Chicago last June," he wrote, "the breakup of the Republican Party was forced by those rotten-borough delegates from the South . . . representing nothing but their own greed for money or office" who had "betrayed the will of the mass of the plain people of the party."

While it met favor from some supporters, particularly in the South, many observers found Roosevelt's stance, to put it charitably, opportunistic. "Bars Southern Negro," the *Baltimore Sun* said in a front-page headline, "But 'T. R.' Welcomes Blacks in States Where Vote Is Factor."

Taft's supporters thought that the statement would help them win black votes in both the North and South. They issued a statement challenging the premise of TR's statement. "There was little venality in the negro delegates from the South at Chicago," Tennessee senator Newell

Sanders said on behalf of the Taft campaign. "This was evidenced by the attempt and failure of the Roosevelt managers to buy them."

TR's new policy was immediately denounced in papers such as the *New York Tribune* and the *New York Times*. A habitual critic of TR, the *Times* carried a scathing editorial. "It is announced in the Colonel's letter to Julian Harris that there will not be a negro delegate from the Southern States in the Bull Moose Convention at Chicago, the fiat having gone forth under the Great Seal of the party that knows no brother, that the rotten borough delegates shall have no part in this second Emancipation Movement. What Mr. Lincoln would say about this can be imagined but not expressed; but the Reincarnated should have pondered long and seriously before determining thus to cut up by the roots the men who have been so loyal and useful to him all these years, and who were watered and attended to by McHarg in his recent wanderings in the South."

The *Times* predicted that what it regarded as the Colonel's cynical move to embrace blacks in the North while excluding them in the South would backfire. "We are told that the lily-white faction is to have its way in the South, where nine-tenths of the negroes live and labor, which is to say that only in the North, where the negroes hold in some States something like the balance of power, are they to be recognized as having any part or a lot in the affairs of the Bull Moose Party, a party whose foundations are established in justice to all men."

At the very least, the paper urged, "the negro delegates in the regular Republican Convention who showed a pliable disposition toward the Bull Moose while he was yet a Republican are entitled to good and regular standing among the Bull Moose people."

That last sentiment was one that the delegates from Mississippi led by Redmond and Howard, who had just arrived in Chicago, could embrace. They still hoped to convince TR to support them, but their dreams were now hanging on a thread. When reporters told the Colonel that his statement "had aroused no little comment," he described it as a statement of principle, a "declaration of his beliefs that he would not retract, no matter what the consequences were." While "he might lose some votes in the South among negroes," he told a reporter for the *New York Times*, he was confident that "he would get more votes in the North than he could possibly lose by any of his utterances."

THE PROGRESSIVE PARTY'S preconvention proceedings started shortly after noon on Saturday, August 3, at the party's headquarters in the Congress Hotel. It was familiar turf to many of the delegates and organizers who had been there just six weeks earlier at the Republican Convention. Although the mood should have been, and for many was, celebratory, the hotel corridors that morning were already "ringing with denunciations of the Roosevelt policy of keeping negro delegates from the South out of the convention." The delegates included some of the most forward-thinking men and women of the era, people who truly believed in social justice. But as the *Boston Globe* put it, TR's "edict started a veritable hornet's nest" of criticism. There were arguments everywhere. At one point, some of the black contestants even threatened to defect to Wilson and the Democratic Party.

When the meeting of the Provisional Committee opened in the campaign's hotel, Joseph Dixon, serving as the temporary chair, talked for two hours about the organization of the new party. Forty of the fifty-seven members of the Provisional Committee were there in person or by proxy. As Dixon took an occasional drag on his big corncob pipe, the delegates described conditions in their states.

It was widely assumed that the committee would quickly seat the all-white delegations from Alabama, Florida, Georgia, and Mississippi despite the presence of contesting groups. But that would not prove so easy. "A group of colored contestants from the State of Mississippi, of which Perry Howard, a negro lawyer from Jackson was the center, clustered just outside the door of the committee room all afternoon," the *New York Times* reported. When white delegates tried to convince them to leave, they refused.

The *Times* described the scene. "Howard, who lacks neither intelligence nor force, invariably came back with this reply," the *Times* reported. "We represent 90 percent of the Republican Party in Mississippi."

While Howard was talking, "T. F. B. Sotham, one of the Colonel's white admirers from Michigan, who has a powerful voice, a quick temper, and a ferocious bunch of bristling black whiskers, came within earshot. Mr. Sotham rushed in to the colored group and made for Howard. The latter, however, stood his ground and Mr. Sotham halted in the middle of his rush.

"If you are Republicans and Democrats to hell with you," Sotham said. "We don't want any of you. Before you come here you had better go home and renounce your old party affiliations and write yourselves down as Progressives. This is the Progressive Party."

"That's exactly what we are trying to do," Howard fired back. "But you won't let us."

Inside the committee room, things were not going as smoothly as Dixon had hoped. During the discussion of the Florida case, which was very much like the case in Mississippi, Edwin F. Tuttle of Rhode Island entered a vigorous protest. An insurance executive from Woonsocket, Tuttle had helped to organize the new party in his state.

"In New England," Tuttle said, "we have long ago passed the stage where we would stand for discrimination against anybody on account of race, religion, or color of his skin. I would not dare to return to my people were I to become a party to any such discrimination."

When the committee reached the Mississippi challenge, Perry Howard appealed to the delegates not to turn away the 900,000 blacks in the state by refusing them any representation at the convention.

"Would you have Roosevelt be the cause of taking from us the liberty that Abraham Lincoln granted us?" he asked.

Dixon asked why Howard's group would not "experiment with white leadership this time."

"That would be alright," Howard said. "We don't want to lead. But we must be recognized in his Progressive Party if we are to do any effective work."

By 10:30 P.M. it had become clear that the black delegates could not be dismissed so easily. Senator Dixon declared a recess until Monday morning. He needed to get further orders from Colonel Roosevelt, who was scheduled to arrive in the city on Monday at 9 A.M.

THE BLACK DELEGATES used Sunday to make their case to anyone who would listen. One of those who understood their concerns was J. Fred Essary of the *Baltimore Sun*. After talking with Perry Howard, he told his readers that "the Southern Negro has forced an issue here that threatens a serious split in the ranks of the convention and a more serious condition after adjournment."

A veteran White House reporter from Tennessee, Essary's legendary career ultimately spanned five decades. "These negroes have refused to be 'steamrollered,'" he wrote. "They are here in force to fight for representation in the party and they are gaining time if they are not gaining ground. They have succeeded in postponing final action until the arrival of Colonel Roosevelt himself, when they will make their last stand. If the Southern negroes are repudiated by the man who has, as they contend, posed as their best friend, they promise to go back home and fight. They promise more. They say they will appeal to the men of their race in the North to repudiate the third party and to hold their vote as a club that could be made dangerous against any political organization."

Essary quoted at length from his interview with Perry Howard. "We are Progressives," Howard told Essary. "We have made fight after fight against the Federal officeholders who control what Republican organization there is in Mississippi. We were defeated there and when the Roosevelt movement came we enthusiastically joined it." But when Benjamin Fridge made it clear that only white men would be allowed at the convention that he had convened, Howard said, "We believed that convention unauthorized and held a convention of our own. We sent a contesting delegation, half white and half black. Now we are told that for political expediency the colored man is not to be recognized by the third party in the South.

"Lincoln was the man who enfranchised us, but this committee, acting in the name of Roosevelt, now seeks to disenfranchise us. We are
told that we are not wanted, not because we are not good citizens, not
because we are not Progressives, but because we are negroes."

Without waiting for further word from the candidate, some delegations began to take a stand on the issue of seating black delegates from
the South. On Sunday morning, the Maryland delegation explicitly
went on record with a resolution stating that "the National Progressive
Party should be neither a class nor a race party."

WHEN HIS TRAIN rolled into Chicago's LaSalle Street Station at 8:55
on Monday morning, TR was greeted by 5,000 cheering supporters. As
he left the station and motored to the Congress Hotel, where a group
of his top aides were waiting for his arrival, a cheering mob followed
close behind shouting, "Teddy, Teddy, our next President." Along the
way he passed a parade of female delegates, proudly marching to their
first convention. But the *Boston Globe* reported that when he reached
the hotel he found that he had become "the storm center around which
has raged a political tornado."

"Outside of his rooms," the paper said, "were a score or more of
expostulating negroes, some of whom had been steamrollered out of
their convention seats by the colonel's Provisional Committee." The
men "felt that they had been "humiliated and wronged by the party
managers." They "demanded to see the colonel and wanted to put the
matter up to him." But TR refused to meet with them, telling them to
"read my letter to Julian Harris of Atlanta. It contains a full statement
of my views."

Elsewhere in the Congress Hotel, the Provisional Committee resumed
its deliberations at 10 A.M., hoping to find some way to resolve the vexing
problem. They had less than two hours to do their work before the start
of the convention. When they reached the case of Mississippi, Senator
Dixon moved that the Fridge delegation be seated and that the Redmond-
Howard challengers be given "honorary certificates of admission."

The resolution met immediate resistance from delegates from Maryland, New England, and California. Perhaps because there were at least six men from all white delegations from the Deep South in the room, including both Parker and Fridge, most comments supporting the black delegates were based on political and tactical considerations rather than a discussion of right and wrong. But from time to time, the debate became candid. At one point Matthew Hale, one of TR's earliest supporters, who, years earlier, had tutored his children, said that "Colonel Roosevelt's letter, to be frank, plucked of its verbiage, is merely saying 'Get out of here, we don't want you.'"

Dixon disagreed, pointing out that there would be a great many black delegates from the North and from border states. He was convinced that their presence would appease those concerned with racial justice, delegates who did not want to be identified with a "white man's party." Indeed, the delegates from Kentucky and Tennessee said that they had added black members to their delegations specifically so that states in the Deep South would not have to do so. "In Kentucky, much against our feelings, we put in a negro as one of the delegates, and we did it simply because we wanted to make it easy for states further south not to put up any," Leslie Combs, a former ambassador to Peru, explained.

But Hale doubted that people in the North would forgive that decision so easily. "All this talk about this not being a 'white man's party' will not go down," he said. If TR hopes to win the presidential election, "you can't make this a 'white man's party.'"

"I have talked with the Massachusetts delegation," he said, "and I find that there is not a single man here that is willing to vote to seat the white delegates from Mississippi."

Connecticut's Herbert Knox Smith, former head of the Bureau of Corporations and a prominent member of TR's "Tennis Cabinet," agreed. "If you make up this temporary roll in this manner," he said, "I don't think you can carry Connecticut and I think it is true of most of the New England States." Edwin Tuttle, who had spoken on behalf of the Rhode Island delegation on Friday, agreed.

George Perkins, representing New York State, jumped in repeatedly to support Dixon's motion. Presumably, he and Dixon knew the Colonel's thinking.

At one point, Hale interrupted Perkins with a question.

"Suppose that in the City of New York the call was issued for all progressives who are not Jews, for all Christians, to come to that convention. Now, would you favor that?" Perkins had no answer.

California's Francis Heney made a similar argument. "You must not forget that there was a Civil War," he said. "There is a public conscience in the North and we must carry the northern states. If we trifle with this question, we are damned to defeat in the North which is where the electoral votes will have to come from for this party." If Dixon and TR disagreed, he said, "they are mistaken as to the public sentiment."

But Dixon and Perkins remained adamant. They rejected Matthew Hale's proposal that the Provisional Committee send a small delegation to meet directly with TR; no such meeting was needed since they knew his wishes. It was clear that Dixon and Perkins could prevail in the committee with the backing of loyalists and the delegates from the South. Parker, who had been responsible for the southern strategy, called the black politicians from Mississippi "the most rotten and corrupt in the United States." Julian Harris continually injected his views of the best course for blacks and whites in Georgia.

Finally, Fridge spoke up, offering a poignant and somewhat heart-rending personal appeal. "I have followed my friend Parker, whose father loaned me money thirty years ago to start a business," he said. If you don't seat my delegation, "I will be a disgraced man in Mississippi when I go home. Please handle me just as nice as you can."

After two hours, by a vote of 22 to 12, the Provisional Committee voted to put the lily-white Fridge delegate slate on the convention's temporary roll.

Matthew Hale was devoted to TR but could not ignore the views of his own state and his own delegation. He added a poignant codicil of his own.

"This is a mighty serious thing that we men from the North are doing," he said. "We of the North, our fathers and grandfathers, fought for the negroes. Now for the first time we are saying publicly and openly that our fathers and grandfathers were wrong and have been wrong since the Civil War."

The battle was over for the morning, in time for them all to join the jubilant crowd at the Coliseum that was creating a new, idealistic Progressive Party featuring women in large numbers for the first time, black delegates from outside the Deep South, and a commitment to social justice and the right of the people to rule. For some, for those who could not understand how such a party could exclude black delegates from Mississippi and elsewhere, there was a cloud over the hall. But they still had some room for hope. The Provisional Committee had made its recommendation that morning, but the ultimate decision on seating would be made in the Credentials Committee, which was scheduled to meet later that night.

THE FIGHT IN the Credentials Committee proved to be even more contentious than the discussion that morning. Frank Knox, who had used his base as chair of the Michigan Republican Party to organize TR's campaign for the Republican nomination, had joined the new party. Having served TR for so long, starting with his days as a Rough Rider in Cuba, he was deemed a reliable chair of the Credentials Committee. The meeting lasted for hours. As it dragged on, many of the exhausted delegates who had traveled long distances to be in Chicago went to bed. Finally at 3 a.m., after two tied votes, the committee made its decision. It sided with Fridge by a 17-to-16 margin. The delegates met in private. Neither the press nor representatives of the black delegate challengers were allowed in the room. But when the meeting adjourned, Julius T. Mitchell, a black delegate from Rhode Island, charged that the decisive vote had been cast by someone with a questionable proxy.

"This isn't just a steam roller. We are under the rock crusher," one black challenge delegate said. "I have felt steam rollers, but they just flatten you out for a time. The machine that Colonel Roosevelt has set to work here is aimed to crush the colored man in the South."

"Fairly sputtering indignation," one paper reported, the black challengers from Mississippi announced that they would take the matter to Col. Roosevelt for a personal ruling. "This matter is not settled yet," they said. "We will lay the matter before Col Roosevelt himself today and if necessary we will carry the fight to the floor of the convention."

For those concerned with practical politics, that was a powerful threat. A battle on the floor of the convention on the seating of black delegates from the Deep South was certain to be disastrous for the new party. Perry Howard, who had organized a skillful campaign in the face of overwhelming odds, knew that the threat of such a fight represented a powerful bargaining chip.

"Charles Banks did not come up to be humiliated for he evidently saw it was in the air," Howard said. "But I wouldn't believe that Roosevelt, who has always professed such love for a fair deal, would not give it to us, so I came. I wanted to find out whether Vardaman had converted Roosevelt." James Vardaman, a former Mississippi governor who was about to be elected to the Senate, was an avowed segregationist who opposed government jobs and education for blacks. He had been associated with support for lynching. His name was poison to northern supporters of the new party.

"I was a Roosevelt delegate up here in June," Howard said, "and Roosevelt and Dixon were very solicitous for us then. We stood up here against all the pressure of sixty-two colored delegates from the south, for Roosevelt, and he would gladly have accepted the nomination at our hands then. Now we come with a delegation composed of ten whites and ten colored men and they put us under the rock crusher because they wish to have a lily white party in the south and they propose to undo the work that Lincoln did in the city where he was nominated."

"What we want," Howard said, "is to get our answer direct from Roosevelt and not through anyone else."

BY TUESDAY MORNING, Roosevelt's refusal to meet with the black challengers was becoming less and less tenable. Some of the angry black delegates from the North and South had joined with men like Redmond and Howard to create what they called the National Progressive Party of Colored Men. About one hundred members of the group met late Monday night. Many threatened to leave the party if they did not get justice. They announced that they would meet again on Tuesday night.

A great many of the white delegates were furious as well. Jane Addams, the famed social worker and founder of Hull House was scheduled to provide the seconding speech for TR's nomination, the first time that a woman had ever been given such an honor at a major national convention. She admired TR enormously and had high hopes for the new party. But she was also a fierce champion of black rights and a member of the board of the National Association for the Advancement of Colored People.

On Monday night, while the Credentials Committee was struggling with the issue, Jane Addams delivered impassioned remarks to the Resolutions Committee, which was holding a simultaneous session. "Some of us are very disturbed that this Progressive Party, which stands for human rights, should even appear not to stand for the rights of the negroes," she said, speaking for herself and other northern reformers. "It seems to us to be inconsistent when on one page of our newspapers we find that this party is to stand for the working man and the working woman, and to protect the rights of the children, and to prevent usurpation of voters' rights by special interests, and on the next page we find that it denies the right of the negro to take part in this movement." She called on the party to "clear up" the appearance of depriving blacks of their rights.

Some of TR's closest advisors finally concluded that the issue had become too hot and too persistent for him to ignore. On Tuesday morning, Frank Knox, having presided over a deeply divided meeting of the

Credentials Committee, finally persuaded the Colonel to meet with the black delegates before the start of the convention that day.

The details of that meeting remain unknown. Simply by having the meeting, Perry Howard and Sidney Redmond had achieved one of their major goals. It gave them a degree of the legitimacy they were seeking. If Roosevelt made any specific promises, they have never come to light.

Realistically, Redmond, Howard, and their colleagues had nowhere to go. They had burned their bridges with the Republican Party and could not form any kind of alliance with the Vardaman-dominated Democratic Party in Mississippi. Under the circumstances, they accepted TR's proposal.

Even though they had lost by a 17-to-16 vote in the Credentials Committee, with one contested proxy, their challenge did not come to the floor of the convention.

SOME WHITE REFORMERS found peace with Roosevelt's decision. Jane Addams spelled out her reasoning in *The Crisis*, the NAACP's official publication. But as many had predicted, the decision to exclude southern blacks from the convention produced a bitter aftertaste for hundreds of thousands of would-be progressives. William Monroe Trotter, the outspoken black editor who had always distrusted TR, said that "women suffrage will be stained with negro blood unless women refuse alliance with Roosevelt."

The son of the great abolitionist William Lloyd Garrison told a niece who had attended the convention not to follow "an unprincipled humbug who cares nothing for suffrage except as it will win him votes and is not to be trusted on that or any other question." One of Garrison's grandsons, the journalist and social activist Oswald Garrison Villard, had a similar view. "I cannot refrain from a little 'I told you so' in connection with Roosevelt's kicking the Southern negro delegates out of the Progressive Party," he wrote Booker T. Washington in early August. "I hope now that the bulk of the colored people who have still clung to this man will realize the falsity of his nature and will no longer follow his leadership." A crusading newspaper editor who had helped to mentor Frank Knox wrote Governor Chase Osborn that TR "never was for women's suffrage and carefully avoids the subject now . . . and he has disenfranchised negroes because they are black."

Blacks who had championed Roosevelt's cause during the primary denounced him. Roscoe Conkling Simmons, the famed black orator who had given speech after speech on his behalf, written articles and letters extolling his virtues, and served as chair of his campaign for black support in New York, wrote an eloquent letter to the *New York Tribune* reproving his former idol. He was as offended by the patronizing tone of TR's letter to Julian Harris in describing men like Redmond and Howard as by his decision to exclude them from the party. "This latest missive, addressed to the son of Uncle Remus and his rabbits, has opened the eyes of a half million voters scattered over the free states; voters who had been led carefully into the colonel's camp," he wrote. "Yesterday men of color thought they discerned in Theodore Roosevelt the personification of the very proper leader in the great cause for 'social justice.' Today they behold him stripped of his robes—the patron of the art of demagogy; the vindictive genius in the great cause of self-aggrandizement. . . . Roosevelt comes to divide them . . . [but he] will lose. He will find that colored men in the North are as zealous of the rights and privileges and political dignity of colored men in the South as they themselves have ever been."

Even Rev. Reverdy C. Ransom, who had served as Roosevelt's cheerleader at the African-American rallies in Chicago during the Republican Convention, turned against him. "Roosevelt's promises are as unstable as water; his covenant with the people is a mask for personal ambition," he told a black congregation in New York shortly after the Progressive Convention. "Here is a new party which proclaims 'the right of the people to rule,' which proposes to devote itself to the cause of political and social justice. Yet, when it comes to deal with the negroes, the people who suffer most from oppression, the people whose men, women and children are the most defenseless victims and greatest sufferers from social and political injustice, Col. Roosevelt, the chief and leader of the herd, lifts his head, waves his antlers high in the air, and sounds the call, and the 'Bull Moose Party' runs amok on the negro question.

"There are some here [in the audience] who have been slaves, and you know that while there was slavery in the South, the negroes in the North were not free," he said to shouts of 'That's right! That's right!'

"Well, if you lose your political rights in the South, you will lose them in the North as well."

During the days that followed, Roosevelt earned the scorn of scores of other black leaders around the country who had once supported him, including Hugh MacBeth, the Baltimore editor who had been one of his strongest supporters; J. Gordon McPherson, often called "the Black Billie Sunday"; and, perhaps most famously, W. E. B. Du Bois, who turned from Roosevelt and ultimately endorsed the Democratic candidate, Woodrow Wilson, on the editorial pages of *The Crisis*, the NAACP publication that Jane Addams used to defend her decision to stick with the Colonel.

Roosevelt even ran afoul of some of his staunchest southern supporters, who deeply cared about social justice. Dr. Louis Edelman, a white delegate to the Progressive Convention from Birmingham, Alabama, sent an angry letter saying, "You have fooled the negro for political gain for more than ten years, and the Republican Party for more than forty years. . . . I appeal to every decent negro who is a registered voter to stay away from the convention and take no part either in the Republican Party or the new party."

Cartoonists had a field day. In the *St. Louis Post-Dispatch*, Robert Minor showed Roosevelt at a card table, throwing a card away. The caption said, "Discarding the Ace."

For Theodore Roosevelt, practical politics had trumped the right of the people to rule.

Epilogue

Woodrow Wilson won the presidential election on November 5, 1912, with 435 electoral votes and 42 percent of the popular vote. If there were a silver medal in presidential contests, TR would have earned it with 88 electoral votes and 27 percent of the popular vote. Taft came in a distant third with only 8 electoral votes (he won Vermont and Utah) and 23 percent of the popular vote. In a high-water mark for fourth- and fifth-party candidates, Eugene Debs won 6 percent of the national vote on the Socialist ticket and Eugene Chafin, the Prohibition Party candidate, won just over 1 percent.

TR's dream of carrying even a single southern state proved to be a fantasy. Wilson won every state in the South with overwhelming margins. In Mississippi, Wilson garnered almost 90 percent of the vote to TR's 5.5 percent. Roosevelt did better in Alabama and Georgia, where he gained almost 20 percent, but Wilson still trounced him in those states by margins of more than 3 to 1.

In some important respects, Theodore Roosevelt's third party had a lasting effect on American politics and policy. The Bull Moose campaign gave greater credibility to innovative ideas such as an eight-hour workday, a form of social security, a federal income tax, and a federal inheritance tax. Some of his ideas found their way into New Deal legislation championed by his cousin, President Franklin Roosevelt, who was elected as a Democrat in 1932.

The most direct impact of Roosevelt's campaign that year, however, was his role as a midwife in the birth of presidential primaries. Even though he didn't win the Republican Party nomination, his campaign transformed the presidential nominating process.

As Jonathan Bourne and the organizers of the Progressive Republican League lamented, TR was a latecomer to the cause of presidential primaries, and there were powerful forces on the Democratic side as well, but once Roosevelt entered the fray, his campaign, more than any other force, popularized presidential primaries and increased the number of states that embraced them. His rhetoric helped to enshrine the cause of popular democracy in the nation's vocabulary. The platform of his own Progressive Party called for a national primary, as did the platform of the Democratic Party that year. President Wilson called for a national primary in his first State of the Union Address. But the idea never gained traction.

There were those who thought that the era of national political conventions was over. "The development of state primaries for instruction and selection of delegates will make national conventions hereafter more of an electoral college than a forum for political maneuver among men mighty in personal influence at home," one commentator predicted that summer with some regret. "With the elimination of national conventions comes the passing of the great political giants and leaders of earlier history who represent a spectacular phase of the country's development." His prediction proved to be premature by at least six decades.

ONE FEATURE OF the 1912 campaign has thankfully disappeared from political life. There are heated debates about registration and voting laws, some of which strike some observers as likely and perhaps even designed to have a dramatic impact on the size and composition of the electorate. But no mainstream figure, candidate, or party today publicly embraces the view that some people, and some races, are not qualified to vote or to play leadership roles. That perspective, which ultimately did not enable TR to win any electoral votes from the South, became a feature of his own new party and a blight on his personal reputation.

Roosevelt had long opposed the concept of universal suffrage. For years he had been warning friends about the dangerous consequences that would follow if every black citizen were allowed to vote. A year earlier, he told Charles Willard the people in Texas and Mississippi would never give the vote to "negroes in the black belt," pointing to what he called "the perfectly sound (although unacknowledged and often highly contested) belief that only certain people are fit for democracy." Roosevelt thought that as few as 5 percent of blacks were equal to whites. But as a bedrock principle, he also argued that all men should be treated equally and that educated blacks should have the same privileges as educated whites.

"If ninety-five percent of the blacks were unfit to hold office," he once explained, "rule those ninety-five out, but not the other five percent simply because of the color of their skin." Speaking specifically of Mississippi, he told Owen Wister that "all I have been doing is to ask, not that the average negro be allowed to vote, not that ninety-five percent of negroes be allowed to vote, not that there be negro domination in any shape or form, but that these occasionally good, well-educated, intelligent and honest colored men and women be given the pitiful chance to have a little reward, a little respect, a little regard if they can by earnest useful work succeed in winning it."

At the end of his trip through Africa and Europe in 1910, he delivered the prestigious Romanes Lecture at Oxford University on the topic "Biological Analogies in History." In his lecture, TR formulated what he called "the great rule of righteousness." He said:

> As regards every race, everywhere, at home or abroad, we cannot afford to deviate from the great rule of righteousness which

bids us treat each man on his worth as a man. He must not be sentimentally favored because he belongs to a given race; he must not be given immunity in wrong-doing or permitted to cumber the ground, or given other privileges which would be denied to the vicious and unfit among ourselves. On the other hand, where he acts in a way which would entitle him to respect and reward if he was one of our own stock, he is just as entitled to that respect and reward if he comes of another stock, even though that other stock produces a much smaller proportion of men of his type than does our own. . . . To more than such just treatment no man is entitled, and less than such just treatment no man should receive.

Roosevelt certainly knew that many of those that he excluded from the Progressive Party caucuses and delegations in 1912 met the "rule of righteousness" standard. With degrees in law and medicine, several of them were, even by his standards, entitled to "respect and reward." He had known such men over the years and, indeed, served as a member of the board of Booker T. Washington's Tuskegee Institute in Alabama (while Taft was on the board of another leading historically black college, the Hampton Institute).

Why, then, did Roosevelt exclude all of the black delegates from the Deep South? Every candidate needs to ask if there is anything he wouldn't do to win an election. Some leaders in the present era, in words that are almost certainly an exaggeration, have been quoted as saying that they would "do anything" to get elected.

TR always believed that once he entered a battle he should hit and hit hard—maybe without restraint. At first he was reluctant to become a candidate, but once he decided to run, he was determined to win. He had no trouble changing tactics and allies and positions as needed to win—moving his base from party bosses and business leaders to social workers and progressives that he had once derided as "extremists;" pretending to be responding to a draft by a group of governors through a process and with letters that Alice Longworth called "somewhat cooked"; changing his views on primaries and women's suffrage; working with unlikely allies where needed, including the conservative faction in North Dakota, party "bosses" in Pennsylvania, and leaders of the Steel Trust when it served his purpose; denouncing Taft for supporting the reciprocity treaty with Canada that he had privately and enthusiastically endorsed; making his family so miserable that Edith and Ethel felt compelled to leave the country; allowing his managers to create false credentials challenges in the South, to threaten gunplay at the caucus in Oklahoma, and to tolerate and perhaps encourage the use of "roughhouse tactics" to get his way at the convention in Chicago; taking "so much money" from George Perkins that TR expected to be "damned in this country." He may even have condoned bribery.

In some cases, TR was acting like many and perhaps most politicians: doing everything necessary to win. Brooks Adams may have been an alarmist, but if TR agreed with his view that his enemies would stop at nothing, including murder, more extreme tactics may have seemed warranted. Seen in one way, his decision to exclude blacks, even those with medical and law degrees, even those who had put their own careers in jeopardy to support him, was simply one more step in that continuum.

Some Roosevelt scholars have concluded that he was in some respects a changed man during the last part of his life, allowing the darker forces of his nature to dominate his actions in the years after he left office. "The extravagance with which he championed proper principles beclouded their merit and vitiated his strength," Yale historian John Morton Blum observed. "The savageness he permitted himself to feel destroyed his judgment about men, about policy, about the instruments of politics he understood so well." Having had power, he could not be fully happy without it. "Hubris conquered," Blum wrote. "This was tragedy."

In deviating from his own "rule of righteousness," TR may also have been motivated by the belief that once he won office he could achieve even more progress for all people, including for blacks in the North and

South; or he may have been motivated by his longstanding affinity for southern whites, by his desire to heal the wounds of the Civil War, or by his ambition to return to glory.

His hopes of winning support in the South were unrealistic, but heartfelt. "If I could carry one of the eleven ex-Confederate states," he told Parker that summer, "I feel as though I could die happy."

ROOSEVELT'S THIRD-PARTY CANDIDACY helped to elect a Democrat, Woodrow Wilson, who was backed by several charter members of the National Progressive Republican League that had started in La Follette's home. When Louis Brandeis endorsed Wilson in July, he made national news by calling on "progressives, irrespective of party affiliation," to back the Democratic candidate. The role of J. P. Morgan and the Steel monopoly remained an issue during the campaign, not only for Taft but also for Wilson, who denounced TR for turning to those interests for both money and ideas. In office, Wilson achieved goals advanced by some progressives, such as creating the Federal Trade Commission to help enforce antitrust laws and regulate big business, creating the Federal Reserve System, and supporting constitutional amendments that would create a graduated income tax and the direct election of U.S. senators. But he was a bitter disappointment to black supporters, including W. E. B. Du Bois.

"I espoused the cause of Woodrow Wilson, fully aware of the political risk involved and yet impelled to this path by the reaction of Taft and disappointment at Roosevelt," Du Bois later explained. "I wrote in the *Crisis* just before the election: 'We sincerely believe that in the face of promises disconcertingly vague, and in the face of the solid cast-ridden South, it is better to elect Woodrow Wilson President of the United States and prove once and for all if the Democratic Party dares to be democratic when it comes to black men.'" Du Bois called the campaign that he and others ran for Wilson "an unusually successful effort" that garnered a hundred thousand black votes in the North.

The result of Wilson's election for blacks in America was a disaster.

"As many Negroes had feared," Du Bois ruefully admitted, "it brought disappointment and encouraged unexpected reaction" ushering in what he called "a time of cruelty, discrimination and wholesale murder." Wilson's first Congress, Du Bois wrote, generated "the greatest flood of bills proposing discriminatory legislation against Negroes that has ever been introduced into an American Congress. There were no less than twenty bills advocating 'Jim Crow' cars in the District of Columbia, race segregation of Federal employees, excluding Negroes from commissions in the army and navy, forbidding the intermarriage of Negroes and whites, and excluding all immigrants of Negro decent."

ROOSEVELT'S PROGRESSIVE PARTY quickly dissipated as a force in American politics. The party backed a number of candidates in 1914, including prominent reformers such as Albert Beveridge in Indiana, Gifford Pinchot in Pennsylvania, James Garfield in Ohio, and Francis Heney in California. Roosevelt had just returned to the country from an excursion to the Amazon's "River of Doubt" that almost cost him his life and left him physically weak. He campaigned for many of his friends, but they were virtually all defeated, often by very conservative opponents. After the election, Roosevelt was despondent. He told William Allen White that the country had turned against reform in a change that "is more than temporary." As for the Republican Party, he said, "the dog has returned to its vomit."

Meeting again in Chicago in 1916, delegates from around the country, bound together by their love of the former President, nominated TR for a second time, and nominated John M. Parker as Vice President. Roosevelt refused to run and immediately announced his support for the Republican Party's candidate, Charles Evans Hughes. Some of his supporters were deeply disappointed, but others followed him back into the Republican fold. Parker's name appeared on some state ballots as a vice presidential candidate without anyone at the top of the ticket.

More than twenty-five years later, Harold Ickes, a prominent Bull Mooser from Chicago who became Franklin Roosevelt's powerful Secretary of the Interior, wrote an article claiming that George Perkins had never believed in progressive principals and had almost single-handedly destroyed the Progressive Party.

ROOSEVELT NEVER SUPPORTED voting rights for blacks in the Deep South. In late 1916, when Senator Boies Penrose of Pennsylvania introduced a "Force" bill to give the federal government power to enforce voting rights in the South, Roosevelt wrote a letter to Senator Lodge, his close friend who had proposed a similar bill in 1890. "Nothing good can come of such a bill, or of such a movement," he said. "As in so many things, clear recognition of an evil may be accompanied by equally clear recognition of the fact that the effort to get rid of it, in the present time, may lead only to worse disaster." TR had two reasons for opposing the legislation. "I believe the movement would be politically unwise," he said. "Moreover, I believe that the great majority of the negroes in the South are wholly unfit for suffrage" and that extending the franchise to them could "reduce parts of the South to the level of Haiti."

Despite the way they had been treated in 1912, however, and despite Roosevelt's belief that most southern blacks were "wholly unfit for suffrage," some black leaders from Mississippi hoped he would be nominated by the Republican Party in 1916. While he was willing to "work with any available line-up," Charles Banks said that he favored TR. Booker T. Washington, who supported Taft in 1912, died in the fall of 1915. His former private secretary, Emmett Scott, who knew his thinking as well as anyone, told Banks that he had "reviewed the whole field myself without being able to see anybody on the horizon but the Colonel."

Many people hoped that Roosevelt would be the Republican Party's candidate again in 1920. He would have been sixty-two years old. Five of the twenty-eight presidents elected by that date had been over sixty. But his health was much worse than was generally understood. The public did not know that he had been suffering from inflammatory rheumatism for twenty years, that he had serious arthritis, and that he had never recovered from his near-death experience during his expedition on the River of Doubt in the jungles of Brazil. Edmond Morris wrote that when Roosevelt died on January 6, 1919, "a common reaction among the millions of Americans who had imagined him to be indestructible, and headed again for the presidency, was a sense of shock so violent they took to refuge in metaphor." Morris quotes one poet who said, "A wind had fallen, a light had gone out, a military band had stopped playing."

Had he lived and become a candidate in 1920, some of the men from Mississippi might have been with him once again. By that time, however, most of his black champions from the South had moved north, generally to Chicago, as part of what became known as the "Great Migration." In the years following World War I, the South became increasingly dangerous and inhospitable, particularly for those who were successful and for black officers returning home from the war. Neil McMillen described Vicksburg in the summer of 1918 as "one of the most racially tense communities in the wartime lower south." Dr. J. A. Miller, who had degrees from Williams College and the University of Michigan Medical School, was charged with sedition by a group of city leaders, presumably for helping to organize a local chapter of the NAACP. Dr. Miller was tarred and feathered, and then "paraded through town, displayed near city hall, put in jail and finally banished under threat of death. That same day, three other black 'disloyalists,' a dentist, a pharmacist and an attorney were all scheduled by the committee for tar and feathering." Willis Mollison, William Attaway, and W. P. Harrison left Vicksburg to escape Dr. Miller's fate.

The men from Mississippi who had been kept out of the Progressive Convention prospered in the North. Samuel A. Beadle, who had been born a slave in Georgia, moved to Chicago, where he continued to practice law. His poetry is now included in various anthologies. His son, Richard Henry Beadle, became a successful photographer in Jackson, Mississippi.

Willis Mollison quickly established a successful law practice in

Chicago. His son Irwin, who earned both an undergraduate and a law degree from the University of Chicago, was appointed to the United States Customs Court in 1945 by President Truman, the first African-American named to a federal court in the continental United States.

William Attaway's daughter Ruth became a noted actor, starting in 1936 when she was part of the original Broadway cast of George S. Kaufman and Moss Hart's Pulitzer Prize–winning comedy *You Can't Take it with You.* His son, William A. Attaway, found fame as an author, writing novels, contributing to popular television shows, and composing music, including Harry Belafonte's still-popular "Banana Boat Song."

Perry Howard and Sidney Redmond were brothers-in-law, married to daughters of Hiram Rhodes Revels, the first black United States senator, who later became the president of Alcorn College. A third daughter, Susan Sumner Revels, met Horace Roscoe Cayton while they were both students at Alcorn. The couple moved to Seattle, Washington, where they edited and published the *Seattle Republican.* After studying at the University of Chicago, their son, Horace R. Cayton, Jr., became a leading scholar, particularly of life on Chicago's South Side, including the ways in which that world changed as blacks from the South moved north. *Black Metropolis: A Study of Negro Life in a Northern City,* which Cayton coauthored with St. Clair Drake, is still considered a classic.

Charles Banks remained in Mississippi until his death in 1923. Although he had been considered the most powerful black man in the state, his financial world began to crumble at around the time that Beadle, Mollison, Attaway, and Harrison were moving north. "The years from 1919 to 1922 brought economic disaster for the town of Mound Bayou," Banks's biographer wrote. As World War I drew to a close, he wrote, "its Golden Age had come to an end." When Banks died in 1923, a huge crowd gathered in Clarksdale. The white-owned *Jackson Daily News* noted that although he had been active in Republican politics, Banks "was more interested in the industrial welfare of his race than in matters political, and he had earned and deserved the respect and confidence of the white people of the commonwealth."

Redmond remained in Mississippi for most of his life. By some accounts, he became one of the ten wealthiest black men in the United States. His career in Mississippi included stints as a doctor, a lawyer, and a bank president. Redmond made much of his fortune as a real estate investor. At one point he owned at least 100 houses. When he died in 1948, he left his heirs an estate worth $604,000, which now would be the equivalent of more than $20 million. Newspaper accounts called him the richest black man in the state's history. Today, the Sidney D. Redmond House in Jackson, Mississippi is on the National Trust for Historic Preservation's list of important African American homes, and Redmond Avenue in that city bears his name.

Redmond's son, Sidney Revels Redmond, earned a degree from Harvard Law School and joined his father's law practice in Jackson. By the late 1920s, the white legal establishment in Jackson had made their professional lives intolerable. The younger Redmond moved to St. Louis, where he won major cases and national acclaim as a civil rights attorney. He served as a delegate to the 1940 Republican Convention and was elected the city's first black alderman in 1944.

Perry Howard returned to the Republican Party, becoming a national fixture for almost forty years. After several attempts to unseat the Mississippi party's white leadership, in 1924 he was elected as the state's representative on the Republican National Committee. By that time, he had moved to Washington, D.C., as a special assistant to Harry M. Daugherty, President Warren Harding's Attorney General, where he was the highest-paid black federal employee. Thanks to his political clout, Howard was able to place people in federal positions ranging from postal carriers to revenue collectors and even U.S. marshals. He was indicted but never convicted for selling those positions for fees ranging from $500 to $2,500.

In 1931, Howard had a bitter falling out with his former brother-in-law. Sidney Redmond called him unfit as a leader and charged Howard with using his position for personal gain rather than for the people of the state. "I am opposed to Mr. Howard's reelection," Redmond said in an open letter to the press, because "his re-election would mean nothing whatever to anyone but Mr. Howard." Over the years, he was attacked by a range of black leaders. A. Philip Randolph, founder and president of the Brotherhood of Sleeping Car Porters, called him "persona non grata among negroes." Walter White, executive director of the NAACP, said that "Negroes like Perry Howard for the sake of political gain would knife every Negro in the country." Ralph Bunche called him "a better lily-white than a white Mississippian could be."

But he prevailed. His firm, Cobb, Howard & Hayes , became a leading—some observers said *the* leading—black law firm in Washington, D.C. With the same combination of eloquence and cunning that he had used to plot a strategy for the 1912 Progressive Convention, Howard remained a member of the Republican National Committee and a delegate to every Republican Convention until 1960.

THEODORE ROOSEVELT, JR., served in World War I as a battalion commander in France, where he was gassed and wounded in the battle of Soissons on July 19, 1918. His brother Quentin, TR's youngest son, had been killed in battle five days earlier.

The war ended on November 11, 1918, with an armistice signed by the Allies and Germany that ended the fighting in Western Europe. By that time, Ted had earned the rank of Colonel.

When TR died on January 6, 1919, Ted was still in France. Six weeks later, John J. Pershing, who led the American Expeditionary Forces during the war, asked Ted to help to found a new organization to support the troops who would be returning home from the war. That organization, which ultimately had a much broader purpose, became known as the American Legion.

Perhaps as a result of coming to know some of the black American soldiers in France, Ted wanted the new organization to be fully integrated. He "envisioned a non-segregated and therefore boldly progressive brotherhood of former soldiers," Steven Trout explained in *On the Battlefield of Memory*. The leaders of the new organization loved Ted and pleaded with him to become the group's first president. But the forces arrayed on the other side were just too powerful. "By the end of its first convention," Trout wrote, "the legion not only rejected a policy of non-segregation but it also insured that black veterans would remain largely excluded from the organization's ranks."

For the rest of his life, Ted championed the cause of civil rights. He became involved with countless organizations, serving as a director and honorary president of the National Health Circle for Colored People and a trustee of Howard College. As assistant secretary of the navy under Presidents Harding and Coolidge, he spoke to the NAACP's annual convention and often served as an intermediary with top administration officials. In 1931, the NAACP Convention exploded with wild applause when he attacked lynching, "whether by mobs or courts."

Ted never achieved his father's success as a politician, serving twice as a member of the New York State Assembly and running unsuccessfully for governor of New York in 1924. But he did become an even greater military hero than his father, earning a Medal of Honor for his service as the only general to storm the beaches of Normandy on June 6, 1944. When General Omar Bradley was asked to name the single most heroic action he had ever seen in combat, he replied: "Ted Roosevelt on Utah Beach."

In 1939, the man who had once spoken so coldly of the intelligence of black voters was elected to the board of the NAACP.

MANY OF THE CONCERNS, problems, and opportunities that surfaced before and during TR's campaign remain a part of the political landscape. Some continue to be hotly contested, and the parties make changes in each election cycle both to perfect the process and to make sure that it works to the advantage of a particular party, candidate, or state. For a range of reasons, Iowa and New Hampshire always want to have the earliest contests—a caucus in Iowa and a primary in New Hampshire. Some other state parties want early primaries to increase the state's political influence, to generate more funding from candidate advertisements and campaigning, or to help a particular faction or candidate gain strength. Rules sometimes give extra delegates to states that have voted for the party's candidate in the last presidential election, a process that reinforces the power of the party's base but may also make it less likely that the nominee will be more centrist.

As in 1912, the delegate selection rules have continued to be established by the national parties through their Call to the Convention. Those rules are only enforceable by the party itself. Parties can assure adherence to the rules by threatening to reduce the voting power of noncomplying states and even by denying a delegation the right to participate. In 1968, the Democratic Convention refused to seat the "regular" all-white delegation from Mississippi, which had been selected by the state party rules, and instead seated an integrated delegation of "loyalist" delegates selected through a series of widely attended but unofficial caucuses. When Florida and Michigan held primaries earlier than the Democratic Party's rules allowed in 2008, their delegate power at the convention was initially cut in half.

Though it may seem arbitrary or surprising to many observers, party rules trump state laws. As the U.S. Supreme Court has explained, "since our national political parties first came into being as voluntary associations of individuals, the convention itself is the proper forum for determining intra-party disputes as to which delegates shall be seated." Elihu Root may have said it best when he observed that "I don't know if it is the best rule, but it was the rule under which they were elected even though there may be a better rule."

HAVE PRESIDENTIAL PRIMARIES upgraded the quality of the candidates selected by the major parties? Could the process be improved? Those are questions that have been debated by academics, reporters, and political operatives in living rooms in Washington, D.C., bars along the campaign trail, political science courses, and on Sunday morning talk shows.

From 1912 to 1968, starting with Taft's defeat of TR, the parties were able to ignore or overcome the results of the primaries. On March 2, 1952, Senator Estes Kefauver of Tennessee defeated incumbent president Harry Truman in the New Hampshire primary. Truman withdrew from the race. Kefauver went on to win eleven of the twelve primaries that he entered and was favored in the final Gallup Poll before the national convention. Nevertheless, the party leaders drafted Governor Adlai Stevenson of Illinois, who had not been a candidate in any primary. That same year, Senator Robert Taft of Ohio, William Howard Taft's son, came into the convention with a plurality of delegates, having won six primaries, whereas General Dwight Eisenhower had won five. But the party turned to Eisenhower, who had the support of most of the Republican governors and looked stronger in public opinion polls.

After 1968, however, when the Democratic Party nominated Hubert Humphrey, who had not won a single primary, both parties adopted rules that have made it difficult if not impossible to nominate a candidate who has not competed successfully in the process. The number of presidential primaries changes from year to year, but primaries generally account for about 80 percent of the delegates.

The precise rules will continue to change from election cycle to election cycle, but the virtues of popular democracy have generally supported the thesis that the public should select the parties' nominees. Without primaries, several of the candidates selected in the past sixty years might not have been chosen. When he launched his campaign in 1960, John F. Kennedy was worried about Senators Stewart Symington and Lyndon Johnson. Both had strong ties to party leaders. Knowing that neither man seemed likely to run in any primaries, Kennedy argued that no nominee should be selected unless he had faced the voters. "If the voters don't love them in March, April or May," he told an audience in New Hampshire, "they won't love them in November." For fifty years, he maintained, since the advent of primaries in 1912, "no Republican or Democrat has reached the White House without entering and winning at least one contested primary."

What's more, Kennedy's campaign team doubted that party leaders would select him unless he could prove that a Catholic could win
in a predominantly Protestant state. After he defeated Hubert Humphrey in West Virginia on May 10, 1960, it was almost impossible for
opponents to derail his campaign. According to one of his top aides,
during the convention JFK warned one of the party's most powerful
bosses that he "had better think what was going to happen to the
Democratic Party if the candidate who'd won all the primaries and
amassed all the delegates could be denied the nomination simply for
being an Irish Catholic."

"Could you imagine me, having entered no primaries, trying to tell
the leaders that being a Catholic was no handicap?" Kennedy asked at
the time. For some men, he said, "primaries are not only good, they are
absolutely vital."

When Ronald Reagan ran for president in 1980 at sixty-nine, his age
was a continuing issue. The primaries provided him with a means to
prove his vitality. "Reagan was being attacked by Republican operatives
supporting [George Herbert Walker] Bush, [John] Connally and [Philip]
Crane, most especially over the age issue but also by the media," the
author of one leading biography of Reagan explained. "Polling showed
pluralities and majorities opposed to Reagan based on his age, especially when asked if they would support a man who would be 70 years
of age one month after his inauguration." But by "campaigning fero-
ciously and demonstrating his vitality," Reagan used the primaries to
overcome those objections.

Similarly, it seems doubtful that the Democratic leadership would
have turned to Barack Obama in 2008 if he had not used the caucuses
and primaries to assuage their fears. "A black man winning in mostly
white Iowa was like John F. Kennedy, a Catholic, winning in Protestant
West Virginia in 1960," one study noted, "crossing a threshold that
needed to be crossed before prudent party leaders could be expected to
sign on."

For better or worse, or both, presidential primaries have also helped to reduce the power of traditional political leaders and of the political parties themselves. The primary process has produced a new class of political leaders and insiders who are not necessarily representative of the general public or even of the party. To win a party's nomination, candidates often feel compelled to appeal to the activist wing of the party, sometimes called its "base," taking controversial positions that may not reflect the views of the candidate or of a majority of the members of the party and that can make it more difficult to reach for the center in the general election or to reach a consensus with political opponents after the election.

Moreover, primary campaigns have become so costly that candidates are forced to spend much of their time raising money and trying to win the hearts of a few very large donors. Thanks to a series of rulings by the Supreme Court, a handful of wealthy individuals or organizations can dominate the system, sometimes by running "independent" efforts. Fabulously wealthy donors have become virtual political parties of their own. In some respects, today's heirs to George Perkins and Frank Munsey have become as powerful as the parties' leaders.

In the era of popular democracy, there may be some highly qualified candidates who simply decide not to run. After having been the Democratic Party nominee in both 1952 and 1956, Adlai Stevenson said that primaries should be abolished. "It is terribly expensive, it's exhausting physically, you burn yourself up, you burn up your ammunition, you burn up your means," he said. "It's a very, very questionable method of selecting presidential candidates. . . . All it does is to destroy some candidates."

Whatever shortcomings they may have brought with them, however, the presidential primaries that TR did so much to create and popularize in 1912 have, indeed, given the people the right to rule. And they almost certainly deserve some of the credit for enabling the candidacies of our first Catholic president, the first man to take office on the eve of his seventieth birthday, and the first African-American President of the United States.

Acknowledgments

With the help of material from dozens of previously unknown and unused manuscript collections, this book provides a fresh perspective on the 1912 campaign, the birth of the presidential primary, and Theodore Roosevelt's decision to exclude black delegates from the Deep South from his Progressive Party Convention. Contemporary news accounts; the diaries, letters, and memoirs of his most important supporters and allies; as well as unpublished letters by and to Roosevelt make it possible to understand his motives and the events of the era with a fresh eye.

Some newly unearthed letters, including those of Ormsby McHarg, one of Roosevelt's key political operatives, were in private hands; others were in locations seldom visited by TR scholars, such as the letters of Arthur Hill, a Roosevelt acolyte who later became a distinguished Boston lawyer, which are at the Portsmouth Athenaeum in Portsmouth, New Hampshire; others had remained unused in huge collections, such as the constant stream of intimate political reports from Franklin Knox, the former Rough Rider who, as his friend and the chair of the Michigan Republican Party, carried out secret missions for TR during the 1912 campaign. After the campaign, Knox purchased a paper in New Hampshire that became known as the *Manchester Union-Leader*, later moved to Chicago, where he published the

Chicago Daily News, ran for Vice President in 1936 as Alf Landon's running mate, and, after the United States entered World War II, served as Franklin Roosevelt's Secretary of the Navy. The Knox letters are in the papers of Governor Chase Osborn at the Bentley Historical Library at the University of Michigan. Still other letters have been held under seal, such as the volumes of notes and letters about the 1912 campaign marked "highly confidential" that were collected by TR's Harvard classmate and friend Charles Washburn. Those documents were unavailable to researchers and readers until the librarians at the American Antiquarian Society Library in Worcester, Massachusetts, agreed that they could be released since more than seventy-five years had passed since the death of most of those involved, including Washburn, Roosevelt, and Henry Cabot Lodge.

In addition to George Mowry's *Theodore Roosevelt and the Progressive Movement*, which helped spark my interest in primary reform in 1968, the events of the era are covered in a range of memoirs of participants and studies of TR, Taft, La Follette, and other leaders of the era. There are hundreds of excellent scholarly works, including some unpublished doctoral dissertations. I benefited enormously from the vast library of more recent books about Theodore Roosevelt, several of which treat some aspect of the 1912 campaign. Among the most relevant are James Chace's *1912: Wilson, Roosevelt, Taft, and Debs—The Election That Changed the Country*; Patricia O'Toole's *When Trumpets Call: Theodore Roosevelt After the White House*; Lewis Gould's insightful *Four Hats in the Ring: The 1912 Election and the Birth of Modern American Politics*; Edmund Morris's *Colonel Roosevelt*, the third volume in his splendid trilogy; and Doris Kearns Goodwin's *Bully Pulpit: Theodore Roosevelt, William Howard Taft, and the Golden Age of Journalism*, a unique blended study of the press, history, and politics.

There are countless more general discussions of the institution and development of the primary election, including Byron Shafer's *Bifurcated Politics: Evolution and Reform in the National Party Convention* and *Quiet Revolution: The Struggle for the Democratic Party and the Shaping of Post-Reform Politics*; Rhodes Cook, *The Presidential Nominating Process*; James W. Davis, *Presidential Primaries: Road to the White House*; Alan Ware's *The American Direct Primary*; and Louise Overacker's *The Presidential Primary.*

Although no book has explored the story of the black delegates from Mississippi to the 1912 conventions and TR's motives for excluding them, books that have proved invaluable include Casdorph, *Republicans, Negroes, and Progressives in the South, 1912–1916*; Smith, *Emancipation: The Making of the Black Lawyer, 1844–1944*; Sewell and Dwight, *Mississippi Black History Makers*; McMillen, *Dark Journey*; Jackson, *A Chief Lieutenant of the Tuskegee Machine: Charles Banks of Mississippi*; Hobbs, *The Cayton Legacy*; Hamilton, *Beacon Lights of the Race*; Sinkler, *The Racial Attitudes of American Presidents*; and Bradley, *The Imperial Cruise.*

One of the great joys of using original material in writing history is the chance to engage in a form of time travel by reading letters and journals, some of which have never been used before. A number of manuscript collections, maintained by archivists who are often the unsung heroes of the historian's craft, provided large quantities of personal correspondence between the major political figures and players in the 1912 presidential primary campaigns. The Library of Congress houses the papers of many important political figures whose dealings are detailed in this book, including Theodore Roosevelt, William Howard Taft, Amos Pinchot, Gifford Pinchot, Albert J. Beveridge, James R. Garfield, and Elihu Root. While most of TR's important outgoing correspondence has been published in Morison's eight-volume *Letters of Theodore Roosevelt*, his unpublished and seldom-consulted incoming correspondence is almost equally interesting. The Charles Dewey Hilles Papers at Yale University, Hiram W. Johnson Papers at the University of California, Berkeley, and the Papers of Ormsby McHarg, held in the private collection of Paul A. Ryan, each proved highly useful in constructing a narrative of the primary campaign from the writings of participants in both TR's and Taft's campaigns. Other valuable collections include the Henry Cabot Lodge Papers at the Massachusetts Historical Society; the

William Kent Family Papers at Yale University; the Papers of Arthur Hamilton Lee at the University of London; the Francis J. Heney Papers at the University of California, Berkeley; the George Walbridge Perkins and Herbert Parsons Papers at Columbia University; the John Milliken Parker Papers at the University of Louisiana at Lafayette; the Charles Grenfill Washburn Papers at the American Antiquarian Society; the Frank B. Kellogg Papers at the Minnesota Historical Society; the E. W. Scripps Papers at the Ohio University Library; the Chase S. Osborn Papers at the University of Michigan; the Herbert S. Hadley Papers and the Western Historical Manuscripts Collection at the University of Missouri; the Nicholas Roosevelt Papers at Syracuse University; the Arthur Dehon Hill Family Papers at the Portsmouth Athenaeum; the Miles Poindexter Papers at the University of Washington; the William E. Glasscock Papers at West Virginia University; and the Joseph M. Dixon Papers at the University of Montana. A number of those involved in the events of the era left useful oral histories, among them Ormsby McHarg and Stanley Washburn.

Throughout the process, I have been aided immeasurably by outstanding research assistants, starting with Jeff Berry, who logged countless hours at the Library of Congress and elsewhere and helped me to find doctoral students and others who had the time and stamina to plow through papers and libraries around the country and, in one case, England.

It was a joy to work with and benefit from the talent of a wide array of young (and sometimes more seasoned) scholars that included Jeremy Sabella, Emily Johnson, Chris Byrnes, Thomas Kaplan and Mary Greenfield at Yale University; Sarah Hartwell at Dartmouth; Xiaofei Wang and Jason Kehe at USC; Gwen McCarter at Harvard and then at Duke; Allison Badger and David Brock at the University of Missouri's Western Historical Manuscripts Collection; Tim Boyd and Alan Sun of Vanderbilt University; Barbara Russell at Washington State University; Carolyn Marvin at the Portsmouth Athenaeum in New Hampshire; William Bolt at the University of Tennessee; Alden Stoner in London;

Craig Schiffert and Melvin Barrolle at Howard University; Margot Edelman and Vanessa Tantillo at Harvard; Hemanth Kadambi of the University of Michigan; Daniel Koehler at the University of Chicago; Nathan Grossman, who conducted research at the Library of Congress; Eugene T. Neely and Yusuf Yusufov of Adelphi University; Charles Disantis at the University of Wisconsin; Jan Hillegas in Mississippi; Benjamin Skomsky at Syracuse University; Kevin Clutter at the Newberry Library in Chicago; Ann Trevor at Stanford University; Alex Morrow at the University of Washington; Jessica Bowman at the University of Idaho; Corey Sherman at Columbia University; Michael Workman at West Virginia University; Zsuzsa Mitro at Dartmouth University; Molly Kennedy at the University of Illinois; Christian Peterson at Ohio University; Timothy Giles at the Kansas State Historical Society; and Thomas Kinzinger and Sophie Jacobson, who were my assistants in the book's home stretch.

Though there are no surviving participants from the era, in an effort to understand the perspective of the black leaders from Mississippi, I tracked down a number of their impressive offspring and am indebted to them for their memories and insights. Those who helped with that stage of my research include: Frances Minor, along with Chicago librarian Michael Flug; Susan Cayton Woodson; Bret, Paul, and Gwen Mollison; Alfredteen Harrison; Barbara Beadle Barber; Jeanne Middleton; Louise Howard; Revels Cayton; Frances Scott Attaway; Noelle Attaway Kirton; and William Attaway.

As a member of the faculty of the University of Southern California, I have been privileged to have some great colleagues, access to a first-rate library, and research funding supplied by the Annenberg Foundation through my Annenberg Family Chair in Communication Leadership as well as from a special fund created by the provost—first Max Nikias and then Beth Garrett—to support the work of University Professors. Some of the early research was made possible by my year as a Fellow at Harvard's Shorenstein Center.

Several leading authors were kind enough to read the manuscript and to suggest improvements. Professor Lewis Gould, who has spent decades studying and writing about some of the events and people in this book, read the manuscript with great care. Professor Byron Shafer, a leading scholar on the history of the delegate selection process, provided the benefit of his considerable expertise and wisdom. Professor Matthew Holden, best known for his work in political science, was born in Mound Bayou, Mississippi, and has spent years studying some of the black leaders of that state; he brought insight to the coverage of the men who were denied entry to the Progressive Party convention of 1912. Reporter and political analyst Ron Brownstein provided extremely valuable advice on the enduring relevance of the events of 1912, as did Mickey Kantor and Bob Shrum, who have organized and run presidential nominating campaigns and presidential elections. Adam Hochschild, who teaches narrative writing when not writing great books of his own, provided sage stylistic advice as did noted screenwriter and playwright David Rintels. I am indebted to all of them and other readers, including my favorite historian (and my sister), Holly Cowan Shulman, former NBC reporter Heidi Schulman, and amateur historian John Cooke.

Once again I am indebted to my agent, Peter Matson, who supported this book with wisdom, enthusiasm, and elan. My editor, John Glusman, believed in this book from the start and improved it at every stage, and his talented assistant, Alexa Pugh, provided invaluable support. Ruth Fecych used her expertise to help edit early drafts.

Above all, I have benefited from the love, enthusiasm, and wisdom of my son, Gabriel Cowan, my daughter, Mandy Wolf, my son-in-law, Jonathan Wolf, and particularly my wife, Aileen Adams, who (while serving as a cabinet secretary in California and deputy mayor of Los Angeles) always found time to read drafts of this book and to provide loving support for it—and for me. We were together on Martha's Vineyard, on the opening night of the 1972 Democratic National Convention, about to leave the house for the evening, when we heard the voice of Howard K. Smith telling his ABC Network News audience that a huge picture of "young Geoffrey Cowan" should have been hanging on the wall of the Miami Beach Convention Center that night because Cowan had "done more to change conventions than anyone since Andrew Jackson first started them"; and she has been with me more than forty years later as a somewhat older Geoffrey Cowan completed work on this book and tried to make sense of TR and the changes that he (and, to a small extent I) had wrought.

ABBREVIATIONS

ADH   Arthur Dehon Hill Family Papers.

AHL   Arthur Hamilton Lee Papers

AJB   Albert J. Beveridge Papers

AP   Amos Pinchot Papers

CDH   Charles Dewey Hilles Papers

CGW   Charles Grenfill Washburn Papers

CSO   Chase S. Osborn Papers

ER   Elihu Root Papers

EWS   E. W. Scripps Papers

FBK   Frank B. Kellogg Papers

FJH   Francis J. Heney Papers

GP   Gifford Pinchot Papers

GWP   George Walbridge Perkins Papers

HCL   Henry Cabot Lodge Papers

HP   Herbert Parsons Papers

HSH   Herbert S. Hadley Papers

HWJ   Hiram W. Johnson Papers

JM   James Manahan Papers

JMD   Joseph M. Dixon Papers

JMP   John Milliken Parker Papers

JRG   James Rudolph Garfield Papers

NR   Nicholas Roosevelt Papers
OM   Papers of Ormsby McHarg
RNC   Republican National Committee Papers
TRP   Theodore Roosevelt Papers
WEG   William E. Glasscock Papers
WHT   William Howard Taft Papers
WK   William Kent Family Papers

NOTES

PROLOGUE

1   **the result of legislation promoted by Roosevelt's operatives:** Experts have differed on the number of primaries attributable to Roosevelt's efforts. Doris Kearns Goodwin gives TR credit for creating direct presidential primaries in seven states: Pennsylvania, Massachusetts, Maryland, Ohio, South Dakota, Illinois, and New York. Goodwin, *The Bully Pulpit*, p. 687.

1   **more than half of the popular vote:** There has been a debate among historians over the exact number of primaries and the totals of the popular and delegate votes attributable to primaries, with some scholars excluding New York. Edmund Morris has a good discussion of that debate and argues that "in their general tendency to emphasize TR's popularity among rank-and-file GOP voters, these historians mystifyingly exclude New York." Including New York, which was certainly treated as a primary by the participants at the time, Morris gives the popular numbers as follows: TR—1,214,969; Taft—865,835; and La Follette—327,357. Of the delegates selected in primaries, he gives TR 294 and Taft 126. La Follette had 36 delegates. Morris, *Colonel Roosevelt*, pp. 188, 193, and accompanying footnotes.

2   **In his most important speeches:** With the title "The Right of the People to Rule," Roosevelt's speech was widely reprinted. It is collected in Davidson, *The Wisdom of Theodore Roosevelt*. Those who want to hear it in his own voice can listen online to a version of a recording that he made later that spring. https://www.youtube.com/watch?v=ZmDhFCTAaPM

2   **"The hopes of the Roosevelt managers":** *New York Times*, June 16, 1912.

3   **change the party's delegate selection rules:** For an account of the events in 1968, see Shafer, *Quiet Revolution*. Also see Tichenor and Fuerstman,

"Insurgency Campaigns and the Quest for Popular Democracy"; Stricherz, *Why Democrats are Blue*; and Harold Hughes, *The Honorable Alcoholic*. The rules reforms owe a special debt to the late Eli Segal. The report of the commission that inspired the rules reforms, which was chaired by Governor Harold Hughes of Iowa, was called "The Democratic Choice." The other members of the commission were Donald M. Fraser, Harry Ashmore, Alexander Bickel, Julian Bond, Frederick Dutton, and Doris Fleeson Kimball. The staff administrator was Tweed Roosevelt, one of TR's great-grandsons, who went on to lecture and write about TR and to serve as president of the Theodore Roosevelt Association.

3   **Smith, in a bit of inflated rhetoric:** Smith's source may have been the account in Theodore White's *Making of the President, 1968*. Interested readers can find the Smith July 10, 1972, editorial in the Vanderbilt Television Archives or online at http://dev-tvnews.library.vanderbilt.edu/broadcasts/21423.

4   **divide the history of presidential nominations into four periods:** For example, Cook, *The Presidential Nominating Process*.

5   **two-thirds of the delegates:** The two-thirds rule helped to preserve the power of the South within the Democratic Party. In 1924, it took more than 100 ballots to nominate the party's candidate. At the urging of Franklin Roosevelt, the rule was eliminated by voice vote at the party's national convention in 1936.

5   **might have won the election:** Gould, *America in the Progressive Era*, p. 64. Kermit Roosevelt reportedly said that "Pop is praying for the nomination of Champ Clark." Cooper, *The Warrior and the Priest*, p. 161.

6   **Though they were not seated:** In a hotly debated "compromise," the party agreed to allow two members of the MFDP to be seated in 1964. The members of the party left the convention rather than agreeing to that arrangement. A successor group to the MFDP was seated at the 1968 convention. For accounts of these events, see Kotz, *Judgment Days;* Mills, *This Little Light of Mine;* Nash and Taggart, *Mississippi Politics;* Williams, *Eyes on the Prize;* and Gitlin, *The Sixties*.

6   **"there are striking parallels":** Milkis, *Theodore Roosevelt*, p. 176.

6   **ensure the seating of the all-white delegation:** Kotz, *Judgment Days*. The episode was memorably dramatized in *All the Way*, Robert Schenkkan's powerful Tony Award–winning play about LBJ.

6   **the men TR had excluded:** Most importantly Perry Howard, Sidney D. Redmond, Charles Banks, Willis E. Mollison, William S. Attaway, William P. Harrison, and Samuel Beadle.

6   **"represent the very worst type"**: TR, Jr., to Parker, July 24, 1912, JMP.

CHAPTER ONE

9   **jumped off of the train:** *New York Sun*, February 25, 1912; *Boston Globe*, February 25, 1912.

9   **"I am really an old man":** TR to Cecil Arthur Spring Rice, August 22, 1911, Morison, *The Letters of Theodore Roosevelt*, Volume VII, p. 334. All of the letters that use citations from Morison volumes are in the public domain, and almost all are available in the Library of Congress. Reference to the pages in Morison are supplied to make research easier for interested readers and scholars.

9   **complained of rheumatism:** TR to Arthur Hamilton Lee, September 25, 1911, Morison, Volume VII, pp. 345–347.

9   **"the most loveable personality":** Butt, *Taft and Roosevelt: The Intimate Letters of Archie Butt, Military Aide* (hereafter: Butt, *Letters*), December 10, 1908, pp. 232–233.

10   **a dozen taxicabs filled with reporters and cameramen:** *New York Sun*, February 25, 1912.

11   **March 4, 1909:** Until the ratification of the Twentieth Amendment in 1933, the inauguration took place on March 4.

12   **youngest former President:** President James Garfield died in office just before his fiftieth birthday.

12   **"When the two were in the White House together":** Sullivan, *Our Times*, p. 290.

12   **"it's always that way when they're together":** Ibid.

12   **"He is going to be greatly beloved":** Butt, *Letters*, December 10, 1908, pp. 229–230.

13   **governor of the Philippines:** Taft had been named governor of the Philippines by President McKinley.

13   **Roosevelt had publicly described Taft:** *New York Times*, September 19, 1908.

13   **"I believe that Taft":** TR to Sir George Otto Trevelyan, June 19, 1908, Morison, Volume VI, p. 1085.

13   **opportunities afforded a brilliant First Lady:** Helen Taft was a "qualified" suffragist and an outspoken activist for the rights of factory workers. Two months after Taft took office, Mrs. Taft suffered a stroke from which she never fully recovered. In 1912, she worked with the wife of the Japanese ambassador to plant 3,020 Japanese cherry trees on the Washington Tidal Basin.

13   **"Let the audience see"**: Roosevelt to Taft, September 11, 1908, Morison, Volume VI, p. 1231.

14   **"Hit them hard, old man!"**: Ibid.

14   **"It's true that I myself"**: Sullivan, *Our Times*, pp. 305–306.

14   **told Taft what subjects to discuss**: Longworth, *Crowded Hours*, pp. 147–148.

14   **1.2 million votes**: Out of almost 15 million votes cast.

15   **an unlikely but nevertheless intimate friend**: Morris, *The Rise of Theodore Roosevelt*, p. 249.

15   **"say nothing about your own political intentions"**: Lodge to TR, December 27, 1909, HCL.

15   **"he slept on the floor"**: Sullivan, *Our Times*, pp. 385–386; for more on his family, see Char Miller, *Gifford Pinchot and the Making of Modern Environmentalism*.

16   **compelled to fire him**: The Pinchot-Ballinger controversy later became a widely studied episode in American history. Penick, *Progressive Politics and Conservation: The Ballinger-Pinchot Affair*.

16   **"The tendency of the administration"**: Pinchot to TR, December 31, 1909, TRP.

17   **"Ugh! I do dread"**: TR to Lodge, May 5, 1910, Morison, Volume VII, p. 80.

17   **his mood reflected**: Brands, *TR*, p. 675.

17   **editor of *The Outlook***: *The Outlook*, Volume 132 (1922), p. 416, obituaries and tributes to Abbott; Schwartz, *Abraham Lincoln and the Forge of National Memory*.

17   **Abbott announced that TR would join**: Lawrence F. Abbott, *Impressions of Theodore Roosevelt*, pp. 13–15; *New York Times*, November 5, 1908. The *New York Times* included the full text of the announcement, which was published in *The Outlook* on November 7.

18   **he would be sixty years old**: TR to Ted Jr., August 22, 1911, TRP.

19   **wired from Cheyenne, Wyoming**: Harbaugh, *Power and Responsibility*, p. 293.

19   **traveling on the train with him**: Gardner, *Departing Glory*, p. 188.

19   **Pinchot wrote a muscular alternative draft**: William Allen White helped Pinchot with the draft.

20   **"maneuvered a retreat from Osawatomie"**: Pinchot, *History of the Progressive Party: 1912–1916*, pp. 113–116.

20   **"folly of the ultra-insurgents"**: Taft to Root, October 19, 1910, ER.

20   **"a better president than McKinley or Harrison"**: Taft to Ted Jr., August 22, 1910, TRP.

20   **"Any change of decision"**: TR to Washburn, November 29, 1915, CGW.

20   **there were areas of bitter disagreement:** Yale historian John Morton Blum,
      who spent years studying TR, concluded that "three of Taft's policies espe-
      cially aroused him." He listed the arbitration treaties, Taft's antitrust suits
      against U.S. Steel and United Harvester, and their differences concerning
      "conservation and control of natural resources." Blum, *The Republican Roo-
      sevelt*, p. 146.

21   **reciprocity agreement for trade with Canada:** On January 12, 1911, Roo-
      sevelt told Taft that "what you are proposing to do with Canada is admirable
      from every standpoint. I firmly believe in free trade with Canada for both
      economic and political reasons." But TR later denounced Taft in order to
      appeal to farmers in the West, a political ploy that Doris Kearns Goodwin
      denounced as "dishonorable opportunism" in *The Bully Pulpit*, p. 694.

21   **giving his brother Charley more credit:** "I owe my election more to you than
      to anybody else except my brother Charley," Taft wrote TR in November,
      1908. Wister, *Roosevelt*, p. 275

21   **"the last straw":** Leary, *Talks with T.R.*, p. 27. Leary was a member of what
      TR called his "tennis cabinet." In his notes, Leary referred to the "Rural Life
      Commission," but William Henry Harbaugh concluded that TR was actu-
      ally referring to "Taft's failure to reappoint the Country Life Commission."
      Harbaugh, p. 543. According to Leary's diary record of a conversation with
      TR on April 8, 1916, he also said that "the break in our relations was due
      to no one thing but to the cumulative effect of many things—the abandon-
      ment of everything my Administrations stood for, and other things." Leary,
      Talks with T.R., p. 27.

21   **while he was in office:** On January 14, 1912, for example, Archie Butt had
      lunch with TR's sister Corinne at the Longworths' and they discussed all
      aspects for the relationship. "She left in my mind the impression that the
      breach was irrevocable and that the Colonel would never forgive the President
      for introducing or allowing his name to be introduced into the Steel suit."

      "Oh, Major Butt," she said, "it is too late now. If it had not been
      for that Steel suit! I was talking with Theodore only last week, and
      he said that he could never forgive."

      "Of course you know," I said, "that the President never saw that
      suit until it was filed."

      "Yes," she said, "and that in his eyes is the worst feature of the
      case—that such a thing could have been done without his knowledge."
      Butt, *Letters*, pp. 812–813.

22   **"wild-eyed ultra-radicals"**: In one letter to Ted Jr., he wrote that "the wild-eyed ultra radicals do not support us because they think we have not gone far enough. I am really sorry to say that good Gifford Pinchot has practically taken his place among the latter." TR to Ted Jr., October 19, 1910, TRP.

22   **"What the people of the Middle West"**: Sullivan to George Loftus, December 27, 1911, JM.

22   **"the professed reformers"**: TR to Washburn, November 29, 1915, CGW. The Colonel explained his concerns about La Follette in a series of confidential letters, most directly in a letter that he wrote three years later to his old college friend Charles Washburn, who was writing a sympathetic biography and wanted to understand TR's motives for entering the race. Washburn deemed those letters so sacred that he donated them to the American Antiquarian Society, along with other materials and correspondence about the campaign, with the stipulation that they never be made public. The documents are on shelves in the American Antiquarian Society that are marked "confidential." The librarian and president of the society agreed that after seventy-five years it seemed time to release that restriction and agreed to provide access to this author. Email from Thomas Knoles to Geoffrey Cowan, June 10, 2009.

22   **reflected the consensus of leaders in the East:** R. David Myers, "Robert La Follette."

23   **"raise a division of cavalry"**: TR to Taft, March 14, 1911, Morison, Volume VII, pp. 243–244.

23   **"his restless and combative energy"**: Adams, *The Education of Henry Adams*, pp. 417–418.

23   **"found the Colonel"**: Lloyd Griscom quoted by Archie Butt in letter of January 19, 1911, Butt, *Letters*, p. 579.

23   **like a son to both TR and Taft:** On December 3, 1911, Alice told Butt that "Father looks upon you as a son, almost." Butt, *Letters*, p. 776.

23   **"If she could have her wish"**: Butt's description of visit by Lloyd Griscom in January 1911. Butt, *Letters*, pp. 579–582.

24   **"If he could only fight!"**: Letter of January 19, 1911, quoted in Butt, *Letters*, p. 581.

24   **"because of your temperament"**: Root to TR, February 12, 1912, TRP.

25   **"We believe that unless"**: "Charter of Democracy," speech by TR, February 21, 1912.

25   **"In their decision"**: Ibid.

26   **did not like decisions that they had rendered:** "Have you heard what John-

son succeeded in doing?" Gifford Pinchot wrote to his brother on February 15, after reading the latest draft of the speech. Gifford to Amos Pinchot, February 15, 1911, GP. E. W. Scripps was convinced that TR's comments on the judiciary came from Hiram. "Roosevelt's Outlook editorial on 'Judicial Encroachment' warmed me up to at least momentary enthusiasm. His speech before the Constitutional Convention [in Columbus] better explained to me Governor Johnson's actions than all of your reports of his meetings with La Follette. This speech not only explained Johnson's actions, but the fact that Johnson was where he was, when he was, leads me to suspect that the speech was at least partly Johnson's speech and not wholly Roosevelt's." Scripps to Gilson Gardner, February 24, 1911, EWS. But O. K. Davis says in his memoir that the idea for the recall of judicial opinions originated with Dr. Van Hise, the president of the University of Wisconsin. Davis, *Released for Publication*, p. 264.

26 **"I differ with you, Colonel":** Amos Pinchot to TR, February 14, 1912, TRP.

26 **With its powerful statement:** William Kent to Louis Edleman, February 26, 1912, WK.

26 **"Roosevelt's Columbus speech":** Kent to W. H. Cameron, March 1, 1912, WK.

26 **"the greatest speech":** George Miller of the *Detroit Press* to TR, February 23, 1912, TRP.

27 **Roosevelt's friends and former cabinet members:** Some people like Ormsby McHarg could let it pass. "It was so far fetched that I just treated it as a joke," he said later. "I thought he was trying to out-devil La Follette." McHarg oral history.

27 **"responsible for the determination":** Davis, *Released for Publication*, p. 266. Alice Longworth said that the judicial decision recall proposal "more than any other thing, lost him the nomination. It gave his opponents the angle from which to attack him as a dangerous radical, and really distressed many of his most sincere friends and supporters." Longworth, *Crowded Hours*, p. 186.

27 **they could not support his campaign:** Gardner issued a statement saying that "I had intended to support Roosevelt until I read his Columbus speech. With very real regret, I find that his fundamental views are so different from my own that I cannot support him." Quoted in *New York Times*, February 27, 1912.

28 **They disagreed too deeply with his position:** Longworth, *Crowded Hours*, p. 187.

28   **"I never thought":** Lodge to TR, February 28, 1912, TRP.

28   **"Roosevelt's Columbus speech":** Lodge to Brooks Adams, March 5, 1912, HCL.

28   **"missed the old friends":** Longworth, *Crowded Hours*, p. 188. She specifically listed Root, Lodge, and Philander Knox, who had been TR's Attorney General and then Taft's Secretary of State.

28   **"the Republican intriguers":** S. Morris, *Edith Kermit Roosevelt*, p. 376.

28   **"Politics are hateful":** Edith to Kermit, quoted in S. Morris, *Edith Kermit Roosevelt*, p. 376.

29   **"Father's hat is not":** *New York Tribune*, February 25, 1912.

29   **"I was forced to be away":** Edith to Arthur Lee, April, 1912, quoted in S. Morris, from Lee's papers in England, pp. 550–551.

29   **Everyone in the press:** *New York Times*, February 26, 1912.

29   **"bubbling over with enthusiasm":** *New York World*, February 26, 1912.

29   **"It has been a very quiet day":** *New York Times*, February 26, 1912.

31   **Roosevelt's planned campaign:** White, *Autobiography*, p. 452.

31   **"I can name forty-six Senators":** Grant to James Ford Rhodes, March 22, 1912, Morison, Volume VIII, pp. 1456–1461.

32   **"realized that the probabilities":** Ibid.

CHAPTER TWO

34   **local caucuses and state conventions:** The first convention was actually held in Baltimore in 1831 by the Anti-Masonic Party.

34   **it had never happened:** Millard Fillmore, who became President when Zachary Taylor died in office, failed to gain the Whig Party nomination in 1852. Andrew Johnson, a Democrat who ran with Lincoln, had been denied renomination by either party in 1868.

34   **creating primaries:** The nation's first primary laws for state officeholders were adopted in the 1890s. The movement gained national attention in 1903 when Governor Robert La Follette led a successful campaign to create such a law in Wisconsin. Ware, *The American Direct Primary*, p. 248; Overacker, *The Presidential Primary*, pp. 10–15; Jackson and Crotty, *The Politics of Presidential Selection*, p. 21; and Ceaser, *Presidential Selection*, pp. 213–214.

36   **Wisconsin Supreme Court ruled:** *Washington Post*, October 6, 1904.

36   **"under no circumstances":** La Follette, *La Follette's Autobiography*, p. 141.

36   **TR refused to intervene:** Ibid., pp. 137–141; Thelen, *Robert M. La Follette and the Insurgent Spirit*, pp. 42–45; Unger, *Fighting Bob La Follette*, p. 133; Wol-

raich, *Unreasonable Men,* pp. 1–8; *Chicago Tribune,* May 19, 1904; *Chicago Tribune,* June 4, 1904; *New York Tribune,* June 12, 1904; *New York Tribune,* June 23, 1904; *Washington Post,* October 6, 1904.

37   **similar delegate selection laws:** Some accounts give Florida the credit for creating the first law permitting the election of delegates in 1900. In 1908, four states held primaries where delegates were elected. A great many accounts of the evolution of the delegate selection process appear in the list of sources. The first major and still valuable account is Louise Overacker's 1926 study, *The Presidential Primary.*

37   **"because that's the type of man he is":** The quote is from a letter from Mrs. Margaret Fitzpatrick dated August 29, 1955, Pike, "Jonathan Bourne Jr., Progressive," p. 3.

38   **"political interests tended to coincide":** Ibid., p. 2.

38   **amend the federal mining law:** Ibid., p. 53, citing letters that Bourne sent in December 1903.

38   **pouring substantial amounts of his own money:** Ibid., pp. 58–59.

38   **"millionaire dinner":** *The Oregonian,* April 3, 1907, quoted in Pike, *Jonathan Bourne Jr., Progressive,* p. 78.

38   **"almost daily":** Bourne to Borah, April 13, 1907, William Borah Papers, quoted in McKenna, *Borah,* p. 71.

38   **"fanatic" on the subject:** *Saturday Evening Post,* December 12, 1908.

39   **"a sincere fanatic":** Roosevelt to William Hutchinson Cowles, March 18, 1908, Morison, Volume VI, p. 975.

39   **Bourne wouldn't give up:** Bourne may have believed that he had the President's secret support. See Schlup, "Republican Insurgent," p. 230.

39   **"has ceased to amuse me":** TR had another reason for distrusting Bourne. While trying to get Roosevelt to run for another term, Bourne was also trying to get him to agree to drop the government's antitrust suit against Standard Oil. On several occasions, he attempted to arrange meetings between TR and the company's president, John D. Archbold. TR was forced to write Bourne that "it is not only a waste of my time but inadvisable to try and carry on the negotiations through you." TR to Bourne, July 3, 1908, Morison, Volume VI, p. 1107.

39   **"I wish you would":** Bourne to TR, May 14, 1910, TRP.

39   **"below average":** TR to White, November 7, 1914, Morison, Volume VIII, p. 835.

40   **"Without being egotistical":** Bourne to TR, June 23, 1910, TRP.

40   **"As soon as I get":** TR to Bourne, July 3, 1910, TRP.

40   **"I know you are"**: Bourne to TR, July 13, 1910, TRP.

40   **take the movement national:** Pike, *Jonathan Bourne Jr., Progressive*, p. 135.

40   **skeptical about both the messenger:** "Bourne misunderstands me," he
       wrote, "and I cannot begin to make him understand me." TR to White, Janu-
       ary 24, 1911, Morison, Volume VII, p. 213.

41   **"nonsense to make the Initiative and Referendum":** TR to White, December
       12, 1910, Morison, Volume VII, pp. 181–185.

41   **"merely as means to ends":** TR to Bourne, January 2, 1912, Morison, Volume
       VII, pp. 196–198.

41   **"I don't wish to say anything":** Pusey, *Charles Evans Hughes*, p. 265.

41   **told Robert La Follette:** TR to La Follette, September 29, 1911, Morison, Vol-
       ume VII, pp. 347–348; TR to White, December 12, 1910, Morison, Volume
       VII, pp. 181–185.

42   **"fanatics":** TR to Ted Jr., August 22, 1911, TRP.

42   **later served as his press secretary:** TR to O. K. Davis, May 31, 1911, Morison,
       Volume VII, p. 274.

42   **"Godlike as a maker of men":** TR to Willard, February 27, 1911; Willard to
       TR, April 1911; TR to Willard, April 28, 1911; Willard to TR, June 9, 1911;
       TR to Willard, June 20, 1911. The entire exchange appears in *The American
       Scholar*, Autumn 1934, pp. 465–486.

43   **shortcomings of popular government in the South:** But he also pointed out
       that the white majorities in the South had acted unwisely in leaving the
       Union.

43   **"No one now seriously contends":** TR to Willard, April 28, 1911, Morison,
       Volume VII, p. 255.

43   **preserve the rights of black voters:** Dalton, *Theodore Roosevelt*, p. 125. Grant
       and Grant, *The Way It Was in the South*, p. 198. The legislation passed in
       the House but was defeated in the Senate by a filibuster. Roosevelt later
       expressed opposition to such efforts. TR to Lodge, December 4, 1916, Mori-
       son, Volume VIII, p. 1132.

44   **"Roosevelt needs time":** William Kent to R. H. Ross, September 11, 1911,
       WK. Known more for his strong conservation views than for political
       reform issues, Kent had been a longtime admirer of TR and Pinchot before
       his election to Congress in 1910. For an interesting description of his career,
       see Hyde, "William Kent," pp. 34–56.

44   **"the direct election of delegates":** La Follette, *La Follette's Autobiography*, pp.
       495–496.

44   **"paramount purpose":** Francis J. Heney to Woodrow Wilson, July 2 1916, FJH.

"The primary and paramount purpose of the organization of the National Progressive Party was to place in the hands of the voters of each and every political party . . . a national direct presidential preference primary." Wilson came out for a national primary in September 1911.

44 **founding members of the National Progressive Republican League:** The group included newly elected Californian William Kent, Louis Brandeis, Ray Stannard Baker, Frances Heney, William Allen White, and Gifford Pinchot.

44 **"The ultra-radicals have been":** TR to Ted Jr., January 2, 1911, Morison, Volume VII, p. 195.

45 **few political observers were paying close attention:** *Washington Post*, July 12, 1911.

46 **"When I wake up":** La Follette, "The Reed Congress and the New National Issues," *American Magazine*, Volume 73, p. 144. (Though this is an excerpt from La Follette's autobiography, the story does not appear in the autobiography itself.)

46 **"The wild-eyed ultra-radicals":** TR to Ted Jr., October 19, 1910, Morison, Volume VII, p. 145.

46 **come out for La Follette immediately:** Amos Pinchot to Garfield, October 3, 1911, AP.

47 **terrible pain:** S. Morris, *Edith Kermit Roosevelt*, p. 373.

47 **"We have kept the accident":** TR to Ted Jr., October 13, 1911, TRP.

47 **had a long talk:** Garfield Diary, October 9, 1912, JRG.

47 **free to select its own progressive delegates:** Garfield Diary, October 10, 1912, JRG.

48 **"United States Senator Robert":** *Chicago Tribune*, October 18, 1911.

48 **"Two hundred Progressive Republicans":** *New York Times*, October 17, 1911.

48 **"appeared to be expressing":** *New York Tribune*, October 17, 1911.

48 **"sentiment of the people":** Garfield diary entry, October 16, 1911, JRG.

48 **"will drop him like a hot potato":** Amos Pinchot to William Kent, October 19, 1911, WK.

CHAPTER THREE

51 **actively opposed primaries:** *New York Times*, June 2, 1910.

51 **"The President was":** The brief was prepared by Jacob McGavock Dickinson who served as Taft's Secretary of War from 1909 to 1911 and then signed on as a special assistant attorney general to prosecute the case against U.S. Steel.

51   **"Roosevelt Was Deceived":** *New York Times*, October 27, 1911. Pringle has a good account in *The Life and Times of William Howard Taft*, Volume II, p. 670.

52   **the new savior of business:** *The Outlook*, November 18, 1911.

52   **George W. Perkins, a director of U.S. Steel:** Annual Report of U.S. Steel, 1912.

52   **battle against the Sherman Act:** For an account of this episode, see Garratty, *Right Hand Man*.

53   **antitrust laws were stifling business:** Geisst, *Deals of the Century*, p. 28; Cummins to Perkins, August 26, 1911, GWP; Cummins to Keeley, August 26, 1911, GWP.

53   **changing the antitrust laws:** Perkins to TR, September 2, 1911, GWP.

53   **"TRUST BOOMING TR":** *Washington Post*, January 16, 1912. The *Washington Post* article first appeared in the *Indianapolis News*. *Current Literature* ran a more complete account with the cute quip that the story made it appear that "the 'big interests' are ready, like Jack the Ripper, to disembowel the Republic." *Current Literature*, February 1912.

53   **"As I have written":** Horace Taft to Hilles, January 15, 1912, CDH. Six weeks later, Charles Taft wrote Hilles that "of course it is the steel crowd that is backing up Roosevelt and putting the money into his campaign. It remains to be seen whether the steel corporation can control the Government of the United States." Charles Taft to Hilles, February 26, 1912, CDH.

53   **Ward had personal credibility:** On December 1, 1911, he attempted to recruit Herbert Parsons. See HP letters. Later that month, he acted as TR's representative on the RNC.

54   **he and others had concluded:** Parsons to TR, December 2, 1911, HP; Parsons to Hilles, December 13, CDH; TR to Parsons, December 6, 1911, Morison, Volume VII, p. 452; Parsons to John B. Townsend, February 6, 1912, HP.

54   **"stated that he had come":** Parsons to Hilles, December 13, 1911, HP.

54   **Parsons turned him down:** After Parsons shared his version of the conversation with TR, the Colonel playfully disagreed with his reasoning on the third-term issue and later started to address him as *Dear Brutus*, asking that he give his love to *Mrs. Brutus*. TR to Parsons, December 13, 1911, TRP, and January 9, 1912, Morison, Volume VII, p. 476.

54   **"a well-defined movement":** *Boston Globe*, December 11, 1911.

54   **"the fear of friends of Col. Roosevelt":** Ibid.

55   **wanted all delegates to go to the convention:** P. D. Barker to Hilles, January 1, 1912, CDH. Barker was a member of the RNC from Alabama who

told Hilles that TR was already a candidate and that his close friends "are doing everything they can to make his nomination possible." For example, he wrote, during the RNC meeting, that Cecil Lyon of Texas "called a caucus of the southern and western members, at which I was present, the purpose of which was to have them agree 1st that no office holder should go as a delegate to the National Convention, 2nd There should be no instructions."

55 **"kept all eyes and ears open":** Letter of December 12, 1911, quoted in Butt, *Letters*, pp. 783–788.

55 **"You know, Ward is delicate":** *New York Times*, December 12, 1911.

55 **"if it were tendered to him":** *Baltimore Sun*, December 12, 1911.

55 **"to leave matters":** Ibid.

56 **"Ward is for Roosevelt":** *New York Times*, December 12, 1911.

56 **"A National Convention":** *New York Times*, December 12, 1911.

56 **"giving every member of the party":** Bourne to Kellogg, October 11, 1911, FBK.

56 **whether or not you support the plan:** Gardner to Kellogg, October 25, 1911, FBK.

57 **results would not be binding:** *New York Times*, December 12, 1911, quoting Arthur I. Vorys, the national committeeman from Ohio.

57 **"it would not do for me to come to *The Outlook* office":** Ward to TR, December 14, 1911, TRP.

57 **Roosevelt asked a friend:** TR to Florence La Farge, December 16, 1911, TRP.

57 **resonated with Ormsby McHarg:** McHarg oral history.

58 **one of Roosevelt's friends:** The friend, Cleveland Dodge, was a Princeton classmate and lifelong friend of Woodrow Wilson but also a friend of TR. See for example Dodge to Roosevelt, August 11, 1902, offering TR the use of his yacht, TRP. After Dodge was indicted in the New Mexico land fraud cases, TR invited him to the White House in a gesture that reporters called Roosevelt's "official stamp of disapproval of the indictment." *St. Louis Post-Dispatch*, November 20, 1907.

58 **remove McHarg from the case:** Larson, *New Mexico's Quest for Statehood*, pp. 259–260; *Baltimore Sun*, November 14, 1907; Curry, *George Curry, 1861–1947: An Autobiography*, p. 209; TR to Llewellyn, July 29, 1907, OM.

58 **"a trimmer":** *Washington Post*, August 28, 29, 30, and November 5, 1909.

58 **"acting as if he were the Lord":** *Washington Post*, August 30, 1909. During the presidential campaign of 1908, McHarg worked closely with Richard Ballinger, who was named Secretary of the Interior by Taft. McHarg once said that he loved Ballinger "as I love my brother"; he sided with the Secre-

tary when he fired Pinchot. Penick, *Progressive Politics and Conservation*, p. 124.

58   **"I believe we have nobody"**: Larson, *New Mexico's Quest for Statehood*, p. 260; Curry, *George Curry, 1861–1947*.

58   **"he wants the Colonel eliminated"**: *Washington Post*, November 6, 1912.

58   **"the most dangerous figure in public life"**: *New York Tribune*, May 27, 1912, quoting the *New York Herald* story dated November 7, 1910.

59   **"I just thought he"**: McHarg oral history.

59   **"look the situation over"**: McHarg oral history.

59   **drum up support for Roosevelt**: McHarg to TR, January 2, 1912, TR; TR to Ward, January 9, 1912, Morison, Volume VII, p. 474; P. D. Barker to Hilles, January 13, 1912, describing McHarg's work in Alabama, CDH; *Atlanta Constitution*, January 14, 1912; *New York Times*, January 16, 1912; Hadley to TR, January 18, 1912, TRP; Hilles to Horace Taft, January 18, 1912, CDH; Pearl Wight to TR, January 23, 1912, TRP.

59   **"yield to the pressing demands"**: *Atlanta Constitution*, January 15, 1912.

59   **holding personal meetings and sending regular updates**: TR to McHarg, December 29, 1911, OM; McHarg to TR, January 2, 1912, TRP; TR to Ward, January 9, 1912, Morison, Volume VII, p. 474.

60   **arranged to meet him again in person**: McHarg to TR, January 8, 1912, OM.

60   **"If we can win delegates"**: McHarg to TR, January 19, 1912, TRP.

60   **"the first person to come out"**: McHarg to TR, March 4, 1912, TRP.

60   **"I have no time"**: *New York Herald*, January 17, 1912.

60   **seemed to have a special reason to like Roosevelt**: As examples, in a letter to Horace Taft, Charles Hilles listed Judge Oscar R. Hundley of Alabama, who had been given two recess appointments by President Roosevelt and one by Taft, but was not appointed a fourth time, and William J. Oliver of Tennessee, who had crossed swords with Taft while bidding on a contract to build the Panama Canal. Hilles told Horace Taft that "Judge Hundley of Alabama was not appointed a Federal Judge. He went to the Outlook office two weeks ago, and now he is an ardent Roosevelt boomer." Hilles to Horace Taft, January 18, 1912, CDH. Instead of appointing Hundley, Taft nominated William Grubb, a Democrat who had been Horace Taft's roommate at Yale College.

60   **"laying mines throughout"**: Hilles to Horace Taft, January 18, 1912, CDH.

60   **He published an account of those adventures**: O'Laughlin, *From the Jungles Through Europe with Roosevelt*.

61   **Cal had won pledges of support**: O'Laughlin to TR, December 10, 1911, TRP; December 21, 1911, TRP; January 8, 1912, TRP; January 15, 1912, TRP;

and January 29, 1912, TRP; quoted in Howland, *Theodore Roosevelt and His Times*.

61 **"The Progressives will want"**: O'Laughlin to TR, December 10, 1911, TRP.

61 **"I am afraid the Post"**: O'Laughlin to TR, January 15, 1912, TRP.

61 **bullet tore through Knox's hat**: TR, *The Rough Riders*, pp. 135–136; Beasley, *Knox*, p. 20–21.

62 **Encouraged by Ward**: Conspiracy theories were everywhere. Charles Hilles (presumably speaking for Taft) was convinced that TR's backers had paid Walter Brown at least $50,000 for his support—with $25,000 coming from Perkins and $25,000 from Dan Hanna. Hilles to Vorys, January 18, 1912, CDH.

63 **"Many of the party leaders"**: Michigan newspaper story around December 14 in TRP.

63 **"the whole plan"**: The business leader was Otto Bannard. Letter of December 20, 1911, quoted in Butt, *Letters*, p. 799.

63 **meet with Taft individually and in groups**: Knox to Osborn, January 5, 1912, CSO.

63 **when "the need arose"**: Roosevelt to Taft, September 11, 1908, Morison, Volume VI, p. 1231.

64 **confirmed by documents**: While challenging a few of the book's conclusions, the *New York Times* review, written by one of TR's closest friends in the press corps, said that the book lifted the veil on events of that year. Charles Willis Thompson, "A Political Mystery," *New York Times*, May 25, 1913. On the TR-Thompson relationship see Thompson, "To Know Roosevelt was to Love Him," *New York Times*, January 7, 1919; "The Charley Thomson Club" in Leary, *Talks with T.R.*, pp. 16–18.

64 **"leadership of the Progressive movement"**: La Follette, *La Follette's Autobiography*, p. 229.

65 **causing just enough confusion**: Ibid., p. 228.

65 **sent a copy to Roosevelt**: Miller to TR, December 11, 1911, TRP.

65 **began to consider deserting**: La Follette, *La Follette's Autobiography*, p. 228.

65 **scheduled to launch his formal campaign**: Ibid., p. 245.

66 **reported that Osborn planned to denounce**: *New York Times*, December 31, 1911.

66 **"settle upon Theodore Roosevelt"**: *New York Times*, January 2, 1912.

66 **"There was no doubt about it"**: Osborn to Charles Townsend, February 24, 1912, CSO.

66 **Osborn sent the speech**: Osborn to TR, January 4, 1912, TRP.

66   **"instantly and enthusiastically agreed"**: Knox to Osborn, January 9, 1912, CSO.

66   **refused to make any such promise**: Pinchot, *History of the Progressive Party: 1912–1916*, p. 132

67   **"spontaneous" letter**: Howland, *Theodore Roosevelt and His Times*, quoting from his diary entry for January 22, 1912, p. 210–211.

67   **"he considered TR"**: Pinchot, *History of the Progressive Party: 1912–1916*, p. 133.

67   **fight on alone**: Ibid., p. 134.

67   **"The Senator has decided"**: Gifford Pinchot to Colver, February 2, 1912, AP.

68   **"If ever a man played"**: Kent to his mother, February 1, 1912, WK.

68   **some of the features of a trade association**: See, for example, Wilder Testimony, Hearings Before the Committee on the Post-Office and Post-Roads of the House of Representatives on Second Class Mail, 1910, p. 24.

69   **important and potentially receptive**: *New York Times*, February 3, 1912.

70   **"For ten minutes or so"**: W. A. White, *Autobiography*, p. 449.

70   **"shook his fist at them"**: Wister, *Roosevelt*, p. 300.

71   **practically empty**: Sullivan, *Our Times*, p. 474; Wister, *Roosevelt*, p. 301.

71   **campaign was over**: Pinchot, *History of the Progressive Party: 1912–1916*, p. 135.

71   **seemed to be at an end**: For example, Buenker, *The History of Wisconsin, Volume IV*, pp. 662–664; John Fackler to Hiram Johnson, April 1, 1912, HWJ.

71   **"il gran rifiuto"**: Robert Grant to James Ford Rhodes, March 22, 1912, Morison, Volume VIII, pp. 1456–1461.

71   **"somewhat cooked"**: Longworth, *Crowded Hours*, p. 185.

71   **letter was his idea**: On January 18, in the postscript of a letter to Chase Osborn, he said: "What do you think of having you and Governor Glasscock of West Virginia, Governor Stubbs of Kansas, Governor Osborn of Michigan [*sic*], and Governor Bass of New Hampshire write me a letter to which I could answer." He then asked if Osborn would "mind writing to Governor Johnson on the subject." TR to Osborn, January 18, 1912, Morison, Volume VII, p. 485. He wrote almost identical notes to Governors Hadley and Stubbs. The complete note, changed slightly for each participant, said: "I have been thinking over matters a good deal the last few days, and even since I dictated this letter. It may be the best and wisest thing for me to come straight out and answer the questions you put to me in some public statement. Now if so, it seems to me very important that it should be done in the right way. What do you think of having you and Governor Hadley of Mis-

souri, Governor Stubbs of Kansas, Governor Osborn of Michigan, and Governor Bass of New Hampshire write me a letter to which I could answer? I mention these men because I have received letters from them about the time I received yours. It seems to me that if such a group of four or five Governors wrote me a joint letter, or wrote me individual letters which I could respond to at the same time and in the same way, that such procedure would open the best way out of an uncomfortable situation. I am inclined to think as I did not even think as late as a month ago, that the evil of speaking in public is less than the evil of my refraining from speaking. The letter to me might simply briefly state the writer's belief that the people of his State, or their States, desire to have me run for the Presidency, and to know whether in such a case I would refuse the nomination. I want to make it very clear that I am honestly desirous of considering the matter solely from the standpoint of the public interest, and not in the least from my own standpoint; that I am not seeking and shall not seek the nomination, but that of course if it is the sincere judgment of men having the right to know and express the wishes of the people and that the people as a whole desire me, not for my sake, but for their sake to undertake the job, I would feel in honor bound to do so." TR to Osborn, January 18, 1912, Morison, Volume VII, p. 484.

71 **and then he wrote it:** The letter asked him to declare whether he would run, saying that "a large majority of the Republican voters of the country favor your nomination and a large majority of the people favor your election as the next president of the United States." Shortly thereafter, the governors also issued a statement that started with this paragraph: "It is nothing to us that Theodore Roosevelt is not a candidate for the Republican nomination. We believe the people have decided to make him their candidate. It is for the people to determine who shall be their leader, irrespective of the wishes of the citizen selected. Knowing of the high sense of public purpose with which Col. Roosevelt is imbued, we are satisfied that he will not refuse to heed the call of the people." *Washington Post*, February 11, 1912.

71 **visit those governors:** The governors were William E. Glasscock of West Virginia; Chester H. Aldrich of Nebraska; Robert P. Bass of New Hampshire; Joseph M. Carey of Wyoming; Chase Osborn of Michigan; William R. Stubbs of Kansas; and Herbert Hadley of Missouri. They were later joined by Governors R. S. Vessey of South Dakota and Hiram Johnson of California. For the tone of their personal responses, see Hadley to TR, January 22, 1912, TRP, and Glasscock to TR, January 22, 1912, TRP.

72 **asking him to work with Knox:** Knox to TR, January 9, 1912, TRP; TR's sec-

retary to Knox, January 17, 1912, TRP; TR to governors, January 20, 1912, TRP.

72 **"propose presidential primaries"**: Howland, *Theodore Roosevelt and His Times*, pp. 209–214, quoting from his contemporaneous diaries from mid-January 1912.

72 **"the genuine rule of the people"**: *The Outlook* printed the full exchange of letters, *The Outlook*, Volume 100, p. 475.

73 **"There is as yet no evidence"**: *The Outlook*, January 20, 1912.

73 **"come out unconditionally"**: Pike, *Jonathan Bourne Jr., Progressive*, p. 163.

73 **"If we lose, we bolt"**: W. A. White, *Autobiography*, pp. 452–455.

73 **"We were all hypnotized"**: Ibid., p. 453.

CHAPTER FOUR

75 **"conditions in Alabama"**: McHarg to TR, January 2, 1912, TRP.

75 **"I felt a great admiration"**: TR, *Theodore Roosevelt: An Autobiography*, p. 27.

75 **a Democrat and former Confederate soldier**: Edward D. White of Lousiana.

75 **a Confederate war veteran from Tennessee**: Jacob Dickinson later served as the special attorney general who prosecuted the case against U.S. Steel and presumably wrote the brief in October 1911 that called TR naïve for approving U.S. Steel's acquisition of the Tennessee Coal, Iron & Railroad Company.

76 **"The power of public office"**: Wight to TR, February 16, 1912, TRP.

76 **"If we can get"**: Ibid., February 26, 1912.

77 **"amazingly complete" portrait**: Chamberlain, *Farewell to Reform*, p. 135. Doris Kearns Goodwin provides an invaluable description of the role and power of the new magazines in *The Bully Pulpit*.

77 **His last-ditch gamble worked**: Britt, *Forty Years*, pp. 81–83.

77 **700,000 people**: Chamberlain, *Farewell to Reform*, pp. 124–127.

78 **"Munsey knew nothing"**: Commager, *The American Mind*, p. 72.

78 **Munsey "saw muckraking as an attack"**: Britt, *Forty Years*, p. 93.

78 **Though indifferent or unsympathetic**: Greene, "America's Heroes: The Changing Models of Success in American Magazines," p. 173.

78 **Munsey and Perkins had been intimate friends**: Editorial obituary for Perkins in June 1920, quoted in Britt, *Forty Years*, p. 145.

78 **the company's largest shareholder**: Britt, *Forty Years*, pp. 143–150.

78 **Munsey "owed that phenomenal amount"**: Geisst, *Deals of the Century*, p. 28. For more on Munsey's ownership, see *Magazine of Wall Street*, Volume 28,

p. 525, and *Financial World,* July 6, 1912. Munsey once told a friend that he had made at least $11 million on his investment in International Harvester, Britt, *Forty Years,* pp. 130–131.

78 **"one subject":** Britt, *Forty Years,* p. 94.

79 **"greatness of United States Steel":** Ibid.

79 **first White House speechwriter:** *Time,* November 2, 1925; *New York Times,* April 15, 1943; Hertzberg, *Politics,* p. 113. See also Schlesinger, *White House Ghosts: Presidents and Their Speechwriters,* which was inspired by the Judson Welliver Society. Welliver later became a publicist for the American Petroleum Institute and the Sun Oil Company.

79 **congressional inquiries:** *Hampton's Magazine,* August 1910–August 1911.

79 **national attention:** Hechler, *Insurgency,* p. 13.

79 **"the charmed circle of Roosevelt favorites":** *Hampton's Magazine,* March 1910, May 1910, August 1911; Hertzberg, *Politics,* p. 115; Mott, *American Journalism,* p. 607; Essary, *Covering Washington,* pp. 97–98.

79 **a most useful man":** TR to Perkins, July 9, 1912, TRP; *New York Times,* October 8, 1912.

80 **La Follette would withdraw:** La Follette and La Follette, "Robert M. La Follette," p. 375.

80 **lead story for *Munsey's* February issue:** *Munsey's Magazine,* February 1912.

80 **cast an electoral vote for a Republican:** In 1876, Rutherford B. Hayes won the vote in Florida, Louisiana, and South Carolina.

81 **only 730 registered black voters:** Casdorph, *Republicans, Negroes, and Progressives in the South, 1912–1916,* pp. 57–58.

81 **"a wretched farce":** *Munsey's Magazine,* February 1912.

81 **reproducing almost the entire text:** *Chicago Tribune,* February 12, 1912.

82 **based on the state's representation:** Sherman, *The Republican Party and Black America,* p. 19.

82 **"One Mississippi Republican":** Welliver, "Catching Up with Roosevelt."

82 **reduce the South's representation:** The Senator was Thomas C. Platt. Perman, *Struggle for Mastery,* p. 243.

82 **"If you will nominate Roosevelt":** Morris, *The Rise of Theodore Roosevelt,* pp. 765–767; Sherman, *The Republican Party and Black America,* pp. 20–21.

83 **"He found that":** Sherman, *The Republican Party and Black America,* p. 46.

83 **"one of the most determined efforts":** *New York Tribune,* June 18, 1908.

83 **block Taft's nomination:** *Washington Post,* June 18, 1908.

83 **"I object strongly to the proposal":** TR to Herbert Parsons, April 10, 1908, Morison, Volume VI, p. 999.

84   **"Along toward evening":** Watson, *As I Knew Them*, p. 129.
84   **"had that resolution passed":** Ibid.

CHAPTER FIVE

85   **"gleefully" distributing telegrams:** *New York Times*, February 27, 1912.
85   **should not be seated:** On January 18, 1911, Hilles wrote a leader from the South asking for information from Louisiana and Mississippi and warning that "the national Committee may refuse next June to seat delegates who were elected prematurely." Hilles to Prelate D. Barker of Alabama, January 18, 1911, CDH.
86   **convince more states to hold primaries:** Pearl Wight was happy to support his old friend with a public endorsement, but he sent TR a private note warning that Taft was virtually certain to win all of the delegates from Louisiana. Pearl Wight to TR, February 26, 1912, TRP.
86   **$100,000 to kick things off:** The equivalent of about $2.5 million today.
86   **to replace McHarg:** In his oral history, McHarg claimed that he was marginalized for a time at Frank Munsey's insistence. However, contemporaneous records, including his ongoing correspondence with Roosevelt, indicate that he remained very much involved even while on the sidelines. McHarg oral history.
86   **"a great smoother":** Davis, *Released for Publication*, p. 286. Much of the material about Dixon comes from Jules Karlin's very valuable biography, *Joseph M. Dixon of Montana*.
86   **sign on as the campaign's secretary:** Davis, *Released for Publication*, p. 268.
86   **"objective" journalists by day:** Ibid. In his memoir, Davis explains the political motivation for their request. He says that he, Cal, and others crafted Dixon's challenge to McKinley that was dated March 5, 1912. At the time, however, he was still with the paper. He sent a letter to TR on *Times* stationery five days later, praising him on the exchange with McKinley and offering to be of service. Dixon to TR, March 10, 1912, TRP.
86   **dared the President to face the voters:** Davis, *Released for Publication*, p. 269.
87   **"I hereby challenge you to a test":** *New York Times*, March 6, 1912.
87   **William B. McKinley:** William B. McKinley was a member of Congress from Illinois and later a United States senator. He was not related to President William McKinley.
87   **"the primary question is the most troublesome thing":** *New York Times*, March 6, 1912.

87   **idealistic young associate editor:** Sullivan also became a noted conservative. He was the subject of *Time*'s cover story on November 18, 1935, which called him "the Jeremiah of the U.S. Press." It said that "thrice weekly in the arch-Republican *New York Herald Tribune* and 92 other newspapers, and on Sunday in the *Herald Tribune* and 72 others, he croaks fearfully against the New Deal."

87   **adopt a primary bill:** *Boston Globe*, March 12, 1912.

87   **Roosevelt used that victory to call on Taft:** *Washington Post*, March 20, 1912.

87   **"to have something doing every minute":** O'Laughlin to TR, March 4, 1912, TRP.

87   **withdrawing the nomination:** Morison, Volume VII, p. 516. This took place on February 19, 1912.

87   **"put the offices on the auction block":** TR to Richmond Pearson, March 2, 1912, TRP.

87   **"flagrant prostitution":** Karlin, *Joseph M. Dixon of Montana*, p. 140.

88   **pressure on southern postmasters:** For example, see the front-page stories that day (March 4, 1912) in the *New York Times* and *Washington Post*. The senator was Joseph Bristow.

88   **"in great shape":** O'Laughlin to TR, dated March 4, 1912, TRP.

88   **"a drop in the bucket":** McHarg to TR, March 5, 1912, TRP.

88   **"declared the primary vote":** *New York Times*, March 11, 1912.

89   **"has told his friends":** Knox to TR, March 15, 1912, TRP.

89   **send his most sensitive messages in code:** Dixon told TR's secretary that a secret code "should be used in confidential telegrams to this office." Dixon to Harper, March 12, 1912, TRP.

89   **"The action of our opponents":** TR to Colonel Nelson, owner of the *Kansas City Star*, March 15, 1912, TRP. "Every Federal officeholder, the whole congressional delegation, all the old-school politicians, all the newspapers, and an unlimited supply of money make a hard combination to fight," he told New Hampshire governor Bass. "It is the kind of combination that is against us practically everywhere." TR to Bass, March 11, 1912, TRP.

89   **"Our fellows put up":** Knox to TR, March 17, 1912, TRP.

90   **"no effort should be spared":** Letter in TR files, February 8, 1912, TRP.

90   **"an unholy alliance of enthusiasts and stand-patters":** Morison, Volume VII, p. 524. "Stand-patter" being the term used to describe the conservative wing of the party.

91   **invigorate the slightly discouraged troops:** Knox to TR, March 11, 1912, TRP.

91   **victory in North Dakota:** *Chicago Tribune,* March 14, 1912.

91   **campaign there was in deep trouble:** Knox to TR, March 11, 1912, TRP.

91   **"It will be a misfortune":** TR to Knox, March 12, 1912, TRP; Morison, Volume VII, p. 525.

91   **"If La Follette shall carry":** Hiram Johnson to Amos Pinchot, March 19, 1912, AP.

92   **"a gathering of the Clan":** *New York Times,* March 15, 1912.

92   **"I have six weeks":** TR to Arthur Lee, February 2, 1911, AHL.

92   **"It is your duty":** Stubbs to TR, March 8, 1912, TRP.

92   **"I do not think":** TR to Dixon, March 5, 1912, TRP.

93   **"the Clan":** Some later accounts also placed Medill McCormick in the meeting.

93   **"become alarmed, feeling":** *New York Times,* March 16, 1912.

93   **According to Stoddard's account:** Stoddard, *As I Knew Them,* p. 400.

94   **"a soldier of fortune":** *New York Tribune,* May 27, 1912.

94   **"flub-dubbing around":** McHarg oral history.

94   **"You two will get McHarg":** McHarg oral history; *New York Tribune,* May 27, 1912.

94   **"In Control of the Colonel's Forces":** *New York Times,* March 17, 1912. Somewhat deceptively, TR said that he did not know what McHarg had been doing and that "McHarg had not toured the South with his authority." But in fact, McHarg had been sending direct reports to Roosevelt from the South for more than two months.

94   **explaining that Dixon was still in charge:** *New York Times,* March 17, 1912.

94   **"I haven't seen McHarg":** Ibid.

95   **Roosevelt had continued to correspond with McHarg:** In early March, TR and McHarg exchanged at least five letters about McHarg's efforts in the South. On March 4, McHarg called the allegations of misuse of patronage "a drop in the bucket compared to what can be shown." He went on to praise Judge Hundley for single-handedly organizing a "marvelous" campaign in Alabama that "has turned that state upside down." McHarg urged TR to send an appreciative letter to Judge Hundley. On that same day, TR sent a letter to McHarg asking whether he had been involved in bribing potential delegates. That letter, which seems to have been crafted as a document that could be shared with others, asked McHarg for "your personal assurance" that he had never done anything improper. March 4, 1912, in TRP and in Morison. On March 5, McHarg sent a "complete and unequivocal denial" to TR, which also seems to be written to be shared with others. McHarg to TR, March 5, 1912,

TRP. On the following day, McHarg wrote to TR repeating his belief in the wisdom of the southern strategy that he had proposed. "I have not the slightest hesitation in saying to you that if the plan that I had originally outlined for handling the southern situation had been followed, we would have driven the office-holding crowd out of the field, and given an opportunity to the rank and file, three-fourths of whom are your friends." Referring to the improper use of patronage by Taft, he said, "There is an abundance of such material which can be easily gathered in each one of the Southern States. I am calling this to your attention now because of the importance of the delegations to be secured in the Southern States where conventions have not been held. If this matter is vigorously to be pushed, it will likely control the situation in Tennessee and Kentucky, particularly, and without doubt will be very important in Texas." McHarg to TR, March 6, 1912, TRP. On March 8, 1912, TR wrote a response to McHarg's letters, including his denial of any impropriety. That letter is in the private papers of McHarg's grandson, Paul Ryan, but does not seem to be in the TR Papers. TR said: "That is fine! [Exclamation mark written in hand, with a typed period turned into an exclamation mark.] I am very much obliged to you for the letter. I was sure of your ground already, but it was good to get a definite statement from you. Will you communicate about those abuses of patronage to Joseph Cotton, 32 Liberty Street, New York City? I have already written to Judge Hundley." TR to McHarg, March 6, 1912, OM.

95   **create delegate challenges:** The *New York Tribune* said he would be Dixon's "chief aide." It reported that "within a day or two of that secret conference, McHarg went to Washington, where he spent a day or two in and around the Roosevelt headquarters. Then he went merrily on his way to the south, blazing his trail with a series of contesting delegations." When he had finished in the South, the paper reported, "McHarg returned to New York where he speedily became one of the most intimate of the Roosevelt satellites." *New York Tribune*, May 27, 1912.

95   **reduce the number of delegates:** Martin, *Ballots and Bandwagons*, p. 111, quoting Munsey's *Washington Times*.

95   **"I not only believe it":** *New York Times*, March 17, 1912.

96   **"Beat Roosevelt in North Dakota":** *New York Times*, March 20, 1912.

CHAPTER SIX

97   **Roosevelt's first speech:** The AP called it "the first speech of the campaign." *Baltimore Sun*, March 21, 1912.

97   **Carnegie Lyceum:** Now known as the Judy and Arthur Zankel Hall. The
       5,000 figure comes from TR's letter to Dixon, March 21, 1912, Morison,
       Volume VII, p. 529.

98   **cheered for another two minutes:** These details come from accounts in the
       New York Times, Chicago Tribune, Baltimore Sun, Washington Post, and *New
       York Tribune,* all of March 21, 1912. A recording of the speech is available at
       the Library of Congress and on the web. Importantly, the recording is not
       of the speech as delivered in Carnegie Hall. He recorded it on cylinder for
       the Edison Company, apparently in August 1912. See LOC description at
       American Memory Home, http://www.loc.gov/item/99391599/.

98   **"All your friends":** Truman Newberry to TR, March 14, 1912, TRP.

98   **"If a strong chord":** Elon Hooker to TR, March 13, 1912, TRP.

98   **hoping that Roosevelt would heed his advice:** *New York Tribune,* March 21,
       1912. Hooker later served as treasurer of the Bull Moose Party.

98   **"La Follette is a wonder":** *New York Times,* March 21, 1912.

98   **"La Follette is really for Taft":** TR to Bass, March 21, 1912, Morison, Volume
       VII, p. 530.

99   **some of his friends found frightening:** Describing the reaction to one of
       TR's speeches, William Allen White said that "I was disturbed, I suppose
       a little frightened, at the churning which he gave the crowd." W. A. White,
       Autobiography, p. 464.

100   **three brilliant young lawyers:** The lawyers were Learned Hand, George
       Rublee, and Joseph Cotton. McClure, *Earnest Endeavors,* pp. 65–74; Rublee,
       The Reminiscences of George Rublee; Gunther, *Learned Hand,* pp. 202–226.

100   **pace back and forth on the platform:** *New York Tribune,* March 21, 1912.

102   **"the best speech you ever made":** Gilson Gardner to TR, March 21, 1912,
       TRP.

102   **"a reckless maligner":** *New York Times,* March 21, 1912.

102   **"deliberately inverted the truth":** TR to Dixon, March 21, 1912, Morison, Vol-
       ume VII, p. 529.

103   **"pessimistic outpourings":** TR to Arthur Hamilton Lee, March 21, 1912,
       Morison, Volume VII, pp. 530–531. By "ultramontane Catholics," TR was
       referring to those who felt that the policies of the church should be deemed
       to dominate those of the state. In an essay called "True Americanism,"
       TR wrote: "We maintain that it is an outrage, in voting for a man for any
       position, whether State or national, to take into account his religious faith,
       provided only he is a good American. When a secret society . . . tries to pro-
       scribe Catholics both politically and socially, the members of such society

show that they themselves are as utterly un-American, as alien to our school of political thought, as the worst immigrants who land on our shores. Their conduct is equally base and contemptible . . . they strengthen the hands of its ultra-montane enemies; they should receive the hearty condemnation of all Americans who are truly patriotic." Roosevelt, *The Forum*, April 1894. Some such Catholics had been offended by an exchange of messages between TR and the Vatican in 1910 when TR had refused, in advance of a meeting with the Pope, "to make any stipulations or submit to any conditions which in any way limit my freedom of conduct." TR to Ambassador John Lieshman, March 25, 1910, quoted in Bishop, *Theodore Roosevelt and His Time*, Vol. II, p. 197.

103 **"between reaction on behalf"**: TR to John St. Loe Strachey, March 26, 1912, Morison, Volume VII, pp. 531–532. Strachey was editor of *The Spectator*.

103 **turned down repeated requests:** On March 1, 1912, Matthews sent the following note to TR on U.S. Senate Press Gallery stationery. Acknowledging a request from TR, Matthews said: "I shall do whatever I can unofficially. Circumstances make it impossible for me to join your national organization. But I will do you more good *from the outside.* . . . The great trouble in this campaign is the late start and want of organization. It is really discouraging. I'll be glad to get Mr. Harper's address." Matthews to TR, TRP. See also Gilson Gardner to TR, February 22, 1912, TRP.

103 **"I am very sorry"**: Matthews to Harper, March 23, 1912, TRP.

104 **The new law was exceptionally confusing:** *New York Tribune*, January 14, 1912.

105 **introduced a bill providing for a statewide vote:** *New York Times*, March 9, 1912.

105 **"There is no more demand for this bill"**: *New York Tribune*, March 20, 1912. Smith later became the governor of New York and the Democratic Party's candidate for President in 1928.

105 **money that they were pouring into:** Pringle, *The Life and Times of William Howard Taft*, pp. 788–789.

106 **"Letting the people rule"**: Taft to G. B. Edwards, quoted in Pringle, *The Life and Times of William Howard Taft*, p. 789.

106 **using the names of people who had moved:** *New York Tribune*, March 25, 1912.

106 **stole money from the Taft camp:** Davis, *Released for Publication*, pp. 277–278.

106 **hired private detectives:** *New York Tribune*, March 26, 1912.

107 **precisely the same falsetto tone:** Ibid.

108 **"Be quiet all of you"**: *New York Tribune,* March 26, 1912; *New York Times,* March 26, 1912.

108 **conservatives and liberals alike:** In the summer of 1912, Maud Malone announced that she was joining TR in his new Progressive Party. *New York Times,* August 11, 1912. That fall she was arrested for "heckling" Woodrow Wilson. *New York Tribune,* October 20, 1912.

108 **disrupted a speech by Otto Bannard:** *New York Times,* October 9, 1909.

109 **"the mayor and the police have refused to help":** *Washington Post,* March 27, 1912.

109 **predicted that Roosevelt would win a majority:** Ibid.

109 **prospects in both states seemed grim:** On top of that, Taft, a graduate of Yale, defeated TR, who went to Harvard and was a member of the University's Board of Overseers, in a straw poll at Harvard. The vote was 783 to 488. *Boston Globe,* March 27, 1912.

109 **"farcical primaries":** Davis to Harper, March 26, 1912, TRP.

110 **"In more than one half":** Dixon to TR, March 26, 1912, TRP.

110 **"primary election in this city":** Judge Charles Holland Duell to TR, March 26, 1912, TRP.

110 **promised to challenge the results:** *Washington Post,* March 27, 1912.

110 **"Republicans do not need":** *New York Times,* March 27, 1912.

110 **before arriving in Chicago:** Ibid.

111 **"I have had to make some promises":** Harry New to Hilles, March 3, 1912, and March 26, 1912, CDH.

111 **"fixed the Evansville":** Dudley Foulke to TR, March 17, 1912, TRP.

112 **announced that they would seek justice:** *New York Times,* March 27, 1912.

112 **"Indiana is seething":** Dixon to TR, March 27, 1912, TRP.

112 **"Taft Gets Indiana; Roosevelt Men Bolt":** *New York Times,* March 27, 1912.

112 **"Roosevelt Rout in New York":** *Washington Post,* March 27, 1912.

112 **"In every congressional district":** *New York Times,* March 27, 1912.

112 **"The events of last week":** *Literary Digest,* April 6, 1912.

113 **"The result in North Dakota":** Hiram Johnson to Ben Lindsay, March 27, 1912, HWJ.

CHAPTER SEVEN

114 **promised that victories in Illinois and Michigan:** O'Laughlin to Hiram Johnson, March 25, 1912, HWJ. He also told readers of the *Tribune* that "the moral effect of a victory in Illinois would be tremendous." *Chicago Tribune,* April 1, 1912.

115   **"the plans went to smash":** *Chicago Tribune,* November 16, 1911.

115   **came out for the law:** Ibid., December 22, 1911.

115   **"a rich candidate's advantage":** Statement of the Republican Editorial Association, quoted in *Chicago Tribune,* November 29, 1911.

116   **"mad clear through":** *Chicago Tribune,* March 27, 1912.

116   **"Probably Illegal":** Ibid.

116   **"a weasel word in it":** Ibid., March 28, 1912. His draft speech was called "A Charter of Business Prosperity."

116   **"not just a farce but a criminal farce":** *Chicago Tribune,* March 29, 1912. Over the next few days, he kept turning up the heat. A few days later, he issued a statement saying: "Owing to the suppression of news by the majority of the New York newspapers and the deliberate choking of the channels of information to the public, people in New York do not realize how deeply stirred the country has been by the infamy of the so-called primaries on Tuesday last in this city. . . . [B]y every species of fraud imaginable, the men who had Mr. Taft's interests in New York in the keeping, in the most barefaced manner, cheated the people out of their right to an honest vote. . . [T]he men elected by these fraudulent primaries cannot, if they are honest men, consent to take their seats in the Chicago convention." *Chicago Tribune,* April 1, 1912.

117   **"Teddy, Teddy, hurrah for Teddy":** Ibid., March 28, 1912.

118   **diverse reading list:** The list of books is from Travers Carman to Medill McCormick, April 4, 1912, TRP.

118   **"We fight to make this country a better place":** *Chicago Tribune,* April 4, 1912.

118   **"thundering his disapproval":** *Chicago Tribune,* April 7, 1912.

118   **"Lincoln declared this":** *Washington Post,* April 9, 1912.

119   **"Colonel Talks Bolt":** *Washington Post,* March 28, 1912.

119   **"Believed here that Roosevelt managers":** McKinley to Adams, March 28, 1912, RNC.

119   **"Roosevelt managers are framing":** George Evans Roberts to Hilles, March 28, 1912, CDH.

119   **"It is no secret":** Roberts to Hilles, March 28, 1912, CDH. George Roberts, the former president of the Commercial Bank of Chicago, told Hilles that "I have been apprehensive from the beginning that Roosevelt's candidacy would end in an attempt to organize and lead a new party and I am confirmed in that opinion by daily developments." Roberts was convinced that TR's supporters had always intended to bolt and were only seeking an excuse. He wrote a paper

in Sioux City that "Roosevelt managers are framing up a case upon which they may withdraw from the National Convention and run him as the candidate of a new party. It is no secret that the original plan of Pinchot and Garfield was to organize a new party. They are fanatics, self-centered and eager to be founders of a new party. These men have already demonstrated their influence over Roosevelt.... His blood is hot and he is working himself into a more unreasoning frenzy every day.... The question now is will he have enough votes in the Convention to make such a movement respectable. It would be ridiculous for him to bolt with only a handful of delegates. What will the La Follette forces do in such a contingency? What will the Cummins delegates from Iowa do?"

119   **"Others say he is drinking, but I do not think so":** Charges that Roosevelt was drinking to excess plagued him throughout the campaign. He admitted to having an occasional glass of wine, but denied that he drank whisky. As Mark Will-Weber points out in *Mint Juleps with Teddy Roosevelt*, he could have modified that to say that, at least while in the White House, he did enjoy having a mint julep, made with rye whisky, after playing tennis, as Archie Butt described in his diaries. In his famous memoir, *Child of the Century*, Ben Hecht, who at nineteen was covering the Republican Convention in Chicago for the *Chicago Daily Journal*, claimed that he and other reporters were in TR's suite in the Congress Hotel on June 22, 1912, the night that TR left the party. "I was with my hero in his hotel suite," Hecht recalled. "He sat on a couch beaming and tossing whisky after whisky down his gullet. He also pretended to be writing a speech. He grinned at us, ordered us to stop whispering, chewed up his pencils, drew comic elephants on note paper, opened a second bottle of whisky, and wrote nothing." Hecht, who later wrote the famous play *Front Page*, idolized TR. Hecht says that he rushed to the convention hall to be there for TR's great speech, worried that the candidate, who had been drinking for two hours, would stagger from the wings. Hecht, pp. 170–173. Also see Watkins, *Righteous Pilgrim*. Roosevelt rebutted such charges in various letters, including a July 5, 1912, letter to Paul Ewert. The following May, TR filed a successful libel suit in Marquette, Michigan, which was designed to settle the issue. *Roosevelt vs. Newett: A Transcript of the Testimony Taken and Depositions Read at Marquette, Michigan.*

119   **"Roosevelt really seems":** Taft to Charley Taft, April 1, 1912, WHT.

119   **"The conduct of the Colonel":** Taft to Joseph Doddridge Brannan, April 10, 1912, quoted in Pringle, *The Life and Times of William Howard Taft*, p. 771.

120   **"All semblance of restraint":** *The Nation*, April 4, 1912.

120   **"In Illinois there has":** *Washington Post*, April 7, 1912.

120   **"Before April 9th men"**: Davis, *Released for Publication,* p. 280.

121   **"In light of the Illinois vote"**: *Chicago Tribune,* April 10, 1912.

121   **"I fully believed"**: Amos Pinchot to McCormick, April 10, 1912, AP.

121   **"The news this morning"**: Dixon to Beveridge, April 10, 1912, AJB.

122   **The most important force:** Taft's supporters knew that they needed a paper in their corner and ultimately bought one. In late 1911, Delavin Smith of the *Indianapolis News* suggested that Taft enlist John M. Harlan, then a Chicago lawyer, to help in Illinois. He said that Taft needs a "more loyal" newspaper in Chicago and suggested that Taft's supporters buy *The Inter-Ocean,* which "can be had for about $250,000, bargain figures, with the prospect of putting the paper on a splendid business basis." Gus Karger to Hilles, December 8, 1911, CDH. *The Inter-Ocean* was purchased on October 9, 1912, by H. H. Hohlsaat, a friend of TR's, who supported Taft in 1912.

122   **might seem unethical or even illegal a century later:** "With the powerful support of the *Tribune,* the Roosevelt forces simply ran away with the April 9 primary," O. K. Davis wrote in his memoir. O. K. Davis, *Released for Publication,* p. 280.

122   **"the handsomest cowboy in Kansas"**: *Chicago Tribune,* October 27, 1912. For a colorful account of the events in Kansas, see W. G. Bissell, "The Cow-Man's Last Stand," *World Wide Magazine,* January 1906.

123   **"a machine boss"**: In an admittedly biased contemporaneous account, *La Follette's Weekly* described Dewey as the "machine boss of the 2d ward" who was supporting Roosevelt because Taft refused to appoint him to a variety of public offices. *La Follette's Weekly,* April 13, 1912. The *Chicago Tribune* once described him as "the silk stocking boss of the Second Ward." *Chicago Tribune,* October 26, 1927.

123   **Taft refused to appoint him:** *Chicago Tribune,* April 11, 1911.

123   **no longer running the *Tribune*:** Much of the Medill family history comes from Lloyd Wendt's *Chicago Tribune,* Richard North Smith's *The Colonel,* and James Webber Linn, *James Keeley, Newspaperman.*

124   **gave almost dictatorial power to Keeley:** On May 15, 1910, the board passed a resolution giving Keeley "entire charge of the affairs of the corporation." Wendt, *Chicago Tribune,* p. 381. For another very useful account of this episode, see Smith, *The Colonel.*

124   **"I repeat. My authority is absolute"**: Quoted in Wendt, *Chicago Tribune,* pp. 369–370.

124   **"cigar-chomping, ambulance chasing"**: Smith, *The Colonel,* p. 74.

124   **"commands attention, gets circulation"**: Ibid.

125 **a blaze that consumed the Iroquois Theater:** In a spirt of full disclosure, it should be noted that two of the author's mother's cousins, Helen and Hazel Regensburg, who were young children, were killed in the blaze. For a list of the victims, see Marshall Everett, *The Great Chicago Theater Disaster.*

125 **"I wish the *Tribune*":** Wendt, *Chicago Tribune,* p. 380.

125 **"Keeley is safe":** O'Laughlin to TR, December 31, 1912, TRP.

125 **Keeley met with TR:** O'Laughlin to TR, January 3, 1912, TRP.

125 **asked O'Laughlin for a list:** O'Laughlin to TR, January 8, 1912, TRP.

125 **kept his role hidden:** But O'Laughlin made sure that TR knew the truth. O'Laughlin to TR, January 15, 1912, TRP.

125 **Keeley's name was nowhere to be found:** *Chicago Tribune,* January 21, 1912.

126 **been no contact with TR:** *New York Times,* January 29, 1912. A memo sent the next day said that the *Times* story was correct except that it omitted Keeley's name. Memo dated January 30, 1912, TRP.

126 **"acting under Mr. James Keeley's directions":** Dewey to TR, January 23, 1912, TRP.

126 **"Tell Keeley that":** TR to O'Laughlin, January 29, 1912, TRP.

126 **"will expect you to make arrangements":** Travers Carman to Keeley, April 3, 1912, TRP. There were several such messages between TR and the campaign, some offering instructions to TR, some to Keeley. For example, in another note Carman wrote Keeley that speeches in Rockford, Bloomington, and Springfield should be "under cover if possible; otherwise very short, and to cut out every other stop wherever possible because necessary to save voice. Have wired Hotel Leland Springfield for private suite and eight single rooms with bath from Saturday to Monday to accommodate Roosevelt party and five newspaper men. Mr. Roosevelt obliged to decline everywhere invitations to private houses. On Monday unless speaking in private halls, speeches must be very short. Please communicate with Medill McCormick." Carman to Keeley, April 4, 1912, TRP. TR even started to treat Keeley as a member of his publicity team, suggesting ways for Keeley to edit political stories. TR to Keeley, January 30, 1912, TRP.

CHAPTER EIGHT

127 **"greenhorn":** Davis, *Released for Publication,* pp. 277–280.

128 **"almost ceaseless work":** Knox to Mary Handrich, February 17, 1912, CSO.

129 **"Illegal meeting of state central committee":** Knox to TR, April 10, 1912, TRP.

129   "stiffen him up": Medill to Valkenburg, April 9, 1912, TRP.

129   "We are all ready for them": Knox to TR, April 10, 1912, TRP.

129   "the liveliest day of his campaign": *Washington Post*, April 11, 1912.

129   a priest from Wilkes-Barre: Roosevelt, *Theodore Roosevelt*, pp. 484–485. The priest was Father John J. Curran.

129   "I can call it nothing but gigantic": Wister, *Roosevelt*, p. 307.

129   four hundred policemen were lining the streets: Much of this account comes from the *Washington Post*, April 11, 1912.

130   "Both your wires received": Newberry to TR, April 10, 1912, TRP.

130   "Delegates Riot": *Chicago Tribune*, April 12, 1912.

130   "Republican Riot Splits Michigan": *New York Times*, April 12, 1912.

131   Knox and Newberry should be replaced: *New York Tribune*, April 12, 1912.

131   called an emergency meeting: *Washington Post*, April 10, 1912; *Los Angeles Times*, April 11, 1912. Alex Groesbeck, who later served as governor of Michigan, replaced Knox as chair of the State Committee. Grant Fellows replaced Newberry as the temporary chair of the convention. See Alice Porter Campbell, *The Bull Moose Movement in Michigan*.

131   admit those with red credentials: *Chicago Tribune*, April 12, 1912; *Baltimore Sun*, April 12, 1912.

131   "Six fat policemen": *Baltimore Sun*, April 12, 1912.

132   only Taft's delegates from Detroit were present: *Chicago Tribune*, April 12, 1912.

132   "resting on a doorstep": *Baltimore Sun*, April 12, 1912.

132   "The Taft machine": Dixon to Hiram Johnson, April 11, 1912, HWJ.

132   No one could claim control: *Chicago Tribune*, April 12, 1912.

132   fell to the ground: *New York Times*, April 12, 1912. Leslie Arndt in *The Bay County Story* says Gordon suffered injuries from which he never recovered, p. 455.

133   decided by the national convention: *New York Times*, April 12, 1912.

133   "Almost all of this" : Osborn to Knox, April 14, 1912, CSO.

134   "Taft Backers Stunned": *Chicago Tribune*, April 14, 1912.

134   "a crushing defeat": *New York Times*, April 15, 1912.

134   exceeded the campaign's own internal predictions: Ibid. Garfield predicted TR would win half of the delegates. Garfield to TR, April 1, 1912, TRP.

134   Hiram Johnson was impressed: "Pennsylvania was more wonderful than Illinois," Hiram Johnson wired Dixon. April 14, 1912, HWJ.

135   "when it is by and for": Taft to Horace Taft, April 14, 1912, CDH.

135   "The allies of the Steel Corporation": Hilles to Horace Taft, April 19, 1912, CDH.

136   "It seems difficult to hold our ground": Hilles to Horace Taft, April 17, 1912, CDH.

136   "The situation is very critical": Ibid.

136   "If Mr. Taft": *The Nation*, April 18, 1912.

137   "I shall not withdraw": Taft to Horace Taft, April 14, 1912, CDH.

137   "not be Rooseveltian and wildly radical": Ibid.

137   "If Mr. Taft had his way": *Chicago Tribune*, April 24, 1912.

138   to attack TR in ways: "There is no use in trying to conceal the fact that a severe blow has been dealt us in Illinois and Pennsylvania," Taft's secretary told a friend. "I am not sure that our campaign can any longer be successfully conducted with dignity and decency as the watchwords on one side and every variety of unfair tactics on the other side." Hilles to Hon. Franklin Murphy, April 15, 1912, CDH.

138   "Roosevelt with his own weapons": *Washington Post*, April 16, 1912.

138   Archie was exhausted: Society columnist Daily Fitzhugh Ayers quoted in Behe, *Archie*, Volume III, p. 474.

138   Butt was likely to suffer a complete collapse: Ibid., p. 552.

138   planned a trip to Italy in early March: In *A Night to Remember*, Walter Lord says that "Frank Millet badgered Taft into sending Butt with a message to the Pope—official business but spring in Rome, too."

139   planning to return long before the campaign was over: Butt to Clara, February 25, 1912, Butt to Kitty, February 27, 1912, *Letters*, Volume II, pp. 849–852. Francis Davis Millet was a talented artist and head of the American Academy of Art in Rome who had shared a home in Washington with Butt for a number of years. They were joined in Rome by Millet's wife, Lily.

139   "According to some reports": *New York Times*, March 21, 1912.

139   "to open diplomatic negotiations with the Vatican": Hilles to Horace Taft, April 19, 1912, CDH.

139   there had been no such discussions: Butt wrote long letters to President Taft and Charles Hilles describing his forty-five-minute meeting with the Vatican's Secretary of State and his half-hour audience with the Pope. Those letters are quoted at length in Behe, *Archie*, Volume III, Chapter 24.

139   the stuff of legend: "Archie Butt had a dozen different endings—all gallant, none verified." Lord, *A Night to Remember*.

CHAPTER NINE

140   "After a tremendous battle": Perkins to Alex G. Hawes, April 22, 1912, GWP.

140 **"Reports from the South":** Churchill Goree to Hilles, April 17, 1912, CDH.

141 **"The federal office holding clique":** Ibid.

141 **"Southern delegates":** Dixon to Hiram Johnson, April 17, 1912, HWJ.

141 **"The desertion of Taft delegates":** Knox to Osborn, April 20, 1912, CSO.

141 **"Massachusetts will send a solid delegation":** *New York Tribune,* March 3, 1912.

141 **"A great, free people":** *Christian Science Monitor,* March 4, 1912.

141 **former Roosevelt family tutor:** TR's sister Corinne Roosevelt Robinson described Hale as "tutor to my nephew Theodore Roosevelt, Jr.," in "My Brother Theodore Roosevelt," *Scribner's Magazine,* July 1921, p. 88. He was preparing Ted for college in 1903–1904. Gilman, *Roosevelt,* p. 205.

141 **threatening to run candidates against:** *Boston Globe,* March 5, 1912.

142 **"Roosevelt Supporters Claim Victory over Machine":** Ibid., March 12, 1912.

142 **"If we lose in the primaries":** Hilles to Horace Taft, April 18, 1912, CDH.

143 **built his reputation:** Chernow, *The House of Morgan,* pp. 109–111.

143 **fat target for anyone:** Ibid., pp. 110–113.

144 **convinced him to intervene:** *New York Sun,* March 2, 1912.

144 **"We are going to carry":** Ibid.

144 **"Please don't file the suit":** Quoted in *New York Times,* April 24, 1912.

145 **"that after all the endeavors":** Quoted in *New York Times,* April 25, 1912.

145 **"It is a very practical question":** Ibid.

145 **top aides exchanged a series of telegrams:** For example, TR to Bonaparte and Bonaparte to TR, April 21, 1912, TRP; O'Laughlin to TR, April 23, 24, 29, and 30, 1912, TRP; Dixon to TR, April 24, 1912, TRP; *The Outlook* staff to TR, April 25, 1912, TRP; Garfield to TR, April 25, 1912 TRP; Gilson Gardner to TR, April 25, 1912, TRP; Herbert Knox Smith to TR, April 25, 1912, TRP.

146 **"without any kind of promise":** Noonan, *Bribes,* p. 622.

146 **"supported Roosevelt because":** Miller Center Report, http://millercenter .org/president/roosevelt/essays/biography/3.

146 **threatening prosecution:** See Goodwin, *The Bully Pulpit,* pp. 416–420.

146 **"political contributions by corporations":** *New York Times,* October 25, 1904.

147 **proposal became law in 1907:** Tillman Act of 1907.

147 *Buckley v. Valeo:* Buckley v. Valeo, 424 U.S. 1 (1976) "The contribution provisions, along with those covering disclosure, are appropriate legislative weapons against the reality or appearance of improper influence stemming from the dependence of candidates on large campaign contributions, and the ceilings imposed accordingly serve the basic governmental interest in

safeguarding the integrity of the electoral process without directly imping-
ing upon the rights of individual citizens and candidates to engage in political debate and discussion." 424 U.S. 23–38. Of almost equal concern as the
danger of actual quid pro quo arrangements is the impact of the appearance of corruption stemming from public awareness of the opportunities
for abuse inherent in a regime of large individual financial contributions.
Congress could legitimately conclude that the avoidance of the appearance
of improper influence "is also critical . . . if confidence in the system of representative Government is not to be eroded to a disastrous extent." 413 U.S.
565. In *Citizens United*, however, speaking of independent expenditures
on behalf of candidates, Justice Anthony Kennedy wrote, "The appearance
of influence or access . . . will not cause the electorate to lose faith in our
democracy."

147   **"contains all of the things":** *The Outlook*, August 17, 1912; A. Davis, "The
Social Workers and the Progressive Party," p. 676.

148   **few Progressive Era figures exemplified the movement's ideals better:** Fink,
Progressive Intellectuals and the Dilemmas of Democratic Commitment, Chapter 3, "The People's Expert: Charles McCarthy and the Perils of Public Service," pp. 80–113.

149   **Perkins felt so strongly about the issue:** McCarthy's memo dated August 12,
1912, is reproduced and discussed in Fitzpatrick, *McCarthy of Wisconsin*, pp.
160–163. The fight over the exact language to be included in the platform
continued during the convention and became an issue in the campaign.

149   **"saw Gussie Gardner daily":** Longworth, *Crowded Hours*, p. 175.

149   **"best and oldest friends":** Ibid., p. 268.

149   **Gardner challenged Roosevelt:** Gardner to TR, April 16, 1912, TRP.

149   **"no reason for my holding":** *Christian Science Monitor*, April 18, 1912.

149   **repeated the challenge:** *Chicago Tribune*, April 21, 1912.

150   **"show that the Morgan interests":** Gardner also challenged Roosevelt on
another matter, his claim that Taft had been a supporter of Senator William Lorimer of Illinois, who had been charged with corruption and was
later removed from office by the Senate. Gardner's telegram said: "You
have given the public the impression that Senator Lorimer has had President Taft's assistance and support. I charge you with knowing that this is
not the fact. I assert that the best evidence to the contrary is contained in
the correspondence between you and the President at the time of the first
agitation on the subject. A mistaken sense of delicacy, as I am told, pre-
vents President Taft from publishing the correspondence. I know that this

correspondence exists and in behalf of square dealing I call upon you and President Taft to produce it." Gardner to TR, April 22, 1912, TRP.

150   **"Gussie Gardner was one of those"**: Longworth, *Crowded Hours*, p. 192.

150   **"get ready today and tomorrow copies"**: TR to George D. Wardrop, April 22, 1912, TRP.

150   **"When you hit, hit hard"**: Franklin Knox to TR, April 29, 1912, TRP.

150   **"Frenzied and shameful"**: Beveridge to TR, April 23, 1912, TRP.

150   **"mash the colonel to a pulp"**: *New York Tribune*, April 23, 1912.

150   **"After remaining silent"**: *New York Times*, April 26, 1912.

151   **Taft grew increasingly aggressive**: Ibid.

151   **"split the colonel wide open"**: *Washington Post*, April 26, 1912.

151   **The platform and streets were packed**: *Hartford Courant*, April 26, 1912.

151   **"a monster meeting"**: *Christian Science Monitor*, April 26, 1912.

151   **"President Accuses Predecessor of Double Dealing"**: *Washington Post*, April 26, 1912.

152   **"Crooked: So Roosevelt"**: *Atlanta Constitution*, April 27, 1912.

152   **"Roosevelt Hurls Savage Answer"**: *Boston Globe*, April 27, 1912.

152   **"Roosevelt in Scathing Terms"**: *Chicago Tribune*, April 27, 1912.

152   **"Roosevelt Accuses Taft"**: *Hartford Courant*, April 27, 1912.

152   **believed what they wanted to believe**: Frank Munsey's *Boston Journal* played an active role on behalf of TR, acting as publicity organ for the campaign and not simply a source of news. Writing from Boston on April 27, Henry Stoddard told TR that "Munsey's paper certainly is doing great work here. Besides 130,000 extra papers distributed daily through the state, he put out 500,000 last Thursday and 500,000 this morning. Today's half million was made up of your Boston speech last night. In full . . . It has gone all over the state of Massachusetts." Stoddard to TR, April 27, 1912, TRP. George Britt said that "in the three states where Munsey owned papers, Pennsylvania, Maryland and Massachusetts, his staffs were drafted not merely for journalistic support but for general political errands." Britt, *Forty Years*, pp. 175–176.

152   **he had been away from Washington**: *Boston Globe*, April 29, 1912.

153   **"conflict of evidence probably will puzzle"**: *Chicago Tribune*, April 29, 1912.

153   **"Arthur D. Hill was"**: *Boston Globe*, April 28, 1912.

154   **hard to predict the outcome**: *New York Times*, April 29, 1912.

154   **"by a scant margin"**: *Washington Post*, April 28, 1912.

154   **superior organization**: *Los Angeles Times*, April 29, 1912.

154   **confidently predicted victory**: *Washington Post*, April 28, 1912.

154   "I am a better warrior": *Boston Globe*, April 30, 1912.

154   "win the nomination without the aid of Massachusetts": Ibid.

154   "Even the President's closest friends": *Baltimore Sun*, April 28, 1912.

154   Taft had gained 32 delegates: *Washington Post*, April 28, 1912.

154   "If Theodore Roosevelt": Ibid.

155   "a very ugly fight": Hilles to Horace Taft, April 28, 1912, CDH.

155   "the order in question": Goodwin, *The Bully Pulpit*, p. 515.

155   "Only his innermost circle": Ibid.

156   "The issue of all race-loyal": See generally Fox, *The Guardian of Boston*, p. 164–166.

156   "an occurrence absolutely unique": *Boston Globe*, April 28, 1912.

156   estimated at 500,000: *New York Times*, April 30, 1912.

156   "he's got a lot of people to believe it": *Boston Globe*, April 30, 1912.

156   "Condemn me if you will": *Chicago Tribune*, April 30, 1912.

157   "When we are running for office": *New York Times*, April 30, 1912.

157   "I should not be here": Ibid.

157   war of personalities: *Boston Globe*, April 30, 1912; *Los Angeles Times*, April 30, 1912.

157   "Party Suicide by Primary": *New York Times*, May 1, 1912.

157   "advantages over this Massachusetts plan are obvious": Ibid.

158   "wasn't the hero-worshiping": *Boston Globe*, April 30, 1912.

158   "Massachusetts has ended": *Chicago Tribune*, May 1, 1912.

158   "The victory of Col. Roosevelt in that state is conceded": Ibid.

159   "Barometer readings": Ibid.

159   "The Colonel was almost": *New York Times*, May 1, 1912.

CHAPTER TEN

160   instruct his at-large delegates to vote for Taft: *Chicago Tribune*, May 2, 1912; *Boston Globe*, May 2, 1912. At first the delegates said they would ignore TR's instructions and vote for Roosevelt. Then they agreed that each delegate should decide for himself, based on what his conscience dictated.

160   "an entirely correct position": *Boston Globe*, May 2, 1912.

160   "Let the people rule": *Chicago Tribune*, May 2, 1912.

161   "the revised returns": Ibid.

161   important battles were about to be waged: Those states would have lost some of their power under the resolution that Roosevelt and Taft had narrowly defeated in 1908. Now political insiders knew that they could be decisive.

161 **"A Wolf Hunt in Oklahoma":** *Scribner's Magazine,* November 1905.

162 **"amassed a fortune":** Casdorph, *Republicans, Negroes, and Progressives in the South, 1912–1916,* p. 57.

162 **had served as the party's "referee":** Pearl Wight to Taft, February 25, 1912, WHT.

162 **"organize your county":** Quoted in *Collier's,* June 8, 1912.

162 **"I have never had to fight":** Pearl Wight to TR, April 17, 1912, TRP.

163 **"in Texas and Louisiana":** Hilles to Booker T. Washington, March 22, 1912, CDH. Hilles told Horace Taft that "under the direction of Cecil Lyon the party has lost an average of 9,000 votes a year, at which rate it would be only three years until we reach the vanishing point." Under Lyon, he said, "the negroes have been eliminated and hoi polloi has been banished." As a result, "we have gone in to demolish the Lyon machine." Hilles to Horace Taft, April 17, 1912, CDH.

163 **all or almost all of the delegates:** O'Laughlin, *Chicago Tribune,* April 8, 1912.

163 **"Until the elections":** In addition, MacGregor said, "Col. Lyon has been flooding the state with . . . post cards and circulars raising the negro question," saying that if Taft won, MacGregor would turn control of the party back to black leadership." MacGregor to Hilles, May 3, 1912, CDH.

163 **"if Massachusetts goes alright":** MacGregor to Hilles, April 19, 1912, CDH.

164 **"A. Buckley, colored":** Confidential Memo from Moseley and Mulvihill to Hilles, April 27, 1912, CDH.

165 **expose his tactics:** *Baltimore Sun,* May 1, 1912.

165 **"The personal fight":** *New York Times,* May 2, 1912.

165 **Republicans in the Maryland Senate:** *Baltimore Sun,* February 27, 1912.

165 **"Maryland has followed":** *Chicago Tribune,* April 1, 1912.

166 **campaigning in Maryland:** *Christian Science Monitor,* May 1, 1912.

166 **500 young supporters:** *Baltimore Sun,* May 1, 1912.

166 **thundered to tumultuous applause:** Ibid., May 4, 1912.

166 **"a monster mass meeting":** Ibid., May 5, 1912.

166 **Convinced that his speeches:** Ibid., May 2, 1912.

166 **"reply to any new attacks":** Ibid., May 3, 1912.

166 **"an exhibition of National politics":** *New York Times,* May 5, 1912.

166 **every unsavory argument that they could find:** Ibid.

167 **"Much Depends on Negro Vote":** *Baltimore Sun,* May 1, 1912.

167 **"the fight revolves around negro preachers":** Ibid., May 2, 1912.

167 **"pivotal states":** *New York Times,* March 14, 1912.

167 **"as long as William":** *Chicago Defender,* April 5, 1912.

168   Roosevelt courted black voters: *New York Times*, May 4, 1912.

168   "I want to enlist": *Baltimore Sun*, May 4, 1912.

168   by some estimates as much as $30,000: Ibid., May 6, 1912.

168   "Every one of these statements": *Chicago Tribune*, May 8, 1912.

169   "because he is more favorable": *Baltimore Sun*, April 29, 1912.

169   they reported directly to him: In two stories, the *Baltimore Sun* listed the names of the three men running for delegate on TR's slate in Howard County as: Joseph T. Jenson, Benjamin A. Greene (or Benjamin H. Greene), and John F. Scott.

169   "the negroes will support Roosevelt": *Baltimore Sun*, May 6, 1912

169   "one county after another": Davis, *Released for Publication*, p. 282–283.

169   planting corn: *Baltimore Sun*, May 8, 1912. The headline read: "Preferred to Plant Corn: White Republicans Did Not Go to Polls in Howard."

169   Thanks to a few young blacks: When O. K. Davis told TR about the role of the three black delegates "to whom we owed the victory in Maryland," Roosevelt asked for their names so that he could write them a personal letter of appreciation. George Henry Payne to Frank Harper, May 15, 1912, TRP.

170   at least 8 of Maryland's delegates would be with Taft: *Boston Globe*, May 8, 1912. The headline said: "Result Hinged on One County: Taft Men Not Ready to Concede."

170   "sole raison d'être": Olin, *California's Prodigal Sons*, p. 3.

170   "We have met the enemy": Meyer Lissner to La Follette, December 15, 1909, quoted in Olin, p. 19.

171   a Republican senator who had represented Oregon: Senator John H. Mitchell.

171   "ruthless conduct of the graft": Olin, *California's Prodigal Sons*, pp. 20–21.

172   a "bug" inserted in the party rules: Hiram Johnson to Ben Lindsay, October 27, 1911, HWJ; Hiram Johnson to Freemont Older, October 31, 1911, HWJ.

172   with the blessings of Roosevelt: TR to Johnson, October 27, 1911, TRP.

173   "The preferential primary law": Johnson to Walter Houser, December 13, 1911, HWJ.

173   similar message to La Follette: Johnson to La Follette, December 13, 1911, HWJ.

173   internal battle among the state's progressive forces: Mowry, *The California Progressives*, pp. 158–195.

173   "I would not feel": TR to Johnson, October 27, 1911, TRP.

174   "come East to consult": TR to Johnson, January 18, 1912, TRP.

174   La Follette's was a lost cause: Mowry, *The California Progressives*, p. 167.

174 "did not like the people": Ibid., p. 168.

174 "took on the air": Ibid., p. 173.

174 "taking the wrong road": Johnson to Kent, February 16, HWJ.

174 "I will hardly be able to forgive": Scripps to Gilson Gardner, February 24,
     EWS.

174 "half a loaf": Scripps to Amos Pinchot, April 10, 1912, AP.

174 "I am inclined to believe": Scripps to Gilson Gardner, February 24, 1912,
     EWS.

175 "We have discovered": Johnson to Ben Lindsay, April 15, 1912, HWJ.

175 "the scene of the bitterest fight": Johnson to Amos Pinchot, April 15, 1912,
     HWJ.

175 "is coming to California": Johnson to Dixon, April 2, 1912, HWJ.

175 "There is in the state": Johnson to Edward Dickson, March 7, 1912, HWJ.

176 "The old machine": Johnson to O'Laughlin, March 30, 1912, HWJ.

176 "Every rat in the state": Johnson to Lindsay, April 15, 1912, HWJ.

176 TR had been inconsistent on hot issues: *San Francisco Chronicle*, May 9,
     1912.

176 Roosevelt could not be trusted: Ibid.

176 carried the statewide election: Roosevelt, 138,563; Taft, 69,345; and La Fol-
     lette, 45,876.

177 La Follette came in a distant third: According to the *New York Times*, TR car-
     ried about 90 percent of the women's vote. *New York Times*, May 17, 1912.

CHAPTER ELEVEN

178 "TR now has enough votes": Munsey to Hiram Johnson, May 15, 1912, HWJ.

178 "The Roosevelt candidacy": George Record to Hiram Johnson, May 15, 1912,
     HWJ.

179 501 of the 540 delegates needed to win: *Washington Post* and *New York Times*,
     May 15, 1912.

179 "Things are looking very good": TR's assistant secretary to Knox, May 16,
     1912, TRP.

179 called Roosevelt's claim "ludicrous": *New York Tribune*, May 20, 1912.

179 "the vote in Ohio": *Chicago Tribune*, May 16, 1912.

179 "Taft Men in Gloom": *New York Times*, May 22, 1912.

180 "Some of our opponents": *Chicago Tribune*, May 20, 1912.

180 "There is no further room": Dixon telegram to the press enclosed in Dixon
     to TR, May 21, 1912, TRP.

180 "It was the greatest victory": Stubbs to TR, May 22, 1912, TRP.

180 planted by Roosevelt's allies: *New York Tribune*, May 20, 1912.

180 talking to Senate colleagues: *New York Times*, May 22, 1912.

180 "the result in Ohio has settled the contest": *Chicago Tribune*, May 22, 1912.

181 "a complete surrender": John A. Stewart to TR, May 29, 1912, TRP.

181 "The fight is won": O'Laughlin to TR, May 30, 1912, TRP.

181 "In the course of long experience": *New York Tribune*, May 30, 1912.

182 425 delegates were reliably for Taft: Ibid., May 19, 1912.

182 435 for Taft and 430 for Roosevelt: Ibid., May 26, 1912.

182 539 delegates on the first ballot: Ibid., June 6, 1912.

183 key operatives who arrived that week: *Chicago Tribune*, June 5, 1912.

183 "You bet they ain't a-kickin' Teddy's dawg around": *New York Tribune*, June 5, 1912.

184 "Taft loses and Roosevelt wins": *North American*, April 1, 1912, quoted in Rosewater, p. 82.

184 "You will observe": *North American*, April 1, 1912, quoted in Rosewater, p. 81–82.

185 "The fight has now reached": *Chicago Tribune*, June 6, 1912.

185 "A Hopeless Minority": *New York Tribune*, June 7, 1912.

185 "The first step to overturn": *Chicago Tribune*, June 7, 1912.

186 McHarg would cry "fraud": *Campaign Contributions: Testimony Before a Subcommittee of the Committee on Privileges and Elections*, United States Senate, 1913, pp. 650–654.

186 As Rosewater explained in his memoir: Rosewater, *Back Stage in 1912*, p. 95.

187 "the contests against the Taft delegates": *Chicago Tribune*, June 9, 1912.

187 "There is not the slightest chance": *New York Tribune*, June 9, 1912.

187 "As I have repeatedly said": Perkins to TR, June 11, 1912, TRP.

188 "too preposterous for consideration": *Atlanta Constitution*, June 14, 1912.

188 "I will tell you": Others in the group included Senator Borah and Frank Kellogg of Minnesota.

188 a colorable case for 72: Butler to William Howard Taft, November 12, 1915, quoted in Pringle, *The Life and Times of William Howard Taft*, pp. 806–807.

188 in cases involving 30 to 50 delegates: Mowry, *Theodore Roosevelt and the Progressive Movement*, pp. 238–239.

189 "You haven't met a man": Gould, "Theodore Roosevelt, William Howard Taft, and the Disputed Delegates in 1912."

189 "thrusting his fist": *Boston Globe*, June 16, 1912.

189   **Roosevelt expected to be awarded all 40**: O'Laughlin put them in TR's column, for example, *Chicago Tribune*, April 15, 1912.

189   **TR thought that he would win half of the delegates**: Hilles to Taft, June 9, 1912, CDH.

189   **"owing to the personal strength"**: *Chicago Tribune*, June 15, 1912.

190   **"This is more than plain stealing"**: *Boston Globe*, June 16, 1912.

190   **"MacGregor and Kealing"**: Gould, *Four Hats in the Ring*, p. 55.

190   **"the most scandalous thing"**: *Atlanta Constitution*, May 17, 1912.

190   **TR probably should have won the delegates**: Goodwin, *The Bully Pulpit*, p. 699, citing Gable, *The Bull Moose Years*, p. 15.

190   **they could handle unruly protesters**: Murray, "The Aberdeen Convention"; Lewarne, "The Aberdeen, Washington Free Speech Fight of 1911–1912."

190   **Both camps claimed to represent the county's 121 votes**: With 14 national delegates at stake, and 335 delegates needed to control the state convention, the *Racine Journal News* had the following totals: TR, 285; Taft, 141; La Follette, 1; Contested, 261.

191   **Taft-dominated King County**: H. G. Rowland to National Roosevelt Committee, May 31, 1912, TRP; *Official Report of the Proceedings of the Fifteenth Republican National Convention*, pp. 254–257.

191   **police allegedly threw some of them**: *Washington Post*, May 16, 1912.

192   **named their own slate of 14 delegates**: Murray, "The Aberdeen Convention."

192   **McHarg said he was confident**: McHarg to TR, May 29, 1912, TRP.

192   **"Every effort was made"**: James Vernon to Hilles, May 15, 1912, CDH.

192   **"raised a great disturbance"**: *New York Times*, May 16, 1912.

193   **"to persuade the Colonel"**: Judge Lindsey was a juvenile court judge, leading social reformer, and friend of TR who sent various letters to the Colonel proposing that he be chosen as TR's running mate. He later moved to California and became a judge in that state.

193   **give all women the vote**: *Atlanta Constitution*, June 13, 1912.

193   **"We won't look a gift horse"**: *New York Tribune*, June 13, 1912, quoting Jean Nelson Penfield.

193   **The *New York Times* reminded readers**: *New York Times*, June 13, 1912.

194   **"He is nothing but a faker"**: *New York Tribune*, June 14, 1912.

194   **"is received by the woman suffragists"**: Grace Raymond to TR, June 14, 1912, TRP.

194   **oppose a constitutional amendment**: The 19th Amendment, guaranteeing women the right to vote, was adopted in 1920.

194   **O'Laughlin told his readers**: *Chicago Tribune*, June 15, 1912.

195 **"The great basic truth":** *New York Tribune*, June 16, 1912.

CHAPTER TWELVE

197 **considered eccentric, arrogant, gruff:** Aaron, *Men of Good Hope*, p. 253.

197 **"urged his friend":** Ibid.

197 **"Call it what you will":** Brooks Adams to TR, May 31, 1912, TRP.

198 **Roosevelt announced to his family:** *Chicago Tribune*, June 14, 1912.

198 **"I am taking Ferrero":** Nicholas Roosevelt, "Account of the Republican National Convention at Chicago, June 1912, compiled from notes taken on the spot," typewritten by Corinne Roosevelt at Oyster Bay in July 1912. Guglielmo Ferrero had recently completed his five-volume study *The Greatness and Decline of Rome*.

199 **a passel of friends and family:** In addition to TR, Edith, and Nick, the party included their son Kermit; TR's secretary, Frank Harper, and his wife; ex-Governor Regis Post of Puerto Rico; W. B. Howland of *The Outlook*; Travers B. Carman of *The Outlook*, who was working in the campaign as an aide to TR; and a cousin, George D. Roosevelt.

199 **"I had heard so much":** Nicholas Roosevelt Diary, p. 6, NR. O'Laughlin was actually thirty-nine.

199 **"If necessary":** Nicholas Roosevelt Diary, p. 6, NR.

200 **"I think—and I really mean":** Ibid., p. 7.

200 **After spending a day meeting:** *New York Tribune*, May 27, 1912; *New York Times*, May 27, 1912.

200 **"The Southern delegates will flop":** *Washington Post*, June 3, 1912.

201 **"The bribery charges":** *New York Times*, June 15, 1912.

202 **$75,000 or $100,000:** Equivalent of about $2.5 million in 2014.

202 **"and with hundreds of people":** Banks to William B. McKinley, June 14, 1912, quoted in *New York Times*, June 15, 1912. There had been speculation about Banks for over a month. On May 5, the *New York Times* reported that Booker T. Washington is "at work in Mississippi among the negro delegates to the Republican National Convention to switch them from Taft to Roosevelt." The story specifically cited Charles Banks, calling him Washington's closest friend and ally in Mississippi," saying that Banks would not vote for Taft despite the instructions of the state convention." Washington, who was for Taft, sent a "highly confidential" letter to Banks pointing out that "if you should shift from Mr. Taft it would be very embarrassing to me." He speculated that the "dispatches are fakes, hatched up in Washing-

ton." Washington to Banks, May 20, 1912, Harlan and Smock, *The Booker T. Washington Papers*, Vol. XI, p. 539.

202 **"Yes, I gave Banks the money":** *New York Times*, June 16, 1912.

202 **57 black delegates:** The larger number, often cited, 68, may have included alternates.

203 **men whose votes were for sale:** *New York Times*, June 16, 1912.

203 **"with nothing behind him":** Sewell and Dwight, *Mississippi Black History Makers*, pp. 55–57.

204 **"I have spent considerable time":** Simmons to TR, June 7, 1912, TRP.

204 **"Do you ask why":** *New York Times*, June 19, 1912 (letter dated June 17).

204 **who had just been named editor:** *New York Age*, May 23, 1912.

204 **"We will implore every one":** *Baltimore Sun*, June 17, 1912. The Virginia lawyer was James H. Hayes. For more on Hayes, see Smith, "Emancipation of the Black Lawyer," footnote for p. 322.

205 **"broke his instructions":** The speaker was Nelson Caesar Crews, who was also a successful realtor. *Baltimore Sun*, June 17, 1912.

205 **"He's coming back":** The song later became the anthem of TR's Bull Moose Party. *Chicago Defender*, June 22, 1912.

205 **"That's not a fair question":** *New York Times*, June 17, 1912.

205 **"the Roosevelt leaders are working":** *New York Times*, June 17, 1912.

205 **with a margin of only 2 delegates:** Samuel Blythe, *Saturday Evening Post*, July 27, 1912.

206 **"the charges that they":** Casdorph, *Republicans, Negroes, and Progressives in the South*, pp. 99–100.

206 **"independently wealthy":** Smith, p. 249, n. 40, quoting Henry Lincoln Johnson, Jr.

206 **intended to stick with Taft:** *Atlanta Constitution*, June 18, 1912.

206 **"long green and gold coins":** *Atlanta Independent*, June 22, 1912, quoted in Casdorph, *Republicans, Negroes, and Progressives in the South*, p. 100.

206 **other black delegates:** TR ultimately had the support of four black delegates from Mississippi. In addition to Banks and Howard, his supporters were Daniel W. Gary and W. P. Locker.

207 **"said to me that":** *Chicago Tribune*, June 17, 1912.

207 **"One of the striking developments":** *New York Times*, June 15, 1912.

208 **"I like the Negro race":** *Chicago Defender*, June 22, 1912.

208 **"President Taft has proved":** While both men were scarred among black voters by the decision to give dishonorable discharges to all of the black soldiers in Brownsville, Texas, many observers felt that the men were not

equally culpable. "Senator Dixon ignores the fact that when President Roosevelt dismissed the negro soldiers after the Brownsville riot, he did so over the protest of Secretary of War Taft, who held up the order." *New York Times*, March 14, 1912.

209 **Rev. James W. Shumpert:** Listed as James M. Shumpert in the *Official Report of the Proceedings of the Fifteenth Republican National Convention.*

210 **Dr. Sidney Redmond:** Misspelled "Rodman" in the affidavit.

210 **D. W. Sherrod, made similar charges:** *Atlanta Constitution*, June 18, 1912, which also spells Sherrod "Sherred."

210 **"Yesterday [Sunday]":** *New York Times*, June 18, 1912.

211 **"Lindon Bates wanted":** *Atlanta Constitution*, June 18, 1912; *Chicago Tribune*, June 18, 1912; *New York Tribune*, June 18, 1912.

211 **"By paying for his dues":** Nicholas Roosevelt's unpublished memoir of the convention, written in July 1912, and based on his daily diary entries.

211 **"the practical men at the bargain counter":** Hilles to Taft, June 12, 1912, CDH.

211 **leading journal:** Goodwin, *The Bully Pulpit.*

211 **articles by Ray Stannard Baker:** Baker, *Following the Color Line.*

212 **"police would throw them out":** *American Magazine*, September 1912.

212 **"it is not far from the truth":** Dixon to Caroline Dixon, July 27, 1912, JMD.

212 **"mounted police of literature":** *American Magazine*, 1910, p. 325, quoted in Cohn, *Creating America*, p. 96.

212 **"The struggle was to get":** *Saturday Evening Post*, July 27, 1912.

CHAPTER THIRTEEN

213 **"The temporary roll of the convention":** Karlin, *Joseph M. Dixon of Montana*, pp. 154–155.

214 **"rotten boroughs" of the Old Confederacy:** "Rotten Boroughs" was a term taken from the British system which had allowed special interests to gain undue and unrepresentative influence within the Unreformed House of Commons.

214 **"make the record so plain":** Davis, *Released for Publication*, p. 293.

215 **"add strength to the Roosevelt movement":** Ibid., p. 295.

215 **"it was of the utmost importance":** Ibid.

215 **"They argued for it vigorously":** Ibid.

215 **not turn to a compromise candidate:** Pringle, *The Life and Times of William Howard Taft*, p. 805.

216 **"Battle Today Means Reform or New Party":** *Chicago Tribune*, June 18, 1912.

217   **"As long as we do not fairly meet"**: *Official Report of the Proceedings of the Fifteenth National Republican Convention*, p. 31.

217   **"slim and lithe as a movie actor"**: W. A. White, *Autobiography*, p. 467.

217   **"a politically minded school boy"**: *Time*, July 2, 1923.

218   **Governor Hadley's resolution was out of order**: *Official Report of the Proceedings of the Fifteenth Republican National Convention*, pp. 29–42.

219   **Californians wanted Hadley to appeal to the floor**: George Edwards to Hilles, June 3, 1912, CDH; on threat of force, Taft to D. T. Flynn, June 2, 1912, WHT, cited in Pringle, *The Life and Times of William Howard Taft*, p. 786.

219   **"roughhouse tactics"**: Nicholas Roosevelt Diary, p. 6, NR.

219   **"Not since the Haymarket Riot"**: *American Magazine*, September 1912.

220   **"He would have stood a better chance"**: This explanation is all set forth in an article in the *Kansas City Star*, February 23, 1923, quoting Chester Rowell of the California delegation as the source. A Taft supporter, Upham was a business leader from Chicago who chaired the Armament Committee at the Republican Convention.

220   **"resort to rough stuff"**: Hadley to Henry Haskell, March 8, 1923, HSH.

220   **"the timid and shrinking" men**: Karlin, *Joseph M. Dixon of Montana*, p. 158.

220   **reputation for fairness and judgment**: Jessup, *Elihu Root*, p. 191.

221   **Root was his first choice**: Roosevelt told H. H. Kohlsaat that "Root would make the best President, but Taft the best candidate." Kohlsaat, *From McKinley to Harding*, p. 161. On July 30, 1907, he wrote William Allen White that "Root would be a better President than Taft or me or anyone else I know. I could not express too highly my feeling for him. But at present it does not seem to me that there would be much chance of nominating or electing him." Morison, Volume V, p. 735.

221   **not a man who could easily be dismissed**: A year later, Root was awarded the Nobel Peace Prize for his work using international arbitration to settle major disputes.

221   **"If we should oppose the election"**: Hadley to TR, June 5, 1912, HSH.

221   **he would not object to Root**: TR's secretary to O'Laughlin, June 4, 1912, TRP.

221   **"In the past, Mr. Root"**: Jessup, *Elihu Root*, p. 188.

222   **Roosevelt forces shrewdly nominated**: Twelve delegates from Wisconsin voted for Judge W. S. Lauder of North Dakota, who had placed McGovern's name in nomination, rather than for McGovern.

222   **"Today's proceedings"**: *New York Times*, June 19, 1912.

223   **Washburn later gained fame:** *New York Times*, August 21, 1924; *San Francisco Chronicle*, May 7, 1916; *New York Times*, December 15, 1950.

224   **outstanding orator with piercing blue eyes:** Descriptions of Hiram Johnson are from *Current Opinion*, 1919, and *Literary Digest*, 1920.

224   **"Though I had had":** Washburn oral history.

225   **"It may be true":** Most of the dialogue comes from the *Official Report of the Proceedings of the Fifteenth Republican National Convention*.

225   **A delegate from Pennsylvania:** The delegate was William H. Coleman.

226   **"started a running fire":** *Baltimore Sun*, June 20, 1912.

226   **"The man who holds":** *Jackson Daily News*, June 21, 1912.

226   **opposition had a hand in the demonstration:** Longworth, *Crowded Hours*, p. 199.

226   **"she came marching":** *New York Times*, June 20, 1912.

227   **people had moved back from Hadley:** That night Mrs. Davis gave her account of the episode to the *Boston Globe*. She was twenty-six years old, from Paducah, Kentucky. TR had always been her idol. "I knew that Teddy was being defeated and it made my Kentucky blood boil," she told a reporter. "I could control myself no longer. My emotions were keyed up to the point that something had to give way. I saw a man sitting near me with a large lithograph of him and I snatched it out of his hands, unfurled it over the balcony and shouted with all my might, "Hurrah for Teddy." *Boston Globe*, June 20, 1912.

227   **"buoyant and cheerful as ever":** *New York Times*, June 20, 1912.

228   **"If I were picking":** Watson, *As I Knew Them*, p. 151.

228   **"arranged a coup":** Ibid., p. 152.

228   **"immediately landed on Hadley":** Ibid., p. 157.

229   **"the cool heads":** *New York Times*, June 21, 1912.

229   **felt it necessary to stay:** Gould, *Four Hats in the Ring*, p. 128.

229   **"The Roosevelt camp has gradually divided":** *Washington Post*, June 21, 1912, quoting George Record.

230   **"Heney, Beveridge, Pinchot":** Hadley to Haskell, March 8, 1923, HSH.

230   **"dear and beloved friends":** W. A. White, *Autobiography*, pp. 467–468.

231   **"Roosevelt cried for a moment":** Ibid., p. 470. The Roosevelt campaign told reporters that "while Governor Hadley would satisfy them, he was not eligible for the reason that he is not physically strong enough to stand the strain of a long, hard campaign." "The Governor is a sick man," one of TR's managers said. "He has to lie down every afternoon, and so it would be impossible for him to undergo a national campaign." *New York Times*, June 21, 1912.

231 **no intention of running for President:** Hadley to Haskell, February 10, 1923, HSH.

232 **reserved the right to leave:** *Washington Post*, June 21, 1912.

232 **"Any man nominated":** Ibid.

233 **"cheat the Republican voters":** *Chicago Tribune*, June 21, 1912.

233 **"two delegates from each":** *Official Report of the Proceedings of the Fifteenth Republican National Convention*, pp. 30–31.

234 **Several court decisions:** *Cousins v. Wigoda*, 419 U.S. 477 (1975); *Democratic Party of the United States v. Wisconsin*, 450 U.S. 107 (1981), said that "The National Party and its adherents enjoy a constitutionally protected right of political association under the First Amendment, and this freedom to gather in association for the purpose of advancing shared beliefs is protected by the Fourteenth Amendment from infringement by any State, and necessarily presupposes the freedom to identify the people who constitute the association and to limit the association to those people only."

235 **"Yes, yes, let the people rule":** *Chicago Tribune*, June 22, 1912.

236 **6 delegates from Illinois:** Ibid.

236 **6,798 for TR and 4,134 for Taft:** Ibid.

236 **"if Roosevelt could not win in this contest":** Lewis, *The Life of Theodore Roosevelt*, p. 363.

236 **Mrs. Roosevelt, who had been watching:** *New York Times*, June 22, 1912.

237 **Supreme Court has made it clear:** *Cousins v. Wigoda* 419 U.S. 477 (1975); *Democratic Party v. Wisconsin ex rel. La Follette*, 450 U.S. 107 (1981). There is one exception: if there is a compelling state interest, such as a violation of a fundamental right, state or federal law may trump the power of private association. For example, a party today could not exclude voters or delegates on the basis of their race or gender.

237 **"I don't know if it is the best rule":** Root to Philip Jessup, September 13, 1930, quoted in Jessup, pp. 190–191.

238 **"One very embarrassing feature":** *New York Times*, June 22, 1912.

238 **described the scene twenty years later:** Pinchot's *History of the Progressive Party* was written between 1930 and 1933, but the manuscript was not published until 1958 after Helene Maxwell Hooker edited it and provided an introduction.

238 **"My fortune, my magazines and my newspapers are with you":** Pinchot, *History of the Progressive Party*, p. 165; Stoddard, *As I Knew Them*, p. 306. There is some dispute about when this promise was made. Morris places it

on Wednesday evening, June 19, or early Thursday morning; Gable places it on Thursday evening, June 20, or Friday morning. Without certainty, but based on my reading of the flow of events and on the date of the *New York Times* story referenced above saying that TR's financial backers were unwilling to support a third-party campaign, which would have been written on Friday for Saturday's papers, I believe that this scene took place late Friday night, June 21, or early Saturday morning. See Morris, *Colonel Roosevelt*, p. 642.

239 **championing his candidacy since early 1910:** *New York Times*, January 30, 1910.

239 **"I am going to ask Mr. Allen":** Henry J. Allen, "What Happened at Chicago," unpublished manuscript in HSH.

239 **"My friends":** *Washington Post*, June 22, 1912.

CHAPTER FOURTEEN

240 **"Theodore Roosevelt is out":** *New York Tribune*, June 22, 1912.

242 **a crowd started to sing:** Much of the color in this description comes from the *Boston Globe*, June 23, 1912.

242 **"The Chair is ready to rule":** The convention dialogue is from the *Official Report of the Proceedings of the Fifteenth Republican National Convention*, pp. 254–262.

245 **reporters claimed that he was in a jovial mood:** *Boston Globe*, June 23, 1912.

245 **"sent back word":** Although the AP story said that TR called for seating 78 delegates, presumably he said or intended to say 72 since that had been his consistent demand.

246 **"another attempt to paint himself as a hero":** *New York Times*, June 25, 1912; also in the *Washington Post* and *Baltimore Sun*.

246 **"offer of a block of votes":** Britt, *Forty Years*, pp. 176–178. Britt's book appeared in 1935, when many of the key participants in the campaign were still alive, was well reviewed, and there is no record that the facts were contested. *New York Times*, December 29, 1935; *Boston Globe*, November 9, 1935; *Wall Street Journal*, December 6, 1935.

246 **Stuart Oliver:** Stuart Oliver, who was also a successful playwright, bought the *Baltimore News* from Munsey in 1915 for $4 million. Hall, *Baltimore: Its History and Its People*.

248 **"the right persons in each State":** Moseley and Mulvihill to Hilles, April 27, 1912, CDH.

248 **"politics being what they were"**: Pinchot, *History of the Progressive Party*, pp. 162–163.

248 **Roosevelt's top advisors gathered:** The group included Munsey; Garfield; several governors, including Johnson, Stubbs, Bass, and Hadley; a few journalists; and the Pinchot brothers.

248 **"I never told Roosevelt":** The account of this meeting all comes from Pinchot, *History of the Progressive Party*, p. 162.

249 **"a deafening noise of cheers, whistling":** *New York Times*, June 23, 1912.

249 **"Mr. Chairman":** Most of the convention floor dialogue is from the *Official Report of the Proceedings of the Fifteenth Republican National Convention.*

250 **"yelling like maniacs":** *Chicago Tribune*, June 23, 1912.

250 **"the cheering, flag waving":** *Baltimore Sun*, June 23, 1912.

251 **"a masterpiece of ironic sarcasm":** W. A. White, *Autobiography*, p. 472.

251 **counted at least three fistfights:** *Baltimore Sun*, June 23, 1912.

251 **"Montana man clawed up":** Quoted in O'Toole, *When Trumpets Call*, p. 185.

251 **"We have pleaded with you":** Allen's speech, along with the interjections by delegates, is set forth in the *Official Report of the Proceedings of the Fifteenth Republican National Convention*, pp. 332–335.

252 **Taft was renominated:** With 540 needed to nominate, the vote was: Taft, 561; Roosevelt, 107; La Follette, 41; Cummins, 17; and 344 not voting (most or all of whom were for TR) and 6 absent.

CHAPTER FIFTEEN

253 **joined scores of others who had been denied:** AP account in the *Chicago Tribune*, June 23, 1912.

254 **singled it out for several paragraphs of praise:** "Address at the Laying of the Corner Stone of the Colored Young Men's Christian Association Building, Washington, D.C.," November 26, 1908, Roosevelt, *Presidential Addresses and State Papers*, pp. 1887–1890.

254 **The group also included Willis Mollison:** Smith, *Emancipation: The Making of the Black Lawyer, 1844–1944*, pp. 291–293; Mollison, "Negro Lawyers in Mississippi."

255 **white members of the group as well:** *Official Report of the Proceedings of the Fifteenth Republican National Convention*, p. 248; *Natchez Daily Democrat*, July 31, 1912.

255 **lost his credentials challenge:** *Official Report of the Proceedings of the Fifteenth Republican National Convention*, p. 245.

255   **"Many of the Federal officeholders"**: Redmond to TR, May 25, 1912, TRP.

256   **"From what you say"**: TR to Redmond, June 11, 1912, Morison, Volume VII, p. 561.

256   **sent identical telegrams to some**: Orme to Parker, June 21, 1912, JMP.

257   **Great Mississippi Bear Hunt**: Black and Barnwell, *Touring Literary Missis-sippi*, p. 62. The others on that famous hunt were Huger Lee Foote, grand-father of writer Shelby Foote, and John McIlhenny, founder of the Tobacco company in New Iberia, Louisiana.

257   **inspired two toy store owners**: The store owners were Rose and Morris Michtrom.

257   **accept a job as a bond salesman**: Ted joined Berton, Griscom & Company in the spring of 1912 according to his statement in Harvard's *Sexennial Report* for the Class of 1909, published in 1915, p. 250.

257   **"We recognize that practically"**: TR, Jr., to Parker, July 24, 1912, JMP.

258   **"a white man's plank"**: Jeffers, *Theodore Roosevelt, Jr.*, p. 200.

258   **"wish it understood"**: TR, Jr., to Parker, July 24, 1912, JMP.

258   **Roosevelt sent O. K. Davis**: TR, Jr., to Parker, July 24, 1912, JMP.

258   **"an uneducated man"**: *Proceedings of the Provisional National Progressive Committee*, August 5, 1912, p. 259.

259   **was pleased to sign up**: Ibid., p. 258.

259   **"This is strictly a white man's party"**: *Magnolia Gazette*, July 27, 1912.

259   **"COL. ROOSEVELT THROWS NEGRO LEADERS"**: *Jackson Daily News*, July 27, 1912.

259   **Bull Moose**: Roosevelt had used the phrase for years. When asked how he felt during a White House reception in 1905, he told the gathering "as strong as a Bull Moose." *Boston Globe*, October 1, 1905. When planning his postinauguration trip to Africa, he told reporters "I feel as strong as a Bull Moose." *Washington Post*, August 7, 1908. His first use of this phrase during the 1912 campaign appears to have been on May 28, on the morning after the New Jersey vote, when a reporter visiting his office at *The Outlook* noted how well he looked even after weeks of strenuous campaigning. "Just like a Bull Moose—that's the way I feel," the Colonel said. The reporter noted that people used to call New York Assembly Speaker Ed Merritt the "Bull Moose." "I don't know where Merritt got it," TR replied, "but I know they used to call me 'Bull Moose' 30 years ago. I certainly didn't borrow the title from him." *Baltimore Sun*, May 29, 1912; *New York Times*, May 29, 1912.

260   **"I am sure that"**: Howard to Dixon, July 12 1912, JMD.

260   **"both the old Republican and Democratic Parties"**: Miles Taylor to Howard, July 14, JMD.

260 "excommunicated": *Vicksburg Evening Post*, July 25, 1912.

260 "the regular Republican leaders": Ibid.

260 "unless they can attach themselves": *Vicksburg Evening Post*, July 29, 1912.

260 "The most terribly tragic": *Jackson Daily News*, July 21, 1912.

261 "to cancel our Call": Redmond Letter, *Vicksburg Evening Post*, July 26, 1912.

261 William A. Attaway: TR knew Attaway's business partner, Wayne Cox. In 1906, he told Owen Wister that Wayne and his wife, Minnie Cox, were "well to do and were quite heavy taxpayers," liked by "the best people of the town." A graduate of Fisk College, Minnie Cox was the postmistress of Indianola, appointed by President Harrison and reappointed by President McKinley. She was forced to resign in 1903 when threatened by whites who did not want blacks to hold such offices. TR, who had become President in 1901, was furious and knew the story well. He told Owen Wister that while he could agree that 95 percent of blacks should not vote, Wayne and Minnie Cox were the kind of "good, well-educated, intelligent and honest colored men and women" who should be given such rights. April 27, 1906, in Wister, *Roosevelt*, pp. 248–256.

261 William P. Harrison: Harrison was profiled in the *Chicago Defender*, August 10, 1912.

261 "In view of the conferences": *Jackson Daily News*, July 25, 1912.

262 "fairly large" crowd: *Vicksburg Evening Post*, August 1, 1912.

262 "There is no place": Ibid.

262 believed that TR had been informed: Most accounts by those in the black community seem to have placed the blame for bribery or attempted bribery with TR or at least his supporters. A prominent black barber in Cleveland named George A. Myers regularly exchanged letters with famed historian James Ford Rhodes. He told Rhodes that "of the sixty-eight negro delegates, I am acquainted with over fifty." Based on those relationships, he told Rhodes that "Previous to the Republican National Convention Mr. Roosevelt and his cohorts invited the 'Brother,' with extended arms. They even attempted to debauch him with their filthy lucre; of which they seemingly had an abundance. . . . The Southern delegate was just as susceptible to the money influence as was the Northern delegate; but from the personnel of the delegates to the 1912 Convention, they could not buy ten." Garraty, *The Barber and the Historian*, pp. 11–12.

263 "did not seem to be the least bit worried": *Vicksburg Evening Post*, August 1, 1912.

263 "We had a very fine convention": Quoted in *Boston Globe*, August 3, 1912.

263 **"You will never be seated":** Fridge statement in *Official Report of the Proceedings of the Fifteenth Republican National Convention*, p. 258.

264 **"These unscrupulous hounds":** Davis to TR, July 31, 1912, TRP.

265 **"If the people have":** J. E. Sistrick to TR, August 5, 1912, TRP.

265 **"In the Convention at Chicago":** TR to Julian Harris, August 1, 1912, TRP.

265 **"But 'T.R.' Welcomes Blacks":** *Baltimore Sun*, August 3, 1912.

265 **"There was little venality":** *Baltimore Sun*, August 4, 1912.

266 **TR's new policy was immediately denounced:** *New York Tribune*, August 3 and 4, 1912.

266 **"the negro delegates":** *New York Times*, August 3, 1912.

267 **"he might lose some votes in the South":** *New York Times*, August 4, 1912.

267 **"edict started a veritable hornet's nest":** *Boston Globe*, August 3, 1912.

268 **When the committee reached the Mississippi challenge:** Most of this account comes from the *New York Times*, August 4, 1912.

270 **"Lincoln was the man":** *Baltimore Sun*, August 5, 1912.

270 **Maryland delegation explicitly went on record:** Ibid. The delegation also named Colonel E. C. Carrington to the Convention's Provisional Committee with instructions to be sympathetic to the cause of black voters in the South.

270 **"Outside of his rooms":** *Boston Globe*, August 6, 1912.

270 **Provisional Committee resumed its deliberations:** All of the dialogue comes from the transcript of the *Proceedings of the Provisional National Progressive Committee*, August 5, 1912, TRP.

273 **questionable proxy:** *Janesville Daily Gazette*, August 6, 1912.

273 **"This isn't just a steam roller":** *Sandusky Register*, August 8, 1912.

274 **"This matter is not settled yet":** *Janesville Daily Gazette*, August 6, 1912.

274 **"What we want":** Ibid.

275 **They announced that they would meet again:** *Boston Globe*, August 6, 1912.

275 **She called on the party:** *New York Tribune*, August 6, 1912. Jane Addams and others were also unsuccessful in asking the Platform Committee to include a strong section on race. Gustafson, *Women and the Republican Party*, p. 128.

276 **meet with the black delegates:** *Janesville Daily Gazette*, August 6, 1912.

276 **Jane Addams spelled out her reasoning:** Addams, "The Progressive Party and the Negro," *The Crisis*, November 1912.

276 **"suffrage will be stained with negro blood":** Fox, *The Guardian of Boston*.

276 **"an unprincipled humbug":** Quoted in Gustafson, p. 128.

276 **"I cannot refrain from":** Oswald Garrison Villard to Booker T. Washington, August 5, 1912, Harlan and Smock, *The Booker T. Washington Papers*, p. 575.

277 **"never was for women's suffrage"**: Frank Sparks to Osborn, October 5, 1912, CSO.

277 **"This latest missive"**: *New York Tribune*, August 8, 1912.

278 **"Well, if you lose your political rights"**: *New York Times*, August 26, 1912; *Chicago Defender*, October 19, 1912.

278 **"You have fooled the negro"**: Edelman to TR, August 6, 1912, TRP.

EPILOGUE

279 **Wilson garnered almost 90 percent:** The Socialist candidate, Debs, won more than 3 percent of the vote in Mississippi, edging out Taft for third place.

279 **but Wilson still trounced him:** Wilson did even better in South Carolina, with 95 percent. In Florida, where Wilson had 70 percent, Debs came in second with over 9 percent. David Leip's Atlas of U.S. Presidential Elections, http://uselectionatlas.org/RESULTS /national.php?year=1912.

280 **popularized presidential primaries:** At the very least, TR's efforts were essential in Illinois, Maryland, and Massachusetts. In *Bully Pulpit*, Goodwin also gives his campaign credit for Ohio, New York, Pennsylvania, and South Dakota. For a good contemporary review of these issues, see C. S. Potts, "The Conventions System and the Presidential Primary," *Review of Reviews*, May 1912.

280 **The platform of his own Progressive Party:** December 2, 1913; Morton and Williams, *Learning by Voting*.

280 **"With the elimination of national conventions"**: "The Passing of National Conventions," *National Magazine*, August 1912.

281 **For years he had been warning:** In 1908, for example, he told Lincoln Steffens that "an absolutely representative government in Yazoo [County, Mississippi] would bring about the condition of Haiti." TR to Steffens, June 5, 1908, Morison, Volume VI, p. 1051.

281 **"negroes in the black belt"**: TR to Willard, April 28, 1911, TRP.

281 **he also argued that all men:** For an extensive review of Roosevelt's views on race, see Sinkler, *The Racial Attitudes of American Presidents*.

281 **"If ninety-five percent"**: Ibid., p. 354.

281 **"all I have been doing"**: TR to Wister, April 27, 1906, Wister, *Roosevelt*, p. 256.

281 **"As regards every race"**: Theodore Roosevelt, "Biological Analogies in His-

tory," speech delivered on June 7, 1910, at Oxford University, collected in *African and European Addresses.*

282 **"do anything":** Wicker, *George Herbert Walker Bush,* p. 211.

282 **derided as "extremists":** "Gifford Pinchot has joined the extremists," TR to Ted Jr., January 2, 1911, TRP.

283 **"The extravagance with which":** Blum, *The Republican Roosevelt,* pp. 142–143.

284 **"If I could carry":** TR to Parker, July 15, 1912, TRP.

284 **"progressives, irrespective of party":** *New York Times,* July 11, 1912.

284 **Wilson, who denounced TR:** Wilson, *The New Freedom.*

284 **"an unusually successful effort":** "We estimated that in the North a hundred thousand black voters had supported Woodrow Wilson in 1912, and had been so distributed in strategic places as to do much to help his election." Du Bois, *Dusk of Dawn,* p. 235.

285 **"As many Negroes had feared":** Ibid., p. 118.

285 **Roosevelt's Progressive Party:** Parties using the same name and with some of the same supporters remained a part of the country's political life. In 1924, Senator La Follette ran for president on a somewhat differently constituted Progressive Party ticket, and in 1948 Vice President Henry Wallace ran as a Progressive Party candidate with a different lineage.

285 **change that "is more than temporary":** Collin, "Theodore Roosevelt's Visit to New Orleans and the Progressive Campaign of 1914."

285 **Harold Ickes, a prominent bull Mooser:** Ickes, "Who Killed the Progressive Party?" pp. 306–337.

286 **a "Force" bill:** *Nashville Tennessean,* December 6, 1916.

286 **"Nothing good can come":** TR to Henry Cabot Lodge, December 4, 1916, Morison, Volume VIII, p. 1132.

286 **"reviewed the whole field":** Quoted in Jackson, *A Chief Lieutenant of the Tuskegee Machine,* p. 151.

286 **Five of the twenty-eight presidents:** John Adams was sixty-one when he took office. The others were Andrew Jackson, William Henry Harrison, Zachary Taylor, and James Buchanan.

287 **near-death experience:** Millard, *The River of Doubt.*

287 **Roosevelt died on January 6:** Morris, *Colonel Roosevelt,* p. 552. The death certificate said that he died as the result of an "embolism of the lung, with multiple arthritis as a contributing factor." The quote is from Yale professor and poet Henry A. Beers.

287 **"one of the most racially tense":** McMillen, *Dark Journey,* pp. 30–32. Also, Harris, *Deep Souths,* p. 231.

287 **W. P. Harrison left Vicksburg:** On Harrison's escape from the KKK, see David D. Foote, "Mississippi: Then as Now," *The Crisis*, March 1965, p. 167. In Chicago, Harrison left pharmacy and became the "major domo of the Grand Hotel" and a leading figure in the Negro Baseball Leagues. *Chicago Defender*, August 26, 1933; *Pittsburgh Courier*, July 5, 1941.

288 **William Attaway's daughter:** Tracy, *Writers of the Black Chicago Renaissance*. Ruth Attaway was a stage and film actress. Her movies included *Conrack* (1974), *Porgy and Bess* (1959), and *Being There* (1979). William A. Attaway's novels were *Let Me Breathe Thunder* and *Blood on the Forge*. He described the evolution of the nation's music in *Hear America Singing*. Attaway later wrote for the stage and for television.

288 **Perry Howard and Sidney Redmond:** Perry Howard married Maggie Revels, who died shortly after their wedding. Sidney Redmond married Ida Revels. Hobbs, *The Cayton Legacy*, p. 10.

288 **Susan Sumner Revels:** She was named for the abolitionist senator from Massachusetts who was Revels's colleague and friend.

288 **met Horace Roscoe Cayton:** For one study of the family, see Hobbs, *The Cayton Legacy*.

288 **"The years from 1919 to 1922":** Jackson, *A Chief Lieutenant of the Tuskegee Machine*, p. 204.

288 **Banks "was more interested in":** Quoted in Jackson, p. 206.

289 **one of the ten wealthiest:** Nercessian, *Against All Odds*.

289 **His career in Mississippi:** Sidney Dillon Redmond bought a home in Washington, D.C., in the summer of 1929 and set up a law practice there. He ultimately decided to move back to Jackson. "50,000 people in Mississippi had petitioned and appealed to me to return to the state," he later explained, and he concluded that "I might do more needed service in Mississippi than in Washington." *Pittsburgh Courier*, January 25, 1930; *Chicago Defender*, October 3, 1931; Smith, *Emancipation*, pp. 297–300; *Pittsburgh Courier*, August 21, 1948.

289 **Redmond's son, Sidney:** McMillen, *Dark Journey*, p. 168; *The Crisis*, November 1943; *Jet*, June 6, 1974. Sidney R. Redmond's oral history can be found at http://shs.umsystem.edu/manuscripts/collections/transcripts/s0829/t0025.pdf.

289 **highest-paid black federal employee:** Gates and Higginbotham, *African American Lives*, pp. 417–419.

289 **"I am opposed to Mr. Howard's":** *Chicago Defender*, October 3, 1931.

290 **"a better lily-white":** Lisio, *Hoover, Blacks, and Lily-Whites*, pp. 70–71.

290 **But he prevailed:** Many details and quotes are from McMillen, "Perry W. Howard, Boss of Black and Tan Republicanism in Mississippi, 1924–1960," pp. 205–224.

290 **Theodore Roosevelt, Jr.,:** Although he was actually Theodore Roosevelt III, Ted was generally known as Theodore Jr.

290 **Ted was still in France:** Jeffers, *Theodore Roosevelt Jr.,* pp. 123–126.

290 **He "envisioned a non-segregated":** Trout, *On the Battlefield of Memory,* pp. 89–90.

291 **Ted championed the cause:** Eleanor Butler Alexander Roosevelt [Mrs. Theodore Roosevelt, Jr.] *Day Before Yesterday,* p. 369.

291 **"whether by mobs or courts":** *The Crisis,* August 1931, p. 271.

291 **"Ted Roosevelt on Utah Beach":** Roosevelt died of a heart attack in July 1944, a month after the landing. That September, he was awarded a posthumous Medal of Honor "For gallantry and intrepidity at the risk of his life above and beyond the call of duty." Balkosksi, *Utah Beach,* pp. 332–333.

291 **the board of the NAACP:** Jeffers, *Theodore Roosevelt Jr.,* p. 200; *Baltimore Afro-American,* January 7, 1939.

292 **all-white delegation from Mississippi:** Nash and Taggart, *Mississippi Politics,* pp. 30–31.

292 **When Florida and Michigan:** On May 31, 2008, the Democratic Party's Rules and Bylaws Committee decided to seat the entire Florida and Michigan delegations but said that each delegate would only be allowed to cast one-half a vote. Three months later, on August 24, the day before the convention started, when it was clear that he would win the nomination, Senator Barack Obama asked the Credentials Committee to restore full voting strength to the delegates from Michigan and Florida.

292 **"since our national political parties":** *O'Brien v. Brown,* 409 U.S. 1 (1972).

292 **"I don't know if it":** Root to Philip Jessup, September 13, 1930, quoted in Jessup, *Elihu Root,* Volume II, pp. 190–191.

293 **Nevertheless, the party leaders:** Patterson, *The Vanishing Voter*

293 **But the party turned to Eisenhower:** Cook, *The Presidential Nominating Process,* p. 34.

293 **80 percent of the delegates:** There are those who still debate which Democratic Party candidate won the most votes in the 2008 primaries. Senator Hillary Clinton won 18,055,516 votes in the primaries, whereas Senator Barack Obama won 17,628,560. Clinton's margin, however, came with an asterisk. Some 328,000 of her votes came from Michigan, where Senator Obama was not on the ballot. Senator Obama's margin of victory came from caucus states where he earned two-thirds of the vote.

293 **"If the voters don't love them":** Sorensen, *Kennedy*, pp. 147–169.

294 **"had better think":** Matthews, *Jack Kennedy*, p. 275, quoting Lawrence O'Donnell.

294 **"Could you imagine me":** Quoted in Davis, *Presidential Primaries*, p. 64. The website of the John F. Kennedy Presidential Library and Museum notes that "the people of West Virginia handed him a stunning victory that he credited with securing the Democratic nomination for President. Sweeping a state in which Catholics comprised barely 5 percent of the population, Senator Kennedy proved that a Catholic candidate could win votes." http://www.jfklibrary.org/Exhibits/Past-Exhibits/Winning-West-Virginia.aspx.

294 **"Reagan was being attacked":** Craig Shirley quoted by Byron York, "Age Was issue for Ronald Reagan in 1980, Will Be for Hillary Clinton in 2016," *Washington Examiner*, April 27, 2014; also see Cannon, *Governor Reagan*.

294 **"A black man winning":** Cohen et al., *The Party Decides*, p. 347.

295 **"It is terribly expensive":** *New York Herald Tribune*, June 2, 1958; *Washington Post*, June 9, 1958. Also see Patterson, *The Vanishing Voter*.

ACKNOWLEDGMENTS

297 **Knox purchased a paper in New Hampshire:** In 1946, after his death, Knox's widow, Annie Reid Knox, sold the paper to William Loeb, Jr., whose father had been TR's executive secretary. Bradlee, *A Good Life*, p. 103.

SELECT BIBLIOGRAPHY

MANUSCRIPT COLLECTIONS

Adelphi Academy—Garden City, NY
    Timothy Woodruff Papers
American Antiquarian Society—
    Worcester, MA
    Charles Grenfill Washburn Papers
Atlanta History Center—Atlanta, GA
    Long, Rucker, and Aiken Family
    Papers
Chicago History Museum—Chicago,
    IL
    James Keeley Papers
Cincinnati Historical Society
    Library—Cincinnati, OH
    Gustave Karger Papers
    Mixter Family Papers
Columbia University—New York, NY
    Herbert Parsons Papers
    George Walbridge Perkins Papers
Cornell University—Ithaca, NY
    Charles W. Thompson Letters
Harvard University—Cambridge, MA

Lucius N. Littauer Papers
    Roscoe Conkling Simmons Papers
Hoover Institution Archives—
    Stanford, CA
    Mark Sullivan Papers
Kansas Historical Society—Topeka,
    KS
    Records of Governor W. R. Stubbs
Library of Congress—Washington,
    D.C.
    Albert J. Beveridge Papers
    Charles J. Bonaparte Papers
    James Rudolph Garfield Papers
    Harold L. Ickes Papers
    Ben B. Lindsey Papers
    Whitefield McKinlay Papers
    Victor Murdock Papers
    Amos Pinchot Papers
    Gifford Pinchot Papers
    Republican National Committee
    Papers

Theodore Roosevelt Papers
Elihu Root Papers
Arthur B. Springarn Collection
William Howard Taft Papers
Stanley Washburn Papers
Booker T. Washington Papers
William Allen White Papers
Massachusetts Historical Society—
    Boston, MA
    Henry Cabot Lodge Papers
    James Ford Rhodes Papers
Minnesota Historical Society—St.
    Paul, MN
    Frank B. Kellogg Papers
    James Manahan Papers
Mississippi Department of Archives
    and History—Jackson, MS
    Percy Family Papers
New York State Library—Albany,
    NY
    Lillian Wald Papers
Ohio Historical Society Library—
    Columbus, OH
    George A. Meyers Papers
Ohio University—Athens, OH
    E. W. Scripps Papers
Portsmouth Athenaeum—Ports-
    mouth, NH
    Arthur Dehon Hill Family Papers
Princeton University Library—
    Princeton, NJ
    William Hard Papers
Private collection of Paul A. Ryan
    Ormsby McHarg Papers
Stanford University—Stanford, CA
    Meyer Lissner Papers
Syracuse University—Syracuse, NY
    Nicholas Roosevelt Papers

University of California, Berkeley—
    Berkeley, CA
    Francis J. Heney Papers
    Hiram W. Johnson Papers
University of Chicago—Chicago, IL
    Charles E. Merriam Papers
University of London—London,
    United Kingdom
    Arthur Hamilton Lee Papers
University of Louisiana at Lafayette—
    Lafayette, LA
    John Milliken Parker Papers
University of Michigan—Ann Arbor,
    MI
    Chase S. Osborn Papers
University of Missouri—Columbia,
    MO
    Herbert S. Hadley Papers
University of Montana—Missoula, MT
    Joseph M. Dixon Papers
University of North Carolina—Chapel
    Hill, NC
    John Milliken Parker Papers
    James Graham Ramsey Papers
University of Pennsylvania—Philadel-
    phia, PA
    William Draper Lewis Papers
University of Rochester—Rochester, NY
    Huntington-Hooker Family Papers
University of Tennessee—Knoxville, TN
    Governor Ben W. Hooper Papers
University of Washington—Seattle, WA
    Miles Poindexter Papers
West Virginia University—Morgan-
    town, WV
    William E. Glasscock Papers
Yale University—New Haven, CT
    Charles Dewey Hilles Papers

James Weldon Johnson Papers

William Kent Family Papers

Charles Nagel Papers

Thomas Collier Platt Papers

James Rockwell Sheffield Papers

Henry L. Stimson Papers

NEWSPAPERS AND PERIODICALS

Afro-American, 1912

American Magazine, 1912

American Scholar, 1934

Atlanta Constitution, 1912

Atlanta Independent, 1912

Baltimore Sun, 1911–1912

Baltimore Afro-American, 1939

Boston Globe, 1911

Chicago Defender, 1912–1933

Chicago Tribune, 1911–1912

Christian Science Monitor, 1912

Collier's, 1912

Colored American, 1900

The Crisis, 1912–1943

The Crusader, 1912

Current Literature, 1912

Current Opinion, 1919

Financial World, 1912

The Forum, 1894

Hampton's Magazine, 1909

Hartford Courant, 1912

The Independent, 1912

Jackson Daily News, 1912

Janesville Daily Gazette, 1912

Jet, 1974

Kansas City Star, 1923

Literary Digest, 1920

Los Angeles Times, 1912

Magazine of Wall Street, 1926

Munsey's Magazine, 1912

Natchez Daily Democrat, 1912

Nashville Tennessean, 1916

The Nation, 1912

National Magazine, 1912

New York Age, 1912

New York Herald, 1912

New York Sun, 1912

New York Times, 1904–1950

New York Tribune, 1912

New York World, 1912

North American Review, 1912

The Outlook, 1911

Pittsburgh Courier, 1930–1948

The Oregonian, 1907

Racine Journal News, 1912

San Francisco Chronicle, 1912

Sandusky Register, 1912

Saturday Evening Post, 1908, 1912

Scribner's Magazine, 1912

Seattle Republican, 1912

St. Louis Post-Dispatch, 1907

The Survey, 1912

Time, 1923

Uncle Remus's The Home Magazine, 1908–1912

Vicksburg Evening Post, 1912

Wall Street Journal, 1935

Washington Bee, 1912

Washington Examiner, 2014

Washington Post, 1909–1911

World's Work, 1912

World Wide Magazine, 1906

BOOKS

Aaron, Daniel. *Men of Good Hope: A Story of American Progressives*. New York: Oxford University Press, 1951.

Abbott, Lawrence F. *Impressions of Theodore Roosevelt*. New York: Doubleday, Page & Co., 1919.

Abrams, Richard M. *Conservatism in a Progressive Era: Massachusetts Politics 1900–1912*. Cambridge, MA: Harvard University Press, 1964.

Adams, Henry. *The Education of Henry Adams*. Boston: Houghton Mifflin Co., 1918.

Anderson, Judith Icke. *William Howard Taft: An Intimate History*. New York: W. W. Norton & Company, 1981.

Arndt, Leslie E. *The Bay County Story: Memoirs of the County's 125 Years*. Bay County, MI: Huron News Service, 1982.

Arnold, Peri E. *Remaking the Presidency: Roosevelt, Taft, and Wilson, 1901–1916*. Lawrence: University Press of Kansas, 2009.

Auchincloss, Louis. *Theodore Roosevelt*. New York: Times Books, 2001.

Baker, Ray Stannard. *Following the Color Line: An Account of Negro Citizenship in the American Democracy*. New York: Doubleday, Page & Co., 1908.

Balkoski, Joseph. *Utah Beach: The Amphibious Landing and Airborne Operations on D-Day, June 6, 1944*. Mechanicsburg, PA: Stackpole Books, 2008.

Beasley, Norman. *Frank Knox: American*. New York: Doubleday, Doran & Co., 1936.

Behe, George. *Archie*. Raleigh, NC: Lulu.com, 2010.

Betts, Charles H. *Betts-Roosevelt Letters: A Spirited Discussion*. Lyons, NY: Lyons Republican Co., 1912.

Bishop, Joseph. *Theodore Roosevelt and His Time Shown in His Own Letters*. New York: Charles Scribner's Sons, 1920.

Black, Patti C., and Marion Barnwell. *Touring Literary Mississippi*. Jackson: University Press of Mississippi, 2002.

Blum, John Morton. *The Republican Roosevelt*. Cambridge, MA: Harvard University Press, 1954.

Bowers, Claude G. *Beveridge and the Progressive Era*. Boston: Houghton Mifflin Co., 1932.

Bradlee, Ben. *A Good Life: Newspapering and Other Adventures*. New York: Simon & Schuster, 1996.

Bradley, James. *The Imperial Cruise: A Secret History of Empire and War*. New York: Little, Brown & Co., 2009.

Brands, H. W. *T.R.: The Last Romantic*. New York: Basic Books, 1998.

Britt, George. *Forty Years—Forty Millions: The Career of Frank A. Munsey*. New York: Farrar & Rinehart, 1935.

Bromley, Michael L. *William Howard Taft and the First Motoring Presidency*. Jefferson, NC: McFarland & Co., 2007.

Bryn-Jones, David. *Frank B. Kellogg: A Biography*. New York: G. P. Putnam's Sons, 1937.

Buenker, John D. *The History of Wisconsin*, Volume IV: *The Progressive Era, 1893–1914*. Madison: Wisconsin Historical Society Press, 1998.

Buhle, Mary Jo, Paul Buhle, Harvey J. Kaye, eds. *The American Radical*. Oxford, UK: Routledge Press, 1994.

Burns, James MacGregor, and Susan Dunn. *The Three Roosevelts: Patrician Leaders Who Transformed America*. New York: Grove Press, 2001.

Burton, David H. *Taft, Roosevelt, and the Limits of Friendship*. Madison, NJ: Fairleigh Dickinson University Press, 2005.

Burton, David H. *Theodore Roosevelt, American Politician: An Assessment*. Madison, NJ: Fairleigh Dickinson University Press, 1997.

Butt, Archibald Willingham. *Taft and Roosevelt: The Intimate Letters of Archie Butt, Military Aide*. Garden City, NY: Doubleday, Doran, & Co., 1930.

Campbell, Alice Porter. *The Bull Moose Movement in Michigan*. Detroit: Wayne State University Press, 1939.

Cannon, Lou. *Governor Reagan: His Rise to Power*. New York: PublicAffairs, 2003.

Caroli, Betty Boyd. *The Roosevelt Women*. New York: Basic Books, 1998.

Casdorph, Paul D. *Republicans, Negroes, and Progressives in the South, 1912–1916*. Tuscaloosa: University of Alabama Press, 1981.

Ceaser, James. *Presidential Selection: Theory and Development*. Princeton, NJ: Princeton University Press, 1976.

Chamberlain, John. *Farewell to Reform: Being a History of the Rise, Life, and Decay of the Progressive Mind in America*. New York: Liveright, 1932.

Chase, James. *Emergence of the Presidential Nominating Convention, 1789–1832*. Champaign: University of Illinois Press, 1973.

Chernow, Ron. *The House of Morgan: An American Banking Dynasty and the Rise of Modern Finance*. New York: Grove Press, 2010.

Citrin, Jack, and David Karol. *Nominating the President: Evolution and Revolution in 2008 and Beyond*. Lanham, MD: Rowman & Littlefield, 2009.

Cohen, Marty, et al. *The Party Decides: Presidential Nominations Before and After Reform*. Chicago: University of Chicago Press, 2008.

Cohn, Jan. *Creating America: George Horace Lorimer and the Saturday Evening Post.* Pittsburgh: University of Pittsburgh Press, 1990.

Commager, Henry. *The American Mind: An Interpretation of American Thought and Character Since the 1880's.* New Haven, CT: Yale University Press, 1959.

Cook, Rhodes. *The Presidential Nominating Process: A Place for Us?* New York: Rowman & Littlefield, 2003.

Cooper, John Milton, Jr. *The Warrior and the Priest: Woodrow Wilson and Theodore Roosevelt.* Cambridge, MA: Belknap Press, 1985.

Cordery, Stacy A. *Alice: Alice Roosevelt Longworth, from White House Princess to Washington Power Broker.* New York: Penguin Group, 2007.

Crunden, Robert M. *Ministers of Reform: The Progressives' Achievement in American Civilization, 1889–1920.* Urbana: University of Illinois Press, 1984.

Curry, George. *George Curry, 1861–1947: An Autobiography.* Albuquerque: University of New Mexico Press, 1995.

Dalton, Kathleen. *Theodore Roosevelt: A Strenuous Life.* New York: Vintage Books, 2004.

David, P. T. *The Politics of National Conventions.* Washington, DC: Brookings Institution Press, 1960.

Davidson, Donald. *The Wisdom of Theodore Roosevelt.* New York: Philosophical Library, 2010.

Davis, James W. *Presidential Primaries: Road to the White House.* New York: Thomas Y. Crowell Co., 1967.

Davis, Oscar K. *Released for Publication: Some Inside Political History of Theodore Roosevelt and His Times, 1898–1918.* Boston: Houghton Mifflin Co., 1925.

De Witt, Benjamin Parke. *The Progressive Movement.* Seattle: University of Washington Press, 1968.

Du Bois, W. E. B. *Dusk of Dawn: An Essay Toward an Autobiography of a Race Concept.* New York: Harcourt Brace & Co., 1940.

Dyer, Thomas G. *Theodore Roosevelt and the Idea of Race.* Baton Rouge: Louisiana State University Press, 1980.

Essary, Jesse. *Covering Washington: Government Reflected to the Public in the Press, 1822-1926.* Boston: Houghton Mifflin Co., 1927.

Everett, Marshall. *The Great Chicago Theater Disaster.* Chicago: Publisher's Union of America, 1904.

Fausold, Martin L. *Gifford Pinchot: Bull Moose Progressive.* Syracuse, NY: Syracuse University Press, 1961.

Felsenthal, Carol. *The Life and Times of Alice Roosevelt Longworth.* New York: St. Martin's Press, 1988.

Fink, Leon. *Progressive Intellectuals and the Dilemmas of Democratic Commitment.* Cambridge, MA: Harvard University Press, 1999.

Fitzpatrick, Augustus. *McCarthy of Wisconsin.* New York: Columbia University Press, 1944.

Fox, Stephen R. *The Guardian of Boston: William Monroe Trotter.* New York: Charles Scribner's Sons, 1971.

Gable, John Allen. *The Bull Moose Years: Theodore Roosevelt and the Progressive Party.* Port Washington, NY: Kennikat Press, 1978.

Gardner, Joseph L. *Departing Glory: Theodore Roosevelt as Ex-President.* New York: Charles Scribner's Sons, 1973.

Garraty, John. *The Barber and the Historian: The Correspondence of George A. Myers and James Ford Rhodes.* Columbus: Ohio Historical Society, 1956.

Garraty, John Arthur. *Right Hand Man: The Life of George W. Perkins.* Westport, CT: Greenwood Press, 1978.

Gates, Henry Louis, and Evelyn Brooks Higginbotham. *African American Lives.* Oxford, UK: Oxford University Press, 2004.

Gatewood, Willard B., Jr., *Theodore Roosevelt and the Art of Controversy: Episodes of the White House Years.* Baton Rouge: Louisiana State University Press, 1970.

Geisst, Charles R. *Deals of the Century: Wall Street, Mergers, and the Making of Modern America.* Hoboken, NJ: John Wiley & Sons, 2005.

Gilman, Bradley. *Roosevelt: The Happy Warrior.* Boston: Little, Brown & Co., 1921.

Gitlin, Todd. *The Sixties: Years of Hope, Days of Rage.* New York: Bantam Books, 1993.

Goodwin, Doris Kearns. *The Bully Pulpit: Theodore Roosevelt, William Howard Taft, and the Golden Age of Journalism.* New York: Simon & Schuster, 2013.

Gould, Lewis L. *America in the Progressive Era: 1890–1914.* New York: Pearson Education Limited, 2001.

Gould, Lewis. *Four Hats in the Ring: The 1912 Election and the Birth of Modern American Politics.* Lawrence: University Press of Kansas, 2008.

Gould, Lewis. *The Presidency of Theodore Roosevelt.* Lawrence: University Press of Kansas, 1991.

Grant, Donald, and Jonathan Grant. *The Way It Was in the South: The Black Experience in Georgia.* Athens: University of Georgia Press, 2001.

Grondahl, Paul. *I Rose Like a Rocket: The Political Education of Theodore Roosevelt.* New York: Simon & Schuster, 2004.

Gunther, Gerald. *Learned Hand: The Man and the Judge.* New York: Oxford University Press, 2011.

Gustafson, Melanie S. *Women and the Republican Party, 1854–1924*. Champaign: University of Illinois Press, 2001.

Hall, Clayton C. *Baltimore: Its History and Its People*. New York: Lewis Historical Publishing Co., 1912.

Harbaugh, William Henry. *Power and Responsibility: The Life and Times of Theodore Roosevelt*. Newtown, CT: American Political Biography Press, 1997.

Harlan, L. R., and R. W. Smock. *The Booker T. Washington Papers*. Champaign: University of Illinois Press, 1981.

Harris, William. *Deep Souths: Delta, Piedmont, and Sea Island Society in the Age of Segregation*. Baltimore: Johns Hopkins University Press, 2003.

Hawley, Joshua David. *Theodore Roosevelt: Preacher of Righteousness*. New Haven, CT: Yale University Press, 2008.

Hechler, Kenneth. *Insurgency: Personalities and Politics of the Taft Era*. Kent, UK: Russell & Russell, 1964.

Hecht, Ben. *A Child of the Century*. New York: Plume, 1985.

Hertzberg, Hendrik. *Politics: Observations and Arguments, 1966–2004*. New York: Penguin Press, 2004.

Hobbs, Richard. *The Cayton Legacy: An African American Family*. Pullman: Washington State University Press, 2002.

Holt, James. *Congressional Insurgents and the Party System, 1909–1916*. Cambridge, MA: Harvard University Press, 1967.

Howland, Harold. *Theodore Roosevelt and His Times*. New Haven, CT: Yale University Press, 1921.

Hughes, Harold. *The Honorable Alcoholic*. Grand Rapids: Zondervan Publishing Co., 1983.

Jackson, David. *A Chief Lieutenant of the Tuskegee Machine: Charles Banks of Mississippi*. Gainesville: University Press of Florida, 2008.

Jackson, John S., and William Crotty. *The Politics of Presidential Selection*. London: Pearson Longman, 2000.

Jeffers, H. Paul. *Theodore Roosevelt Jr.: The Life of a War Hero*. New York: Presidio Press, 2002.

Jessup, Phillip C. *Elihu Root: 1845–1909*. Hamden, CT: Archon Books, 1964.

Johnson, Claudius O. *Borah of Idaho*. Seattle: University of Washington Press, 1936.

Karlin, Jules. *Joseph M. Dixon of Montana*. Missoula: University of Montana Press, 1974.

Kohlsaat, H. H. *From McKinley to Harding: Personal Recollections of Our Presidents*. New York: Charles Scribner's Sons, 1923.

Kotz, Nick. *Judgment Days: Lyndon Baines Johnson, Martin Luther King Jr., and the Laws that Changed America*. Boston: Houghton Mifflin Co., 2005.

La Follette, Robert M. *La Follette's Autobiography: A Personal Narrative of Political Experiences*. Madison: University of Wisconsin Press, 1960.

Larson, Robert W. *New Mexico's Quest for Statehood, 1846–1912*. Albuquerque: University of New Mexico Press, 2013.

Leary, John J., Jr. *Talks with T.R.: From the Diaries of John J. Leary, Jr.* Boston: Houghton Mifflin Co., 1920.

Lewis, William Draper. *The Life of Theodore Roosevelt*. Philadelphia: John C. Winston Co., 1919.

Link, Arthur S. *The Higher Realism of Woodrow Wilson and Other Essays*. Nashville: Vanderbilt University Press, 1971.

Linn, James Webber. *James Keeley, Newspaperman*. Indianapolis: Bobbs-Merrill Co., 1937.

Lisio, Donald. *Hoover, Blacks, and Lily-Whites: A Study of Southern Strategies*. Chapel Hill: University of North Carolina Press, 1985.

Longworth, Alice Roosevelt. *Crowded Hours: Reminiscences of Alice Roosvelt Longworth*. New York: Charles Scribner's Sons, 1933.

Lord, Walter. *A Night to Remember*. New York: R & W Holt, 1955.

Lovejoy, Allen Fraser. *La Follette and the Establishment of the Direct Primary in Wisconsin*. New Haven, CT: Yale University Press, 1941.

Lower, Richard Coke. *A Block of One: The Political Career of Hiram W. Johnson*. Stanford, CA: Stanford University Press, 1993.

Lowry, Edward G. *Washington Close-Ups: Intimate Views of Some Public Figures*. Boston: Houghton Mifflin Co., 1921.

Madison, Charles A. *Critics and Crusaders: A Century of American Protest*. New York: Henry Holt & Co., 1947.

Manners, William. *TR & Will: A Friendship That Split the Republican Party*. New York: Harcourt, Brace & World, 1969.

Martin, Ralph. *Ballots and Bandwagons: Three Great Twentieth-Century Conventions*. New York: New American Library, 1964.

Matthews, Chris. *Jack Kennedy: Elusive Hero*. New York: Simon & Schuster, 2013.

McClure, Marc E. *Earnest Endeavors: The Life and Public Work of George Rublee*. Westport, CT: Greenwood Press, 2003.

McCormick, Thomas J., and Walter LaFeber, ed. *Behind the Throne: Servants of Power to Imperial Presidents, 1898–1968*. Madison: University of Wisconsin Press, 1993.

McCullough, David. *Mornings on Horseback*. New York: Simon & Schuster Paperbacks, 1981.

McKenna, Marian C. *Borah*. Ann Arbor: University of Michigan Press, 1961.

McMillen, Neil. *Dark Journey: Black Mississippians in the Age of Jim Crow*. Champaign: University of Illinois Press, 1990.

Milkis, Sidney. *Theodore Roosevelt, the Progressive Party, and the Transformation of American Democracy*. Lawrence: University Press of Kansas, 2009.

Millard, Candice. *The River of Doubt: Theodore Roosevelt's Darkest Journey*. New York: Doubleday, 2005.

Miller, Char. *Gifford Pinchot and the Making of Modern Environmentalism*. Washington, DC: Island Press, 2004.

Miller, Nathan. *Theodore Roosevelt: A Life*. New York: William Morrow & Co., 1992.

Mills, Kay. *This Little Light of Mine: The Life of Fannie Lou Hamer*. Lexington: University Press of Kentucky, 2007.

Morison, Elting. *The Letters of Theodore Roosevelt*. Cambridge, MA: Harvard University Press, 1954.

Morris, Edmund. *Colonel Roosevelt*. New York: Random House, 2010.

Morris, Edmund. *The Rise of Theodore Roosevelt*. New York: Random House, 2001.

Morris, Edmund. *Theodore Rex*. New York: Modern Library, 2002.

Morris, Sylvia Jukes. *Edith Kermit Roosevelt: Portrait of a First Lady*. New York: Modern Library, 2001.

Morton, Rebecca, and Kenneth Williams. *Learning by Voting: Sequential Choices in Presidential Primaries and Other Elections*. Ann Arbor: University of Michigan Press, 2001.

Mott, Frank. *American Journalism: A History of Newspapers in the United States*. London: Routledge/Thoemmes Press, 2000

Mowry, George E. *The California Progressives*. New York: Times Books, 1963.

Mowry, George E. *Theodore Roosevelt and the Progressive Movement*. Madison: University of Wisconsin Press, 1946.

Nash, Jere, and Andy Taggart. *Mississippi Politics: The Struggle for Power, 1976–2008*. Jackson: University Press of Mississippi, 2009.

Nercessian, Nora. *Against All Odds: The Legacy of Students of African Descent at Harvard Medical School Before Affirmative Action, 1850–1968*. Hollis, NH: Puritan Press, 2004.

Noonan, John T. *Bribes: The Intellectual History of a Moral Idea*. Oakland: University of California Press, 1987.

Nye, Russel B. *Midwestern Progressive Politics: A Historical Study of Its Origins and Development, 1870–1958.* New York: Harper Torchbooks, 1959.

O'Laughlin, Cal. *From the Jungles Through Europe with Roosevelt.* Boston: Chapple Publishing, 1910.

Olin, Spencer. *California's Prodigal Sons: Hiram Johnson and the Progressives.* Oakland: University of California Press, 1968.

O'Toole, Patricia. *When Trumpets Call: Theodore Roosevelt After the White House.* New York: Simon & Schuster, 2005.

Overacker, Louise. *The Presidential Primary.* New York: Macmillan Co., 1926.

Patterson, Thomas. *The Vanishing Voter: Public Involvement in an Age of Uncertainty.* New York: Vintage Books, 2003.

Penick, James L. *Progressive Politics and Conservation: The Ballinger-Pinchot Controversy.* Chicago: University of Chicago Press, 1968.

Perman, Michael. *Struggle for Mastery: Disenfranchisement in the South, 1888–1908.* Chapel Hill: University of North Carolina Press, 2001.

Pinchot, Amos, and Helene Maxwell Hooker. *History of the Progressive Party: 1912–1916.* Westport, CT: Greenwood Press, 1978.

Pinkett, Harold T. *Gifford Pinchot: Private and Public Forester.* Urbana: University of Illinois Press, 1970.

Pringle, Henry F. *The Life and Times of William Howard Taft.* Newtown, CT: American Political Biography Press, 1998.

Pusey, Merlo J. *Charles Evans Hughes.* New York: Columbia University Press, 1963.

Renehan, Edward J. *The Lion's Pride: Roosevelt's Family in Peace and War.* Oxford, UK: Oxford University Press, 1998.

Robinson, Corinne Roosevelt. *My Brother Theodore Roosevelt.* New York: Charles Scribner's Sons, 1921.

Roosevelt, Eleanor Butler Alexander. *Day Before Yesterday: The Reminiscences of Mrs. Theodore Roosevelt, Jr.* Garden City, NY: Doubleday & Co., 1959.

Roosevelt, Nicholas. *A Front Row Seat.* Norman: University of Oklahoma Press, 1953.

Roosevelt, Nicholas. *Theodore Roosevelt: The Man As I Knew Him.* New York: Dodd, Mead & Co., 1967.

Roosevelt, Theodore. *African and European Addresses.* New York: G. P. Putnam's Sons, 1910.

Roosevelt, Theodore. *Politics and People: The Ordeal of Self-Government in America.* New York: Charles Scribner's Sons, 1925.

Roosevelt, Theodore. *Presidential Addresses and State Papers: November 15, 1907 to November 26, 1908.* New York: Review of Reviews Co., 1910.

Roosevelt, Theodore. *The Rough Riders.* New York: Charles Scribner's Sons, 1899.

Roosevelt, Theodore. *Theodore Roosevelt: An Autobiography.* New York: Macmillan Publishing, 1913.

Roosevelt, Theodore, Jr. *All in the Family.* New York: G. P. Putnam's Sons, 1929.

Roosevelt vs. Newett: A Transcript of the Testimony Taken and Depositions Read at Marquette, Michigan. Privately Printed, 1913.

Rosewater, Victor. *Back Stage in 1912: The Inside Story of the Split Republican Convention.* Philadelphia: Dorrance & Co., 1932.

Rozwenc, Edwin C., ed. *Roosevelt, Wilson, and the Trusts: Problems in American Civilization.* Boston: D. C. Heath & Co., 1950.

Rublee, George. *The Reminiscences of George Rublee.* New York: Columbia University Press, 1972.

Russell, Thomas H., ed. *The Political Battle of 1912.* American Association of Political and Social Science, 1912.

Sageser, A. Bower. *Joseph L. Bristow: Kansas Progressive.* Lawrence: University Press of Kansas, 1968.

Samuels, Peggy, and Harold Samuels. *Teddy Roosevelt at San Juan: The Making of a President.* College Station: Texas A & M University Press, 1997.

Schlesinger, Robert. *White House Ghosts: Presidents and Their Speechwriters.* New York: Simon & Schuster, 2008.

Schwartz, Barry. *Abraham Lincoln and the Forge of National Memory.* Chicago: University of Chicago Press, 2003.

Sexennial Report: Class of 1909 Harvard College. Boston: Press of George H. Dean, 1915.

Sewell, George A., and Margaret L. Dwight. *Mississippi Black History Makers.* Jackson: University Press of Mississippi, 1977.

Shafer, Byron E. *Quiet Revolution: The Struggle for the Democratic Party and the Shaping of Post-Reform Politics.* New York: Russell Sage Foundation, 1983.

Shaw, Albert. *A Cartoon History of Roosevelt's Career.* New York: Review of Reviews Co., 1910.

Sherman, Richard B. *The Republican Party and Black America: From McKinley to Hoover, 1896–1933.* Charlottesville: University Press of Virginia, 1973.

Sinkler, George. *The Racial Attitudes of American Presidents: From Abraham Lincoln to Theodore Roosevelt.* New York: Doubleday, 1971.

Smith, J. Clay, Jr. *Emancipation: The Making of the Black Lawyer, 1844–1944.* Philadelphia: University of Pennsylvania Press, 1999.

Smith, Richard N. *The Colonel: The Life and Legend of Robert R. McCormick, 1880–1955*. Evanston, IL: Northwestern University Press, 2003.

Sorenson, Theodore. *Kennedy*. New York: Harper & Row, 1965.

Southern, David W. *The Progressive Era and Race: Reaction and Reform, 1900–1917*. Wheeling, IL: Harlan Davidson, 2005.

Steen, Harold K., ed. *The Conservation Diaries of Gifford Pinchot*. Durham, NC: Forest History Society, 2001.

Stoddard, Henry L. *As I Knew Them: Presidents and Politics from Grant to Coolidge*. New York: Harper & Brothers, 1927.

Stoddard, Henry L. *Presidential Sweepstakes: The Story of Political Conventions and Campaigns*. New York: G. P. Putnam's Sons, 1948.

Stricherz, Mark. *Why the Democrats Are Blue: Secular Liberalism and the Decline of the People's Party*. New York: Encounter Books, 2007.

Sullivan, Mark. *Our Time: 1900–1925*. New York: Charles Scribner's Sons, 1972.

Thelen, David P. *Robert M. La Follette and the Insurgent Spirit*. Madison: University of Wisconsin Press, 1986.

Thompson, Charles Willis. *Presidents I've Known and Two Near Presidents*. Indianapolis: Bobbs-Merrill Co., 1929.

Tracy, Steven. *Writers of the Black Chicago Renaissance*. Champaign: University of Illinois Press, 2011.

Trout, Steven. *On the Battlefield of Memory: The First World War and American Remembrance, 1919–1941*. Tuscaloosa: University of Alabama Press, 2012.

Unger, Nancy C. *Fighting Bob La Follette: The Righteous Reformer*. Madison: Wisconsin Historical Society Press, 2008.

Wagenknecht, Edward. *The Seven Worlds of Theodore Roosevelt*. New York: Longmans, Green & Co., 1958.

Walker, Dale L. *The Boys of '98: Theodore Roosevelt and the Rough Riders*. New York: Tom Doherty Associates, 1998.

Ware, Alan. *The American Direct Primary*. Cambridge, UK: Cambridge University Press, 2002.

Washburn, Charles. *Theodore Roosevelt: The Logic of His Career*. Boston: Houghton Mifflin Co., 1916.

Watkins, T. H. *Righteous Pilgrim: The Life and Times of Harold L. Ickes, 1874–1952*. New York: Henry Holt & Co., 1990.

Watson, James E. *As I Knew Them: Memoirs of James E. Watson*. Indianapolis: Bobbs Merrill, 1936.

Wendt, Lloyd. *Chicago Tribune: The Rise of a Great American Newspaper*. Skokie, IL: Rand McNally, 1979.

White, Theodore. *The Making of the President 1968.* New York: Atheneum Books, 1969.

White, William Allen. *The Autobiography of William Allen White.* Lawrence: University Press of Kansas, 1990.

Wicker, Tom. *George Herbert Walker Bush.* New York: Penguin Group, 2004.

Williams, Juan. *Eyes on the Prize: America's Civil Rights Years, 1954–1965.* New York: Viking Press, 1987.

Wilson, Woodrow. *The New Freedom: A Call for the Emancipation of the Generous Energies of a People.* New York: Doubleday, Page & Co., 1913.

Wister, Owen. *Roosevelt: The Story of a Friendship.* Whitefish, MT: Kessinger Publishing, 2004.

Wolraich, Michael. *Unreasonable Men: Theodore Roosevelt and the Republican Rebels Who Created Progressive Politics.* New York: Palgrave Macmillan, 2014.

Wood, Frederick S. *Roosevelt As We Knew Him.* Philadelphia: John C. Winston Company, 1927.

ARTICLES

Abramowitz, Jack. "John B. Rayner—A Grass Roots Leader." *Journal of Negro History,* Vol. 36, No. 2 (April 1951), pp. 160–193.

Abramowitz, Jack. "The Negro in the Populist Movement." *Journal of Negro History,* Vol. 38, No. 3 (July 1953), pp. 257–289.

Alilunas, Leo. "The Rise of the 'White Primary' Movement as a Means of Barring the Negro from the Polls." *Journal of Negro History,* Vol. 25, No. 2 (April 1940), pp. 161–172.

Aylsworth, L. E. "Presidential Primary Elections—Legislation of 1910–1912." *American Political Science Review,* Vol. 6, No. 3 (August 1912), pp. 429–433.

Barnett, James D. "The Presidential Primary in Oregon." *Political Science Quarterly,* Vol. 31, No. 1 (March 1916), pp. 81–104.

Bellush, Jewel. "Reform in New Hampshire: Robert Bass Wins the Primary." *New England Quarterly,* Vol. 35, No. 4 (December 1962), pp. 469–488.

Boyer, Hugh E. "The Bull Moose in the Upper Peninsula: William J. Macdonald and Michigan's Twelfth Congressional District in 1912." *Great Lakes Review,* Vol. 9/10, No. 2/1 (Fall 1983–Spring 1984), pp. 37–50.

Bromley, Michael L. "The Constitution's Bodyguard: William Howard Taft and His Defense of the Constitution During the Election of 1912." Self-published paper (2004).

Campbell, Alice Porter. "The Bull Moose Movement in Michigan." *Michigan History Magazine*, 1939.

Carleton, William G. "The Revolution in the Presidential Nominating Convention." *Political Science Quarterly*, Vol. 72, No. 2 (June 1957), pp. 224–240.

Casdorph, Paul D. "The 1912 Republican Presidential Campaign in Mississippi." *Journal of Mississippi History*, Vol. 33, No. 1 (February 1971), pp. 1–19.

Colby, David D. "The Voting Rights Act and Black Registration in Mississippi." *Publius*, Vol. 16, No. 4 (Autumn 1986), pp. 123–137.

Collin, Richard. "Theodore Roosevelt's Visit to New Orleans and the Progressive Campaign of 1914." *Louisiana History: The Journal of the Louisiana Historical Association*, Vol. 12, No. 1 (Winter 1971), pp. 5–19.

Davis, Allen F. "The Social Workers and the Progressive Party, 1912–1916." *American Historical Review*, Vol. 69, No. 3 (April 1964), p. 671–688.

De Santis, Vincent P. "Republican Efforts to 'Crack' the Democratic South." *Review of Politics*, Vol. 14, No. 2 (April 1952), pp. 244–264.

Dickey, Francis W. "The Presidential Preference Primary." *American Political Science Review*, Vol. 9, No. 3 (August 1915), pp. 467–487.

Dodd, W. F. "Social Legislation and the Courts." *Political Science Quarterly*, Vol. 28, No. 1 (March 1913), pp. 1–17.

Ferrell, Robert H. "Who Are These People?" *Presidential Studies Quarterly*, Vol. 32, No. 4 (December 2002), pp. 664–671.

Gatewood Jr., Willard B. "A Republican President and Democratic State Politics: Theodore Roosevelt in the Mississippi Primary of 1903." *Presidential Studies Quarterly*, Vol. 14, No. 3 (Summer 1984), pp. 428–436.

Gatewood Jr., Willard B. "Theodore Roosevelt and Arkansas, 1901–1912." *Arkansas Historical Quarterly*, Vol. 32, No. 1 (Spring 1973), pp. 3–24.

Gatewood Jr., Willard B. "Theodore Roosevelt and the Indianola Affair." *Journal of Negro History*, Vol. 53, No. 1 (January 1968), pp. 48–69.

Gatewood, Willard B. "William D. Crum: A Negro in Politics." *Journal of Negro History*, Vol. 53, No. 4 (October 1968), pp. 301–320.

Gerstle, Gary. "Theodore Roosevelt and the Divided Character of American Nationalism." *Journal of American History*, Vol. 86, No. 3 (December 1999), pp. 1280–1307.

Gertz, Elmer. "Chicago's Adult Delinquent: 'The Tribune.'" *Public Opinion Quarterly*, Vol. 8, No. 3 (Fall 1944), pp. 416–424.

Glad, Paul W. "Progressives and the Business Culture of the 1920s." *Journal of American History*, Vol. 53, No. 1 (June 1966), pp. 75–89.

Gould, Lewis L. "Theodore Roosevelt, William Howard Taft, and the Disputed

Delegates in 1912: Texas as a Test Case." *Southwestern Historical Quarterly,* Vol. 80 (July 1976– April 1977) pp. 33–56.

Green, G. N. "Republicans, Bull Moose, and Negroes in Florida, 1912." *Florida Historical Quarterly,* Vol. 43, No. 2 (October 1964), pp. 153–164.

Greene, Theodore. "America's Heroes: The Changing Models of Success in American Magazines." *Business History Review,* Vol. 45, No. 4 (Winter 1971), pp. 543–546.

Hahn, Harlan. "President Taft and the Discipline of Patronage." *Journal of Politics,* Vol. 28, No. 2 (May 1966), pp. 368–390.

Hahn, Harlan. "The Republican Party Convention of 1912 and the Role of Herbert S. Hadley in National Politics." *Missouri Historical Review,* Vol. 59, No. 4 (July 1965), pp. 407–423.

Halsell, Willie D. "James R. Chalmers and 'Mahoneism' in Mississippi." *Journal of Southern History,* Vol. 10, No. 1 (February 1944), pp. 37–58.

Haney, James E. "Blacks and the Republican Nomination of 1908." *Ohio History,* Vol. 84, No. 4 (1975), pp. 207–221.

Hyde, Anne. "William Kent: The Puzzle of Progressive Conservationists." In *California Progressives Revisited.* Edited by William Deverell and Tom Sitton. Oakland, CA: University of California Press, 1994, pp. 34–56.

Ickes, Harold. "Who Killed the Progressive Party?" *American Historical Review,* Vol. 46, No. 2 (Jan. 1941), pp. 306–337.

James, Felix. "The Civic and Political Activities of George A. Myers." *Journal of Negro History,* Vol. 58, No. 2 (April 1973), pp. 166–178.

Kaye, Andrew M. "Colonel Roscoe Conkling Simmons and the Mechanics of Black Leadership." *Journal of American Studies,* Vol. 37, No. 1 (2003), pp. 79–98.

La Follette, Belle, and Fola La Follette. "Robert M. La Follette." *Journal of Politics,* Vol. 17, No. 2 (May 1955), p. 375.

La Follette, Robert. "The Reed Congress and the New National Issues." *American Magazine,* Vol. 73 (November 1911–April 1912), p. 144.

Ledbetter, Calvin R., Jr. "Presidential Politics in Arkansas from 1909–1912: The Visits of Taft, Roosevelt, and Wilson." *Arkansas Historical Quarterly,* Vol. 53, No. 2 (Summer 1994), pp. 191–210.

Lewarne, Charles P. "The Aberdeen, Washington Free Speech Fight of 1911–1912." *Pacific Northwest Quarterly,* Vol. 66, No. 1 (January 1975), pp. 1–12.

Lincoln, A. "My Dear Senator: Letters Between Theodore Roosevelt and Hiram Johnson in 1917." *California Historical Society Quarterly,* Vol. 42, No. 3 (September 1963), pp. 221–239.

Lincoln, A. "Theodore Roosevelt, Hiram Johnson, and the Vice-Presidential Nomination of 1912." *Pacific Historical Review,* Vol. 23, No. 3 (August 1959), pp. 267–283.

Link, Arthur S., ed. "Correspondence Relating to the Progressive Party's 'Lily White' Policy in 1912." *Journal of Southern History,* Vol. 10, No. 4 (November 1944), pp. 480–490.

Link, Arthur S. "A Decade of Biographical Contributions to Recent American History." *Mississippi Valley Historical Review,* Vol. 34, No. 4 (March 1948), pp. 637–652.

Link, Arthur S. "The Negro as a Factor in the Campaign of 1912." *Journal of Negro History,* Vol. 32, No. 1 (January 1947), pp. 81–99.

Link, Arthur S. "The Underwood Presidential Movement of 1912." *Journal of Southern History,* Vol. 11, No. 2 (May 1945), pp. 230–245.

Maxwell, Robert S., ed. "A Document on the Progressive Campaign of 1912." *Mississippi Valley Historical Review,* Vol. 36, No. 1 (June 1949), pp. 113–115.

McMillen, Neil, "Perry W. Howard, Boss of Black and Tan Republicanism in Mississippi, 1924–1960," *Journal of Southern History,* Vol. 48, No. 2 (May 1982), pp. 205–224.

Meier, August. "Booker T. Washington and the Town of Mound Bayou." *Phylon,* Vol. 15, No. 4 (Winter 1954), pp. 396–401.

Mollison, Irvin C. "Negro Lawyers in Mississippi." *Journal of Negro History,* Vol. 15, No. 1 (January 1930), pp. 38–71.

Monnet, Julien C. "The Latest Phase of Negro Disenfranchisement." *Harvard Law Review,* Vol. 26, No. 1 (November 1912), pp. 42–63.

Mowry, George E. "The California Progressive and His Rationale: A Study in Middle Class Politics." *Mississippi Valley Historical Review,* Vol. 36, No. 2 (September 1949), pp. 239–250.

Mowry, George E. "The South and the Progressive Lily White Party of 1912." *Journal of Southern History,* Vol. 6, No. 2 (May 1940), pp. 237–247.

Mowry, George E. "Theodore Roosevelt and the Election of 1910." *Mississippi Valley Historical Review,* Vol. 25, No. 4 (March 1939), pp. 523–534.

Murphy, Gary. "'Mr. Roosevelt is Guilty': Theodore Roosevelt and the Crusade for Constitutionalism, 1910–1912." *Journal of American Studies,* Vol. 36, No. 3 (2002), pp. 441–457.

Murray, Keith A. "The Aberdeen Convention." *Pacific Northwest Quarterly,* Vol. 38, No. 2 (April 1947), pp. 99–108.

Myers, R. David. "Robert La Follette." *The American Radical.* Ed. Mary Jo Buhle et al. New York: Routledge, 1994, pp. 159–166.

Olin, Spencer, Jr. "Hiram Johnson, the California Progressives, and the Hughes

Campaign of 1916." *Pacific Historical Review,* Vol. 31, No. 4 (November 1962), pp. 403–412.

Overacker, Louise. "Direct Primary Legislation in 1928–29." *American Political Science Review,* Vol. 24, No. 2 (May 1930), pp. 370–380.

Parker, Elliott. "Political Power and the Press: Charles Fairbanks." Presented at Association for Education in Journalism and Mass Communication in Toronto, Canada (August 2004).

Pinchot, Nancy Pittman. "Amos Pinchot: Rebel Prince." *Journal of Pennsylvania History,* Vol. 66, No. 2 (Spring 1999), pp. 166–198.

Ponder, Stephen. "'Nonpublicity' and the Unmaking of a President: William Howard Taft and the Ballinger-Pinchot Controversy of 1909–1910." *Journalism History,* Vol. 19, No. 4 (Winter 1994), pp. 111–121.

Robinson, Edgar Eugene. "Distribution of the Presidential Vote of 1912." *American Journal of Sociology,* Vol. 20, No. 1 (July 1914), pp. 18–30.

Rosewater, Victor. "Republican Convention Reapportionment." *Political Science Quarterly,* Vol. 28, No. 4 (December 1913), pp. 610–626.

Rowell, Chester R. "Remarks on Mr. Herbert Croly's Paper on 'State Political Reorganization.'" *Proceedings of the American Political Science Association,* Vol. 8 (1911), pp. 140–151.

Scheiner, Seth M. "President Theodore Roosevelt and the Negro, 1901–1908." *Journal of Negro History,* Vol. 47, No. 3 (July 1962), pp. 169–182.

Schlup, Leonard. "Republican Insurgent: Jonathan Bourne and the Politics of Progressivism, 1908–1912." *Oregon Historical Quarterly,* Vol. 87, No. 3 (Fall 1986), pp. 229–244.

Sherman, Richard B. "Charles Sumner Bird and the Progressive Party in Massachusetts." *New England Quarterly,* Vol. 33, No. 3 (September 1960), pp. 325–340.

Smith, Duane A. "Colorado and Judicial Recall." *American Journal of Legal History,* Vol. 7, No. 3 (July 1963), pp. 198–209.

Solvick, Stanley D. "William Howard Taft and the Payne-Aldrich Tariff." *Mississippi Valley Historical Review,* Vol. 50, No. 3 (December 1963), pp. 424–442.

Stagner, Stephen. "The Recall of Judicial Decisions and the Due Process Debate." *American Journal of Legal History,* Vol. 24, No. 3 (July 1980), pp. 257–272.

Stephenson, Wendell H. "William Garrott Brown: Literary Historian and Essayist." *Journal of Southern History,* Vol. 12, No. 3 (August 1946), pp. 313–344.

Tichenor, Daniel, and Daniel Fuerstman. "Insurgency Campaigns and the Quest for Popular Democracy: Theodore Roosevelt, Eugene McCarthy, and Party Monopolies." *Polity,* Vol. 40, No. 1 (January, 2008), pp. 49–69.

Tidmarsh, Jay, and Stephen Robinson. "'The Dean of Chicago's Black Lawyers': Earl Dickerson and Civil Rights Lawyering in the Years Before Brown." *Virginia Law Review,* Vol. 93, No. 5 (September 2007), pp. 1355–1387.

Tinsley, James A. "Roosevelt, Foraker, and the Brownsville Affray." *Journal of Negro History,* Vol. 41, No. 1 (January 1956), pp. 43–65.

Van Deusen, John G. "The Negro in Politics." *Journal of Negro History,* Vol. 21, No. 3 (July 1936), pp. 256–274.

Vogt, Daniel C. "A Note on Mississippi Republicans in 1912." *Journal of Mississippi History,* Vol. 49, No. 1 (February 1987), pp. 49–55.

Warner, Robert M. "Chase S. Osborn and the Presidential Campaign of 1912." *Mississippi Valley Historical Review,* Vol. 46, No. 1 (June 1959) pp. 19–45.

Weiss, Nancy J. "The Negro and the New Freedom: Fighting Wilsonian Segregation." *Political Science Quarterly,* Vol. 84, No. 1 (March 1969), pp. 61–79.

Welliver, Judson Churchill. "A Vitally Illuminating Article on a Criminally Corrupt Condition in the Republican Party." *Munsey's Magazine,* Vol. 46 (February 1912), 619–628.

Welliver, Judson Churchill. "Catching Up with Roosevelt." *Munsey's Magazine,* Vol. 46 (March 1912), pp. 791–804.

Wynne, Lewis N. "Brownsville: The Reaction of the Negro Press." *Phylon,* Vol. 33, No. 2 (Summer 1972), pp. 153–160.

COURT PROCEEDINGS AND DOCUMENTS

Buckley v. Valeo. 424 U.S. Supreme Court. 1976.

Citizens United v. Federal Election Commission. 558 U.S. Supreme Court. 2010.

Cousins v. Wigoda. 419 U.S. Supreme Court. 1975.

Democratic Party of the United States v. Wisconsin. 450 U.S. Supreme Court. 1981.

McCutcheon v. Federal Election Commission. 572 U.S. Supreme Court. 2014.

O'Brien v. Brown. 409 U.S. Supreme Court. 1972.

SPEECHES, TESTIMONIES, AND PUBLIC DOCUMENTS

Annual Report of U.S. Steel, 1912.

Testimony of Ormsby McHarg, *Campaign Contributions,* Testimony Before a Subcommittee of the Committee on Privileges and Elections, United States Senate, 1912.

Miller Center Report. "American President: Theodore Roosevelt: Campaigns and

Elections."   http://millercenter.org/president/roosevelt/essays/biography/3. Accessed 14 November 2014.

Official Report of the Proceedings of the Fifteenth Republican National Convention. 1912.

Proceedings of the Provisional National Progressive Committee. 1912.

Roosevelt, Theodore. "A Charter of Democracy." Speech. Ohio State Constitutional Convention. Columbus, Ohio, February 21, 1912.

Testimony of George Wilder, Hearings Before the Committee on the Post-Office and Post-Roads of the House of Representatives on Second Class Mail. 1910.

Tillman Act of 1907.

Hughes, Harold. *The Democratic Choice: A Report of the Commission on the Democratic Selection of Presidential Nominees.* August 1968.

ORAL HISTORIES

Ormsby McHarg. Interview, Oral History Research Office, Columbia University, February 1951–March 1951.

John Lord O'Brian. Interview, Oral History Research Office, Columbia University, 1952.

William Ambrose Prendergast. Interview, Oral History Research Office, Columbia University, 1951.

Sidney R. Redmond. Interview, Oral History Collection, State Historical Society of Missouri, 1970.

George Rublee. Interview, Oral History Research Office, Columbia University, December 1950–February 1951.

William Henderson Wadhams. Interview, Oral History Research Office, Columbia University, 1950.

Stanley Washburn. Interview, Oral History Research Office, Columbia University, 1950.

PH.D. THESES

Haney, James E. "Theodore Roosevelt and Afro-Americans, 1901–1912." Kent State University, Ph.D. dissertation, 1971.

Lobdell, George, Jr. "A Biography of Frank Knox." University of Illinois at Urbana-Champaign, Ph.D. dissertation, 1954.

Pike, Albert, Jr. "Jonathan Bourne Jr., Progressive." University of Oregon, Ph.D. dissertation, 1957.

IMAGE CREDITS

Maud Malone: Library of Congress, Prints & Photographs Division, [LC-DIG-ggbain-16068]

TR in Massachusetts: N.C.

Taft in Massachusetts: Library of Congress, Prints & Photographs Division, [LC-DIG-ggbain-11216]

Republican Convention in Chicago: Library of Congress, Prints & Photographs Division, [LC-DIG-ggbain-10562]

California delegates: Library of Congress, Prints & Photographs Division, [LC-DIG-ggbain-10544]

"The Free and Independent Colored Delegates": N.C.

Perry Howard: Center for Research in Black Culture, Jean Blackwell Hutson General Research and Reference Division, The New York Public Library. "Perry W. Howard." *The New York Public Library Digital Collections.* 1923

Progressive Party convention: Library of Congress Prints & Photographs Division, [LC-USZ62-116075]

TR addressing the Progressive Party convention: Library of Congress Prints & Photographs Division, [LC-DIG-ggbain-11285]

Jane Addams: Library of Congress, Prints & Photographs Division, [LC-USZ62-53516]

"Discarding the Ace": *St. Louis Post-Dispatch*

INDEX

Page numbers beginning with 307 refer to endnotes.